AFTER BLAIR

David Cameron
and the Conservative Tradition

Icon Books

Distributed in the UK, Europe, South Africa and Asia
by TBS Ltd, TBS Distribution Centre, Colchester Road,
Frating Green, Colchester CO7 7DW

This edition published in Australia in 2007
by Allen & Unwin Pty Ltd,
PO Box 8500, 83 Alexander Street,
Crows Nest, NSW 2065

Distributed in Canada by
Penguin Books Canada,
90 Eglinton Avenue East, Suite 700,
Toronto, Ontario M4P 2YE

ISBN-10: 1-84046-795-9
ISBN-13: 978-1840467-95-6

Typesetting by Hands Fotoset

Printed and bound in the UK by
Bookmarque Ltd, Croydon, Surrey

Contents

Acknowledgements

I'm not entirely sure how this happened. In my day job I research computing and the World Wide Web and all that sort of stuff. *After Blair* developed out of some research I did in my spare time with members of the School of Politics at the University of Nottingham. I would like to thank Andrew Denham, David Stevens, Mat Humphrey and Pru Hobson-West for giving their time and expertise freely, and also David Willetts, who was very generous with his comments and criticisms of the first edition. After the first edition appeared the whole thing took on a momentum of its own, and I ended up being asked to engage the political part of my brain almost as often as the techie bit. Which is nice.

Icon Books has been very encouraging of this project, and I am particularly grateful to Peter Pugh, who took a firm interest in the book from the beginning, and who bought me the lunch over which I convinced him that a second edition would be desirable for the Cameron era. Thanks also to Duncan Heath, who has overseen the writing process and made it painless, Andrew Furlow, Ruth Nelson, Lucy Leonhardt and Tansy Hiner.

The School of Electronics and Computer Science at the University of Southampton has, as ever, been a delightful employer, and has given me plenty of space to pursue what must seem very recondite research interests. Particular thanks to Nigel Shadbolt and Wendy Hall for providing that research environment, and to Susan Davies for helping in countless ways.

Conversations with Rebecca Hughes and Yorick Wilks have been very influential on certain sections of the book. I would also like to acknowledge the often intangible but nonetheless real contributions of various people with whom I have discussed the ideas behind this project, including: Hugo de Burgh, David Evans, Anthony Freeman, Mark Garnett, Edward Leigh, John Penrose, Tom Richmond, Andy Robinson, Keith Sutherland, Simon Tormey and Peter Wilby. My thanks to Robin Hutchison and Ladbrokes for their provision of the odds for the 2005 Tory leadership contest. And my experiences working with the think tank Agora have been invaluable in all sorts of ways.

ABOUT THE AUTHOR

Kieron O'Hara is Senior Research Fellow at the University of Southampton, and a fellow of the Web Science Research Initiative, researching into the politics of knowledge, technology and computing. He is the author of several books, including *Trust: From Socrates to Spin* and *The Referendum Roundabout* and a co-author of *inequality.com* (with David Stevens) and *A Framework for Web Science* (with Sir Tim Berners-Lee and others). He is currently working with Andrew Denham on *Cameron's Mandate* about Tory leadership elections.

For NW, smallest of small 'c' conservatives

PREFACE

When the levee breaks ...

Society is a fragile thing. Such was the theme of *After Blair: Conservatism Beyond Thatcher*, the first edition of this book. As thinking, political beings, we are constantly attempting to improve the world, to raise standards of living and quality of life, for as many people as possible, and quite right too. But the philosophy of conservatism counsels caution in the face of that fragility.

It is often thought that improvements are easy to achieve. But the world is a dynamic, complex place, and tinkering with one part of a deeply interconnected system can cause surprises elsewhere. Progressive political thinkers discover what is wrong with the societies we have – and let's face it, there is plenty for them to discover – and envisage ways to engineer out the problems, injustices or inefficiencies. This is a noble endeavour, but not necessarily a wise one. The conservative, by contrast, is mindful of the amazing fact that societies operate at all, that systems function, and that people get along more or less well, without a hint of a retreat to a Hobbesian war of all against all. This, for the conservative, is the noteworthy point. And re-engineering a society to improve it might, on occasion, undermine precisely the relationships and structures that make the society work in the first place. The conservative does not claim that he or she knows when this will happen – but does claim that the progressive thinker is heedless of the risks.

Any doubts about society's fragility, even in the rich Western world where so many people benefit from the great wealth and prosperity produced, were swept away along with so much else on 29 August 2005, when Hurricane Katrina hit New Orleans. A well-known, laid-back city, the home of wondrous jazz and blues, the 'Big Easy' collapsed into looting, violence and anarchy, in the heartland of the richest country in the world. There was much commentary, suitably outraged, about many aspects of the calamity – our impotence in the face of nature at her worst, the incompetence of the Bush administration's response. But for our purposes, the thing to note is the speed with which civilisation crumbled when the disaster hit. People did not band together, mutual aid did not happen, society did not work in those circumstances. Society will not work in all circumstances.

One reason for a new edition of this book is the amount of disparate work that has appeared in the intervening period that has confirmed what Katrina suggested: that the complexity of society makes it vulnerable to sudden upheaval, and resistant to top-down masterplans – work reported in fascinating books such as: Jared Diamond's *Collapse*, which describes the failure of many apparently robust civilisations;[1] Paul Seabright's *The Company of Strangers*, which points out how much society depends on mutual trust, and how friable that trust can be;[2] James Surowiecki's *The Wisdom of Crowds*, which shows how large groups make more effective decisions and analyses than individual experts;[3] William Easterly's *The White Man's Burden*, which chronicles the difficulties in getting development aid to the people who need it;[4] and Francis Fukuyama's *After the Neocons*, which demonstrates the failure of neoconservatism to achieve desirable social change beyond America.[5]

A new Tory leader

The first edition of *After Blair* traced the history of the link between complexity and fragility, expanded on its consequences, and applied it to the British political scene at the beginning of the 21st century. The conservative tradition is most obviously associated with the Conservative Party in the United Kingdom, though it is not the only tradition that features in its history. But at the time of publication, the Conservatives were in some disarray. They were on their third leader in four years, unable to dent the poll leads of Tony Blair's Labour government, approaching a third general election thrashing, and about to veer off to the right with unpalatable policies about immigration and the like. The rather creepy campaign slogan, 'Are you thinking what we're thinking?' seemed to confirm the suspicion that Tory policies and thought were not quite ... *polite*. *After Blair* tried to use the older conservative tradition to motivate a set of policies that would appeal to the post-Blair voter, the basically tolerant and liberal urban professionals who used to vote Tory overwhelmingly, who had drifted to Labour but who now, thanks to Iraq and the obvious staleness of Mr Blair's government, were looking for somewhere else to go. For make no mistake, these people are actually the Tory core vote: *After Blair* put forward the genuine core vote strategy.

By the time *After Blair* emerged in January 2005, the outline of Michael Howard's leadership had already ossified, with attacks on asylum seekers and illegal immigrants prominent, and as coverage of these attacks swamped some of the more imaginative pronounce-ments about education, health and the like, defeat in 2005 became inevitable. But then one of the points *After Blair* made was that, from their current position, the Tories had to be in for the long haul. Patience was the virtue here; a reputation (or, if you prefer modern managementspeak, a brand) had to be restored. Would *After Blair*'s message be heard in the longer term?

It is very gratifying to see many of *After Blair*'s strategic pointers taken on board following the general election, under the leadership of David Cameron. And even more gratifying, of course, that the new direction has led to encouraging progress, both in the polls and electorally – first steps only, but more than the Conservatives have seen in their nine years of opposition (and five years of government preceding that). It is nice when one is shown to be right.

The first review of *After Blair* appeared in the *Guardian* newspaper: a generous, though critical, review written by an up-and-coming Tory policy wonk guy who was coordinating the drafting of the 2005 election manifesto; a chap called, er, well, David Cameron, actually.[6] Now, far be it from me to suggest that this little extra-curricular assignment for Mr Cameron is entirely responsible for the Tory revival. Egotistical, *moi*? But at least we know that as early as January, even while he was drafting what was a truly awful election-losing manifesto, he was beginning to agree that a move towards the centre of politics would be 'at least part of the road map for a sustained conservative recovery in modern Britain' ('sustained' being the key word here), and that it would be consistent with Tory traditions.

Such a move could be, and indeed is being, characterised as a 'sell-out'. Another distinguished reviewer, Danny Kruger, concluded another generous review with his dissenting worry that *After Blair* 'provides a comfortable mooring at which exiled lefties can quietly dock with the Tories'.[7] But that, in a way, is the point. A party that hopes to govern a diverse country has to appeal widely; it is the exiled lefties, put crudely, to whom the Tories have to appeal. *After Blair* tried to demonstrate that, *pace* 30 years of divisive ideological conflict around Thatcherism, there are many strands in the conservative tradition that could appeal to the middle ground voters who 'hated Thatcherism but dislike Blair's messianic tendencies'.[8] When Mr Cameron put forward the slogan 'Vote blue, go green', that was music to my ears, if not Mr Kruger's.

Like the Labour Party, the Conservative Party covers a lot of ground, and of course is heir to a number of traditions, not only conservative. It could emphasise any or all of them, appealing to many different groups of voters. My main message was, and is, that the conservative ideology has been somewhat drowned out of late; secondarily, I hoped to suggest that revitalising it would help Tory fortunes.

Mr Cameron has certainly done that, in the short time available to him. Hence I, and Icon Books, felt that it was time for an appraisal of his work in the context of the conservative tradition.

Well, *some* change is desirable ...

Of course, some overhaul to *After Blair* was felt necessary (Mr Cameron did not appear at all in the first edition: such has been the speed of his rise, he now appears on the cover). As before, the book is divided, like Goscinny and Uderzo's Gaul, into three-and-a-bit parts. A substantially rewritten introduction sets out the task facing Mr Cameron, and gives us the context we need for examining conservative history. Part One sets out the conservative tradition from the Ancient Greeks to the influence of Thatcherism on the Conservative Party, and defines the philosophy; this has been fairly extensively revised in parts to take on board new scholarship. Part Two has been given a very substantial upgrade, looking at Mr Cameron's thinking with respect to markets, society and trust of politics and politicians, through the lens of the conservative philosophy. Part Three, entirely new, summarises the threats and opportunities with which Mr Cameron will be presented on the road to 2009 (or 2010), with respect to the ongoing debate about the modernisation of the Tory Party – a proxy war about Tory ideology – and in general whether his policies can really make a difference to our scary and dangerous world.

But though the form of the book has changed to reflect the dramatically altered context after May 2005, the aim and ideological arguments remain the same (and, I should say, though I have deleted a great deal of discussion from the first edition, that is purely for reasons of space – I'm not disavowing anything). As I said in the Preface to the first edition, the ideology I have in mind is the sceptical conservatism that reached its zenith at the turn of the last century, under the leadership of the Marquess of Salisbury and Arthur Balfour. It is therefore essential to establish that such an ideology is tenable in today's very different world. This involves meeting two influential arguments. One, made by academics such as Michael Freeden and Robert Eccleshall, is that there is no genuine distinction between Mrs Thatcher's radical liberalism and Salisbury's pessimistic scepticism. The other, whose most prominent exponent is John Gray, is that, though sceptical conservatism is distinct from Thatcherism, changes in society (including many changes wrought by Thatcherism itself) have rendered conservatism obsolete.

Of course, revival will serve the interests of the Tories – but paradoxically will serve those of Labour as well. As with Mrs Thatcher's third term of office from 1987 to 1990, much of the legislation served up by Mr Blair has been sloppy, much of his strategy error-strewn. I think the reason for this is the lack of effective opposition. Mr Blair is not kept on his toes – domestically anyway. Improved Tory performance will, in and of itself, provoke improved Labour performance, and indeed Lib Dem and nationalist performance where devolution has brought them close to office.

Ideology, in politics, is not everything. Indeed, it is often not very much at all, and Lord Salisbury himself would have been the first person to say that. But ideology can send important signals. Few people care about the intricacies of socialist ideology, and fewer still care about the exact content of the 'Third Way'. But the ideological switch from Old Labour to New Labour conveyed a message to the electorate that the Labour Party was serious about governing once again. Whatever New Labour is, the fact that it was distinct from Old Labour drew centrist voters: those voters are getting fed up with Mr Blair, but at the moment they don't really have anywhere else to go.

So it is in *all* our interests that the Tories cut a more attractive ideological figure. This is therefore a book for all of us.

CHAPTER ONE

WELL, I WOULDN'T START FROM HERE ...

How long shall mine enemy be exalted over me?

Psalm 13:2

A dire situation

The circumstances of the general election of May 2005 were very propitious for Britain's Conservative Party. After several years of disastrous leadership under Michael Howard it was rediscovering the virtues of unity and purpose, and no longer looked like a rabble. For the first time in a long time, Tory infighting was not the story, and an Australian called Lynton Crosby was beginning to be thought of as the new Alistair Campbell. The Tories ran an effective guerrilla campaign from January onwards, focusing on popular and press discontent about supposed abuse of the immigration and asylum systems, and the reluctance of middle-class parents to endorse the policy that their offspring should pay even highly subsidised fees for their tertiary education.

Meanwhile the Labour Party was struggling in the polls as its 'big tent' coalition became increasingly fissile. Tony Blair had always run an explicit strategy to ignore his core voters. The reasoning behind this was simple: there were more centrist moderates than committed left wingers, and anyway the latter were concentrated in inner city seats where they commanded large majorities (and so their votes were relatively worthless), and had no one else they could vote for.[1] But the isolation strategy was beginning to look less effective after eight years of government, as Labour was losing councillors and activists – the people who push envelopes through front doors – and starting to show signs of the 'hollowing out' that befell the Tories in the 1990s. Furthermore, parties were exploiting the weakness to Labour's left. RESPECT: The Unity Coalition (Respect, Equality, Socialism, Peace, Environment, Community, Trade Unionism) was in many ways an opportunistic and implausible coalition of disgruntled socialists, trades unionists and Islamists grouped around former Labour MP George Galloway. More serious was the strategy of Charles Kennedy's Liberal Democrats to pitch some key high-profile policy announcements to the left of Labour – most noticeably his condemnation of the Iraq war.

There was trouble on Mr Blair's right flank too. The moderates were getting fed up with bad news from Iraq (the war had never been popular, but the incompetence marking the post-war nation-building, combined with the inability to stifle the insurgency alienated many who had initially bought into the Bush/Blair vision), hefty tax increases and a general sense of weariness. Mr Blair's initial plan for the election was to energise the centre, to try to reinvigorate the reformist programme that had characterised his second term of office in 2001–05. To that end, he appointed Alan Milburn, a former Cabinet minister and supporter to run the election campaign and sideline Gordon Brown. But the Tories' hit-and-run tactics during campaigning discomfited Mr Milburn, and Mr Brown ended up being a central asset to Blair's campaign. The price of Brown's support was Blair's announcement that he would stand down as leader sometime during the 2005–10 Parliament.

The final piece of good news for the Tories was that the Liberal Democrats, as noted, were unspecific as to their positioning. They did this deliberately of course, in order to pick up voters to Labour's left and right simultaneously, but ultimately that is a hard trick to pull. Their most visible policies, in the context of the campaign, were those to the left, on the war, the abolition of council tax and an increase in the top rate of income tax. Some in the party worried that this leftward move away from traditional liberal centrism looked like opportunism, and a cynicism about their positioning began to spread, particularly when they unveiled Bennite MP Brian Sedgemore as their latest recruit from Labour's ranks.[2] Finally, Mr Kennedy's troubles with alcohol, which finally cost him his job at the end of the year, began to impinge on the campaign after his faltering, bleary-eyed performance at the launch of the Lib Dem manifesto.

How could the Tories fail?

With ease. In the end, they got 198 seats, less than Michael Foot's Labour Party in the disastrous election of 1983. Their support in terms of a percentage of the vote barely budged, while the Lib Dems profited somewhat from Labour losses. Their position remains dire: to win a majority of 50 seats in 2010, they will need a 9 per cent swing, to give them a further 140 seats.[3] The first-past-the-post electoral system does not currently favour them. The Tories are now concentrated in the South of England, and have virtually surrendered the North, Midlands, Wales and Scotland to Labour and the Lib Dems. Labour seats, being disproportionately in the inner cities which are losing population, tend to have fewer voters, while Tory seats (the suburbs and shires) are growing all the time and therefore have inefficiently large majorities. Low turnout in the cities also helps make Labour votes more powerful. Furthermore, the anti-Tory tactical voting by Labour and Lib Dem voters has remained, to some extent, in place: being a Tory is still not *comme il faut*.

A shame, then, that Mr Howard's election campaign didn't try to address that problem. As a number of commentators pointed out,[4] beginning an assault on Labour with a cry about immigration was a bad idea, and the shrillness continued throughout the campaign, orchestrated by the unsavoury 'Are you thinking what we're thinking?' slogan. In the abstract, people were concerned by stories about large numbers of immigrants arriving, but their worries given voice in public sounded paranoid and unpleasant.

The Tories needed a new start. They had lost all credibility and popularity, rather as Labour had in the 1980s, and they needed to change people's minds about them – to borrow an oft-used phrase, they needed to repair their damaged brand.[5] A famous, or infamous, polling result showed that, even if voters agreed with Tory policies, they were less likely to endorse them once they were aware they were *Tory* policies. Mr Howard improved much about the party, but failed to understand that a thoroughgoing change could not be carried out (or conveyed to the electorate) while quick dashes for short-term gain were the main drivers of policy. A deep analysis of polls before and after the election by Michael Ashcroft set out the scale of the Tories' problems in their relationship with voters; if the Tories manage to take these lessons on board, the document could be of historical significance.[6]

This is a journey that Labour has already taken. Mr Blair is often accused of being a 'closet Tory'. This is actually not true, as plenty of his policies – pumping money into public services, setting up a minimum wage, constitutional reform, setting stiff targets for eliminating child poverty, meeting the UK's targets on the Kyoto environmental protocol, increasing international aid – are particular totems of the left. Indeed, it is striking how far he has got with the implementation of a traditional left-wing slate; certainly much further than any previous Labour Prime Minister, with the possible exception of Clement Attlee. He has recognised that Mrs Thatcher deliberately changed Britain to rid it of socialism. She failed; but what Mr Blair represents is the mutation of socialism to function in the post-Thatcher ecosystem.

The Tories now need to find a way of living in the post-Blair world. In the same way that the trades unions had appeared to be a regrettable but necessary part of the scene in the 1950s, 60s and 70s, Thatcherite policies had seemed vital in the 1980s and 90s, without generating much enthusiasm. The Tories had become associated with them, rightly taken the credit for them, and had yet to realise that voters had regarded them as medicine that, once the illnesses of the 1970s had seemed to be cured, they wanted to stop taking. The Tories had become the party of economics, of the bottom line, of atomised society, of selfishness, of greed. This was to a very large extent a caricature, but like any caricature it contained a germ of truth and that needed to be addressed, partly by remaking the image, partly by reconstructing the reality.

How did the Tories, who just twenty years earlier were musing on the possibility of becoming the hegemonic party of permanent government, come to such a pass? How did the most efficient election-fighting machine in British politics falter so badly? The Tories need to understand their achievements, and their vulnerabilities, if they are to flourish in the world After Blair.

The Conservative century

The Tories began the 20th century as they left it, in fairly bad shape. The long Victorian twilight of Lord Salisbury ended with political failure: he was succeeded in 1902 by Arthur Balfour, a philosopher of some note but not a man of great political skill. Balfour, incidentally, was Salisbury's nephew, and his rapid rise was attributed less to his genius and more to his family connections (Salisbury's given name was Robert Cecil, and his uninhibited promotion of his nephew gave rise to the expression 'Bob's your uncle!').[7]

The Tories fell apart over the issue of tariff reform, rather as they fell apart over Europe in more recent memory. As with monetary union today, the issue was central to economic and political affairs, although the recondite arguments, fanatical certainties and lack of consensus left voters cold. It took the Tories a decade to become electable again, after which, although they didn't always furnish the Prime Minister, it was the Tory majority in the Commons that underpinned a number of coalitions. The Tories dominated the inter-war years, in both election results and policy, and even when the appeasement-minded Tory governments of Baldwin and Chamberlain in the 1930s were discredited, it was the opposition of brilliant up-and-coming Tories that propelled another Tory (of liberal instincts), Churchill, to the position of war leader.

The period 1945–79 was driven by a dialectic of corporatist doctrine (an extension of wartime measures of control and management) with the new libertarian free market ideas being developed by thinkers such as Hayek. Even when corporatism flourished, and a roughly left-wing consensus seemed in the ascendancy, as often as not the nation trusted the Tories to administer such policies. Since 1979, the Tories have set the intellectual agenda (indeed, it was from about this time that business-oriented terminology, like 'agenda', became so sadly *de rigeur* in political discourse, reaching its apotheosis in the dreary functionaries of New Labour).

The Tories' is an impressive record of success. Indeed, the 20th century has been called 'the Conservative Century'.[8] Why was that the case, and why have they lost their golden touch so spectacularly?

The unideological party

In their revues of the 1950s, Flanders and Swann poked gentle fun at middle-class mores of the day. One of Michael Flanders' introductory monologues (improbably to a song about a gnu) included the following passage:

> Well, I wrote to the local council about this. Very nice about it, you know, elections coming up and so on. We have got a jolly decent lot of old burghers on our council. Get them sticking up flags on the town hall, I'll tell you that much. But then our council is, of course, strictly non-political. They're all Conservatives.[9]

In our own time, after Mrs Thatcher and Sir Keith Joseph, after the infatuations with monetarism and Hayek, this is not a joke that one could make. Far from bumbling along, the Tories have often made a point of maintaining that much was wrong with Britain and that they knew what was right; they have torn up many long-standing institutions and replaced them with new ways of doing things.

Historically, this is a very odd situation. The 19th-century progressive philosopher John Stuart Mill famously called the Tories the 'stupid party'. What an insult that was intended to be, redolent of Thackeray's *Vanity Fair*, of fat claret-swilling swells living off the income of giant swathes of inherited land, their consumption, travels, gambling and snobbery supported by hard-working tenants in desperate poverty. How surprised Mill would have been to see the Tories not only be unoffended by his insult, but almost welcome it positively. Many Tories' self-image, at least until 1975, was that of a group of sensible and responsible people unconcerned with political ideas, because ideas were the causes of trouble. They had ideas in France, which was why they had revolution and tyranny. They had ideas in Germany; indeed the German language furnishes them with lots of big abstract nouns, all made to look even more important by beginning with capital letters. No wonder they bequeathed us such disruptive thinkers as Hegel, Marx and Nietzsche, whose undoubted brilliance hardly compensates for the trouble they caused. And the same was true nearer home: those few Tories who tried to be clever, like Iain MacLeod or Enoch Powell, were much more trouble than they were worth.*

The Tories were conservative, with a small 'c'. The wisdom of Britain, such people thought, was contained not in its books or universities, but in its ramshackle system that had grown up piecemeal over 1,000 years, embodied in the parish church, in the pattern of agriculture, in the Briton's practical inventiveness and in the judgements laid down – the same judgements, to rich and poor alike – in its courts. No doubt the system was not perfect, but

---

* MacLeod was famously dismissed as being 'too clever by half'.

the perfect is so often the enemy of the good. The system worked, conflict was rare, and that in itself was valuable. It was the duty of the British politician, on the Tory view, to make sure that everything continued to trundle on in its own way.

Commentators have long been dubious about these claims to be unideological. For example, Michael Freeden argues:

> Remarkably, proponents of conservatism have shared this deep-rooted image of anti-intellectualism. As one of them, F.J.C. Hearnshaw, remarked without a hint of apology: 'It is commonly sufficient for practical purposes if conservatives, without saying anything, just sit and think, or even if they merely sit.' Supporters and opponents notwithstanding, this line of argument cannot be adopted. Like any other concatenation of political ideas that refer to the real worlds of politics, conservatism *is* an identifiable ideology, exhibiting awareness among its producers and amenable to intelligent analysis.[10]

Political scientist Robert Eccleshall concurs:

> Nor should much credence be given to the suggestion that conservatism is different from other political doctrines because it belongs outside the realm of ideology. Those who characterise conservatism as a frame of mind often denigrate ideology as a perverted or 'alien' form of knowledge … consisting of speculative notions which foster the illusion that the political order can be dramatically improved. Conservatives, in contrast, allegedly attain genuine understanding of human affairs because of their pragmatic attachment to existing institutions. This insistence that conservatism is not an ideology is itself an ideological ploy by those sympathetic to the doctrine, part of the rough-and-tumble of political argument rather than an analytical exercise.[11]

I think Freeden and Eccleshall are right. Conservatism *is* an identifiable ideology, and I am going to try to describe it, and discuss how it might function in a rapidly changing world. As will become clear, I do not agree with either of them about how conservatism should properly be described. I also think conservatism is a special kind of ideology, in a way that I will try to explicate later on, and which will explain why conservatives have traditionally been able to pretend disingenuously that they are such unideological creatures.

The party of stability – and free markets

The Tories are traditionally the party of stability. They abhor uncertainty and they are suspicious of innovation. There are many reasons for this. First, stability and certainty are good for planning ahead. Everyone needs to plan, because people take such big risks in the normal course of events. Second, if a society functions reasonably well – as the Tories claim most Western societies do – then one should have a very good reason to change the way that it works. Third, industry and wealth depend on sensible, timely and lucrative investment, and investment is higher, other things being equal, when there are fewer uncertainties about the future. Fourth, cooperation between people (and organisations such as firms, charities or governments) is greater if everyone behaves predictably and does business along familiar lines.

The institutions that Tories have traditionally looked towards in order to promote stability in Britain are a relatively small set, although that is no reason why they shouldn't look for more in the future. They fall into two groups: the institutions over which their governments have had control; and the independent institutions of which they approve.[12]

Institutions that Tory governments have traditionally controlled include the financial system; in particular, the currency. Tories look for a stable pound (and if we join the euro, with or without their support, they will look for a stable euro). Governments usually spend more money than they can really afford, and in order to pay for the excess they are often tempted to print more money. This is an inflationary pressure, and the value of one's cash, one's investments and one's debts will vary unpredictably, making planning and investment hard. Sound money is one important Tory credo.

Another is the rule of law. Clear laws, applied to rich and poor, strong and weak alike, which have the support of most people, make social interaction stable, and – if crafted well – promote the kind of behaviour Tories instinctively approve of. Lawbreaking is a serious issue for Tories, and just because a law is thought to be unjust, for example, that is no reason to break it out of adherence to a policy of civil disobedience (this in complete opposition to the liberal idea that civil disobedience is one of the institutions of the rule of law). The wrong caused by the disobedience will almost always, says the Tory, outweigh the wrong caused by the unjust law, because the former will undermine the rule of law in its entirety.

A third is the defence of the realm. The Tories are wary of disruption from within, but are also mindful of the dangers without. Hence a strong defence capability is essential – and indeed military muscle is very important to project Britain's voice on the world stage. The real peace dividend at the end of the Cold War was not that a country could spend less on defence, but that the money it *did* spend would buy more power internationally. The Tories are keen to ensure that the system of international relations enables Britain's interests to be pursued successfully.

A fourth is property. It is essential, for the Tories, that everyone feels included in a society, and that as few people as possible should think it worth their while to change it. Property is a key element in making people feel that they are part of a society, that they benefit from being in the society, and so the Tories have generally supported a mild materialism, often expressed through the owner-ship of one's own home.

The independent institutions of which the Tories approve

include the Church (specifically the Church of England, which used to be known as the Tory Party at prayer), the family and business. However, these are proving disappointing. The Anglican Church is becoming a pretty left-wing organisation, to the left of the Labour Party, never mind the Tories. Even when it takes a moral lead, it is often not the moral lead that the Tories would be interested in. And its adherents are smaller in number every year (for the Tory, these facts are not unconnected).

Fewer and fewer people live in the stable family units that the Tories prefer, and more families than ever are dysfunctional. Business, which likes a winner, has also migrated to the hegemonic Labour Party, creating a rather vicious circle for the Tories. The Tories need money to make inroads into the Labour majority, but as long as that majority looks invincible, the people with lots of money will continue to back the winning horse and ignore the also-rans, however ideologically agreeable. However, some types of business retain Tory support, for example private health care organisations and private schooling.

Given all this, a major problem for the Tories, which we will discuss in Chapter Five, and throughout Part Two of this book, is how their philosophy can function in a world that is changing all the time, that appears to be inherently unstable and uncertain, and in which the Tories' traditional allies no longer share their basic instincts.

Another interesting issue, which we will discuss in Chapter Six, is the Tories' long-standing support for free markets. There are many good reasons for such support. But one thing that has to be said about free markets is that they are not inherently stable. Indeed, stability has been substantially greater under the Chancellorship of Gordon Brown than under the eighteen years of Tory government that preceded it, which began with an engineered bust, then proceeded with an engineered boom, which turned to bust once more; since 1997, in contrast, growth has been steady, and for good measure better than most of the UK's competitors most of the time.

Indeed, one commentator has gone so far as to claim, at some length, that the adoption of the free market ideology, and the rapid altering and reconfiguring of many of the institutions of government under the Thatcher and Major governments, have destroyed the traditional Tory philosophy. The institutions that provide the continuity essential for stability have all gone, and the comfortable middle-class life, to which the upwardly mobile Tory voters of the Thatcher years aspired, has gone with them. There is, no doubt, more money to be made for the enterprising, but that requires entrepreneurial energy – and the spectre of bankruptcy and insecurity makes the effort of climbing the greasy pole seem less worthwhile. Tory policy during the 80s and 90s, according to this analysis, was self-undermining. It relied on aspirational Tories for votes, at the same time that the lifestyle to which they aspired was being destroyed by Thatcherite reforms.[13] We will address this argument in detail in Chapter Five.

The glory days

Ironically, the Tories' troubles stem from their post-war glory days: Mrs Thatcher's period of office from 1979 to 1990. After the mildly left-wing corporate consensus broke down in the 1970s under a tidal wave of strikes and poor economic performance, Mrs Thatcher acted decisively to shift Britain's politics rightward. After experiments in monetarism, Thatcherism was born, though maybe accidentally,[14] as a programme for the removal of government influence from industry, the introduction of market-based methods of incentive in those public services that could not, for philosophical, economic or political reasons, be privatised, and a shift of the onus of care from the state to individuals or, as a second best, voluntary organisations. Mrs Thatcher's ascent to the leader-ship in 1975 does not represent a big discontinuity in Tory ideas; in many ways she continued Mr Heath's early rhetorical programme and exploited ideas that had been influential in Tory circles since the war: for example, the writings of Hayek. But on the other hand, the effect of her repositioning of Britain is clear when we compare the current political consensus in Britain with, say, those of France or Germany, whose corporatist assumptions appear outdated to British eyes.

Thatcherite policies were intended to capture or recreate the spirit of public service and self-reliance that characterised the Victorian era, which throughout the 20th century had been a deeply unfashionable time. The irony, though, is that in so far as Mrs Thatcher genuinely recreated the Victorian ethos, it was the policies of the Victorian Liberal Party that she brought in, not those of the Tories of the day.[15]

Post-Thatcher blues I: John Major

The Tory slide began in Mrs Thatcher's third term, after 1987, when her previously sure touch seemed to desert her. As well as a number of odd incidents ('we are a grandmother'), she seemed to alienate most of the people of real talent around her, notably Nigel Lawson and Sir Geoffrey Howe. Her policy instincts also went awry, with the disaster of the poll tax being only the most prominent. Finally, a boom engineered in the run-up to the 1987 general election became a recession after it. The Tories lost council elections and the party lost grass-roots members; it began to 'hollow out'.

The Tories, sliding in the polls, were faced with the classic twist-or-stick dilemma: should they carry on with Mrs Thatcher as leader, hoping that she would get back on track and continue her exemplary record of winning elections, or make a change? One attempt to change the leadership went off half-cocked in 1989, but after Howe's devastating resignation speech in the Commons in 1990 (in Mrs Thatcher's own words, 'cool, forensic, light at points, and poisonous. ... this final act of bile and treachery'[16]), Michael Heseltine was emboldened to strike, wounding her fatally. Since then, the Tories have been divided largely between those who regret that incident and those who thought it necessary for victory in 1992.

John Major's problem was that he was neither as combative as Mrs Thatcher, nor as ideologically driven. He had the advantages of being neither (a) a toff, like Douglas Hurd for instance, and therefore supposedly more acceptable in our egalitarian age, nor (b) tainted by plotting or faction membership, having risen from pretty well nowhere, nor (c) Michael Heseltine. But it soon went wrong. Mrs Thatcher unhelpfully (and arguably inaccurately[17]) decided that Mr Major had betrayed the ideological cause. He proved incapable of steering a course between the pro-Europeans and the Euro-sceptics, whose antagonism was multiplied tenfold as Europe was the ostensible issue that brought Mrs Thatcher down. Major's Chancellor Norman Lamont became a laughing stock after Black Wednesday (one of Mr Lamont's advisors at the time was a certain D. Cameron). And Labour came up with not one but two consecutive electable leaders. After the euphoria of Mr Major's 1992 election victory, his experience of the premiership became very sour, and he resigned immediately after his heavy defeat in 1997. The long period of unpopular Tory government had merely cemented their bad reputation with the voters.

Post-Thatcher blues II: William Hague

In opposition, the first tangible note of progress was the laying to rest of the European issue; a thoroughgoing yet moderate Euro-scepticism prevailed, having been initiated by Mr Major's successor William Hague. But Mr Hague otherwise failed to dispel the general dislike of the Tories. Having tried to make the Tories inclusive and 'modern', he panicked in the face of poor poll ratings and moved the party sharply to the right.[18] Big mistake.[19] He also managed to wound the party still further by introducing a truly terrible method of electing the leader, who can be fired by the parliamentary party but is hired by the grass-roots members.[20]

Mr Hague forever seemed to be casting around for the big idea, without the sticking power to make such an idea work. The problem grew worse with the splits in his Shadow Cabinet. But he had made a good start by fixing a clear line on Europe; he took a mild eurosceptic line and held a referendum of party members on it, which was carried suitably impressively (85 per cent to 15 per cent, with a 60 per cent turnout of members). This tactic was much derided, and it was thought that the most likely effect would be to exacerbate party divisions. In fact, the argument died down quite quickly. A number of pro-Europeans dissented, and a couple of Shadow Cabinet members resigned. But Mr Hague's move was cannier than many had thought. In the first place, the lack of response to the pro-Europeans' protests merely drew attention to their isolation within the party. And second, as Mr Major's period of office had shown, it was the eurosceptics who were troublesome, and who were in effect responsible for putting Mr Blair into Number 10; the Europhiles were comparative pussycats.

But Mr Hague couldn't pull the same trick with the public services. His deputy, Peter Lilley, tried to edge the party away from the Thatcherite tradition with a speech in April 1999 about how market mechanisms were of limited efficacy in certain markets and for certain purposes; on this ground he attempted to rule out privatisation of education or health. The speech was moderate and sensible – and indeed the only direction the party could realistically move in, given the public consensus – but the unfortunate coincidence of the speech with a dinner to celebrate the twentieth anniversary of Mrs Thatcher's election victory, and reports that Mrs Thatcher herself had hit the roof, killed the initiative. Mr Lilley was sacked shortly afterwards.

Given the lack of an overarching political philosophy (in itself not necessarily a handicap), together with the failure of an important initiative, Mr Hague was in trouble. He was also landed with two rather nasty contingencies. First, Mr Blair's government was actually doing OK, and Mr Brown's stewardship of the economy showed a strong continuity with the successful policies of former Tory Chancellor Kenneth Clarke. And second, the Shadow Cabinet was unmanageable.

In the end, he decided on the core vote strategy; if all committed

Tories voted, even though that would not be enough people to threaten Mr Blair's victory, it would still be a sufficient number to cut his majority, and give the youthful Mr Hague a second crack at the whip in 2005/6.

Oops.

The issues that excited Tory ultras resonated badly in the Blairite nation. Mr Hague supported the rights of Tony Martin, a farmer who had killed a burglar on his property. This was all very well, and highlighted the Tory issue of crime. But Mr Martin seems to have become obsessed with the idea of being burgled, and – to say the least – was not the sort of person that the urban professionals who had deserted the Tories could identify with in the slightest. Another dubious character with whom Mr Hague had problems was the Tory candidate for the London mayoralty election in 2000, Jeffrey Archer, a copious creator of fiction whose integrity (not widely believed to be his long suit) Mr Hague very publicly endorsed. Shortly afterwards, Mr Archer retired from the election after revelations of past perjury.

When protesters against the high price of petrol brought the country to a near standstill, Mr Hague not only supported the campaign but seemed to speak in favour of lawbreaking. He made an attack on the 'liberal elite' – much, if some accounts can be believed, to the chagrin of Michael Portillo[21] – in the wake of the Macpherson report on institutional racism in the Metropolitan Police. In the run-up to the 2001 general election, he made a speech about how Britain was becoming a 'foreign land' to its own citizens.

This last appeared to be a further sideswipe at the 'floods' of 'bogus' asylum seekers that had been the focus of Tory ire for some time. That was bad enough, as once more this was not a topic that would engage the new Blair voters; but it was interpreted by one or two on the Neanderthal right as *carte blanche* (pardon the pun) to flirt with racism in the election campaign. Outgoing Tory MP John Townend took the opportunity of lamenting the decline of the British into a 'mongrel race', and Mr Hague's dissociation of himself and his party from the remark seemed to take an age.

The final straw was the ill-fated election campaign in June 2001, which Mr Hague presented as Britain's last chance to save the pound. Events, of course, have shown the theory to be wrong, but it seemed silly even at the time. He ended up with the nickname 'Billy Bandwagon'. Rather than a pragmatic opportunism, which would be defensible and actually not that far from Mr Blair's own style, Mr Hague seemed to produce knee-jerk responses to whatever seemed to be discomfiting Mr Blair most at the time, sending him off further and further right, ceding the centre to Mr Blair without a fight.

Post-Thatcher blues III: Iain Duncan Smith

Mr Hague failed to improve Tory fortunes in the 2001 general election, and resigned, like Mr Major, with some relief. The first leadership election under the controversial system that Mr Hague had put in place proved as worrying as many thought it would.[22] A series of votes in the parliamentary party eliminated one of the favourites, Michael Portillo, while the final ballot of all Tory Party members saw the other favourite Kenneth Clarke beaten convincingly by Iain Duncan Smith. At this stage in their recovery, the Tories might not actually have been leadable. Mr Portillo, handsome and media-savvy, was pronounced dubious because of his sudden change from being a hard right-winger to a touchy-feely inclusive type (with a gay past, to boot), while Mr Clarke's Europhilia probably did for him. Mr Clarke later opined memorably that a choice between himself and Mr Portillo would force the Tories to decide whether they were more europhobic than homophobic or *vice versa*.[23]

But if Messrs Portillo and Clarke were problems for the Tories in 2001, Mr Duncan Smith was not the solution. He had difficulty not only commanding the support of the parliamentary party, but also in improving the Tories' organisation, and was widely derided as an inept leader. His years as a rebel against John Major made it impossible for him to appeal to loyalty. So, despite his producing an interesting and thoughtful set of policies,[24] he was eventually deposed after poor opinion polls and unfounded allegations of financial scandal involving his wife.

Mr Duncan Smith's policy concerns were signalled with a visit to the Easterhouse estate in Glasgow in 2002,[25] which inspired a volume of essays[26] in which Mr Duncan Smith and his collaborators make, even if only implicitly, two important points. First of all, there is a clear need for the Tories to concern themselves with poverty. Certain communities were disembowelled by the shift from manufacturing to services in the British economy; mining towns suffered massively from the wiping out of that industry. With the fading of memories of the bad old union-dominated days of the 60s and 70s, public attention has focused on ordinary people left behind, ill-equipped educationally and financially to weather the storms of unemployment.

Second, government is not capable of addressing the problems of poverty with any assurance.

> If Conservatives are to build on our past, we must also learn from Labour's current mistakes. Labour's most serious error is its failure to understand how society works. They got into power by characterising the Conservative Party as only about individualism and materialism. They were wrong and that has meant that they have gone back to centralisation, as a false alternative. This is a Government that believes that it can only deliver through structures that are imposed on people, not composed of them.[27]

> Huge, centralised bureaucracies are unable to handle the complexity of life and information in society. They lack the subtlety to respond to the infinitely varied needs of patients and pupils. They increasingly undermine the independence and judgement of highly qualified professionals.[28]

This, of course, is a serious conservative point. On the other hand, there is a tradition of governmental action to address poverty; no conservative can afford to neglect that tradition. If independent and charitable organisations do not exist in large enough numbers, the compassionate conservative argument risks being too similar to neo-liberalism.

Anyway, his days as leader were numbered. Mr Duncan Smith had won the support of only a third of MPs. As the polls steadfastly refused to improve, a vote of confidence was called. He was deposed, having never been accepted by the people he was supposed to lead; the introduction of democracy, supposedly to increase the leader's legitimacy, actually worked against it. The botched democratisation of the party doomed him. His lack of leadership skills would have always been a handicap, but he might have got away with it with the help of low expectations. He might have been able to take the necessary longer view had he been elected in a system that conferred any legitimacy on him. The 156,000 votes that he received from the party members were irrelevant; one problem with their overwhelming support was (one of the premises of this book) that those party members were out of step with the rest of society. There is a serious question in the British party system as to whether a party leader is there to represent the views of his or her members, or to win elections. The two do not go – rarely have gone – hand in hand.

Post-Thatcher blues IV: Michael Howard

Despite the vote of no confidence, candidates weren't circling with quite the vulturish relish of 1997 or 2001. Hot favourite was yesterday's man, Michael Howard. The terrifying Home Secretary of the Major years with 'something of the night' about him (Ann Widdecombe's brilliant put-down, cleverly alluding to Mr Howard's Transylvanian ancestry and sleek vampirical appearance), had left front bench politics at one point, but had been risen again, like the Prince of Darkness himself, to act as Mr Duncan Smith's Shadow Chancellor.

The opposition to Mr Howard seemed unwilling to move. His most serious rival was David Davis, who had been the victim of one of Mr Duncan Smith's botched sackings, but who had little chance of winning. The party was in the doldrums, with just 18 months or so before a likely general election, and no one wanted a damaging leadership election that could take weeks. The pressure on Mr Davis was enormous, and he withdrew.[29] To everyone's surprise, including their own, the Tories had actually despatched their leader bloodlessly and replaced him efficiently. Was this a sign that six and a half years of crazy self-destruction were over?

In terms of organisation, the Tories were vastly improved. Between then and the dissolution of Parliament in 2005, their disarray rarely made the news. But Mr Howard, a master tactician, was a poor strategist, and struggled with policy. For instance, Shadow Chancellor Oliver Letwin worried about how to keep up public services without increasing taxes, and plumped for that old favourite, the reduction of waste (Mr Brown trumpeted the results of his own search for bureaucratic waste instantly, thereby undercutting Mr Letwin). Mr Letwin claimed he could cut £35 billion more than Mr Brown by 2012.

This was a mistake. Mr Letwin's claim, even had he been in a position to put his plans into action, was false. Financial forecasts of even a year ahead, never mind eight, are always horribly wrong. So why such manoeuvring? One obvious reason was to impress subtly upon voters that the Tories are the small government party. The Tories do indeed have a low tax brand that they are wise to exploit. But lower taxes than Labour should not rule out tax increases, when circumstances make that imperative (outbreak of foot and mouth, anyone? Iraq war?). The electorate was and is clearly uncertain that its tax pound is being well spent, but the backlash against the perception of the Thatcher years as 'tax cuts for the rich and selfish, poor public services for the poor and needy' has yet to wear itself out.

Mr Howard and Mr Letwin were being squeezed by Labour rhetoric, and by the sense that Labour were vulnerable on the issue of public services. They were tempted to offer better services, while equally driven by their history and instincts to criticise Labour tax rises (and occasionally emboldened to talk of low taxes). It is, no doubt, possible sometimes to achieve both. But voters do not believe it. The Tories' tax-lowering rhetoric sounded hollow.

Mr Howard was well placed to comment on the notion of inclusion, being the child of immigrants. Admittedly, one has to squint with eyes half-closed and be quite sympathetic to be able to look at his previous record in this respect as Home Secretary. But his speech in Burnley about the racist British National Party played well, as did his visits to various areas with large immigrant populations,[30] and his unscripted addendum to his first conference speech as leader, in which he discussed his background as a son of Jewish immigrants who would not have survived the war were it not for Britain and Winston Churchill, was a great success too.[31]

Mr Howard made a splendid beginning, when he countered a move by Home Secretary David Blunkett to put pressure on asylum seekers to leave Britain 'voluntarily' by threatening measures to take their children into care – Mr Blunkett was obviously temporarily confused about the meaning of the word 'voluntarily'. Mr Howard complained that Labour had gone further than any civilised government should go. He was clear about the extent of his sympathy for asylum seekers, but at least his two principles on the topic made a lot of sense.

> Asylum policy should be based on two clear principles. First, Britain has a proud tradition of providing a safe haven for those fleeing persecution. It should continue to do so.
>
> But second, once a set of rules has been agreed to distinguish between such people and those without a genuine claim, then these rules should be enforced.[32]

All well and good. But this was quickly followed by Shadow Home

Secretary David Davis's speech to the 2004 conference, which made an almost Powellite argument that uncontrolled immigration is posing a threat to the nation's values.[33] Quite apart from the facts that immigration is hardly uncontrolled, and that the nation's 'values' are highly contested and arguable, the juxtaposition of Mr Davis's speech and Mr Howard's sent an undoubtedly mixed message. In the end, instinct sent Mr Howard after the core votes, and the main feature of the Tory election campaign of 2005, by common consent, was an attack on immigration, an illiberal message that simply turned voters off.[34]

Mr Howard also loved attacking Mr Blair. Had he been sitting on top of a motivated group of workers and voters, ready and willing to replace Labour in government, and numerically significant enough to stand a chance of doing so, then his tactics of attack would have given them great cheer. The rough and tumble of politics is very exhilarating. Mr Howard was not in such a position. Needing to woo voters who had been voting regularly for Mr Blair, attack was not the way forward. But the Tory campaign was negative and superficial. The aim was to be memorable (shades of Tony Blair's five pledges in 1997 and 2001); the result, summarising the campaign in ten words, was shallow and crotchety. School discipline. More police. Cleaner hospitals. Lower taxes. Controlled immigration.[35] Maybe these are all laudable aims, but the soundbites concealed the coherent vision underneath (if there ever was one).[36]

Mr Howard's tactics, the reversion to something like a core vote strategy, were ultimately his undoing. The general election of 2005 wasn't a disaster, and for once the Tories weren't the story, which was a victory of sorts. But Mr Blair had his third term, with a decent, if reduced, majority (and the reduction in the majority was due to a swing to the Liberal Democrats, not the Tories). Some felt that Mr Howard should stay on to supervise a change in the leadership election rules, so that never again should a leader be in the position of Iain Duncan Smith, but – there were rumours of pressure from supporters of David Davis – Mr Howard quit shortly after the election.

The post-Thatcher blues have shown a marked lack of ideological coherence about the Tories. Mrs Thatcher's own touch had deserted her in her third term, and once Mr Blair had stolen her best ideas there was little to point to as distinctively Tory. Casting around for a lead, the eyes of many Tories had peered over the Atlantic, where they found very congenial company with the neoconservative think-tankers and Republican politicos within the Washington Beltway.[37] Why did the American turn not help?

Looking for ideas: the American turn

The Tories had enjoyed good American connections throughout the post-war period, but strong intellectual debts began to appear during the 80s, when British Tories got themselves interested in ideology in a big way, and while Ronald Reagan's team were redefining what was possible in the US. The close personal friendship between Mrs Thatcher and Mr Reagan encouraged such exchanges. Mrs Thatcher saw much of her thought in American terms; her arguments resonated with puritanism and disdain for the morally weak.

> I was an individualist in the sense that I believed that individuals are ultimately accountable for their actions and must behave like it. But I always refused to accept that there was some kind of conflict between this kind of individualism and social responsibility. I was reinforced in this view by the writings of conservative thinkers in the United States on the growth of an 'underclass' and the development of a dependency culture. If irresponsible behaviour does not involve penalty of some kind, irresponsibility will for a large number of people become the norm. More important still, the attitudes may be passed on to their children, setting them off in the wrong direction.[38]

So in 1997, it was not unnatural for the Tories to try to conceive of their predicament in American terms. Parallels were not hard to find between the Tories and the Republicans. The story went like this. Each had had a period of domestic political hegemony in the 80s, with leaders (Thatcher 1979–90, Reagan 1981–9) who had transformed their respective countries internally, while simultaneously engendering respect abroad. But these two great leaders were followed by timid courtiers hopelessly inadequate to be trusted with the great legacy (Major 1990–7, Bush Sr 1989–93). Meanwhile, useless leftie opposition had remoulded itself, at least superficially, around charismatic but fundamentally empty political geniuses (Blair 1997–, Clinton 1993–2001).

Britain's Conservatives, it was opined, were a little behind the Republicans in the cycle. Following Mr Clinton, various Republican state governors were quietly experimenting with clever ways of dealing with various crises of public service, steering a course between the differing moral visions of a country increasingly divided between puritan Christians and liberals. Ideology was ditched, in favour of fostering cross-party support. Prominent among these governors were Tommy Thompson of Wisconsin, John Engler of Michigan and, not least, the two sons of George Bush Sr, George W. in Texas and Jeb in Florida. Each of these Republicans seduced large numbers of the Democrats' core supporters.[39]

George W. quickly reached a position of pre-eminence as he developed the philosophy of 'compassionate conservatism'. Much of this was a careful deployment of vocabulary, but the idea seemed to have wide appeal. In the Texan context, it generally involved reducing the involvement of government in society, exporting many of its functions to voluntary or faith-based organisations, which, it was assumed, would be less bureaucratic and more efficient at targeting resources where they were needed. Mr Bush held out a hand to the large number of Latino immigrants in his state, becoming fluent in Spanish (in the 1998 midterm elections, Mr Bush took 49 per cent of the Latino vote).[40]

In sum, compassionate conservatism pulled together many strands of American thought. It appealed to the religious right, the small government neoconservatives, the Clintonistas who were interested in creative ways of keeping levels of public service up while saving money at the same time, and those agonising about the atomism and individualism in American society in the wake of Putnam's *Bowling Alone*.[41] Most of all, it appealed to the ordinary Texan, who was repelled by the sterility of partisan debate.

The Tories were keen. The core supporters liked the word 'conservatism'; the modernisers liked 'compassionate'. And it fitted rather nicely into the narrative of British/American parallelism. Mr Clinton looked like being succeeded by Vice President Al Gore, a man of talent and intelligence, but who lacked the appeal of his boss, and indeed harboured a not-so-secret scepticism about much of the Clintonian agenda. Across the pond, the Gore mantle fitted Gordon Brown to a T. And so, were a Republican with a big idea to win in 2000, that big idea, went the argument, could be deployed against Labour in the analogous context of 2001.

The narrative at that stage looked good. And so, drawing upon compassionate conservatism, as well as the 'common sense conservatism' of Canadian politician Mike Harris, Mr Hague developed the philosophy of 'kitchen table conservatism'. The idea was that conservatism could be explained, or discussed, by an ordinary family around a kitchen table. It thereby rather neatly connected a number of images. First of all, it took political ideology out of the think tanks, whose pointy-headed sharp-suited denizens were not viewed with favour by voters, and brought it into people's houses. The concepts would have to be simple, clear and intuitive enough to appeal to all, not just those who owned the complete works of Hayek. Second, it resurrected the Oakeshottian idea of politics as a conversation.[42] This distanced the Hague approach from the ideologically driven Thatcherites, who were seen as arrogant and out of touch, and chimed in with the new humility of a party keen to be seen as 'listening'. Third, it subtly suggested support for the 'normal' family: the nuclear family assembled round the table at important communal moments such as breakfast and dinner, implicitly appealing to traditionalists.

But the idea did not take off.

> The party's hapless attempts to rebrand itself conquered new summits of preposterousness when Mr Hague returned from America espousing 'kitchen table conservatism', and went on to install such a table in Tory headquarters, giving shape if not clarity to this perplexing metaphor.[43]

It, and a series of planned party political broadcasts featuring young couple Chris and Debbie sitting around their – you guessed – kitchen table, were quietly canned.

What went wrong with the big idea? In the first place, the aim – to privilege particular ways of living – was always going to be hard to achieve in our secular and liberal times. No version of conservatism in a diverse democracy can be strongly linked to a 'standard' way of life. The idea of the family sitting round the kitchen table always looked a little anachronistic, but the Tories' timing was masterly. Around about the same time, the famous Oxo family, which played out a comic soap opera over several years of stonking great roasts served with mouth-watering Oxo gravy, was dropped by the advertisers, because 'family life is changing'.[44] Britain's potteries began to slump, as they continued to produce large, ornate dinner services designed for the multi-course family dinners at the table that no one was having any more.[45] Mr Hague leapt on the kitchen table bandwagon just as kitchen tables were on the way out.

Mr Duncan Smith continued Mr Hague's interest in American, particularly Republican, politics (indeed, the Tory conference of 2002 was deliberately designed on American lines, with black, Asian and young people ushered on stage at various times, though Party Chairman Theresa May's kitten heels rather stole the show[46]). The Iraq war complicated matters, but senior Tories were happy to go along with the pro-Americanism. It looked sensible, as not only was George Bush in the ascendant in both American and world politics, but also it was thought that British politics was beginning to look like that of America. Oliver Letwin argued as much on the ground that British political argument, being about the role of the state and how much power should be devolved from the state to lower levels of government, was hard to distinguish from American debate.[47]

One of Mr Howard's first significant ideological acts as leader was to release a set of core beliefs for New Year's Day 2004,[48] a credo, it turns out, with strongly American roots, as hostile commentators enjoyed pointing out.[49] American philanthropist John D. Rockefeller's statement of his beliefs, originally made in a radio broadcast on 8 July 1941 – young Master Howard was one day old – and immortalised in a stone plaque outside the Rockefeller Center in New York, is very similar to Mr Howard's. Mr Howard's *penchant* for tax-cutting was another strongly American theme, chiming in with a new reading of the parallels between Britain and America, according to which Mr Bush's right-wing success was based not on compassionate conservatism, but rather on his trillion-dollar tax cut.

The American turn never worked to dispel the post-Thatcher blues; kitchen-table conservatism, compassionate conservatism, tax cutting all failed either to dent Mr Blair's dominance, or to provide the Tories with a sense of purpose and focus. The real problem lies in the origin of the initiative, in American policy wonkery. Why assume that the solution in America should be the same as the solution in Britain? Britain and America are very different places – obvious, but it is amazing how often one has to point it out explicitly. In particular, America has long and worthy traditions of self-reliance and philanthropic giving that Britain does not have and cannot match. Americans give 1 per cent of GDP to philanthropic causes; Britons just 0.6 per cent (of a much smaller *per capita* figure).[50] In general, America is a much more right-wing place with very different social attitudes (Figure 1). Should we really expect to be able to transplant ideas from a very

Divided by more than the sea

**American and British public opinion
selected issues, %**

	US	Britain
Oppose/disagree with an unlimited right to abortion	46	17
Proud to be 'American'/'English'	97	76
Taxation is 'too low'/support higher taxation (for public services)	1	62
Approve of George Bush's increase in foreign aid	53	90
Believe in the Devil	45	13
Support a ban on the possession of handguns	32	83

Selected social indicators

	US	Britain
People earning 40% or less of median income, %	14	5
Millionaires, % of population	0.74	0.58
Gun deaths, per 100,000 people	10.6	0.3
Average number of executions, per year, 1997–2001	78	0
Defence spending per head, $	1,059	576
Government spending, % of GDP	30	39

Figure 1: Differences between America and Britain[51]

different soil and expect them to grow? Is it, more to the point, a very *conservative* thing to want to do? That question is key to understanding conservatism, and understanding the possibility of progress for the Conservative Party under its fifth leader after Mrs Thatcher, David Cameron.

Ten lessons to be learned

The history of the Tory Party from 1990 to 2005 is one of extra-ordinary decline. It is not easy to turn around a large, failing organisation. There are many factors to be considered, including changes to organisational structures and decision-making procedures, tactical alterations, attempts to put up cuddlier, more photogenic and more diverse candidates and a determined effort to repair the damaged brand.[52] Media analysts, psephologists and assorted young men in suits with computers can wrangle over such issues, and decide whether to change the name of the party, whether to put up all-women or all-ethnic-minority shortlists for selected safe seats, whether to change the party's colour from blue or whatever. But beliefs matter.

This is a book about ideology. Although image is important, few people will vote in a sustained way for a party whose beliefs are not widely shared, or which seems to have no beliefs. A leader with a pretty face can deliver victory, but to be a sustained party of government, to influence the history of a country for decades requires an understanding in the voters of that country of what the party stands for.

A party's ideology – particularly in the British system where parties are essentially large coalitions of diverse interests – will often be as much a blend as a specific philosophy, and the individuals at the head of the party (not just the leader) will determine, in their complex negotiations and trade-offs between themselves, interests within the party, interests outside the party and the voters, exactly what the blend should be. So the Tory Party, for instance, tries to blend free market neo-liberalism, conservatism, business interests, Christianity, strict moralism, ruralism and so on. Different leaders emphasise different things: so for instance Mrs Thatcher's period of leadership was characterised by her strong promotion of neo-liberalism, but was not restricted to that and there was plenty about the policies she created and rhetoric she used to keep adherents to other ideologies (including voters who were not in the party) happy. Although such electoral factors as party unity have nothing directly to do with ideology, a party whose members are comfortable with its ideological direction is more likely to present a united front to voters.

A party's ideology is created in all sorts of ways: in philosophical statements and speeches for sure, but also in the careful selection of arguments made, policy areas addressed and enemies engaged. If this is done judiciously, as Mrs Thatcher certainly did for many years, then the diverse coalition that is the party stays together. If not, then it will fall apart. There has to be something for everyone. Expectations are important. Mrs Thatcher failed at the end because her overconfidence led her to neglect constituencies of opinion which diverged from hers (including the voters'). John Major failed largely because he was seen as a very damp squib following Mrs Thatcher, although in truth his more casual, more conservative and more collegiate leadership style had been amply trailed. William Hague's attempts to appeal to everyone backfired, from the notorious baseball cap (of which he must be heartily sick) to his leaping onto bandwagons. Michael Howard was seen as too illiberal for a liberal nation. Perhaps only Iain Duncan Smith, of recent Tory leaders, failed as a result of other faults; his policy programme was generally seen as at least a partial success.

So ideologies can be adjusted and the balance set differently. It seems clear – polling bears this out – that the Tories are currently perceived by the electorate as way too right wing, and focused on the wrong issues.[53] That is a pragmatic reason to change. It is also not a party that seems at ease with itself; that is a sign that something is wrong. Finally, there are good reasons to think that the world has changed remarkably since the resignation of Mrs Thatcher, and it is essential that the party reinvent itself ideologically in order to keep pace. And our review of the experience of 1990–2005 gives us many lessons that the Tories must learn.

1. The individualism of the Thatcher era must be toned down. There are many reasons for this. First, the individualists to whom the party appealed are not natural party-joiners – this is why the party 'hollowed out' so badly in various areas. Second, many of the serious problems of social breakdown facing Britain at the moment require a more collective view. Third, in a nation that prides itself on its decency (almost all Tory discussions of the state of Britain make that point eventually), a sink-or-swim individualism is simply not appropriate.

2. Libertarianism is similarly inappropriate.

3. Equally, the Tories have to avoid moral prescriptivism. Britain is now a very diverse place, with many immigrants and descendents of immigrants, many people who relish sexual freedom, many people who for good or ill live in alternative family structures to the nuclear family. Perhaps the greatest challenge of the globalised 21st century is how to ensure that diverse, open and multicultural societies can remain societies, and not descend into chaotic conflict.

4. Europe is obviously an important political issue, but the passion and venom that the Tories injected into the debate were clearly out of place, especially when any EU government's freedom of manoeuvre is so limited.

5. The balance between public and private provision of services is fairly delicate, but it is clear that any attempt to shift it too radically in the direction of private enterprise will go against the wishes of many British people.

6. A related point: Britons are neither repelled by, nor suspicious of, the state. They do not mind the state doing things, and indeed seem to want the state to step in

whenever some problem is blown up by the tabloid media (and criticise the government for inaction). There are limits to such indulgence, of course; voters doubt that Gordon Brown's increased taxes have been spent wisely. But equally voters do not slaver after tax cuts.

7. So-called 'core vote' strategies, to shore up the supposed traditional Tory vote, are purely and simply mistakes. In the first place, there are not enough voters in this 'core' to deliver Tory government. Second, policies that resonate with the Tory 'core' are fiercely opposed by most of those outside. And third, surely the real Tory core is the suburban professional middle class, the ABs, who are deserting the Tories in droves and are not impressed with anti-immigrant, Euro-sceptic or illiberal rhetoric.

8. The flip side of the above point is that the Tories have to realise that Britain is a liberal nation, by and large.

9. Strategy matters so much more than tactics. Discomfiting Mr Blair or Mr Brown, securing the resignations of Cabinet ministers, is good newspaper copy, and may secure short-term improvements of poll ratings. But the Tories have to think of the longer term. It is not impossible that they will win a general election in 2009 or 2010, but unlikely. They may have to wait until 2015 for a sniff of government, and all of that time needs to be spent changing voters' perceptions. A positive vision is needed.

10. Britain is not America, and American ideology will not necessarily work in Britain. The success of the Republican Party over the last quarter century has been very inspiring for many Tory thinkers, but that should not imply that the various strains of Republican thought will work in Britain.

These ten ideological lessons stand out from our review of the last fifteen years. Whatever else the new leader does, Mr Cameron needs to bear these in mind.

Post-Thatcher blues V: David Cameron

The leadership election

David Cameron came from nowhere. Reportedly under some pressure from David Davis, Michael Howard announced his impending resignation as Tory leader immediately after the election, although he intended to oversee the transition to a new system of leadership election that would return much of the selection power to MPs. This led to a long period of reflection, perhaps calculated on Mr Howard's part. After all, throughout summer 2005, everyone knew there would be a contest for the Tory leadership, but no one knew the rules under which the contest would be carried out. The general betting was that a vote of the membership would favour Mr Davis, whereas the MPs were a little more suspicious of him, so any change of rules to restrict the say of the ordinary party members would help Mr Davis's opponents. At the beginning of the process Mr Davis was a hot favourite – Ladbrokes made him 5–2 favourite when the contest was called, and he was odds on by June.

At that stage, however, no one knew who those opponents were. Kenneth Clarke was a perennial challenger, and Sir Malcolm Rifkind had been making thoughtful speeches for quite some time. But Mr Howard launched his own favoured candidates, by appointing 34-year-old George Osborne as his Shadow Chancellor, and as Shadow Education Secretary he named Mr Cameron, who at 38 was a little older, but who still appeared very young. Mr Cameron had long been talked about as a potential leader of the party, but his close involvement with the drafting of the disastrous 2005 manifesto seemed to raise doubts about his judgement, and indeed his commitment to bringing the Tories to the centre. All these four were thought to emanate from the left of the party; Dr Liam Fox was also considering a move from the right.

Even though the leadership election process was deeply flawed, and even though a change would speed up the handover of power, Mr Howard failed to get his preferred system agreed, and late in the summer it became clear that the contest would have to take place under the Hague rules. Votes of the MPs would take place after the party conference in October, and the final ballot of members would be completed by early December.[54] In all, seven months elapsed between Mr Howard announcing he was standing down and Mr Cameron's victory speech – one would consider that a record, except that Tony Blair made a similar announcement before the 2005 general election, and was still in place two years later, much to the chagrin of both Gordon Brown (rumoured) and the Labour Party at large (all too evident).

This unwieldy system yielded a distinct advantage to Mr Cameron. Unknown at the commencement of the campaign, he was a household name by the end of it. In that way, the system acted rather like the primary campaigns in the United States, which allow regionally based politicians to achieve a national profile through several months of media exposure. Mr Cameron's campaign – Mr Osborne declined, probably wisely, to stand – reached a climax with his successful conference speech,[55]* and he

* The Ladbrokes odds for the Tory leadership tell the story of a fascinating conference. On 3 October, when the conference began, Mr Davis was 1–2 favourite, Mr Clarke was 5–2, Mr Cameron was 9–1 and Dr Fox 10–1. On the morning of 4 October, Mr Cameron made his speech, and by lunchtime was 9–2, while Mr Clarke had moved out to 100–30. Mr Clarke's own speech in the afternoon didn't affect either set of odds, but by the end of the day, Dr Fox had moved out to 12–1, while Mr Davis was holding steady at 8–15. On 5 October, Mr Davis made his ill-fated speech, followed by Dr Fox. Mr Davis's odds drifted through the day, ending up on 5–6, still favourite, while Dr Fox moved out still further, to 14–1. Mr Clarke was moving in, now at 11–4, but the steamer was Mr Cameron, who ended the day at 9–4, now clear second favourite. On the morning of 6 October, everyone read their newspapers and the true horror of Mr Davis's speech, and its contrast with Mr Cameron's, was revealed. Mr Clarke moved out to 4–1, while Dr Fox moved back in to 12–1. Poor Mr Davis, odds on overnight, continued to drift, and by 2.21 that afternoon, Messrs Davis and Cameron were joint favourites at 5–4. Mr Cameron continued to move in, and was odds on favourite, at 4–5, by the end of the conference. Mr Davis was looking much weaker at 15–8. Dr Fox's own speech had done him little good, but he had capitalised on Mr Davis's weakness and ended the week a little stronger at 9–1, while Mr Clarke was the other big loser of the week, at 11–2. Had you put £100 on Mr Cameron at fixed odds at the beginning of the conference, you would have walked away with £1,000 in December; by the end of the conference, your £100 would have got you a mere £180.

had little difficulty, in the end, in seeing off the three official challengers, Messrs Davis, Fox and Clarke. It seemed to be a victory for modernisation, but, as I consider in more detail in Chapter Nine, two of his three opponents also declared themselves modernising candidates, and the meaning of the term 'modernisation' remains a matter of some dispute.

The successes

Be that as it may, Mr Cameron had immediate successes. His speeches prior to his victory trailed his determination to drag the party to the centre. Labour were certainly worried by this, but the real losers were the Liberal Democrats. Under their leader Charles Kennedy, a likeable, laid-back character, they had pursued a strategy of targeted schizophrenia, appearing right wing when middle-class suburbanites were to be wooed (opposing tuition fees for university students, for example), while sliding to the left to attract disaffected Labour supporters (opposing the Iraq war most obviously, but also trumpeting their determination to raise taxes for the wealthiest). The Tories' neglect of the centre enabled them to persist in this strategy, even though it was obviously unsustainable in the long term (at least if they wanted, as they claimed, to displace the Tories as the major opposition to Labour); opposition from senior Lib Dems was muted by Mr Kennedy's popularity with voters, and with the electoral gains he made.

Mr Cameron's move back to the centre was the final straw. With a centrist Tory Party competing directly for Mr Blair's votes, the Liberal Democrats no longer could be all things to all men. They would have to decide whether they were to the left or to the right (broadly speaking) of Labour. A few weeks of turmoil in the party led to the dramatic events of New Year 2006, when Mr Kennedy's leadership was ended by a rebellion of the parliamentary party. A lacklustre contest, for which the party was ill-prepared (as evinced by a couple of sex stories that quickly surfaced), saw the Lib Dems play for safety, choosing staid, uninspiring Sir Menzies

Campbell as successor. Sir Menzies' job, it quickly transpired, was not to overtake the Tories, but rather to preserve the Lib Dem's strong third place. The election of Mr Cameron was the direct cause of this reduction in scale of Lib Dem ambition.

In fact, Mr Cameron has reinvigorated the Tories as the four previous leaders failed to do. The polls tell their own story (Figure 2). If we look at the period of Tory hegemony and decline, we first see Mrs Thatcher's roller-coaster: ten points down in the polls before the Falklands War in 1981, and recovering to win a spectacular victory in June 1983; the big win in 1987, followed by the incoherent third term, with the poll tax effect giving Labour a twelve-point lead. We should not underestimate Mr Major's achievement in turning that around, in eighteen months or so, to an eight-point election victory. The polls also show the effect of Black Wednesday: Mr Major was three points down in August 1992, ten points down in October, and the Tories only occasionally got within ten points of Labour until Labour's own decline brought them down to the Tories' level in 2005.

That inertia in the Tory vote is what Mr Cameron has to undo. One year after the general election, six months after his ascent to the leadership, he had wrested the lead back from Labour, albeit by a small margin. This is the greatest poll success of any Tory leader against Mr Blair, although individual polls mean little, and there are more hills to climb.

Mr Cameron's successes brought other tangible pluses. Now that the Tories look less moribund, he has also revolutionised the funding situation. Labour had become the party of choice for business after 1997, but following Mr Cameron's victory the moolah is flowing the Tories' way once more. In the first three months of Mr Cameron's leadership, nearly £9 million went to the Tories, as compared with under £3 million for Labour and £700,000 for the Liberal Democrats.[57]

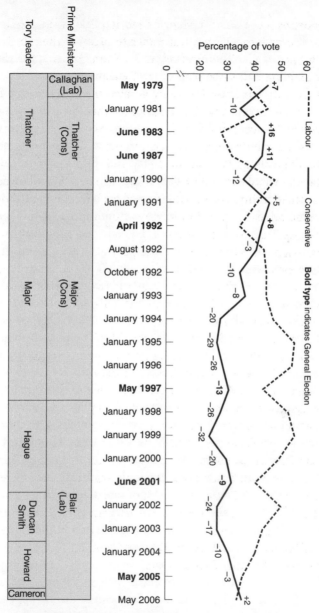

Figure 2: The fall (and rise?) of the Conservative Party[56]

The challenges

But it is not all plain sailing for Mr Cameron. He has spearheaded a Tory revival, and indeed has showed that he has learned from Mr Blair's experience. Like Blair (1997 model), Cameron is a fresh face, and a relaxed man. He understands the centre, and shuns most of the instincts of his activists, though equally he preserves a vestigial trace of traditional Tory obsessions (with strong stands over Europe and the Human Rights Act, for example). He has made a sustained attempt to appear vaguely normal, and wears his Etonian past easily.

Nevertheless, the ground is not as propitious as it was for Mr Blair in 1994. In the first place, Mr Blair was preceded by two important leaders, Neil Kinnock, who led the drive from the far left of politics and crushed the ridiculous Militant Tendency, and John Smith, who not only took Labour directly into the centre but was also much more attractive to voters. Between them, Messrs Kinnock and Smith took eleven years to prepare the ground: Mr Blair's centrism could only appear plausible against that history of patently sincere struggle. Mr Cameron's three predecessors, as we have seen, spent their eight years of opposition messing about, veering wildly from left to right and back again. There is much talk of the need to develop a 'coherent narrative', but a coherent narrative is not just any old narrative. It also has to be coherent (which seems obvious, but sadly needs stating). It can't just be a *post hoc* rationalisation of the random policy trails of 1997–2005 – it has to be a genuine story of how a determined group of people exorcised the self-destructive demons of the previous political generation and remade the Conservative Party and made it relevant once more. Mr Cameron, it is clear, stands at the beginning of that story, not (like Mr Blair) at its end.

So Mr Cameron has a lot of work to do. He is likeable, popular and has made important ideological changes; all well and good. But he has not, and will not, sweep all before him. He appeals, so far, to the affluent voters in the South and East who had deserted the Tories. But at the time of writing, there is little evidence that he is making very much progress anywhere else. The Tories abandoned the North of England, Scotland and Wales many years ago, and it will take a Southerner like Mr Cameron quite a while to win them back. That is not to say that he cannot. But victory in the 2010 general election depends on gaining a few seats in rural Scotland, the suburbs of the Northern cities and the wide open spaces of Yorkshire and further North, and at present there is no reason to think that he will.

This leaves Mr Cameron with another problem that Mr Blair never had in his brief period of opposition. Mr Blair directly challenged the left of his party, and was able to do so with impunity because he could demonstrate, by opinion polls and council election results, that he was pretty certain to deliver a landslide in 1997 (which of course he duly did). The left stayed more or less onside (with the odd grumble by Clare Short and others) because government beckoned. Some of them even persuaded themselves that Mr Blair only sounded like a Tory because he didn't want to jeopardise his lead, and that when he became leader he would be much more left wing – not a good call.

Mutatis mutandis, Mr Cameron has the same problem with his right wing: he is deliberately betraying the right wing's current view of what Tory policy should be, and doing so in order to connect with more centrist voters. His right wing has been duly fractious. Lord Tebbit even compared Mr Cameron with Pol Pot; the charge's very ridiculousness betrays the depth of feeling. In one sense, this is a good thing. Mr Blair enjoyed being at war with his unpopular party, and if moderate voters see that the Tories' right wing is upset they will be much more likely to believe Mr Cameron is sincerely trying to change the party. But Mr Cameron will be unable to show that victory in 2010 is inevitable, because it is highly evitable. Demography, the voting system, time and the size of the Labour lead are all against him. He might, with luck and a following wind, be able to show that he *might* win in 2010; he should be able to point to a clear improvement over 2005. But that is a long way short of the heady prospect of government. Those true believers who loathe Mr Blair might easily assume that the Tory improvement was as a result of New Labour's unpopularity, and that the revival would be even more pronounced without the wet Mr Cameron at the tiller.

And then there is the collapse in Mr Blair's personal ratings. The war in Iraq and the botched occupation have destroyed Mr Blair's credibility amongst voters. Labour, no less than the Tories, have to decide what comes after Blair. But when voters consider the qualities of Mr Cameron they will have the precedent of Mr Blair before them. They will know the great political story of our own time: how a personable, informal 'straight kind of guy' with his denim shirt and coffee mug became a weary warmonger, friend of Bush and ignorer of the United Nations Security Council, implicitly connected with all the evils of Guantánamo and extra-ordinary rendition, while in his own land savaging civil liberties and presiding over growing inequality.

The Tories used to accuse Mr Blair of being left wing while pretending to be right wing. This is obviously not true. But voters now know that while Mr Blair was pretending to be from Venus, he was really from Mars. That deception might well have gone unnoticed had the attacks of 11 September 2001 not changed the world. But they did, and Mr Blair's true colours were raised. Voters wanted to be released from the Tories and were prepared to trust Mr Blair; ironically, one of Mr Blair's most important political legacies to his own party might be his fall from grace. The parallels between Mr Cameron and Mr Blair can only serve to foster suspicions, and any relief that is felt at Gordon Brown succeeding the latter might also work to Mr Brown's advantage against the former.

Changes

Mr Cameron's problems, then, are complex, and his youth and agreeable personality will only get him so far, as he understands. His attempts to change the Tory Party are various, and will hopefully have some effect, but it is not as simple as that. One of Mr Cameron's ideas is to produce an 'A-list' of 100 or so favoured candidates, vetted by Central Office, containing people of the highest calibre. We will talk about this in more detail in Chapter Nine. But Mr Cameron, in trying to escape the Tories' image of the party of the rich, white and middle-aged,[58] has also tried to seed this list with a larger than usual proportion of women and people from the ethnic minorities – all parliamentary parties are unrepresentative of Britain's demographic mix, but the Tories more so than most.[59] These diverse and high-calibre people, it is hoped, will find themselves safe seats to fight the 2010 election.

But the Tories' constituency parties are extremely independent – indeed positively cussed, and the first opportunity to exploit the A-list was turned down in Bromley and Chislehurst.[60] The new candidate eventually won the by-election, but with a dramatically reduced majority of 633.[61] The significance of this isn't clear. Does it mean that Mr Cameron's appeal is limited, and that ignoring the core vote will undermine the Tories?[62] Or alternatively that he was right: an A-lister, rather than your average pinstriped type, might have done better?[63] More data, of course, is needed, but we will speculate further in Chapter Nine.

Policy is another important issue for Mr Cameron. There is absolutely no point in his coming up with a set of policies a long way before he has to face the next general election. Such policies might become outdated between 2007 and 2010. The long run-in would give Labour a long time to counter them. And the Tories might seem somewhat stale if they stick with the same set of policies for several years. Furthermore, Mr Cameron's record as a policy-picker – he is, don't forget, the author of the 2005 election manifesto – is anyway not good.

Mr Cameron's solution was interesting and creative: he set up various policy teams to investigate the key policy challenges of the 21st century, and recruited a few eye-catching names, such as green activist Zac Goldsmith, who is the Vice-Chairman of the Quality of Life board, and rumpled saint Bob Geldof, advisor to the board investigating Globalisation and Global Poverty. The output from these policy teams, reports and recommendations for policy, then become the input to the Tories' team to assemble the draft manifesto for the next election, whose Chairman is Oliver Letwin. We look at policy in more detail in Part Two of this book, but the policy teams have the advantage of being able to think creatively and having deniability. On the other hand, if they came up with inconvenient ideas – or indeed inconsistent ones – if, say, Mr Goldsmith's recommendations clashed with those of John Redwood's board investigating Competitiveness – then whatever policy documents result from the exercise might be much less exciting than the individual policy teams' reports. If interesting ideas end up being mangled, then the Tories might well be worse off for the exercise.

Indeed, letting others do one's thinking for one can be problematic even with deniability. For instance, Policy Exchange, a think tank, published a lengthy paper in 2006 that received a lot of publicity. The paper, unfortunately, was called *Compassionate Conservatism*.[64] The paper makes interesting reading, and makes a number of worthwhile points. But Policy Exchange is Mr Cameron's favourite think tank, and indeed he is prone to call himself a 'modern, compassionate conservative'. But compassionate conservatism does make one think instantly of George Bush, and the Americanism that cannot straightforwardly be transplanted on UK soil. The authors of the paper explicitly want to reclaim the idea from Mr Bush,[65] but maybe a retreat would have been wiser, in the same way that Francis Fukuyama has given up trying to pull the term 'neoconservative' out from Mr Bush's long shadow.[66] The idea that the so-called 'third sector' can take over some state functions, which is the chief burden of *Compassionate Conservatism*, is doubtless not ridiculous and worth exploring, but as we have noted, America has much more robust traditions in this area. Conversely, it is at least doubtful that the enthusiastic amateurs of Britain's volunteer sector could realistically cope with any kind of significant transfer of state function to them.[67]

Meanwhile, on the PR front at least, the idea is open to attack from influential voices on the left with a strong sense of the role of Britain's state in welfare provision.[68] Mr Cameron's closeness to Policy Exchange, and his use of the phrase 'compassionate conservatism', makes deniability trickier than perhaps he might have hoped. The amount of inspiration that can be drawn from the very different American experience is inversely proportional to the risks of drawing it.

The core of Tory policy that was not intended to be undeniable appeared eventually, in summer 2006, in a revised document called *Built to Last*.[69] In its introduction, Mr Cameron discussed the notion of change explicitly, change for both the party and the country. 'The country needs a new direction and new answers', he said, and called for a 'responsibility revolution'.

> A revolution in personal responsibility – giving every individual the skills, the resources, and the confidence to take control of their life.
>
> A revolution in professional responsibility – giving all those who work in our public services the freedom to fulfil their vocation.
>
> A revolution in civic responsibility – giving our neighbourhoods and communities the power to shape their destinies, fight crime and improve the quality of life.
>
> A revolution in corporate responsibility – giving business the encouragement and the incentive to help enhance our environment and improve well-being.
>
> That is the mission of the modern Conservative Party: a responsibility revolution to create an opportunity society – a society in which everybody is a somebody, a doer not a done-for.[70]

The notion of a responsibility revolution is *prima facie* an odd one – conservatives are theoretically opposed to revolutions of any kind, but responsibility is something they warm to. Do we even detect welcome echoes of Flanders and Swann, with their respectable songs for responsible people? Their classic tactic of subverting subversion – 'The purpose of Satire, it has been rightly said, is to strip off the veneer of comforting illusion and cosy half-truth, and our job, as I see it, is to put it back again' – may well have been copied, albeit unconsciously, by a new and energetic generation. In Part Two of this book we will consider exactly what the responsibility revolution consists of.

Tory revival and Tory ideology

The Tories have made decent progress with a decent, personable young leader. If they change their image from being the stern economic party to one interested in the social consequences of economic policies, if they manage to highlight more women and people from the ethnic minorities, if they manage to sound more like the voters they hope to represent, and if they don't obsess about Europe or gay marriage or whatever, then they will make even more progress. But that is not all.

Mr Cameron needs a narrative to explain and express the Tories' move back to the centre, and he needs to filter the results of the policy review boards into something coherent. These matters are not to be addressed simply by clever brand management, new logos and photo shoots. These are philosophical and ideological matters: the Tories need an underlying ideological foundation upon which they can build. If they do not establish that, then their recovery will be built on PR sands. Indeed, Labour have identified this area as one where Mr Cameron is vulnerable. After all the caring, sharing, tree-hugging postmodern Tory leader is also the author of the gung ho blood-and-guts 2005 manifesto. Labour suspect that Mr Cameron is an all-things-to-all-men type of politician – nothing like Tony Blair, then – and at one point carica-tured him as Dave the Chameleon.

There are a number of ideological directions to help the Tories resolve this appearance of vacillation. They could continue the

Thatcherite neo-liberal line of development, or they could ape Mr Blair's third way. In this book, I wish to argue that traditional conservatism, sceptical of human powers and respectful of society, is another way forward, one that will allow them to develop policies relevant to the 21st century while remaining faithful to their past and their intellectual forebears.

The attentive reader will have noticed that I have so far referred to the Conservative Party as the Tory Party, to Conservatives as Tories. There is a reason for that. Conservatism is a philosophy, an ideology, and those who profess it are conservatives. In general, conservatives are members of the Conservative Party; that is, conservatives are Conservatives. Conservatives (with a small 'c'), as their name suggests, prefer where possible to conserve; they are not radical, they distrust innovation. This is not always true of Conservatives with a big 'C' (= members of the Conservative Party); Mrs Thatcher's free market policies changed the political landscape (sometimes even the physical landscape) of Britain, for better or worse, dramatically. She was a radical, of the liberal tradition (which the Conservative Party has continued to an extent since her deposition).[71] Her instinct was not at all to conserve, not at all to avoid disruption.

There is nothing wrong with this *per se* – the Conservative Party is and always has been a broad church. It contains not only liberals and conservatives, but also libertarians, businessmen and women, and moral atavists among others. Understandably, practising Conservative politicians have been keen to emphasise the ideas they hold in common.[72] But there has been a tendency to equate conservatism with 'that which the Conservative Party does', which misses the point, given the different views of its members and leaders.

Michael Freeden calls the idea of several ideologies within the Conservative Party a 'chimera',[73] though one might be forgiven for thinking that the chimera in this case was the hybrid 'ideology' he specifies. Similarly, political theorist W.H. Greenleaf wrote in 1983 about the 'twin inheritance of Conservatism' – note how the issue is confused when the capital letter is used: does that mean an ideological follower of conservatism, or a member of the Conservative Party? The twin inheritance in question is that of Tory paternalism and free market liberalism, the two particularly prominent views held within the Conservative Party.

> There remains the continuing assertion that there *must* be common characteristics in Conservatism (or any other ideology) of a meaningful and distinguishing kind. But, whatever its superficial appeal, this claim must be denied, and the counter-question asked: What *are* the aims, arguments and assumptions that are shared by Stafford Northcote and R.A. Butler, Joseph Chamberlain and Enoch Powell, Mallock and Macmillan, a Central Office pamphlet issued in (say) 1927 and the notions of Sir Keith Joseph? They do not even necessarily oppose the same things.[74]

Greenleaf is wary of distinguishing between party and ideology (but then what is Enoch Powell, who had by then left the Conservative Party in disgust, doing in his list?). And he is of course correct that ideologues of different periods may well have different priorities, depending, among other things, on who their perceived enemies may be. But claiming that conservatism means being a member of the Conservative Party, and *vice versa*, glosses over many interesting phenomena, as well as playing fast and loose with the original definition of 'conservative' – someone wanting to conserve.

Political researcher Bruce Pilbeam thinks that if conservatism is understood in this relatively straightforward sense, the resulting class is too wide, and so the definition is flawed.

> Taking a bare attitude towards change as defining of conservatism leads, on the one hand, to denying the label to the very many avowed conservatives who have actively sought change (such as advocates of dismantling the welfare state), and, on the other, to the inclusion within the ideology's boundaries of

many who would not ordinarily be considered conservatives (such as Soviet communists who defended their regime during the Cold War).[75]

To be honest, it doesn't seem absurd to me to lump together people of different positions who try to avoid change, be they English barons, Soviet generals or Iranian mullahs. But when we examine conservatism a little more closely, as we will in Part One below, we will find an interesting theme running through its history of a robust scepticism, and this in itself will rule out many who simply try to avoid change because they are doing rather well out of the status quo. Such a position is a natural selfishness, rather than anything ideological.

This will be discussed in much more detail in Chapter Four, but the point I have been belabouring in this section is that there is a distinction between conservatives (with a small 'c') and Conservatives. The former occupy an ideological position that I will specify; the latter are members of a particular political party. Many conservatives are Conservatives, and *vice versa*, but it is perfectly possible to be one without the other. The Conservative Party is the natural custodian of the ideology of conservatism, but has rather neglected it for the last 30 years. My argument in this book will be that attempting to re-establish conservatism as a viable philosophy for the 21st century may well be a way for the Conservative Party to regain the political centre while simultaneously providing differentiation from Blairism. But equally, it would be possible for members of other parties to be conservatives in the sense I will describe; when Mr Blair railed against the forces of conservatism in 1999, he did not mean to restrict his bile to members of the Tory Party.[76] It is perfectly possible to be a conservative of the left (for example, defending the current structures of our public services against Blairite reform).

So, in this book, orthography (and proof-reading!) are all-important. When I write 'conservative' with a small 'c' I specifically mean someone who holds the conservative ideology, whichever party he is in, or even if not in any party at all. When I write 'Conservative' with a capital 'C', I mean a member of the party, whatever ideological stance he takes. If there's an ambiguity, because the word appears at the beginning of a sentence for example, I'll take care to disambiguate. That small 'c' is vital to meaning.

With a small 'c'

Having set the scene, we now have three tasks. The first is to raid history and philosophy to gather materials for a firm definition, and intellectual tradition, of conservatism, up to the point at which the Conservative Party became the representative in Britain of the conservative interest. We shall trace conservatism as an attitude to theory and knowledge, from the Ancient Greeks, via the transmission of their work to Renaissance Europe, and thence to Britain, showing how scepticism became a political attitude (Chapter Two). Next, we will follow conservatism in the Conservative Party, and try to show how a version of 19th-century liberalism took over the party, eventually replacing its conservative host in 1975 (Chapter Three). Given that intellectual and political history, we will then try to develop a definition of conservatism that is consistent with it, drawing on the work of more recent conservative thinkers like Michael Oakeshott and Roger Scruton (Chapter Four). The final task of this opening part is to counter arguments that conservatism, along the lines we have defined it, is necessarily dead in the rapidly changing post-Thatcher world (Chapter Five).

The second part of our enquiry looks at what would happen were the Conservatives to make a committed attempt to replace their current liberal free market ideology with a conservatism such as we have described, as an attempt to take a non-Blairite central position. Three particular issues are examined: the key policy areas of economics and markets (Chapter Six), and social affairs (Chapter Seven); and an area where Conservatives currently score rather badly, but where – I shall argue – conservatives might actually do rather well: the collapse of public trust in authority (Chapter Eight).

The final part of the book will look at the particular problems of the Tories in refashioning their ideological stance. First, we will look at the way in which the modernisation debate has cut across party allegiance and direction (Chapter Nine). What does it mean to modernise the Conservative Party, or conservatism, and how can the project be brought forward, given that modernisation is espoused by anyone who is anyone, each of whom means something slightly different by the term? And finally, we will round up the debate, looking at how Mr Cameron is shaping up as a conservative and as a potential election-winner (Chapter Ten). The debate over the Tories' ideological direction is only just beginning and much depends on its outcome.

Part One

What is conservatism?

When, he'd say, we study the various types of industrialization in advanced countries, for example, we find they're like revolutions imposed on those societies from above; they're the work of ruthless minorities who aren't to be swayed from the goals they've set, and regard all obstacles to progress as solvable by technical and rational means. He found this imposed rationalism disturbing, because its advocates chose to view society as being susceptible to rational arrangement through a mixture of acumen and power, and any irrational elements discovered within the societal foundations had to be resolutely mastered and changed in accordance with the needs of the advocates of rationalism themselves.

Jabra Ibrahim Jabra, *In Search of Walid Masoud*
Translated by Roger Allen and Adnan Haydar

People, I have seen the doubt
the lovely ambiguities of light and dusk.
Who wouldn't wish to share
this cherished jamais vu
of knowing next to nothing?

Peter Armstrong, 'Homage to Joe English'

CHAPTER TWO

THE IDEA OF HUMAN IMPERFECTION

Socrates, morality and knowledge

The question this book addresses was posed in Chapter One: how can the Conservative Party regain the centre ground in British politics while retaining the essential continuity with its ideological roots? Of course this is a hard problem! It is easy to see political debate as being obsessed with the affairs of the moment – tuition fees, the Iraq war, congestion charging, tax cuts or whatever – because that is what politicians argue about. But, for a principled politician, ideological considerations always underlie the crude day-to-day parliamentary knock-about. Hence, straightening out those considerations, perhaps altering them, perhaps merely coming to understand them properly, could well lead to a break-through in understanding how a political party, whose fortunes might be waning, could make itself relevant in a new context. It was such a first-principles examination of the socialist tradition that enabled Tony Blair to revitalise the left, for instance by unpicking the neat assumption, formulated during the Second World War, that the state was the essential architect of measures to redistribute wealth and to ensure equitable access to resources.

To pull a similar trick for the Conservative Party, we need a similar examination of their ideological traditions, though the task is complicated by the different ideological strands present within the party. It is of course a matter of taste as to which strand one thinks is most useful and important; I propose to examine its small 'c' conservative strand. Unpicking this tradition requires stripping away the interests of the moment from conservative writings and rhetoric, and understanding what are their basic elements. Surprisingly, the basic ideas of conservatism are concerned not with morality, or economics, or human nature, or any of the standard subject matters of ideologies: conservatism is actually a claim made about human understanding and knowledge of the world, a plea for humility in the face of the widely differing sources of knowledge in the world.

The story of conservatism – the strand of conservatism with which we are particularly concerned – is a long one. We must travel back two and a half millennia, to the Ancient Greeks, to see its beginnings. The Greeks were a fascinating people, gregarious, curious, disputatious. They studied everything, and had theories about everything, many of which were horribly wide of the mark.[1] But that did not stop them arguing about them.

Our interest begins with Socrates (469–399 BC), a philosopher who wrote nothing; he merely argued and for this he was executed. There are first-hand accounts of Socrates still extant, which paint incompatible pictures of him. But the abiding view of him is shaped by Plato, in whose philosophical dialogues Socrates is the main character.[2] In these brilliant vignettes Socrates is witty, original and devastatingly destructive. The only thing he knows, he says, is that he knows nothing. He then takes on his interlocutors – all of whom claim knowledge about some philosophical concept, justice, say, or beauty – and demonstrates, merely by asking suggestive questions, that they actually know as little as he (except that they do not know that they do not know). Doubt everything, says Socrates; take nothing on authority.

We can only guess how much of the historical Socrates has survived in these portraits. But what does seem as certain as anything is that he was concerned with *questioning*. If someone claimed to have knowledge, Socrates would leap in and try to unravel what the content of that knowledge was. Presumably he would often discover that there was nothing to the supposed 'knowledge' beyond meaningless jargon and puffery. No doubt on occasion he punctured assiduously cultivated reputations for wisdom. As a modern parallel, recall the general attitude towards the counter-cultural professors in the universities exhorting their students to revolt in 1968. Socrates was perhaps the earliest exponent of a sceptical attitude towards authority, demanding to know what the basis of the authority was. He would simply ask questions, and lead his opponent into admissions that were either inconsistent or deeply implausible, or otherwise unconvincing, earning him great admiration from those thinkers who had grown impatient with the fantastic proliferation of views, theories and ideas in Greek intellectual life.

The schools of ancient scepticism

Socrates was not as deep a sceptic as it is possible to be, however. Like some of his fellows (Xenophanes, Empedocles or Democritus, for instance), his view seems to have been that knowledge is desirable, and that man had up till then failed to achieve it. If knowledge was necessarily and completely unattainable, that was a matter of regret. Socrates always remained an important role model for sceptics, but he was essentially pessimistic. Scepticism proper began when some philosophers started to think not only that knowledge was unattainable, but that that was a *good* thing; it was not a symptom of man's bleak fate in a world that was doomed to be forever foreign to him, but rather a liberation from certain types of desire, certain types of error and certain types of pressure.[3]

The philosopher who is credited with this discovery is Pyrrho of Elis (c.365–c.275 BC). Like Socrates, he wrote nothing, and all we have of him are some near-first-hand accounts of which we possess only fragments.[4] Pyrrho thought that knowledge about the world was impossible, that the world was, in his reported words, undifferentiated, unmeasurable and unjudgeable. Hence enquiry about the world was pointless. Pyrrho's follower Timon praised him for releasing mankind from the slavery of opinion and the bonds of deceit and persuasion.

Pyrrho's ideas fell into obscurity after the death of Timon, but his name was spectacularly revived by a philosopher called Aenesidemus (who lived sometime at the beginning of the 1st century BC). Falling out with the 'official' sceptics, the intellectual followers of Socrates in the Academy originally founded by Plato, he stalked off, taking his new philosophy with him. In honour of his great predecessor, he called it *Pyrrhonism*.[5] This was focused on methods for creating doubt and uncertainty, ways to show that a dogmatically held theory was false. In particular, he thought that even the sceptics themselves were too dogmatic, not sceptical enough. They asserted dogmatically that knowledge was impossible. Aenesidemus wouldn't even have that. In his version of Pyrrhonism, no doubt some bits of knowledge might be true, but no one could ever know which. Maybe true knowledge was impossible, maybe not; the Pyrrhonist was agnostic over such questions. He wouldn't even claim that Pyrrhonism was true, only that the methods it espoused induced a spiritual calm.

Aenesidemus' work is completely lost, and the intellectual trail of Pyrrhonism goes cold for a while. But with the appearance in the 2nd century AD of an obscure doctor called Sextus Empiricus, Pyrrhonism becomes highly visible indeed.

Sextus Empiricus

Sextus Empiricus was not a great philosopher, nor did he claim to be one. But he does have a giant place in intellectual history, thanks to the ironies of fate. Whereas Aenesidemus, an original figure, remains obscure, Sextus is important because of the historical accident that his work has *survived*.

No doubt much of Sextus's work has been lost,[6] but there is still a decent quantity left. Most crucially, there is a piece called *Outlines of Pyrrhonism*.[7] This work was intended as an introduction for the layman, a textbook of the philosophy of Aenesidemus. It is this that has ensured Pyrrhonism's survival into the modern era, its textbook qualities guaranteeing the work was read much more than the originals.

Despite this relative wealth of material there are many doubts about what Pyrrhonism actually involved. Some maintain that Sextus's argument is that knowledge of *any* type is impossible, that no one can really know anything.[8] Others say that Sextus was really only railing against the wild Greek theories of science, about the speculations of the professors who claimed to have knowledge of, say, how the human body worked, when in reality they didn't. Our ordinary commonsense knowledge of the world is perfectly OK; it is only when we try to go beyond the obvious, to postulate hidden causes, deep mysteries, that we tie ourselves in silly speculative knots.[9] Still others say that Sextus inconsistently flip-flopped between these two views.[10] Others detect a more sophisticated argument in Sextus that has to do with justification: we are never justified in believing what we believe (and hence we should never be tempted to be dogmatic).[11] Indeed, as Sextus was not a philosopher of the first rank, and was bringing together material from several sources, all of these may be the case at different places.

What is Pyrrhonism?

The actual form of Pyrrhonism is of less importance for our purposes than the reaction to it and its influences on later thinkers, which we will trace in this chapter. Sextus left us a method for analysing arguments, based on the philosophy of Aenesidemus,[12] which does contain a nugget of effectiveness.[13] Here is not the place to go into details, but in a nutshell, the basis of Pyrrhonism is this.

Suppose there is some contested issue, let's say the existence of God. This has been debated for centuries and the various positions have become very well worn. Suppose I advance an argument that God in fact does exist, and that He has some particular nature.

Then you will without doubt be able to find arguments, from thinkers greater than I, that God does not exist, and other arguments, from other great thinkers, that He does exist, but that He is very different from the being I supposed. And to your arguments, I will be able to find counter-arguments from equally great thinkers, and so on. The only result of our discussion is to demonstrate the equipollence, or equal strength (*isostheneia*), of the arguments, the fact that each point of view can muster convincing arguments in its favour, arguments moreover that come with the endorsement of great intellectual figures.

Why would I choose one point of view over the other? If more brilliant people than I have failed to show convincingly that they are right and that others are wrong, why would *I* be able to advance the position? If, for example, such geniuses as St Thomas Aquinas or René Descartes cannot prove the existence of God, and other geniuses like Voltaire or Nietzsche cannot prove the opposite, what on earth can I add to the debate? Much better, says Sextus, to forget the question, to cease to worry about the issue. No doubt there is a right and a wrong side of the argument. No doubt either St Thomas or Voltaire is correct. But I don't and can't know which; furthermore, nor did St Thomas or Voltaire. I cannot decide the matter, so why should I let it bother me? I should suspend my belief (*epoche*), and this will lead to a feeling of well-being and relaxation (*ataraxia*) – and after all, isn't a feeling of well-being what we're all really after?

Hence a clever argument (even one I am unable to refute) is not, in itself, evidence that a view is correct. In the face of the complexity and intractability of the world, cleverness will never be enough. There may well be a fact of the matter about which we are speculating, but we are simply not equipped to find it. This sceptical insight is the essential thread that will take us from the Greeks through to the 21st century, for we can see exactly this *isostheneia* in many extremely important social, philosophical, political or economic debates.

Let's take a modern, political example. One premise for

promoting aid for the developing world is that it acts as an investment that enables developing countries to move into self-sustaining growth; we give a chunk of aid now and in ten years' time the recipient country will be standing on its own feet. This is not a silly idea, but it is a disputed one. For many years the debate was fruitless, as there was very little data on which to base a position, but in the mid-1990s, key papers were published by Peter Boone, who argued that aid financed consumption rather than investment-led growth.[14]

Love–fifteen against the supporters of aid. But then World Bank economists Craig Burnside and David Dollar examined the data, distinguishing between the recipient countries' economic and political policies: they discovered that when aid goes to countries with sensible economic policies (low inflation, free trade, small budget deficits), there is a payoff in terms of growth.[15] Fifteen–all. Next, three more economists weighed in, re-examining the Burnside/Dollar data and adding more available data: they discovered that the effects of 'good' policies disappear in the wider data set.[16] Fifteen–thirty. But there was more to come. Three more economists separated out different types of aid and analysed the data concerning them separately: they discovered that aid designed to have an impact on growth in the immediate term did help, whether or not the recipient country had good policies.[17] Thirty–all.

What is the layperson to make of this? Let us not presume that the final paper is the final word. Academics cannot reach a consensus about this most vital of issues – and this is not because they are silly, or idle, or pusillanimous, or indecisive. It is because the data is hard to interpret, and their theories can only be tentative. But these academic results must feed into the deliberations of politicians and activists who understand the debate much less; the politicians and activists must decide which side of the fence they are sitting on, which of these august economists are correct. But how can they? They do not have the expertise to do so. So their choice of whom to believe, if they make a choice, is of necessity uninformed and unjustified. The way in which contradictory evidence makes its way into the political debate on aid is discussed in more detail by former World Bank economist William Easterly.[18]

So the Pyrrhonist claims that knowledge is too hard to find, because even the experts never agree. What about those who reply that he undermines his own argument? If he (the Pyrrhonist) says that such weighty matters as science, metaphysics or whatever cannot be known, and someone else (a scientist, say), says that they can be known, then we have another pair of arguments and more *isostheneia*. The Pyrrhonist's argument is undermined, goes this criticism, by the fact that he takes one side in a debate, and therefore his own arguments apply to his own theories.

The Pyrrhonist replies that he also knows nothing about the *decidability* of these intellectual arguments (for example, between St Thomas and Voltaire, or between the various economists about aid). He does *not* know that nothing is knowable (if he did claim that, then of course he would be contradicting himself: if he *knew* nothing could be known, then he would know *something*, viz., that nothing could be known, and therefore it could not be true that *nothing* could be known). It is only that he is unable to decide between the point of view that the original argument is decidable, and the opposite point of view that it is not decidable. And he can't decide that question for the same reason that he can't decide the original question, i.e. because lots of equally powerful arguments from great thinkers can be piled up on each side of the issue.

Such, then, is Pyrrhonism. Why should Sextus think that Pyrrhonism was attractive? We know very little of Sextus, but the clue is that he seems to have been a doctor. The Greeks had lots of medical theories of how the body worked. Some thought that it was made up of the hot, the cold, the wet and the dry; others that there were bodily humours, for example black bile, yellow bile, blood and phlegm, and so on. The treatment of disease involved rebalancing these humours, for example by purgatives, emetics or bloodletting.[19] There was much fierce argument about exactly what treatment should accompany which symptoms.

We should not, of course, be ungenerous to the Greek physicians, but equally we can't help but note that these scientific theories are all incorrect, to put it mildly. And no doubt many of the treatments came closer to killing than curing. A movement arose in medicine called *empiricism*, which was based as far as possible on eschewing theories and just observing symptoms.[20] If a particular treatment had dealt well with a particular symptom in the past, then that was a *prima facie* reason to try it again – though the physician couldn't know for sure that it would work for a second time. The idea was to build up, slowly and steadily, a portfolio of case studies.

Sextus was almost certainly a physician of this sort of persuasion;[21] indeed the name Sextus Empiricus means 'Sextus the empiricist'. And there is obviously a close link between the empiricist rejection of theory on practical grounds and the Pyrrhonist idea that there are always clever arguments, between which it is impossible to decide, for and against any theory.

Both philosophies were reactions against the intellectual cacophony of the Greeks, the interminable disputation that seemed essential to the Ancient Greek character.

Scepticism and conservatism

This type of scepticism about knowledge and authority, though it might seem revolutionary and even conducive to libertinism, actually promoted a rather acquiescent position. Pyrrho himself, for example, believed that, as no moral standard could be established by reason (or be self-evident), then the wise man should conform to the laws, norms and conventions of the society of the day.[22] Sextus also recommended conformity in a famous and influential passage.

> Adhering, then, to appearances we live in accordance with the normal rules of life, undogmatically, seeing that we cannot remain wholly inactive. And it would seem that this regulation

of life is fourfold, and that one part of it lies in the guidance of Nature, another in the constraint of the passions, another in the tradition of laws and customs, another in the instruction of the arts. Nature's guidance is that by which we are naturally capable of sensation and thought; constraint of the passions is that whereby hunger drives us to food and thirst to drink; tradition of customs and laws, that whereby we regard piety in the conduct of life as good but impiety as evil; instruction of the arts, that whereby we are not inactive in such arts as we adopt. But we make all these statements undogmatically.[23]

In other words, we have to make moral choices in our daily lives, but we can never know which moral choice is correct. It is therefore sensible to adhere to the customs of one's society, which after all are as likely to be correct as any other position.

The wisdom of basing one's moral and political behaviour on the customs of the country was also confirmed from another source. The restless Greeks had explored far and wide, and had amassed quite a literature on other cultures (most notably the works of Herodotus[24]). The variety they found chimed in with the idea that social regularities were accidents, matters of taste rather than manifestations of any kind of moral law.[25] Such accidents were worth attending to:

> For perchance the Sceptic, as compared with philosophers of other views, will be found in a safer position, since in conformity with his ancestral customs and the laws, he declares that the Gods exist, and performs everything which contributes to their worship and veneration, but, so far as regards philosophic investigation, declines to commit himself rashly.[26]

Note here that the sceptic conforms to the norms of his age for his own self-interest. It keeps him from being attacked for nonconformity, and it also saves him having to think too deeply about matters that he cannot resolve – it brings the positive benefits of *ataraxia*. The result is a *type* of conservatism, but the strong element of self-interest means that Pyrrhonism has yet to become the conservatism that we understand today.

The transmission of ancient scepticism to the Renaissance

Sextus gained some celebrity, but was the last of the major sceptics. The world was changing in the 2nd and 3rd centuries AD, and the sceptical, challenging frame of mind had little place in it. The dynamic tension of the Greek city states had been replaced by the bureaucratic vigour and murderous political strife of the Roman Empire. Such conditions do not reward adventurous thinking.

Furthermore, Christianity was on the march, becoming the dominant framework for thought and politics. Scepticism was out; the essence of Christianity was certainty, the word of God through the Bible. The insight of Pyrrhonism – that clever theories are not necessarily informative about the world – was made irrelevant by the increasing acceptance that you could scour your Bible, or works of respected churchmen, for telling evidence one way or the other. The heavy hand of religious authority suffocated scepticism, for the time being at least.

And so the Pyrrhonists were gradually forgotten. In Western Europe there was no mention of Sextus Empiricus for 1,000 years or so. During the long Dark Ages, many ancient texts were lost; there were no doubt major philosophers, mathematicians and thinkers of all stripes of whom we are now totally ignorant. But fortunately some of Sextus's manuscripts were preserved in libraries in Byzantium; Sextus's knack of bringing together arguments from different people, and of summarising the positions of other philosophers, including those of whom he disapproved – the skill of the textbook writer – meant that his work was occasionally consulted by Greek-speaking Byzantines and Arab scholars,[27] while the more technical, and perhaps more philosophically correct, works of his predecessors were neglected. This occasional consultation was just enough to keep the flame burning low.

Three developments in the late medieval period conspired to rekindle scepticism. The first was the nature of the Church. In the centuries following Sextus the Church was for Christians pretty well the only source of hope, of intellectual comfort – one might almost say, of civilisation were it not for the Moorish kingdoms in Spain. But by the Middle Ages it had abused its monopoly so flagrantly that its authority (if not its political and military power) had declined dramatically. Intellectual rebellions against corruption, sales of indulgences and the dissolute lifestyles of supposedly abstemious men, rebellions that were ultimately to lead to the Reformation, were under way. Hence there was once more a space for philosophies that questioned authority.

Second, while Christianity and the Bible remained paramount, other methods of understanding the world were gaining currency. Science, or something like it, was beginning to emerge. Mathematics and logic seemed to provide ways of achieving absolute certainty. This led to an obvious question: would these other methods of acquiring knowledge lead the inquirer to a belief in God? In other words, could you use your *reason* to establish the truth about *God*? What if reason issued in the wrong results? There was scriptural justification for worry about this: St Paul, for example, had often argued that the Holy Word was more important than any learning ('knowledge puffeth up, but charity edifieth'[28]). But logical thought seems so compelling. Is it possible to find things out about God without reading the Bible, without prayer, without faith? This had always been a source of tension for the Church, but as the medieval thinkers gradually recovered their intellectual confidence, the question became more pressing.

Third, the greater curiosity of the age, and the greater stability that allowed more travel and trade, meant that thinkers from the West began to rediscover the classical thinkers, often via translations out of Greek, into Arabic and thence to Latin (though all Sextus's work survived in Greek). Interest in the ancients began to spread, an intellectual movement known as *humanism*.

Sextus was one of the posthumous beneficiaries of the fashion. The first interested Western owner of a manuscript of Sextus's work was Francesco Filelfo (1398–1481), a manuscript that is now probably in Florence.[29] The early Italian humanists were mainly interested in the work for its antiquarian value. But gradually, thinkers began to take more notice of what Sextus's work actually said, and began to re-evaluate Pyrrhonism on its own terms. A number of minor Italian philosophers began to use the destructive critical methods that his work contained, notably Gianfrancesco Pico della Mirandola (1469–1533).[30] But Pyrrhonism's second wind really arrived in the 1560s, when Latin translations began to appear, and the scene of the action switched from Italy to France.

Montaigne

Michel Eyquem de Montaigne (1533–92) was one of the greatest, one of the most likeable and one of the most unsystematic of all European intellectuals. After studying law, and serving for thirteen years as a magistrate in Bordeaux, he retired in 1570, at the age of 37,* to his country estate to read, to think and to escape the fraught political situation of the day.

As he thought, so he wrote; the result was three books of almost unparalleled brilliance and humanity.[31] His short discursive takes on many and various topics provided the original model for the literary form of the essay. Montaigne revelled in the unusual and the immediate – he saw no need for consistency, and his idea was that by ranging over this vast collection of topics, he could portray a human mind in the hopeless task of extracting sense from a vast, complex, patternless world.

The France of Montaigne's adult life was very troubled. The Reformation had created immense tensions between Catholics

---

* Lucky sod.

and Huguenots (Protestants); at the same time the Crown was trying to centralise power. France was almost ungovernable – certainly governed badly – and from 1562 to 1595 it was more often than not in a state of outright religious war.

Montaigne, a Catholic, had no time for religious intolerance – indeed, many of his own family had converted to Protestantism. What appalled him was not just the inhumanity of the wars, but also the way that the inhumanity was provoked by a strong sense of certainty about religion. Both sides naturally assumed that God was on their side. Not for the first time in history, speculative philosophy and theology, subjects that were over most people's heads and whose truths were hard if not impossible to verify, were the excuse for savagery and destruction.

So when Montaigne discovered the joy of Sextus (so to speak), and read in the *Outlines* in Latin translation that nothing is certain, and that arguments on each side of a problem generally if not always cancel each other out, he was delighted. He even struck a medal to commemorate the event, and painted quotes from Sextus on the beams of his study. Much of Montaigne's work was influenced by Pyrrhonism. He also, like Sextus, loved piling up evidence that different societies valued different things, and that none was better than any other. He loved to find travellers' tales of paradoxical societies that functioned perfectly well, and retold the stories to great effect.[32]

Montaigne certainly disliked and distrusted change. His views on human ignorance and imperfection led him to castigate the presumption of those who thought they knew how best to govern:

> ... for my humour, there is no system so bad (provided it be old and durable) as not to be better than change and innovation ...
>
> I find that the worst aspect of the state we are in is our lack of stability and that our laws cannot adopt one fixed form any more than our fashions can. It is easy enough to condemn a polity as imperfect since all things mortal are full of

imperfection; it is easy enough to generate in a nation contempt for its ancient customs: no man has ever tried to do so without reaching his goal; but as for replacing the conditions you have ruined by better ones, many who have tried to do that have come to grief.[33]

Hence scepticism has led to the idea that people simply aren't clever or brilliant enough to understand how a society functions, or how to draft a system that will function better. But whereas Sextus (and the other Greek sceptics) were chiefly concerned with knowledge, science and philosophy, and only tangentially interested in politics, Montaigne was the opposite; he came to find Pyrrhonism exciting precisely because of the political implications he thought it supported.

There is no doubt that Montaigne was a Pyrrhonist sceptic for at least some of his writing life. There has been much scholarly debate about whether he was a conservative. Peter Burke has argued, sensibly enough, that the debate is not terribly interesting. 'Conservative' (small 'c') has a specific meaning and a more general meaning; the former is somewhat anachronistic, the latter is devoid of significance in the 16th-century context.

> His support of outward conformity may suggest that Montaigne was a conservative. The difficulty here is that if we want to use the term in a precise sense, we have to say that a conservative is someone who opposes the liberals. In this sense, no one was a conservative in the sixteenth century. Right and Left, as names of specific parties, were born together at the French revolution. If we resolve to use the term 'conservative' in a vaguer sense, we are faced with the opposite problem. In the weak sense of the word, everyone was a conservative in the sixteenth century, for everyone, Luther no less than the pope, defended his views by appealing to tradition.[34]

And David Lewis Schaefer argues that Montaigne supported many progressive ideas, and that he was a determined anti-religious radical;[35] there is plenty of textual evidence in the *Essays* for this view.

But this leads us to perhaps Montaigne's greatest contribution to the development of conservatism out of ancient scepticism. For – rarely among political thinkers – Montaigne seems to have recognised his own ignorance just as acutely as he did that of the rest of society. He is quite happy to acknowledge that Sextus's sceptical arguments applied just as much to his, Montaigne's own, political ideas as to anyone else's. Schaefer replies that this is an 'extremely shallow' point of view,[36] but shallow or not, this use of scepticism to argue for conservatism has the brilliance and flamboyance of a jewel thief returning a tiara to a pretty girl.

> To speak frankly, it seems to me that there is a great deal of self-love and arrogance in judging so highly of your opinions that you are obliged to disturb the public peace in order to establish them, thereby introducing those many unavoidable evils and that horrifying moral corruption which, in matters of great importance, civil wars and political upheavals bring in their wake – introducing them moreover into your own country. Is it not bad husbandry to encourage so many definite and acknowledged vices in order to combat alleged and disputable error? Is any kind of vice more wicked than those which trouble the naturally recognized sense of community?[37]

However radical he 'really' was, Montaigne's contribution to a humane and civilised conservatism is immense. He did not introduce Pyrrhonism to the West; nor was he the first to associate Pyrrhonism with conservatism. His major intellectual innovation was shifting the focus of scepticism. Ancient scepticism was centred on the well-being of the sceptic himself, in three ways. First of all, the sceptical methods set out by Sextus were to be used by the sceptic to triumph in debate; the aim was a public demonstration of the sceptic's argumentative ability. Second, the use of the sceptical methods was intended to aid the sceptic to rid himself of unsupported belief, and thereby to reach a state of contented wisdom, or *ataraxia*. Third, as can clearly be seen from the quotes from Sextus above, the conservatism that Pyrrhonism supported was intended to protect the sceptic from the bad opinion of a society; it was not intended to benefit the society in any direct way.

Montaigne switched the whole thing around. The aim of Pyrrhonism as he recreated it was to benefit *society*. It was society that suffered when unsupported opinions clashed, and society that suffered when opinions and theories were implemented to right presumed wrongs. Montaigne *externalised* Pyrrhonism; he turned it from an attitude about knowledge, and an attitude towards an interlocutor, into a political attitude towards political interests and purposes. Instead of helping untangle someone's *mind*, Pyrrhonism now became a tool to promote social stability, and protect society from uninformed and unwarranted interference.

Shakespeare and the Elizabethans

In the slightly morbid atmosphere of England at this time, Montaigne's counsel of imperfection would find plenty of nourishment. Edmund Spenser's (1552–99) epic poem *The Faerie Queene*, for example, contains many passages making the point that God alone could possibly know what was best, or what fortune would hold. In one episode, the virtuous Artegall confronts a giant who is trying to restore the 'balance' of the Earth, to recreate order out of the chaos of the time.

> Such heavenly justice doth among them reign,
> That every one do know their certain bound,
> In which they do these many years remain,
> And mongst them all no change hath yet been found.

But if thou now shouldst weigh them new in pound,
We are not sure they would so long remain:
All change is perilous and all chance unsound.
Therefore leave off to weigh them all again,
Till we may be assured that they their course retain.[38]

If you try to impose a fair balance on everything, says Artegall to the giant, you are more likely to upset the present balance than produce a fairer result.

Shakespeare (1564–1616) too wrestled with problems caused by human attempts to redraw the boundaries. Many of his works were concerned with the tribulations of authority and the rejection of legitimacy. Characters try to influence events, but when they do, they quickly lose control of the situation. Such machiavels (as they were called, in honour of the notorious Italian philosopher Machiavelli) could be evil (Richard III), misguided (Macbeth) or even well-intentioned (Brutus). But their intrigues always led in the same direction. First, the new order they created could not supply justice, stability or good government. And second (most graphically demonstrated in *King Lear*), once the threat of the machiavel had been repulsed, it was not possible to restore the old order. Once a traditional society, with a legitimate ruler, had been disrupted, the delicate balance was irreplaceable.[39]

The problems of human imperfection, the vagaries of fortune, the uncertain relationship between the actions of individuals and the tribulations of society; these are all problems that Montaigne wrestled with, under the influence of many authors, Sextus Empiricus prominent among them. Sceptical ideas were spreading around Europe. Had Shakespeare read Montaigne? There is some evidence that he had, and that in particular 'On the Cannibals' could well have been one of the sources for *The Tempest*.[40]

Whatever the truth of that, as England moved from the relative stability of the Elizabethan reign to the beginnings of union with Scotland, and the inept politicking of the Stuart century, a taste for scepticism was developing.

Sir Thomas Browne and the nature of human imperfection

By the 17th century, the scepticism that had begun in antiquity was all the rage in Europe.[41] Montaigne had been championed in England by the philosopher and civil servant Sir Francis Bacon. But perhaps the Englishman most like Montaigne was a relatively minor figure, Sir Thomas Browne (1605–82), a distinguished doctor from East Anglia who had a healthy sense of the variety, unpredictability and mystery of the world. Indeed, he was rather too Montaigne-like for his own equilibrium; a placid man, he felt moved enough by a review of his *Religio Medici* to reply waspishly to his critic:

> The learned Annotator-commentator hath parallel'd many passages with other of Mountaignes essayes, whereas to deale clearly, when I penned that peece I had never read 3 leaves of that Author & scarce any more ever since.[42]

Browne's *Religio Medici* (*The Religion of a Physician*)[43] is an enchanting work, written, like Montaigne's essays, during a period of great religious controversy and strife (in Browne's case, the mid-1630s – the work circulated in pirated copies until Browne published an authorised edition in 1643). It caused controversies of its own: Browne was accused of atheism, and *Religio* was placed on the Catholic Index of Prohibited Works for three years; extreme Protestants were no less scathing, with one critic punning on the Latin title to call it a description of the religion of the notorious Medici family.

Browne was certainly not an atheist, but a moderate Anglican, and his style was informal, tolerant, and mistrustful of clever reasoning when so much of the world is uncertain and paradoxical. Argument is no sensible way of reaching agreement.

A man may be in as just possession of Truth as of a City, and yet be forced to surrender; 'tis therefore far better to enjoy her with peace than to hazard her on a battle.[44]

The Pyrrhonist insistence on the equal power of conflicting arguments was a constant theme.

We do but learn to-day, what our better advanced judgements will unteach to-morrow … the wisest heads prove, at last, almost all Scepticks, and stand like *Janus* in the field of knowledge.[45]

The wisest men and women are perpetually afflicted with doubt, and like the Roman god Janus must face both ways. This leaves room for faith – indeed, theologically it positively invites it – but that faith could never be so positive as to license the religious violence that was seen in France in the 16th century and in England in the 17th. Browne's faith was relatively unusual, whimsical even; he believed strongly in witches (here he was unlike Montaigne), and even testified to that end in a trial in 1664, although characteristically he was unconvinced that witchcraft was responsible for the victims' woes in actual cases.

English Pyrrhonism

Religio Medici had a great vogue in both England and Europe for decades. With it, English scepticism takes on a characteristically Pyrrhonist form. The Pyrrhonism is of a mild strain; the English Pyrrhonist does not espouse the strong form of scepticism (found on the Continent) that says that all knowledge is impossible. Instead, he or she suggests mildly that advanced theories are likely to be incorrect (experience, after all, tells us this), and that a common-sense understanding of the world will be much more important. The implication of this is that we shouldn't sacrifice the actual and concrete for the abstract and speculative, except in extreme circumstances.

Society's ills have their roots in human imperfection. But the word 'imperfection' is ambiguous. We should not focus on man's *moral* imperfection, the fall from grace, the eviction from Eden. If we do, we will be liable to veer into authoritarianism (as if others' moral vices were any of our business anyway). The desire to improve or perfect people quickly becomes the urge to eliminate those who refuse or are unable to be improved to order. Our brief examination of Montaigne and Browne shows us that the sceptical conservatism I am describing has its roots in tolerance, and the avoidance of extremes.

The imperfection of mankind has little to do with moral imperfection, but rather is an *epistemological* imperfection (i.e. imperfection of our means of gaining knowledge). The world is complex, scruffy and difficult to understand. Both Montaigne and Browne thought that God at least could understand it, but that that certainty was vouchsafed to no mortal. Such uncertainty cries out for tolerance.

If we do not keep an eye on the difference between moral and epistemological imperfection, then we risk turning sceptical conservatism from a tolerant creed to an intolerant one. From the 21st-century perspective of a troubled world, riven once more with religious and political strife, we can begin the task of reinventing conservatism as a philosophical and political tool for promoting tolerance and humility, against the malevolent certainties of extremism.

CHAPTER THREE

THE CONSERVATIVE PARTY AS THE CUSTODIAN OF THE CONSERVATIVE TRADITION

Right and left

By the beginning of the 18th century, the British two-party system was already in place. The identities of the parties have often changed; we have had Whigs and Tories, Liberals and Conservatives, Conservatives and Labour. There have often been third forces that have threatened to destabilise the dual hegemony; the Peelites, Irish Nationalists, Social Democrats, Liberal Democrats. Indeed, the Labour Party started out as a disruptive third force, but by displacing the Liberals preserved the traditional duality.

In such a system, ideology is one factor only in the great decisions of policy that parties have to make. Electoral advantage always has to be borne in mind, of course; that may mean bribery of key parts of the electorate, and sometimes the necessity of giving in to distasteful aspects of the *Zeitgeist*. Furthermore, governments (though not oppositions) are under all sorts of unwelcome constraints, such as binding international treaties, human rights law, and the realities of government finance. Finally, each big party must position itself relative to the other, opposing some things, urging more action elsewhere. In particular, conservatives, who by and large are happy with the status quo, find much of their ideological content determined by the radical plans of the opposition, whoever the opposition (liberals, socialists, feminists, etc.) might be at any one moment: a point that students of ideology have made much of.[1]

Hence a party cannot do all it wants, even if its members all agree on the wish list. In a two-party system, in a nation with a rich and varied political life, parties can be nothing more than fluctuating coalitions of interests. The Conservative Party, for example, contains not only conservatives, whose traditions are the focus of this book, but also agricultural interests, business interests (at least from the end of the 19th century), Anglicans (up to the middle of the 20th century) and free marketeers (in the 20th century). It is not trivial to read off the conservative ideology from the actions of the Tories or the Conservative Party.

A further wrinkle, not often discussed in detail, is that the two British parties seem to occupy different points in *psychological* space.[2] At least since Disraeli and Gladstone (of whom more below), certain psychological characteristics have been identifiable in many supporters of the two parties, the party of the right (Tories/Conservatives), and the party of the left (Whig/Liberal/ Labour). If I may resort to caricature, on the right politics is a game, about which it is appropriate to nurture a sense of humour; the left approaches matters with much deeper moral seriousness.[3] The left has the confidence to propose solutions to problems; the right is sceptical. The right is proud of the past, trusting of the institutions of society, and sympathetic to the law-abiding, the unsung, the ordinary; the left wants to free the human spirit, and instinctively sides with rebels and outcasts, those who are pushing the boundaries. The left worries about encroachment from the government, the right from the mob. As Dr Johnson put it, the Tory favours establishment, the Whig innovation. If we were casting film stars as personified political forces, we might put David Niven on the right, and Jack Nicholson on the left, the electorate to decide top billing.

Hence, for all these reasons, it would be impossible to show very much about ideology in Britain without studying the history of political parties in very great detail. What I want to do in this chapter is to pick out some conservative episodes in Conservative history, while thinking too about the simultaneous development of the sceptical conservative ideology, rooted in Pyrrhonism, which we left bubbling away at the close of Chapter Two. Ideologies and history are inseparable, and so this juxtaposition is essential. However, I am very alive to the fact that I am being of necessity extremely selective, and, though the discussion below *illustrates* my point that the conservatism I wish to describe has until recently been written through the Conservative Party like the message in a stick of Blackpool Conference rock, proof is a very different thing.

The emergence of the two-party system

The left/right split in British politics was already implicit with the arrival of the Stuarts in 1603. Everyone could agree that the monarchy's legitimacy came from the proper succession, because during the long reign of Elizabeth I (1558–1603), the question as to what would happen with an unsuitable monarch did not have to be raised. Elizabeth had turned England into a Protestant country, and Catholicism was disapproved of by virtually everybody. But the Stuart kings' open flirtation with Catholicism changed everything.

Rebellion was in the air, and the founders of the Tory tradition began to emerge during the civil war of the 1640s; in particular, men such as Viscount Falkland and Edward Hyde looked for a middle way between the absolutism that the foolish King Charles I demanded and the radicalism of Cromwell's Roundheads, a middle political way that mirrored the middle way in the literature and religion of Sir Thomas Browne. Falkland even furnished conservatism with a splendid dictum, that if it is not necessary to change the state, then it is necessary *not* to change it.

The Tories were in something of a bind. They were Anglicans, supporting the politico-religious establishment; on the other hand, the kings whose legitimacy they defended toyed with undoing that establishment. The problem came to a head when it became obvious that Protestant King Charles II would have no (legitimate) issue, and would be succeeded by his overtly Catholic brother James, Duke of York. This led to a political crisis in 1679–81, the exclusion crisis, when the first attempt was made through Parliament to prevent James from ascending to the throne. It was during this crisis that recognisable parties emerged (political cliques at that stage, rather than organised bodies). Their names were terms of abuse given by their opponents, later worn with pride: a 'Tory' was an Irish cattle thief, satirising their espousal of the cause of a Catholic prince; a 'Whig' a Scottish horse thief, hinting at nonconformity and the undermining of the settled way of the land.

Initially, the Tories were triumphant, seeing off the Whigs in 1681. We can get the measure of the times from the work of poet laureate John Dryden (1631–1700), who was very much in the mainstream that we are describing: sceptical, an admirer of Browne (the title of his poem *Religio Laici* deliberately apes *Religio Medici*) and a defender of the legitimacy of the Stuart kings.[4] Dryden's poetry often spells out the ideal of the constitutional monarchy, the middle way between French-style absolutism and Whiggish democracy, a middle way whose nature was determined by the stoical and phlegmatic nature of the English people.

> Our Temp'rate Isle will no extremes sustain
> Of pop'lar Sway or Arbitrary Reign:
> But slides between them both into the best;
> Secure in freedom, in a Monarch blest.[5]

His epic *Absalom and Achitophel*, written in 1682 reputedly at the behest of Charles II himself, describes the feverish years of the exclusion crisis with the good English sense of the solid roast-beef Tory. Even if people could legitimately get rid of their king, what Englishman would ever want to?

> Yet, grant our Lords the People, Kings can make,
> What prudent man a settled throne would shake?
> For whatsoe'r their Sufferings were before,

That Change they Covet makes them suffer more.
All other Errors but disturb a State;
But Innovation is the Blow of Fate.[6]

But the Tory victory was hollow. James II, as the Duke of York became upon succeeding his brother in 1683, extended the tradition of Stuart incompetence to the point of imbecility, promoting Catholics without consideration of Anglican sensibilities, and making cynical arrangements with Whig nonconformists. He alienated his Tory supporters on almost every level, and consequently they made very little effort to stand in the way when he was overthrown by a *coup* in 1688. James had had a number of Anglican offspring, and the Tories consoled themselves that the involvement of these princesses provided legitimacy for the new government.

Actually, this involved some high-grade mental gymnastics, as not only had James been overthrown, but his son James Edward had also been thrown aside. The new king was the Dutch William III, who was married to James's daughter Mary (now Mary II); on such flimsy ground did the Tories convince themselves, if no one else, that they were remaining loyal simultaneously to their religious principles and the hereditary idea. When first Mary, then William died, James's surviving Protestant daughter Anne succeeded to the throne, but none of her twelve children survived her (six more were stillborn). Then came the crunch.

When Anne died, the only realistic option for a Stuart succession was James's Catholic son James Edward (the Old Pretender). Parliament, however, had ruled out the possibility of a Catholic monarch, and had appointed as heir the non-English-speaking Elector of Hanover, who duly became George I. This was too much for most Tories – and the Scottish Tories (the Jacobites) even moved into open rebellion in 1715, and then again in 1745 in favour of the Young Pretender, Bonnie Prince Charlie, against George II (George I's son). The contradiction between the requirements of legitimacy and religion had been exposed, and, the Jacobite rebellions having failed, the Tories were finished, politically, for two generations. Neither George I nor George II forgave them, instead appointing Whigs to office exclusively. The joint period of their reigns, 1714–60, has been called 'the Whig supremacy'.[7]

Edmund Burke: the Whig who inspired the Tories

In time, the Hanoverian kings forgot their antipathy towards the Tories, and under George III, the first English-born king since James II, they became a serious political force once more. However, bizarrely, the most influential figure in British conservatism was not a Tory at all, but a renegade Whig, the Irishman Edmund Burke (1729–97).

For most of his career, Burke was a model Whig, who served under a number of Whig Prime Ministers, including Lord Rockingham and Charles James Fox, and was a prominent supporter of both the American Revolution, an important victory of the Enlightenment forces upholding the rights of man, and the English 'Glorious' Revolution against James II in 1688. But he is most famous for a sensational attack on the French Revolution of 1789; his *Reflections on the Revolution in France*,[8] published in 1790, has remained the leading work of conservative philosophy ever since.

It is a matter of dispute why Burke should support two revolutions and not the third; the feeling at the time was that he was bribed to oppose the French Revolution by George III himself (Burke was a somewhat Bohemian figure, perpetually surrounded by a large, loud and flamboyantly Irish extended family, and was regarded as slightly shifty). Burke's editor, Conor Cruise O'Brien, suggests that Burke harboured secret revolutionary thoughts and had mild, though suppressed, Jacobite sympathies.[9] Hannah Arendt argues that whereas 1688 and 1776 were conceivable (and conceived by their perpetrators) as organic changes repairing traditions that had been broken by authoritarian governments, where existing bodies politic were confirmed and legalised, 1789 was a conscious breaking of all traditions.[10] However that may be, Burke laid into the French Revolutionary parties with a will.

The French Revolution, initially at least, was popular in Britain; for some time it had generally been felt that the liberties and freedoms available in Britain contrasted favourably with the rigid hierarchies of French society. The French were storing up trouble for themselves, it was thought, and the Revolution seemed to prove the point. The British allowed themselves a smug snicker.

So, for the last few years of his life, Burke was not a popular man; his counter-revolutionary propagandising – for the *Reflections*, despite their laid-back, academic name, were in truth no more nor less than propaganda – were seen as extremist rabble-rousing. Much of this was because the Tories were in power at the time; no doubt he would have been more circumspect had the Whigs been required to dream up a policy to contain the revolutionary virus. But the net result was to alienate him from both sides in British politics. His own Whig party was generally in favour of the Revolution of 1789, as it was of those of 1688 and 1776. These revolutions, the Whigs thought, were prompted by human rationality in the face of superstition and tradition, classic victories of the spirit of Enlightenment over the forces of ignorance. Burke did not agree, and he and the Whigs parted company acrimoniously.

The Tories, on the other hand, never warmed to Burke, at least while he was alive, nor he to them. Burke thought that the French Revolution would bring down the established order with disastrous consequences, unless Britain was prepared for a long war to defeat the revolutionary movement. The Tories were quite happy for a war, but only a short one designed to secure Britain's interests, not to install a counter-revolution.

To the modern reader, Burke's prescience stands out compared with the misplaced optimism about the French Revolution of virtually all his British contemporaries; for instance, Tom Paine anticipated a bloodless revolution that would establish the rights of man.[11] We often forget, reading the *Reflections*, how early they were written, during the initial, relatively benign phase of the Revolution. Burke forecast that the overthrowing of the old order, corrupt and authoritarian though it was, would result in a complete lack of stability, a flourishing of violence and the opposite of the rational Enlightened society that most commentators were expecting to follow. He recognised that the French peasantry was unprepared for the difficult task of self-rule, that the compromise and humanity that such a task required were absent. It was French society that had been beheaded, not just the monarch.

Actually, when the *Reflections* were written, the monarch and his queen had *not* been executed. The September massacres and the Terror had yet to take place. Burke was generally thought to have been exaggerating, but events were to prove him correct. He even predicted that a militaristic despot would ultimately take over; Napoleon finally took control of France two years after Burke's death. In the event, the long war that Burke desired did happen, and did not end until Napoleon's final defeat at Waterloo in 1815.

Burke became a very fashionable figure in the Cold War, as his arguments seemed to apply quite nicely – for hawkish American purposes – to the Russian Revolution of 1917 as much as to the French one.[12] But it is an error to see Burke as a systematic political philosopher. The *Reflections*, and more so his later counter-revolutionary works, were explicitly propaganda, as noted above. Nevertheless, he develops many interesting themes that have been deeply influential on British conservative thought since, and that make their most commanding appearance in the *Reflections*.

First, there is the general worry about the violence of revolutions, that the forces unleashed by the sudden lifting of authority – even if that authority was not benign – will be worse than what they swept away. This is a point with particular 21st-century relevance.

Second, Burke much preferred the realities of practical politics to abstract theorising. The sceptical thread that we have been tracing through political history comes out strongly in Burke's preference for expediency and pragmatism over high-flown theories that may or may not apply to reality. People, not only as individuals, but also *en masse*, are unpredictable, and the real, unique circumstances of any situation count for more than abstract ideas of rationality, human nature, etc.

> I flatter myself that I love a manly, moral, regulated liberty as well as any gentleman of that society, be he who he will; and perhaps I have given as good proofs of my attachment to that cause, in the whole course of my public conduct. I think I envy liberty as little as they do, to any other nation. But I cannot stand forward, and give praise or blame to any thing which relates to human actions, and human concerns, on a simple view of the object, as it stands stripped of every relation, in all the nakedness and solitude of metaphysical abstraction. Circumstances (which with some gentlemen pass for nothing) give in reality to every political principle its distinguishing colour, and discriminating effect. The circumstances are what render every civil and political scheme beneficial or noxious to mankind. Abstractedly speaking, government, as well as liberty, is good; yet could I, in common sense, ten years ago, have felicitated France on her enjoyment of a government (for she then had a government) without enquiry what the nature of that government was, or how it was administered? Can I now congratulate the same nation upon its freedom? Is it because liberty in the abstract may be classed amongst the blessings of mankind, that I am seriously to felicitate a madman, who has escaped from the protecting restraint and wholesome darkness of his cell, on his restoration to the enjoyment of light and liberty? Am I to congratulate an highwayman and murderer, who has broke prison, upon the recovery of his natural rights?[13]

Third, Burke supported moderation, as being a prerequisite for liberty to be properly enjoyed.

Men must have a certain fund of moderation to qualify them for freedom else it becomes noxious to themselves and a perfect nuisance to every body else.[14]

Fourth, a useful mechanism for securing stability is property. This argument has been transposed into the language of 'stakeholding' in New Labour ideology; people must feel they have a stake in society before they will act to preserve it. For Burke, this 'stakeholding' is intergenerational; that is, it is expressed through inheritance. Private property can be appropriated legitimately neither by the state (except via properly instituted tax law), nor by revolutionary forces.

> These professors of the rights of men are so busy in teaching others, that they have not leisure to learn any thing themselves; otherwise they would have known that it is to the property of the citizen, and not to the demands of the creditor of the state, that the first and original faith of civil society is pledged. The claim of the citizen is prior in time, paramount in title, superior in equity.[15]

Though property and moderation are important, and can be undermined by massive inequalities (as indeed happened in the top-heavy French society of the 18th century), this does not mean that equality should be pursued to the extreme. Equality, like liberty, is an abstract idea that no doubt is perfectly sensible in the privacy of the thinker's office, but whose imposition, in a real situation, onto real people, will inevitably cause injustice and strife. The best solution is to avoid centralisation, promote varied and disparate sources of power, and seek to limit the domination of government by big bureaucracies that enjoy a monopoly of effective information.

> The characteristic essence of property, formed out of the combined principles of its acquisition and conservation, is to be *unequal*.[16]

These principles, their careful balance between interests and support for stability and moderation, were an important, if unusual, contribution to 18th-century thought. Their general common sense, and evident usefulness to preserving the status quo, made Burke the hero of conservatives within a few decades. But he wasn't the only Enlightenment thinker who managed to articulate a philosophy of conservatism that went beyond the self-interest of the wealthy and powerful. In Scotland the philosopher David Hume was thinking more explicitly in the Pyrrhonist tradition, and reaching similar conclusions from a more theoretical direction.

David Hume: Pyrrhonism in the 18th century

Pyrrhonism has always been controversial. Does it say that all knowledge is wrong, or just that we should accept what is evidently true while not going beyond the evidence? Does the sceptic break his or her own rules by stating that (some) knowledge is impossible? Is it possible to live life as a sceptic, or is scepticism just an intellectual pose?

As we have seen, Sextus Empiricus himself was ambiguous about the first question, and its interpretation has been a matter of dispute ever since. The second question caused an ancient split between the sceptics, with the Pyrrhonists following Aenesidemus in accusing the sceptics of the Academy of indeed breaking their own rules. The third question has always led to the charge of inconsistency being laid against sceptics, although Sextus, for one, used to say that living a sceptical life was not only possible, but the only means to a serene existence.

However, by the 18th century, scepticism had become a sharp philosophical tool, honed by sceptics such as Pierre Bayle (1647–1706) and non-sceptics such as René Descartes (1596–1650) alike. Their rigorous debate went far beyond the undogmatic moderation promoted by Sextus or Montaigne; Descartes went so far as to doubt everything, to wonder whether the external world existed at all.[17] A large literature developed, with many thinkers charging that scepticism was self-undermining. Pyrrhonism was paradoxical: do you *know* that knowledge is impossible? If yes, then you have contradicted yourself; if no, then by what right do you assert it? And Pyrrhonism was unbelievable: you claim to doubt everything, but when you are about to be run down by a carriage, you don't doubt its existence, you leap out of the way just like everyone else.

David Hume's (1711–76) contribution was to articulate a Pyrrhonist philosophy in the tradition of Sextus and Montaigne that defused such arguments. Being a man of the Enlightenment, he argued much more cogently and rigorously than the deliberately unsystematic Montaigne. In his great works,[18] Hume argued that our knowledge could never be grounded as definitely as we might hope; we could never assemble adequate evidence for us to be certain of our knowledge. We could, of course, assemble evidence, but a properly critical examination of the evidence would reveal that it was at least as uncertain as the propositions it was supposedly evidence for. Even mathematics and logic could let one down.

> In all demonstrative sciences the rules are certain and infallible; but when we apply them, our fallible and uncertain faculties are very apt to depart from them, and fall into error. ...
>
> There is no Algebraist nor Mathematician so expert in his science, as to place entire confidence in any truth immediately upon his discovery of it, or regard it as any thing, but a mere probability. Every time he runs over his proofs, his confidence encreases; but still more by the approbation of his friends; and is rais'd to its utmost perfection by the universal assent and applauses of the learned world. Now 'tis evident, that this gradual encrease of assurance is nothing but the addition of new probabilities, and is deriv'd from the constant union of causes and effects, according to past experience and observation.[19]

We no doubt reason; no doubt the realisation of some things is forced upon us (as Sextus pointed out, we notice that some food is sweet, or that the weather is cold). But we do not have solid foundations or *grounds* for such beliefs, not in the way that scientific rationalists would like to think.[20]

In this way, Hume ingeniously drew a distinction between a *reason* for believing something, and a *cause* of our believing it. I have no *reason* for thinking it is cold; but my belief that it is cold is *caused* by the wind and the rain (and the wiring of my nervous system). In this way, we actually go around believing things about the external world – because nature has wired us up to do so. As the critics of Pyrrhonism claimed, it is impossible to be sceptical about everything. But, says Hume, this is not because it is *incorrect* to be sceptical. Rather, it is because we are what we are that we believe things based on the input to our senses.

> It seems evident, that the dispute between the sceptics and the dogmatists is entirely verbal, or at least regards only the degrees of doubt and assurance, which we ought to indulge with regard to all reasoning. ... No philosophical dogmatist denies that there are difficulties both with regard to the senses and to all science, and that these difficulties are, in a regular, logical method, absolutely insolvable. No sceptic denies that we lie under an absolute necessity, notwithstanding these difficulties, of thinking, and believing, and reasoning, with regard to all kinds of subjects, and even of frequently assenting with confidence and security. The only difference, then, between these sects, if they merit that name, is that the sceptic, from habit, caprice, or inclination, insists most on the difficulties, the dogmatist, for like reasons, on the necessity.[21]

But this psychophysical necessity does not mean that the philosophical arguments adduced by sceptical Pyrrhonists are wrong. The Enlightenment dream of building an understanding of the world on an edifice of reason and self-evident axioms of human nature is undermined just as surely by this modified Pyrrhonist argument.[22]

So Pyrrhonist scepticism kills off the Enlightenment rationalist hope. But it does not prevent the sceptic himself or herself leading a perfectly normal life. How so? Because it would take a literally superhuman effort to worry about it, except when one was being a philosopher.

> Most fortunately it happens, that since reason is incapable of dispelling these clouds, nature herself suffices to that purpose, and cures me of this philosophical melancholy and delirium, either by relaxing this bent of mind, or by some avocation, and lively impression of my senses, which obliterate all these chimeras. I dine, I play a game of back-gammon, I converse, and am merry with my friends; and when after three or four hour's amusement, I wou'd return to these speculations, they appear so cold, and strain'd, and ridiculous, that I cannot find in my heart to enter into them any farther.[23]

Even when Hume is trying to worry about knowledge, science, reason and the external world, a few hours' backgammon with his friends stops him, and he feels rather silly. Would that more academics had that reaction to their work.

Between them, Burke and Hume develop a distinctive conservative position in the tradition of Sextus and Montaigne. Abstract theorising is all very well, but society is not an abstract thing; nor are people abstractions. Political conditions are here and now, *sui generis*, with concrete benefits (and also concrete drawbacks). One should be very wary of attempting to substitute abstract benefits for concrete ones, because the trajectory of human society is inherently unpredictable (Burke), and abstract reasoning is usually flawed (Hume). Removing well-understood institutions will lead to the collapse of those elements of society that the institutions were meant to uphold; removal of sources of power will lead to power vacuums and violence; and all this in the name of some theory or other for which there can be no ultimately persuasive ground.

The moderation of ancient and Renaissance scepticism, that had been lost during the early Enlightenment, had now been restored to it. All that now remained was to translate these insights into political action.

Peel, corn and the origins of the Conservative Party

The development of what we now know as the Conservative Party was pretty murky throughout the 18th century.[24] There are definite continuities from the Tories to the Conservatives, but also several false starts, stalls and dead ends. The inheritances of Burke and Hume, and indeed other thinkers such as Coleridge, were and are argued over. In this book, we have space only to sketch a tradition, and then to map it onto current ideological discourse; hence we will skip a lot of development and jump to the middle of the 19th century, to the premiership of Sir Robert Peel (1788–1850)*, which illustrates some of our themes rather well.

Peel, although even now a household name, was not a successful party leader. He had to deal with a major shock to the political and economic system, and failed to carry his party with him. The problem was the notorious Corn Laws.

These had been introduced in the aftermath of the war against France in 1815. Wartime financial measures, including Britain's first income tax, were repealed. However, the landowning interests foresaw a fall in the price of corn from the high wartime prices (indeed, they were right – prices halved in the months after Waterloo), and ambushed the government of Lord Liverpool, a limited but long-serving Tory Prime Minister. They forced the Liverpool government, which they generally supported, to impose restrictions on imports of corn: not until corn prices reached 80

---

* Prime Minister 1834–5, 1841–6.

shillings per quarter*[25] could foreign corn be brought in. The effect, naturally, was to keep corn prices artificially high, to the benefit of landowners and the detriment of those who spent a large proportion of income on food, including the increasing numbers of working-class people in the towns. The new manufacturers were hit as well, as the high food prices indirectly reduced demand for manufactured goods.

However, in 1832, the Reform Act increased the number of people who could vote, and diluted the parliamentary influence of the big landowners. In the face of the wider franchise, the Tories were forced to reorganise and broaden their appeal; they emerged with a new name, the 'Conservative Party', and a new organisational centre, the Carlton Club.[26] Their leader, the splendidly reactionary Duke of Wellington, recognised the talents of their best middle-class mind, Robert Peel. Peel was undoubtedly correct to recognise, as Prime Minister from 1841, that the Corn Laws were indefensible, not only morally and economically, but also in electoral terms. His calculation, further, was that they would be best repealed by the Conservatives, rather than the Liberals (as the Whigs had become). If change was inevitable, it should be carried out as sympathetically as possible.

Party historian Lord Blake has suggested that the Conservatives, from 1832, really had three alternatives, each interestingly drama-tising the complex dialectic between conservatism and modernity, between pragmatism and distaste for progress. First, they could become the party of solid reaction, opposing change and continuing their pre-1832 protection of landowners' interests. Second, there could be an anti-progressive alliance with the work-ing class against the rising middle class with its liberal economics and 'dark satanic mills'; this would appeal to the Romantic strand in British politics. Third, the Conservatives could recognise the force of the middle class, accept the Industrial Revolution and the

---

* 80 shillings is £4. A quarter is bizarrely difficult to define. A quarter in Liverpool was 480 lb; in London 496 lb; elsewhere 504 lb. Nowhere was it a quarter of a ton, which is 560 lb.

rapid change it brought, the liberalism of economic law, and try to broker acceptable compromises between the three social classes.[27] Peel was temperamentally disposed to the third option, which was probably also the only realistic one. Hence he moved to abolish the Corn Laws.

The result, though, was a catastrophic split in the Conservative Party that put it out of office for two decades. The measure was passed, but only with Liberal support; the 'ultras', hard Conservative reactionaries, voted against. The rebels left the party, though most of the office holders in Peel's government stayed loyal, and Peel kept command of the party machinery. The split toppled the government, and a disastrous election followed in which Peel's support collapsed. There were just 89 'Peelite' MPs as against 243 rebels, and the Peelite rump continued for another ten years or so, tending to side with the Liberals. The rebels took the brand name of 'Conservative' (after toying with others – the 'Protectionists' was popular), and started their party afresh. Blake maintains that 1846 is the best date to take as the beginning of the Conservative Party we know today.[28]

This incident is very interesting from our point of view. It shows the dangers of blanket opposition to change, the problems of deeply reactionary conservatism. There is no doubt that Peel, though tactically inept and personally aloof,[29] was right to repeal the Corn Laws. The party as a whole was wrong to reject change; change sometimes needs to happen, and conservatives need to recognise when we have reached such a time – not that that is always easy.

It also shows the danger of splitting the anti-progressive vote. The Conservative Party in 1846 was the country party, rural, communitarian, traditionalist, of orthodox religious views. These are all no doubt important interests in a country such as Britain, but they had never formed a majority of the electorate since the 1832 Reform Act. If the Conservative interest is restricted to these groups, it cannot win elections; if the conservative ideology benefits only these groups, it stands no chance of influencing governmental policy. Wider coalitions need to be formed; without them, as in many countries in Continental Europe, anti-progressive forces will find themselves losing out to liberal or socialist parties.[30] A new alliance had to be forged, and the man who forged it was an outsider, Benjamin Disraeli.

Dizzy

Disraeli (1804–81[*]) is an outstanding figure of his day, comparable in many ways to Lloyd George or Churchill. After a splendid start in life, helped by writing a series of best-selling novels and marriage to a wealthy widow, he became an MP in 1837. He was driven by pragmatism, personal dynamism and not a small quantity of bloody-mindedness, rather than ideology. He had flirted with the Whigs and radicalism, before settling on being a progressive Conservative.

But having made this choice, and despite his manifest talents, he didn't advance as quickly as he would have liked. Overlooked by Peel in the government of 1841, Disraeli, a man for whom revenge was a dish best eaten hot, then cold, then warmed over for breakfast next day, launched a ferocious campaign of destabilisation.

With some young Romantic aristocrats, he formed a group called Young England (of which Disraeli, a slightly moth-eaten 38-year-old, was much the senior), nourished on a diet of nostalgia and escapism. Peel's stiffness, and the wit and charm of the Young Englanders, ensured that they remained a thorn in Peel's side. Disraeli brought his literary skills to bear, writing a 'state of the nation' novel called *Coningsby* (1844), in which the Young Englanders were lightly caricatured, and Peel mercilessly satirised.

> There was indeed considerable shouting about what they called Conservative principles; but the awkward question naturally arose, what will you conserve? The prerogatives of

* Prime Minister 1868, 1874–80.

the Crown, provided they are not exercised; the independence of the House of Lords, provided it is not asserted; the Ecclesiastical estate provided it is regulated by a commission of laymen. Everything in short that is established, as long as it is a phrase and not a fact.[31]

A sequel, *Sybil* (1845), made more of the increasing divisions between rich and poor, and coined the idea of two nations within one.[32] 'One nation Conservatism' since then has become a coded phrase for Conservative politicians embarrassed by the gap between rich and poor.

The fall of Peel over the Corn Laws was no doubt a great delight to Disraeli. The problem was that actually Peel had adopted the only realistic policy strategy, one that Disraeli might well have gone along with had there been a place for him in the Peel government. The Conservatives found themselves out of step. Furthermore, as the Conservatives' most experienced and talented people had been driven by the backwoods reaction into the arms of the Liberal Party (Gladstone was the most famous man to make that journey), virtually the only man of ability left was Disraeli – but his cosmopolitan background and his Jewishness were a massive turn-off for his colleagues, who overlooked his obvious claims to the leadership for over twenty years.

Had Disraeli died much earlier than he did, he would be remembered only as a talented maverick failure, a sort of Lord Randolph Churchill or Enoch Powell figure (whose torturing of the stiff, awkward, proud Edward Heath irresistibly recalls Disraeli's attacks on Peel). He had a couple of spells as a not-too-successful Chancellor in Lord Derby's brief administrations. But as the pilot of the 1867 Reform Act, he becomes a serious historical person in his own right.

The history of the 1867 Act is complex, and makes little narrative sense.[33] In a nutshell, the Liberals attempted to get their Reform Bill through the House, to try to extend the franchise still further; they failed, thanks to a revolt by the right of the Liberal Party in alliance with the Conservatives, and the government fell. Derby was asked to form a minority administration, and Disraeli, in the Commons, developed a bill that was even more radical than the Liberals' measure, which passed! No one is really sure how this happened.[34] Anthony Trollope satirised the various *voltes faces* in his novel *Phineas Redux* (1873);[35] certainly Disraeli's about-turn was as glaring as that for which he excoriated Peel in 1846.

Nevertheless, the measure actually improved the fortunes of the Conservatives, if not immediately – Disraeli, upon the retirement of Derby, had finally become Prime Minister in 1868, and lost a general election under the new franchise a few months later – at least in the long run (*The Times* famously said that Disraeli saw the Conservative in the working man as Michelangelo saw the angel in the marble). The angels made their first appearance in the general election of 1874.

The Liberal Prime Minister Gladstone,* though concerned, like Disraeli, with the condition of the working man, was rather more concerned with what the working man *ought* to do, than with making it possible for the working man to do what he *wanted* to do. The Education Act of 1870 provided for genuine mass education, but also aggravated sectarian concerns. Trade union laws alienated the leaders of organised labour. And the Licensing Act, aimed more at keeping the working classes from drink, than the drinking classes at work, was not at all popular![36] Since then, brewing companies, at least until very recently, have traditionally been major donors to the Conservative Party.

Hence Disraeli, in the face of Gladstone's reforming zeal, was able to present the Conservatives, in a series of important speeches, as a party with a broad base covering the working classes and the propertied classes generally as well as its aristocratic core. The Liberals were interfering, constantly legislating, while the Conservatives were not. The Liberals 'knew best', while the Conservatives did not claim to. The result was that in 1874 the Conservatives turned a deficit of 100 seats into a majority of

* Prime Minister 1868–74, 1880–5, 1886, 1892–4.

52 over all parties. This method of opposition to an interfering, ideologically driven government that 'knows best' may well have relevance for small 'c' conservatives in the current political climate.

Disraeli's feat was to develop a set of conservative principles adapted for office, appealing beyond the Conservatives' natural constituency. First, he – as befits a follower of Burke – displayed a genuine commitment to various and dispersed centres of power, as opposed to the Gladstonian instinct to centralise. Second, he carefully ensured sufficient continuity of policy between his government and the government that preceded it (Gladstone's) to ensure that politics did not collapse into a left–right bunfight (or at least any more of a bunfight than one would expect an antagonistic system to produce). Disraeli, in a quiet way, produced a series of social reforms that kept relations with the working class open; and though it goes without saying that these policies were much less thoroughgoing than Gladstone would have produced, nevertheless the measures were civilised, just, justified and, as a bonus, electorally sensible. The Sale of Food and Drugs Act, the Public Health Act, the Artisans' Dwellings Act, the Rivers' Pollution Act, and various Factory Acts and other labour legislation were all important measures to protect the weak against the strong.[37] Disraeli went with the flow of the times; he did not try to reverse it. In that way, he held the country together, re-established the Conservative Party as a party of government, accepted the shift in the political mainstream in the Gladstonian direction, and – as a happy by-product – is accepted as a major folk-hero in Tory history. Can David Cameron, from a not dissimilar starting position, pull off the same trick?

Salisbury, man of inaction

Lord Randolph Churchill sketched Disraeli's career thus: 'failure, failure, failure, moderate success, renewed failure, sudden and absolute triumph'.[38] However, there was to be one more failure, if a relatively minor one: the Liberals turned their deficit of 52 into a majority of the same size in the 1880 election. Disraeli, now ennobled, died shortly afterwards in opposition (he remains the only man to have refused the honour of a state funeral). He was replaced by the enigmatic Lord Salisbury (1830–1903*).

Salisbury was a reactionary who had had some difficulty in accepting the low-born Jew Disraeli as his leader. He had vaguely conspired against him in 1869 and again in 1870, was often not on speaking terms with him, and described him in print as a 'mere political gamester'. He resigned from Derby's Cabinet in 1867 over the Reform Act, though he served under Disraeli in the government of 1874–80. As leader of the party, Salisbury's record, though not unblemished, is impressive; several years of effective parity with the Liberals ended with Salisbury's crushing victory in 1895, followed by a second in 1900.

It has been said that Salisbury is difficult to characterise.[39] He was certainly unusual. Politics is essentially a space for action. You go into politics if you want to change the world, to right a wrong. But Salisbury opposed action, tried to avoid intervention wherever he could; in this we can detect the authentic voice of an age-old scepticism in his writings.

> The optimist view of politics assumes that there must be some remedy for every political ill, and rather than not find it, will make two hardships to cure one. If all equitable remedies have failed its votaries take it as proved without argument that the one-sided remedies, which alone are left, must needs succeed. But is not the other view barely possible? Is it not just conceivable that there is no remedy that we can apply to the

---

* The greatest member of an impressive political family. This Salisbury was the 3rd Marquess. The 4th Marquess led the Conservatives in the Lords in 1925–31; the 5th Marquess in 1942–57. Lord Cranborne, who is heir to the seat, led the Conservatives in the Lords from 1994 to 1999, before being summarily sacked by William Hague for independently negotiating a deal with the Labour government to phase out the majority of hereditary peers. The 3rd Marquess was Prime Minister 1885–6, 1886–92, 1895–1902.

Irish hatred of ourselves? that other loves or hates may possibly some day elbow it out of the Irish peasant's mind, that nothing we can do by any contrivance will hasten the advent of that period? May it not, on the contrary, be our incessant doctoring and meddling, awaking the passions now of this party, now of that, raising at every step a fresh crop of resentments by the side of the old growth, that puts off the day when these feelings will decay quietly away and be forgotten? One thing we know we can do in Ireland, for we have done it in India and elsewhere with populations more unmanageable and more bitter. We can keep the peace and we can root out organised crime. But there is no precedent in our history or any other, to teach us that political measures can conjure away hereditary antipathies which are fed by constant agitation. The free institutions that sustain the life of a free and united people, sustain also the hatreds of a divided people.[40]

Indeed, a tragedy early in his ministerial career when he was Secretary of State for India affected him deeply, not only personally, but as a warning against experts and claims for omnipotence of expertise. A famine in the Indian state of Orissa developed, despite warning signs that were ignored by the officials of the Raj. Salisbury always felt responsible for the failings of his department, and denounced the 'experts' and political economists roundly in the House. He remained sceptical of experts to the end of his life.[41]

Although Salisbury liked to give the impression that he did very little other than give the occasional touch on the tiller when the ship of state threatened to go off course, he actually continued the Disraelian strategy of cautious reform, accepting that a very weak concoction of the policies that might appeal to wavering Liberals would help drain their support (for example, Salisbury devoted a lot of effort to improving working-class housing[42]).

So historian John Ramsden is unfair when he accuses Salisbury of failing 'entirely to understand the political trends of his time',[43] though he does have Salisbury's own account on his side.

Salisbury himself found it hard to explain the trends of his political lifetime, for such Conservative dominance in the 1890s defied all the pessimistic, disintegrationist and class-conflictive predictions that had been his stock in trade ever since 1866–7, when he had defied Disraeli over the extension of the franchise; 'the result turned out exactly the other way', he confessed in 1895.[44]

But politicians often fail to understand their environment; Salisbury's incomprehension is hardly unknown elsewhere. In our own day, armed with batteries of opinion polls and platoons of media managers, it is often incredible how little politicians seem to understand of the people who vote for them. That Salisbury, the grandest of grandees, should be taken aback that Disraeli's strategy of reform should work, that he should fail to see the angels in the marble where Disraeli succeeded, is no surprise. Rather, the inevitable condition of politics is surely that of uncertainty in the face of complexity. The issue, as Salisbury appreciated, is how best to navigate blind through choppy waters.

Balfour the philosopher

Salisbury's nephew and successor A.J. Balfour (1848–1930*) is unusual – and helpful to us – for being the most intellectual of Prime Ministers, the author of a number of books of philosophy. These works are interesting not least because Salisbury himself took an interest in them, to the point of suggesting a change of title for the first book,[45] a work of 1879 originally called *A Defence of Philosophic Scepticism*, Salisbury's advice being to call it *A Defence of Philosophic Doubt*.

Balfour's *oeuvre* was not great philosophy, but interesting, building laconically on the work of David Hume. He discusses the idea of scepticism as a presence in the real world, as a philosophical (and political?) tool.

* Prime Minister 1902–05.

I must point out that the word 'scepticism' taken without explanation is ambiguous. It may mean either the intellectual recognition of the want of evidence, or it may mean this together with its consequent unbelief. ...

If, then [as Balfour had argued], scepticism in the second sense be impossible, is scepticism in the first sense – scepticism which merely recognises the absence of philosophical proof or other logical defect in a system of belief – of any but a speculative interest? At first sight it would seem not. Scepticism which does not destroy belief, it is natural to suppose, does nothing. This, however, is by no means necessarily the case. If in the estimation of mankind all creeds stood on a philosophical equality, no doubt an attack which affected them all equally would probably have little or no practical result. The only result it could reasonably produce would be general unbelief, and, as I have just remarked, general unbelief can hardly be regarded as a possible frame of mind. But if in the estimation of mankind there is the greatest difference in the relative credibility of prevalent systems of belief, if now one system now another is raised to the dignity of a standard of certainty, it is plain that a sceptical attack, especially if it deals with the system that happens at the moment to be in favour, may have considerable consequences – consequences, at least, quite as considerable as any which considerations addressed merely to the reason are ever likely to produce.[46]

Balfour's message is implicit in much of Hume and Montaigne. Scepticism shouldn't be espoused to undermine belief; rather, its purpose is to ensure that the believer preserves a questioning attitude, never relaxes into a complacent certainty. He argues that a watertight set of reasons for adopting one system of beliefs over another – in his case, the systems he is interested in are Science and Religion (he capitalises them) – will never emerge, on the basis, more or less, of the arguments put forward by Hume. Brute and unpersuasive causes of belief remain, and these should, and can, be respected by others. This line of thought is the direct descendant of the tolerance of Montaigne.

In the absence then of reason to the contrary, I am content to regard the two great creeds [Religion and Science] by which we attempt to regulate our lives as resting in the main upon separate bases. So long, therefore, as neither of them can lay claim to philosophic probability, discrepancies which exist or may hereafter arise between them cannot be considered as bearing more heavily against the one than they do against the other. But if a really valid philosophy, which would support Science to the exclusion of Religion, or Religion to the exclusion of Science, were discovered, the case would be somewhat different, and it would undoubtedly be difficult for that creed which is not philosophically established to exist beside the other while in contradiction to it – difficult, I say, not absolutely impossible. In the meanwhile, unfortunately, this does not seem likely to become a practical question. What has to be determined now is the course which ought to be pursued with regard to discrepancies between systems, neither of which can be regarded as philosophically established, but neither of which we can consent to surrender; and on this subject, of course, it is only possible to make suggestions which may perhaps commend themselves to the practical instincts of the reader, though they cannot compel his intellectual assent. In my judgment, then, if these discrepancies are such that they can be smoothed away by concessions on either side which do not touch essentials, the concessions should be made; but if, which is not at present the case, consistency can only be purchased by practically destroying one or other of the conflicting creeds, I should elect in favour of inconsistency – not because I should be content with knowledge which being self-contradictory must needs be in some particulars false, but because a logical harmony obtained by the arbitrary destruction of all discordant elements may be bought at far too great a sacrifice of essential and necessary truth.[47]

As he wrote in his 1895 work, *The Foundations of Belief*, we therefore must resign ourselves to error without necessarily relapsing into pessimism or defensiveness.

> Not merely because we are ignorant of the data required for the solution, even of very simple problems in organic and social life, are we called on to acquiesce in an arrangement which, to be sure, we have no power to disturb; nor yet because these data, did we possess them, are too complex to be dealt with by any rational calculus we possess or are ever likely to acquire; but because, in addition to these difficulties, reasoning is a force most apt to divide and disintegrate; and though division and disintegration may often be the necessary preliminaries of social development, still more necessary are the forces that bind and stiffen, without which there would be no society to develop.[48]

Invasion of the liberals

Balfour was probably the most academic of all Britain's Prime Ministers, and one of the most intellectually formidable. It may or may not be a related fact that he was one of the least successful.

Long-term trouble for the Conservatives had been created by what seemed at first to be a disaster for the Liberals, the splitting of the party by Gladstone over the recondite (to the English) issue of Irish Home Rule during his fleeting appearance as Prime Minister from February to July 1886. A group of unionists opposing the splitting up of the United Kingdom followed Joseph Chamberlain (1836–1914), who had been a radical social reformer and President of the Board of Trade under Gladstone in the early 1880s, out of the party.

The Liberal Unionists sat in Parliament as a separate party

during Salisbury's period of office, leaving the official Liberals hopelessly placed (between the general elections of November 1885 and July 1886, they lost 143 seats). The Unionists enjoyed the Empire and the flag-waving jingoism that became popular, and generally voted with the Conservatives. Chamberlain even joined the Salisbury government as Colonial Secretary.

So far, so good. Not only did the defection of the Unionists split the Liberal vote, but they also brought in support for the Conservatives from beyond the traditional rural Tory heartland.[49] Eventually they relinquished their distinct political identity and joined the Conservatives (renamed the Conservative and Unionist Party).

This was a disaster for Balfour. The Conservatives suddenly had to absorb a large number of alien thinkers into their ranks. Liberalism is the ideology of freedom, roughly speaking.[50] All liberals (small 'l', note) value freedom. But freedom can be described in a number of ways. One distinction is between freedom to do things – the lack of restraint on one's personal choices of action – and freedom from things – being unhindered by conditions that restrict one's freedom of choice.[51] The distinction is subtle; suppose I own a factory that has a machine that creates some pollution. The former type of liberal would tend to support my freedom to use the machine (though it may be incumbent upon me to pay for the clean-up afterwards); the latter type would tend to favour legislation to restrict my use of it, to increase the general freedom of everyone else to enjoy an unpolluted environment. The former type of liberal identified with Chamberlain, and gravitated towards the Conservative Party from 1886 on, while the latter type, the high-minded Gladstonians, remained with the Liberals, and are the mainstays of the Liberal Democrat Party even today. Given the influx of liberals into the Conservative Party, it was inevitable that there would be tensions (often creative ones[52]).

The focus of those tensions were a number of political organisations affiliated with the Tory Party about this time that were concerned with reducing the size of government, such as the

Liberty and Property Defence League, founded in 1882 by Conservatives, to prevent the government from meddling in economics. But it is instructive to study the ambivalent relationship its principal publicist, Lord Elcho (later the Earl of Wemyss), had to the party. In 1846, he became a Peelite, the faction that followed Peel during the Corn Law kerfuffle, and which in general drifted towards (and voted with) the Liberals. As it happened, unlike most of the Peelites, Elcho rejoined the Conservatives. The main doctrinal inspiration for the LPDL was the thinker Herbert Spencer (1820–1903), not a member of any party, but a defender of libertarian principles.

In these groups, we see most strongly the tensions between liberals and conservatives. The LPDL contained both Liberals and Conservatives, though the latter predominated over time.[53] We have already seen that the Conservative Party was home to many people who did not share the conservative philosophy – after all, this was the intention of Disraeli's increasing the coalition of members. And if Elcho and their friends thought that the Conservative Party was itself a sufficiently reliable ideological vehicle to promote their free market ideas, then why set up the LPDL at all?[54] Indeed, Elcho was even able to accuse Lord Salisbury, perhaps the most reactionary politician of stature ever in Britain, of crypto-socialism![55]

There were many minor political figures and organisations of similar ilk, but the libertarian free market groups which proliferated at the turn of the century like flowers in the spring have a difficult relation with mainstream politics, as historian E.H.H. Green illustrates.

> Suffice it here to say that from 1880 onwards it becomes easier and more meaningful to identify Conservative individualists. Organizations such as the Liberty and Property Defence League (LPDL) and the British Constitutional Association (BCA), and individuals like Lord Wemyss, Herbert Spencer, A.V. Dicey, Auberon Herbert, and Ernest Benn, all explicitly

espoused individualist ideas and were supporters or members of the Conservative Party. Yet, in spite of their party-political affiliation, the political *philosophy* to which these 'men versus the State' were selfconsciously closest was nineteenth-century Liberalism. Dicey, Herbert, and many others associated with the LPDL and BCA had no great love for Conservatism, but, when faced with the development of a Collectivist New Liberalism, saw the Conservative party as the best chance for preserving old Liberal individualism. This is not to say that *all* individualist sympathizers in the Conservative ranks were former Liberals – Lords Wemyss, Hugh Cecil, and Robert Cecil stand out as Conservatives of long standing – but there is a marked coincidence between the rise of Conservative individualist thought and the arrival in the Conservative party, at all levels, of Liberal defectors.[56]

These tensions exposed the weaknesses of Balfour's scepticism. He was convicted by commentators of the day (probably fairly) of vacillating between various camps in the party, not least between the defenders of free trade and those, like Chamberlain, who wanted a preferential tariff regime for producers in the Empire.[57] His being the author of a book called *A Defence of Philosophic Doubt* hardly helped this perception.[58] Liberal MP Sir Wilfrid Lawson wrote an insulting jingle.

> I'm not for Free Trade, and I'm not for Protection.
> I approve of them both, and to both have objection.
> In going through life I continually find
> It's a terrible business to make up one's mind.
> So in spite of all comments, reproach and predictions,
> I firmly adhere to Unsettled Convictions.[59]

In the period of Salisbury and Balfour, conservatism as a creed of unsettled convictions reached its heyday. But the obvious danger when arguments do flare up is drift: one can be too understanding of opposing points of view, and this is an important lesson for conservatives of all stripes.

Conservatives (small 'c') must be open-minded; but in testing conditions they must be capable of taking a lead, of making stern decisions, and of building new institutions that help deal with changing circumstances; that conservatives oppose change does not – cannot – mean that they can *ignore* change.

Other avowedly conservative Conservatives have made the same mistake. Stanley Baldwin (1867–1947*) for example led Britain through perhaps her most difficult period, through the devastating worldwide depression and the polarisation of world politics between communism and fascism. Though on leaving office he was fêted, as having in particular handled the abdication crisis well, the world system crumbled shortly after he retired, and Churchill made sure that he took a large share of the blame. He failed to see the dangers of the resurgent Germany, and, though his humanity and conciliatory skills no doubt helped to preserve Britain's social harmony during the long depression, in the end the problem was the failure of the prewar economic system, and could not be cured by a benign understanding. Radical action was needed, and Baldwin completely failed to take such action, or even conceive that it was required. Such is the danger of complacent conservatism.

Triumph of the liberals

Whether two different ideologies can co-exist within large coalitionist parties will depend on a number of factors, perhaps most notably on the nature of the forces opposing them. Through most of the 20th century, certainly since the First World War, the main opposition to the Conservatives was formed by the Labour Party, whose commitment to socialism was perhaps never quite as solid as it pretended, but which periodically declaimed that equality was the greatest political good, and that wealth should be redistributed between the classes. Within Labour ranks were also

* Prime Minister 1923–4, 1924–9, 1935–7.

social democrats, who wished to reform capitalism to make its outcomes more equitable, and Gladstonian liberals who had fled the Liberal Party during and after its terminal decline. This opposition coalition shared a rough goal of greater equality (not necessarily total equality).

The 20th-century Conservative Party was united by opposition to Labour's brand of moderate, non-Marxist socialism. Small 'c' conservatives opposed redistribution partly because they opposed the assumption that a society should have any goal to which it should work, partly because they worried about how such meddling in economic structures would affect social relations, partly because they thought the degree of planning involved in such a redistribution of wealth was too great, and partly because they disliked the shift in responsibility for a citizen's welfare from the citizen him- or herself to the state. Free market liberals opposed the interference with market-delivered outcomes.

Because of this happy coincidence of aims of both conservatives and liberals, it has been possible to paint the British conservative as being merely opposed to equality,[60] and the Conservative Party as being made up entirely of conservatives.[61] But this is much too simplistic a picture. At the very least, it leaves unexplained the obvious fact that the 20th century saw a good deal of argument *within* the Conservative Party about whether or not to move in a liberal, free market direction.

The pleasing fact of a common enemy brought conservatives and liberals together, but some thinkers tried to develop a stronger unity between the ideologies. One of the most sophisticated was the fearsomely intellectual, and ideologically driven, Enoch Powell (1912–98). Powell was explicitly conservative, and explicitly drawn to market liberalism. As a conservative, he celebrated, often in poetic terms, the continuity of English traditions,[62] yet he was also very pro-markets, so much so that his speeches on economic topics sound much more modern, to a 21st-century reader, than those of his contemporaries. He found little or no contradiction between free markets and what he called 'the Tory prejudice that, upon the whole, things are wiser than people, that institutions are wiser than their members and that a nation is wiser than those who comprise it at any specific moment'.[63]

Is reconciliation as easy as Powell claims? *Prima facie* evidence for a tension can be found in his fierce reaction to mass immigration, the issue which defined 'Powellism' for a nation and finished his career as a serious politician. Powell was convinced that the long and continuous traditions of which he had written depended to a large extent on a cultural and political homogeneity, a capacity to conceive of the totality of a nation.[64] From his vantage point as an MP for Wolverhampton, with its relatively large immigrant population, he worried about its increasing heterogeneity, until his notorious, and deliberately offensive, 'Rivers of Blood' speech.[65] Ideology in the 1960s was much more robust, much more steak-and-Rioja, than the steamed-chicken-and-mineral-water fare we are served nowadays. But whatever one might think of the tone of the speech, one thing it does is repudiate the free global market for labour in no uncertain terms.

The attempts to meld conservatism and liberalism were only a passing fad. By 1965, Edward Heath* had come down strongly in favour of liberalism, though he retreated under political and economic pressure, famously doing a U-turn to keep Rolls-Royce solvent in 1972 (much to Powell's disgust), and from then on the liberals within Conservative Party ranks preferred to claim that they were the legitimate heirs to the conservative tradition. Sir Keith Joseph, Heath's Health and Social Services Secretary, under-went a noisy period of introspection following double defeats in the elections of 1974, in effect deciding that conservatism, for him, simply meant 'liberalism'.[66] Mrs Thatcher** agreed, and though she went into government in 1979 with a manifesto not unlike Heath's in 1970, she famously did not back down when things went wrong (which they did almost immediately[67]). She persevered, and eventually triumphed.

* Prime Minister 1970–74.
** Prime Minister 1979–90.

There was certainly a grumbling in the ranks. All conservatism, according to the Joseph–Thatcher position, was a species of liberalism, and this formulation, as we shall see in the next chapter, has been accepted by most leading commentators on ideology. But on the contrary, conservatives and liberals are very different creatures, and as the distinction could not be masked, it was ultimately marked – as it would have to be marked, so clear was it – by the use of the nomenclature 'wet' (conservative) and 'dry' (liberal).

From 1975, the liberals were in control at the top of the Conservative Party, by 1981 solidly cemented in place. A similar battle had taken place in the Labour Party, whose founding socialists were invaded by Gladstonian liberals following the decline and collapse of the Liberal Party; the liberals won their decisive victory in that party in 1994, when Tony Blair became leader.[68]

The Liberal Party is no more; its successor, the Liberal Democrats, still only a third force (though of substantial potency). But it is the descendants of Gladstone and Chamberlain that slug it out in 21st-century politics.

CHAPTER FOUR

WHAT IS CONSERVATISM?

What conservatism is not

From Socrates to Margaret Thatcher, we have traced a theme through human thought and political action: a certain type of scepticism, allied to a certain view of society, produces a certain type of conservatism that has often, though not always, been prominent in the thinking of the British Conservative Party. The history is interesting, but what matters with an idea at a particular moment is whether it is *alive*, whether it can be adapted to the world of that moment. In the remainder of Part One, we will go beyond history and take the idea's pulse. In this chapter we will define exactly what we mean by 'conservative'; in the next, we go on to look at the extent of its current relevance.

But to begin with, if we assume, with the dictionaries, that conservatism involves some antagonism towards change (we will examine this assumption carefully later), then I should start by ruling out some specific types of conservative who immediately spring to mind.

First of all, there is the type of person who is personally unsettled by change. This is the person who doesn't like new technologies, and has complained about every innovation as it came along. He or she worried about the waltz, nonrepresentative art, jazz, rock'n'roll, Sputnik, hula hoops, computers, skateboards, mobile telephones, the Internet and digital television. This person is more or less satisfied with his or her life, and doesn't want the bother

115

115

and difficulty of learning new behaviour, mastering more gadgets, talking to new people.

Second, there is the type of person who is doing well out of the status quo, and doesn't want any alteration to it, thank you very much. Never mind if there are deep and obvious structural reasons why the status quo is unsatisfactory; this type of person defends his or her own economic, political or social interests.

It is, of course, the right of such people to resist change. And people of these psychological types (particularly the second) do often happen to support the Conservative Party. Nevertheless, we should avoid calling these people conservatives in the ideological sense that I will define (in the same way that we should avoid calling a hedonistic layabout a 'liberal', a racist football supporter a 'nationalist' or a thief who redistributes wealth from rich people to give to the poor – i.e. himself – a 'socialist').

The reason is fairly clear: such preferences have only an incidental connection with the ideas, and they are certainly not prompted by those ideas. Those timidly afraid of change have no thought that society would be better as a result of stasis, only that their own lives would remain pleasant. Those who do well from the status quo are not really concerned with change so much as with wealth and status; if they were divested of their wealth of a sudden, then their conservatism would vanish along with their loot.[1]

What we are looking for, in an ideology, is the existence of good *arguments*, objective *reasons* for its support. Of course, human nature is such that the ideologies we espouse are often those that will act in our interests; the poor are more often socialist than the rich; the rich are more often market liberals than the poor; you will be unlikely ever to encounter a non-Christian defending fundamentalist Christianity; those dependent on heavy industry for their livelihoods tend not to be environmentalists. So much is to be expected. But when the poor person defends socialism, the rich person market liberalism, the Christian fundamentalism or the hippy environmentalism, you would expect the arguments to be concerned not with the personal circumstances of the arguer, but with reasons that stand alone, reasons that the interlocutor has to engage with. When hippies defend environmentalism, they do not point out their distaste for consumption and artifice; they produce evidence of imminent ecological catastrophe. When business people reply to them, they do not produce their bank statements; they talk of the liberating power of prosperity, and the importance of development. No doubt their ideological beliefs are *caused* by concern with nature or bank balances, but the reasons they produce are different from the causes, and no less valid for not being causes.

The need to articulate one's position so that it is understandable by all citizens irrespective of their preferences or ideas of the good is an imperative of *public reason*, an idea developed by the American political philosopher John Rawls.[2] If I appeal to public reason I have to convince you, not that the ideology is in my interests – you will no doubt be happy to accept that – but instead that your interests, unbeknown to you, are actually allied with mine. This sort of abstraction from individual circumstances, partly to produce an ideology that is more far-reaching and applicable to others' circumstances, and partly to facilitate the persuasion of others that the ideology should be applied in real life, was one of the successful moves made by Rawls as he revitalised liberalism almost single-handedly with his classic text *A Theory of Justice*.

What Rawls did for liberalism needs to be done for conservatism; a Rawlsian turn is strongly recommended, and in this chapter I am going to try to develop a conservatism that appeals to public reason in the same way that Rawlsian liberalism (perhaps the most successful political philosophy of the last three decades) does. The two types of 'conservative' we sketched above are therefore not conservatives in the meaning of the act, because their reasons are purely self-centred. Of course one would expect those who are 'conservative' to be the ultimate beneficiaries of conservative policies; but one must also demand that the conservative be able to explain his or her reasons for conservatism in an intelligible and widely applicable way.

Not all Conservatives are conservatives, and not all conservatives are Conservatives

A genuine conservative, in the ideological sense, isn't necessarily someone who is too rich or staid to welcome change, or someone who reveres Churchill or Mrs Thatcher, or someone who thinks that the Tories are posh and Labour coarse – sizeable though each of those constituencies is.

What about the relationship between the Conservative Party and conservatism? We have already argued that the Conservative Party is the custodian of the conservative tradition. It is time to inquire about the meaning of that statement in more detail.

As the title of this section suggests, I want to argue against assuming that what the Conservative Party does is the be-all and end-all for judging what conservatism is. I have already insisted upon making a conceptual distinction between conservatism and the Conservative Party; in this section, I now have to argue that not only is the distinction conceptual, but it also reflects reality. That involves arguing that either there are conservatives who are not Conservative, or there are Conservatives who are not conservative, or both. That in turn depends on how 'conservatism' is characterised (assuming for the minute that the notion of being a Conservative is unproblematic, which, as for instance in the case of Enoch Powell, it is not).

Surely conservatism, the urge to conserve, is inimical to many of the Tory projects of the last half-century. The politicians who came together in the 1980s under the rubric of the 'new right', armed with references to Friedman, Nozick and Hayek, were enthused by the attack on corporatism and the promotion of supply-side economics, and developed quite an armoury of distinctive social policies, to do with the welfare state, identity and citizenship, as well as the market-driven economics that were the mainstay and chief attraction. But these had little to do with tradition and human imperfection (except in so far as they had common *antagonisms*). Small 'c' conservatives are opposed to non-pragmatic thought, whereas free marketeers can often be very evangelical; many commentators have written of 'market fundamentalism'.[3] Conservatives' suspicion of abstract thought seems also inimical to the neo-liberal theorists' development of systems. Small 'c' conservatives focus on the individual case, whereas liberals are much more interested in system.[4]

This, however, is not to say that conservatism and market economics are unlinked; far from it. Indeed, many of the social structures that underpin free markets (property rights, a work ethic, contract law and respect for the law generally) are exactly those that are valued by conservatives. Hence it is perfectly possible for a conservative to argue that, as an economic regulator of exchange, free markets are as good as any, while nationalised industries (for example) distort valuable relationships within a society.

On the other hand, a conservative is always sensible of outcomes; some pattern of exchanges might well lead to unfortunate outcomes. The new right would reject the whole idea that an outcome of a properly conducted exchange might be 'unfortunate' or 'fortunate'; they would argue strongly against the claim that, if one was a property owner, one might have wider duties to society when it came to exchanging that property.[5]

Why, then, do political scientists insist that conservatism is unrelated to tradition? Most look back at Tory history, and argue that not only do many Tories not shun abstract thinking, they actually prefer it.[6] But these arguments that conservatism is nothing to do with tradition and opposition to change are question-begging.

They go like this. The aim is to show that conservatism is nothing to do with tradition, or allergy to theory, or the avoidance of change, or anything else that conservatives say it is. To prove this, a counterexample is exhibited, often the new right (often Mrs

Thatcher herself), but also sometimes the odd groupuscules of the late 19th century such as the Liberty and Property Defence League, which did propose theories, exhort radical change, and attack established institutions and order. But such arguments rest on the assumption that the new right, or the LPDL, or whatever, are genuinely conservative, *which is precisely the point at issue*. If such thinkers assume exactly what they are trying to prove, then it is not at all surprising that the proof is simple.

But we should not fall for it. Before we have any kind of proof that everyone under the big Conservative Party tent has an ideology in common, we cannot assume that because a Conservative espouses some cause, conservatives in general must.

As W.H. Greenleaf points out,[7] the Conservative Party is so old, and its net drawn so wide, that expecting all its members to espouse the same policies is wrongheaded, but it does not follow that it is wrongheaded to point out that there are deep divisions within the party. If, as Greenleaf and Eccleshall argue, there is no fundamental *ideological* distinction between the majority of Conservative politicians, then it remains a mystery why the same arguments blow up time after time. For example, Harold Macmillan testified to a Cabinet split whose fault line ran directly along the historical divide.

> Meanwhile, the Chancellor of the Exchequer and I worked on a letter to be addressed to both sides of industry proposing the creation of the National Economic Development Council, drawn from trade unions, management and government who could participate in central planning advice. … The discussion about this plan revealed 'a rather interesting and quite deep divergence of view between Ministers, really corresponding to whether they had old Whig, Liberal, *laissez-faire* traditions, or Tory opinions, paternalists and not afraid of a little *dirigisme*'.[8]

If there is no divide within the Conservatives between the paternalist and the libertarian, the wet and the dry, then there needs to be some explanation of why that sort of terminology keeps resurfacing, and why there have been perpetual arguments within the party about precisely these issues. The whole point, surely, is that the arguments between, say, Baldwin and Churchill, Macmillan and Thorneycroft, Heath and Powell, Pym and Thatcher, Major and Redwood, Hague and Portillo, are instances of a common pathology. Surely the oddest explanation for these is that they are all *sui generis* examples of individual vendettas in a uniquely fractious party. The claim of fundamental ideological unity seems to lack explanatory power at the point at which it is most obviously needed.

So there is pretty strong evidence that not all Conservatives are conservative. What about the argument that not all conservatives are Conservative? I have already argued against Bruce Pilbeam that there is nothing *prima facie* unreasonable about assuming that Soviet generals or Iranian mullahs are conservative[9] (though as will be clear, I do not think they are – for different reasons from Pilbeam's).

In general, over the last two centuries, inequality has been decreasing. The poor have been getting generally richer, partly because of socialist reforms, partly because of the operations of the market, partly because of the impact of technology and partly because of the social compacts made by various Conservative governments. Everyone, it is fair to say, Tory, Liberal and Labour, gets some credit. But the effect of the increase in equality is that the rich have been generally keener to halt reform, while the poor have been generally keener to accelerate it. So far, so good: as one would expect. But since 1979, and the Thatcherite market-driven reforms, inequality has been on the increase. It halted in the 1990s under John Major (though it was not reversed), and has been on the increase again under Tony Blair.[10] Hence from 1979 it has been true, as it has not been true before, that the poor might feel (possibly incorrectly) that they could benefit from a slowing-down of the pace of change, that though they do not get very much out of the status quo, it may well be the best that they can hope for. The institutions of society that were constructed in the early part of the 20th century by Gladstonian liberals, and in the third quarter by socialists, are precisely the institutions that they wish to protect from neo-liberal market-led reforms. Such a constituency might well begin to examine the conservative arguments that I will set out in this chapter rather more seriously once they can see that they can benefit from them. As Mannheim said, being a progressive may turn you into a conservative in order to preserve the fruits of revolution.[11]

For instance, an argument along these lines was sketched by political philosopher John Gray in the final years of the Major government; Gray, formerly a leading theorist of the new right, has in recent times switched dramatically to a much more hostile position.[12]

> Nowhere has Tory market corporatism been more destructive than in the National Health Service. It is worth reflecting on Tory policy on the NHS, if only as an object lesson in ideological folly. By any international standard the old, unreformed NHS was a considerable success story. ... Furthermore, and perhaps decisively, the NHS was understood and trusted by the British people. There is not, and never has been, any popular demand for its reform. In fact, there is deep public disquiet about its dismemberment. ... In imposing on the tried and familiar institutions of the old NHS a grandiose scheme of marketizing reforms, whose ultimate outcome even they could scarcely guess at, the Tories proved once again that they have lost the concern for the continuity of institutions that is their only principled *raison d'être*.
>
> There is, then, an overwhelming conservative case – to be sure, one which today's Tories cannot be expected even to understand – for restoring the old National Health Service, as the fundamental institution within which health care is provided in Britain.[13]

The first tenet of conservatism: the change principle

How, then, to describe conservatism? A very fruitful framework for understanding ideologies generally has been developed by political philosopher Michael Freeden.[14] Freeden sees ideologies as coarse versions of political philosophies, made easier to understand and communicate, less subtle but more applicable to the real world. An ideology can be described as a small cluster of basic tenets, principles or concepts. Such tenets, beyond the political group, can be disputed, and open to a number of interpretations. But within a particular group, the meaning of the principle is *decontested*, that is, it is not disputed. The tenet is taken as something that the group holds in common.

So, for example, the term 'liberty' is open to a number of interpretations. But for a particular ideological group – for example, neo-liberal free marketeers – the meaning of liberty is not argued over. Neo-liberals may argue about many things, such as the extent to which markets should determine the distribution of a society's resources, but what they do not argue about is the nature of liberty, and whether such liberty is a good. This does not mean that all neo-liberals necessarily *agree* about the nature of liberty, or about why it is desirable. But, perhaps in the face of some common opponent, they tacitly agree not to subject their basic assumptions to argument and contest within the group.

So what are the decontested ideas of conservatism? Let us begin with the desire to avoid change. Given that we hope to take a Rawlsian turn and appeal to public reason, we need to produce arguments for opposition to change that do not simply boil down to a preference for the status quo.

It is worth noting as well that behavioural evidence shows that innovation is not always the most efficient or 'best' strategy, even if we discount the risks. Both young chimpanzees and human children learn by copying their elders in various tasks. But surprisingly, it is the chimpanzees who try to work things out for themselves while imitating; children imitate their parents much more slavishly, even when they are aware that some of the actions they are imitating are useless.[15] This is ironic: it would appear that more engaged and thoughtful learning strategies are less successful (as chimps grow up to be less intelligent than humans). The counterintuitive result is because of the massive complexity of the human environment; young humans need to learn to do so many more things very quickly, and imitation is more efficient for learning as it provides a guaranteed solution to the problem (even if that solution is itself not the most efficient).[16] Efficiency in problem-solving can be addressed once basic techniques have been learned unintelligently. The moral is that in complex environments, imitation is a better learning strategy than innovation.

On the other hand, children's learning is one thing, politics quite another. And early conservative philosophers soon extended conservatism beyond a focus on the *mere* preservation of traditions and practice, precisely because of the potential for narrow-mindedness and pettiness in that focus.[17]

Can any politician oppose change *tout court*? There are great social forces, and it seems crazy for a politician to stand in their way. Indeed, Tolstoy in the Epilogue to *War and Peace* went so far as to argue that no individual, not even Napoleon, could have any effect on history at all. That view is too extreme, but nevertheless it is fair to say that to try to prevent change utterly would be impossible. Conservative philosopher Roger Scruton suggests that much greater flexibility is desirable here.

> It is a limp definition of conservatism to describe it as the desire to conserve; for although there is in every man and woman some impulse to conserve that which is safe and familiar, it is the nature of this 'familiarity' that needs to be examined. To put it briefly, conservatism arises directly from the sense that one belongs to some continuing, and pre-existing social order, and that this fact is all-important in determining what to do. ... The desire to conserve is

compatible with all manner of change, provided only that change is also continuity.[18]

Scruton's point is well taken; conservatism is *not* intended to preserve the status quo against all comers. It is an ideology *concerned* with the difficulties that change provides, and is intended to manage change and to render it safe to handle. Allowable change is seen as *organic* or *natural*, in contradistinction to imposed or designed change.[19] Conservative philosopher Michael Oakeshott puts it like this.

> Changes, then, have to be suffered; and a man of conservative temperament (that is, one strongly disposed to preserve his identity) cannot be indifferent to them. In the main, he judges them by the disturbance they entail and, like everyone else, deploys his resources to meet them. The idea of innovation, on the other hand, is improvement. Nevertheless, a man of this temperament will not himself be an ardent innovator. In the first place, he is not inclined to think that nothing is happening unless great changes are afoot and therefore he is not worried by the absence of innovation: the use and enjoyment of things as they are occupies most of his attention. Further, he is aware that not all innovation is, in fact, improvement; and he will think that to innovate without improving is either designed or inadvertent folly. ... Innovating is always an equivocal enterprise, in which gain and loss (even excluding the loss of familiarity) are so closely interwoven that it is exceedingly difficult to forecast the final up-shot: there is no such thing as an unqualified improvement. For, innovating is an activity which generates not only the 'improvement' sought, but a new and complex situation of which this is only one of the components. The total change is always more extensive than the change designed; and the whole of what is entailed can neither be foreseen nor circumscribed. Thus, whenever there is innovation there is the certainty that the

change will be greater than was intended, that there will be loss as well as gain and that the loss and the gain will not be equally distributed among the people affected; there is the chance that the benefits derived will be greater than those which were designed; and there is the risk that they will be offset by changes for the worse.[20]

So the reason for the conservative attitude towards change is that 'inorganic' change, innovation, may have bad effects. Existing social structures confer huge benefits, which can be easily overlooked. The fact that 60 million people share the United Kingdom and interact as often and as peacefully as they do, the fact that prosperity spreads reasonably well, if not perfectly, through the nation is in and of itself a reason for celebration. It is something to *value*.

Equally, it is not something to risk lightly, because we know how fragile functioning societies are. Environmental and social depredation has laid many a society low, remarkably and horribly quickly.[21] We have seen many times how peaceful, relatively prosperous populations have been prepared to throw away the advantages of peace and prosperity in favour of murderous civil war, because of wrongs, or imagined wrongs, committed centuries ago (of which many are only dimly aware). In the United Kingdom, there are still communities wavering on the brink of throwing away the benefits of stable society, preferring pointless, barely motivated conflict. In Northern Ireland, the peace process is stalled despite its obvious benefits. In some forgotten towns in the north of England racial tensions threaten the peace. It seems incredible that the disorganised racist rabble that is the British National Party could launch a sustained assault on British society, but stranger things have happened.

The benefits that society brings are often not noticed by their recipients (until they have gone), and are very fragile. Change will therefore entail a risk, and the conservative point is that that risk should be weighed very carefully. We will call this first central tenet of conservatism the **change principle**.

The case for a conservative attitude will depend to a large extent on the particular context. Small 'c' conservatism will be attractive in an attractive society. The concrete benefits of an existing society must, says the conservative, be taken more seriously than potential, abstract benefits that could be gained through applying a social theory. That does not, self-evidently, entail that one should never innovate, nor that the concrete should always be valued more highly than the abstract. It is only to say that there is an *extra* burden of proof on those who are willing change.

So, for example, consider Japan. Japan is a very pleasant country, prosperous, orderly – and conservative. But since the property bubble burst at the end of the 1980s, there has been a prolonged slump from which it is only just emerging. Part of the problem is that the banks took on a lot of bad debt in the preceding boom, and now are reluctant to lend to further clients, which means that it is hard for investors to build up new businesses. The Anglo-Saxon, red-blooded variety of capitalism has a simple solution: let the banks go bust (Mrs Thatcher, of course, famously let much of British industry die). But the Japanese are reluctant to do this, because the social shock will be too great. Are the Japanese right or wrong?

The change principle does not determine right and wrong. From its standpoint, however, the Japanese are undoubtedly correct to value social continuity, and to try to solve their debt problem without wiping out savings, even if those savings are invested unwisely. But there must come a point at which the concrete benefits of the status quo are too small to affect the consideration, particularly when the potential benefits of drastic action are large. Geographer and environmentalist Jared Diamond describes several societies where the traditional ways of doing things, however in tune with the environment initially, led ultimately to catastrophic collapse.[22]

The effect of the change principle is not to prevent change, nor to set out the exact circumstances when change is acceptable, but *to throw the burden of proof onto the innovator*. That burden will become higher when the benefits of an existing society are high, or when (as for instance in early modern Iceland[23]) the environment is so fragile that any innovation at all is virtually guaranteed to make things worse. In this way, the change principle does not direct policy, so much as indicate the proper subject matter of the important political arguments.

The change principle entails that conservatism will vary across societies. Hence, unlike liberals or Marxists, conservatives from different societies will say different things. Marxists from Liberia or Letchworth will agree on policy fundamentals; their conservative opponents will not. This is why it is so hard to lump conservatives together and treat them as a single unit. For example, an American conservative maintains that a written constitution is the guarantor of liberty; a British conservative claims that it would be the first step on the road to tyranny. They cannot agree, because each conservative values the benefits visible in his or her own society.

Furthermore, the nature of the individual societies themselves will determine how change has to be addressed. For instance, Karl Mannheim points out that Britain and Germany, two relatively conservative societies (at least in the early 19th century about which he was writing), had to adopt two different principles to dampen change. In Britain, the relatively high social mobility allowed the gradual evolution of society, and ultimately the avoidance of revolution during the mid-19th century. In Germany, on the other hand, where there was much less mobility, strong institutions had to be put in place by conservatives to prevent change.[24]

The change principle also rules out the idea that conservatism can be a mere exercise in nationalistic nostalgia. Many people claim, or have claimed, to be conservative on the basis of their preference for a 'kinder, gentler age', but no one who accepts the change principle should wish a return to a golden age, even if that golden age is particularly inviting, for the obvious reason that someone turning the clock back is forcing unwelcome, inorganic change every bit as much as someone who speeds the clock forward. Each is ruled out, as conservatism, by the change principle. When the Ayatollah Khomeini set off the Iranian revolution, and returned Iran from a modernising society under the brutal Shah to a 'conservative' one where 9th-century *Sharia* law predominates, he had to change the place, and he and his successors have had to hold the development of Iranian society back, painfully and with great difficulty. The result is a deeply divided country which, despite its being a nominal theocracy, does not seem godlier than anywhere else. The malign consequences of forcing Iranian society back several centuries would have been obvious in advance to anyone who took the change principle seriously.

The roots of social order

The change principle defines a certain type of mild conservatism. It is mild because the politician is exhorted to privilege the present over future possibilities. Nevertheless, this description applies to virtually every British government, including those of Mrs Thatcher and Mr Blair, as the inertia of the massive government machine prevents British governments from making wholesale changes. Something more is required, a second principle, if we are to define a conservatism that is both consistent with the sceptical conservative philosophical and political tradition, while ruling out related non-conservative ideologies.

Michael Freeden's impressive analysis of the conservative ideology supplements the change principle with an idea that cleverly incorporates the conservative acceptance of (or insistence on) human imperfection.

> The defence of a specific, 'normal' type of change [i.e. the change principle] is significantly assisted by a second core component of conservatism that underlies whatever quasi-contingent guises its various manifestations may borrow: a belief in the extra-human origins of the social order, i.e. as

independent of human will. It is undoubtedly a substantive and valorized core concept, though not always recognized as such by its practitioners. The phrase 'extra-human', rather than the more common phrase 'natural', is deliberate because it is an intriguing extension of the latter. The search for harmony, equilibrium, and order – itself a raising of the concern with change to a state of awareness – has adopted many forms. God, history, biology, and science, as understood by different generations, have served in turn as the extra-human anchor of the social order and have been harnessed to validate its practices. In the nineteenth century, conservatives saw stability as a function of the natural order or hierarchy, 'my station and my duties', with their concomitants of status and responsibility anchored in a strong sense of history. In the early part of the twentieth century, the emphasis was on identifying immutable 'psychological' principles of human nature, such as the need to provide incentives to action, or the desire to compete, which justified property-holdings as expressions of human worth and facilitators of human activity. Some contemporary conservatives still adhere to such notions of necessity, invoking the bonds of family or the natural instinct to endorse prevailing practices and institutions. In the era of welfare-state Keynesianism, as well as free-market post-Keynesianism, the appeal has been to another natural order – that of 'scientific' economic laws ostensibly endowed with universal validity.[25]

In other words, the conservative accepts that he or she has no control over the conditions that underlie the natural order. Whether those conditions involve God, free markets or something else, the job of the conservative politician, on this reading, is to ensure that humans do not try to interfere with, or impede, the 'extra-human order'. This inclusion of free markets under the rubric of 'extra-human order', incidentally, makes Freeden's argument that free market liberalism is a type of conservatism completely straightforward.[26]

Roger Scruton's very British conservatism provides an example of a conservative philosophy that Freeden's characterisation includes.[27] He rests his idea of conservatism on an extra-human order to do with institutions, law and family relations, all of which are given (i.e. our relationships with them are not contractual, and therefore not voluntary on our part, and cannot be adjusted or redrawn as we like). His conservatism is based around allegiance and loyalty to these institutions. The change principle ensures (a) that no one should make any attempt to impose their own ideas of right, efficiency or morality on this extra-human order, and (b) continuity from generation to generation that marks out a particular type of life as British (in Scruton's case, English[28]), and confers legitimacy on the institutions as ways of regulating social and economic life.

As a characterisation of conservatism, the change principle plus the adherence to a strong view of the roots of social order has its attractions. Indeed, Danny Kruger, an advisor to David Cameron, singled out my lack of interest in these extra-human roots as his major criticism of the thesis of the first edition of this book;[29] he would prefer a conservatism rooted in what he calls the 'numinous – the quality of the history of England, say, or the unique settlement of the Church of England'. This would allow 'emotional allegiance as well as mental agreement'. My brand of conservatism he finds rather intellectual and dry. Well, maybe so. But let me set out four reasons for thinking that an account of conservatism that depends on a particular view of the extra-human origins of the social order is of necessity inadequate. The combination is too unstable to support a coherent ideology.

The first reason is to do with the communicability of the conservative message. Recall our stricture that conservatives must have public reasons underlying their commitment to the status quo and its slow, organic evolution. Merely disliking change, or wanting to be posh, is not sufficient to be counted as a conservative. We recommended that conservatism take a Rawlsian turn, that it should be prepared to base itself on as few and as uncontroversial assumptions as could bear its weight, partly to provide a stronger philosophical foundation, partly to facilitate the communication of the ideology to others.

The problem with basing conservatism on the extra-human origins of the social order is that whether one accepts conservatism will then depend on one's buying into that account of the social order. If I am asked to become a conservative because God created the world, and man in His image, etc., then the recruitment drive ends there because I do not believe that there is a God. In the United States, where politics is polluted by the incessant screech of the culture wars in the background, the very possibility of a secular brand of conservatism is the subject of live debate.[30] If I am asked to become a conservative because one cannot buck the market, then again I have difficulties. I have a deep respect for market forces, and few moral problems with the idea of free markets, globalisation, etc., but equally it seems perfectly reasonable to me for communities to interfere with market operation when they feel that greater issues are at stake. I cannot be persuaded of the merits of conservatism prior to being persuaded of the merits of the extra-human order in question.

A second point, in direct response to Kruger, that follows is that to reject an account of the extra-human origins of the social order as a *component* of the conservative philosophy does not prevent someone from nevertheless having such a view. Someone who did have a strong faith in something numinous, be it English history or the Anglican settlement, could retain that faith. Nothing about the conservatism I set out in this chapter would contradict that. But equally, the lack of strong commitment in the general philosophy allows such a conservative to do two things. First, he can make common cause with other conservatives who are motivated by a different view of the social order. Any moderate political project will have to seek a balance between the manifold views of the good in civilisation, and that will be much harder to do if the politician refuses to compromise on the good that he himself seeks. We must beware of what Oliver Letwin has called 'false gods'.[31] Rejecting sentimental attachment as a component of conservatism does not require people to have no emotional attachments at all – it merely allows them to make their case logically, without question-begging.

Related to this, there is a third reason to reject Freeden's account of conservatism: the fragmentation of ideas of the social order. There are dozens and dozens of views of the foundation of the social order, and any attempt to form a conservative policy will be fraught with difficulty in the absence of a consensus on what the extra-human origins actually are. A fundamentalist Christian and a free market evangelist could agree about many things, no doubt, but at some point they will come to Christ's evicting the money-changers from the temple.

The final problem is the most serious, and it is that the idea of resting conservatism on the extra-human origins of the social order actually stands in many imaginable circumstances in complete contradiction to the change principle. To state it most baldly, if the current state of the social order was such that it concealed rather than celebrated its extra-human origins, then it would be the duty of the conservative to change the social order, possibly radically. If you have strong beliefs about the extra-human origins of the social order, then you are just as likely to want to change society radically as to preserve it; and alternatively just as likely to try to prevent organic change as to allow it to happen.

So, to revisit a previous example, the Ayatollah Khomeini's Islamic revolution in Iran was clearly based on a particular conception of the extra-human origins of the social order, as all Islamist ideologies are. But Khomeini had to violate the change principle radically, because he found the existing social structures in 1979 Iran to be literally worthless. The present and concrete was not considered for a second to be comparable to the absent, abstract and potential. That the social and moral improvements promised by Khomeini remain absent and abstract – I think I demur at 'potential' – even now is evidence of the value of the change principle.

More germane to the British case is the point that free markets are celebrated as agents of massive and thoroughgoing change (not always for the worse, not always for the better). In the post-Thatcher world, it is almost impossible to understand the pre-Thatcher experience; to read the speeches of, say, Robert Carr or George Brown is to enter a different world. Free marketry cannot inherently be a species of conservatism because free markets deliberately flout the change principle. It is no coincidence that the arch-free-marketeer Hayek (whom we will meet below), a man with very decided views of the extra-human origins of the social order, once wrote a paper explaining 'Why I am not a conservative'.[32]

Planning and targets: a lack of knowledge

We agreed earlier that the change principle would have to be supplemented by something else, and we have seen that the 'extra-human' idea doesn't work. The history of conservatism, on the other hand, suggests that knowledge might be a key to understanding conservatism. From Socrates, to Sextus Empiricus, to Montaigne, thinkers have argued that people are simply incapable of discovering the basic facts that would justify the opinions they have, and that they are very bad at extracting the relevant information from the world. When the philosophers left off, the psychologists got hold of us and managed to prove the situation is at least as bad as the philosophers had expected; we are very irrational and biased creatures, at least as measured against the yardstick of rational decision-making.[33]

Part of the problem in running human affairs has always been the uncertainty of future events. One obvious solution to uncertainty is to plan the development of society in order to reduce uncertainty, specifically to plan the economy. The idea is that, for example, a government, armed with a suitable mandate from its electorate, could make certain decisions to reduce risk for its population. So, for example, it could fix the prices of various products that were determined to be essential; it could fix the price of labour, to ensure that posts deemed to be too important to remain unfilled were attractive to enough people; it could make it harder, or even illegal, to fire people; it could ensure the supply of various commodities; it could raise the price of some imports to make sure that home-based industry could compete on easier terms; it could prevent the purchase of certain firms by foreigners to ensure an indigenous industry; most obviously of all, it could purchase (nationalise) firms to take their demand and supply decisions out of the purview of the market altogether, and in effect fund the losses through taxation. Such policies were routinely pursued in Britain in the 60s and 70s.

Since 1989, however, they have been radically discredited by the collapse of the Soviet Union, the most ambitious planned economy the world has ever known. Other planned economies on a smaller scale, most notably North Korea and Zimbabwe at the time of writing, have also proved abject failures. On the other hand, a large enough economy can live with small planned enclaves, as long as voters/taxpayers are prepared to take up the slack by paying higher prices and losing out on opportunities for trade. One particularly egregious example is the EU's Common Agricultural Policy, designed to enrich a small number of farmers in Europe at the expense of European food consumers (i.e. everybody), and competing farmers in the developing world (i.e. everybody else).

It is recognised by most commentators that planning an economy is simply beyond the ken of most governments. It was hoped that a government could assemble a large enough bureaucratic machine to administer the millions of demand and supply decisions through transparent rules and consistent application of regulations.[34] But the difficulty has been that, though a bureaucracy might be fairly represented as being machine-like, a society cannot be, and the actions of the one upon the other may well be harmful. Added to which, individual bureaucrats are still as prone to error as the rest of us; an enduring image in virtually every British comedy film of the 1950s is the 'men from the ministry', bureaucrats invariably dressed in pinstriped suits and bowler hats, carrying rolled umbrellas and briefcases, usually played by Richard Wattis or Eric Barker, causing more problems than they solve.

So detailed planning is now unfashionable. But the problem with unplanned systems is that they might produce undesirable outcomes. This is difficult for a government with respect to any industry or sector that it feels is strategically important, unless it is prepared to surrender that sector to the disciplines of the market (a surrender that is becoming increasingly popular with governments of all stripes, unfortunately just when it seems to be becoming decreasingly popular with voters). It is particularly difficult when the government actually owns the assets and is responsible for the system involved (as is usually the case with health and welfare systems, for example).

How should a government produce the outcomes it wishes? It could try to govern using artfully crafted market-based incentives and property rights, but this is rather too complex. A recent innovation, championed in the UK by Chancellor Gordon Brown, is to use *targets*. The government sets out a schedule of target values for particular parameters called *performance indicators*. Bureaucrats then are given incentives (e.g. promotion, more funding, bonuses) to ensure that the performance targets are reached. The changes in incentives are important – there is nothing particularly wrong, or indeed unusual, about a government setting out the outcomes that interest it. The target culture begins when the government starts to penalise people or organisations when those outcomes are *not* achieved.

The government picks out parameters that seem to it to go with or indicate good performance. So, for instance, it wants the National Health Service to produce a healthy population, efficient use of NHS resources, and a happy relationship with their patients.

But these are too nebulous and open to interpretation to operate as targets, so the government chooses quantifiable values that theoretically can act as proxies for these desirable outcomes. They might include the number of people waiting for particular operations, the average length of time someone stays in hospital, the number of people surviving some surgical procedure for a certain length of time, and so on. Schools find themselves having to meet targets concerning the number of children who pass particular exams. Universities, to meet concerns about the education of the wider community in the 'knowledge economy', are given targets for the number of admissions of students from certain social groups. The police need to meet crime reduction targets.

Focusing public servants on the outcomes of their actions is no bad thing; too often government services make little or no attempt to consider the requirements of their clients. But the trouble is that attempts to micromanage giant organisations in this way seem not to work. The focus on quantifiable targets means that more useful goals, that may be unquantifiable, get pushed aside. For example, the Ministry of Agriculture, Fisheries and Food (MAFF), in 2002, met ten of its thirteen targets. Pretty good, no? Unfortunately one of the three targets it missed was one to prevent outbreaks of serious diseases; British agriculture was devastated in 2001 by a massive epidemic of foot and mouth disease, which even caused that year's general election to be postponed for a month.[35] In the end, the government, fed up with the long list of MAFF's failings, abolished it. National targeting can be insensitive to local conditions. For instance, sickle cell anaemia, an illness that affects particular ethnic groups, is not a very common condition in the United Kingdom, so does not feature on national targets. But because there are areas of high concentration of the affected ethnic groups, there are certain areas where sickle cell anaemia is a serious problem; nevertheless, because targets are national, hospital managers are given no incentives to tackle it in those areas.[36]

And, lest the reader is tempted to think that we are focusing on New Labour meddling in public services, we should also note that even when targets are relatively hands-off, well-crafted and successful for years, we should be wary of their long-term utility. Perhaps the best example of a useful target regime in the United Kingdom has been inflation-targeting. Following the pound's ignominious ejection from the European Exchange Rate Mechanism in 1992, Chancellors of the Exchequer, Tory and Labour, dropped the tacit policy of massaging exchange rates, and instead focused on targeting inflation – using interest rates to try to keep inflation within an agreed range or around about an agreed target figure (in 2006, this was 2 per cent). As prices go up, or expectations of rising prices begin to take hold, then interest rates increase, to make saving rather than consumption more attractive, and to encourage foreigners to buy the currency. Demand is dampened, and inflation should calm down. So goes the theory. Mr Brown's first significant act as Chancellor was to allow the Bank of England to pursue this target independently of government interference (though the government sets the inflation target that the Bank tries to hit). The result of nearly a decade and a half of inflation targeting in the UK has been low inflation and economic stability. Targets can be successful, and the inflation target most successful of all.

Policies based around targets should not become ossified; one thing is as sure as anything in politics and economics, which is that there is no guarantee that a policy instrument that works today will work tomorrow. Inflation targeting, to repeat, a very successful managerial innovation, which has been responsible for many years of stability and prosperity, has been copied all over the world, with the conspicuous exception of the United States. But its operation in the early 21st century has revealed two preconditions that are required for the method to work, preconditions that are currently not obtaining. The first is that demand stays reasonably constant – if demand picks up dramatically, then the rise in prices reflects the greater demand, rather than any problems in the value of the currency. As China and India increase their global presence, both with relatively open economies, various prices, particularly of commodities – notably oil – have skyrocketed (supply worries caused by the Iraq war and Hurricane Katrina also contributed, of course). This will tend to put prices up worldwide, but that phenomenon should not be confused with inflation proper – raising interest rates to dampen demand may well cause economies to falter in such a situation.

And the second precondition of an inflation target working is that different sorts of price remain in step. In particular, it is a general expectation that consumer prices and asset prices increase and decrease together, as they have always done. The interest rate regime appropriate to regulate the one has, in general, in the past been appropriate to regulate the other as well. However, in 2006, consumer prices are relatively calm, while asset prices, notably house prices, have shot up. As assets affect future consumption, asset prices have something to say about expectations of future prices generally, and that in itself is an important signal to governments and bankers. Consumer spending, furthermore, has remained buoyant across the Western democracies thanks to a borrowing boom on the back of those house prices. So an increase in interest rates to curb asset price inflation risks causing falling house prices, a credit squeeze, falling consumer spending and recession. Decreases in interest rates in response to low consumer price inflation risk fuelling the borrowing boom and the house price bubble, with the danger of a larger crunch later on. There are no easy or right answers here, even with the use of a highly successful policy instrument like inflation targeting.

So, why do targets go wrong? The problem is what organisational theorist Marshall Meyer calls the *performance paradox*.[37] Performance targets will never be able to create the right sort of professional behaviour except in the short term, in circumscribed contexts. According to Meyer, the needs of management are constantly shifting, and so, though managers need lots of measures of performance, static and simple measures lose their informational content over time; they become less significant, and relay less useful information to managers the longer they are in place.

First, the world changes. Targets are crafted, often at great expense, to cope with the world as it is understood at that time. In very complex systems – particularly the giant welfare systems of the big liberal democracies – the inevitable result is that by the time the targets feed back into the management process, the world has moved on, populations will have changed, priorities will have altered, new technologies will be available. And so there is a decent chance that a performance target will be completely uninformative even before it is deployed; if not, it will become less and less informative as time goes on.

Second, not only does the world change, but the system itself changes – most notably in response to the incentives provided by the performance targets. Before a target is in place, a professional will be doing her job as she understands it. Once the target is deployed, then she suddenly has incentives to hit the target. The better-crafted the target, the more likely it is to help her achieve good performance. But when professional priorities change, she may be left with incentives to achieve what are now irrelevant targets. For instance, schoolteachers are given incentives for their pupils to pass GCSE exams. The result is that children are nursed through the exams, so pass rates have increased. This is not necessarily a good thing, since the whole purpose of an exam is as a signalling system; the point is to tell employers and others which students are better than others. If everyone gets a prize, then the signalling value is zero.

Indeed, if targets are badly crafted, or out of date, then the incentives they give become perverse – the professional is actually given incentives to perform badly. For instance, if a hospital is penalised for deaths during operations, then they may have an incentive for not performing operations on patients who are at some risk from the procedure. Or – a real example – Mr Blair's government placed a target on local authorities to collect a certain quantity of recyclable waste. Many authorities insisted that their residents should separate their household waste into that which was recyclable and that which was not, and collected them separately, and therefore met their targets, and were rewarded with more funding. But there is a national shortage of recycling depots. And the target was for *collecting* recyclable waste, not for recycling it. So some authorities then put the recyclable waste back with the rest, and buried or incinerated it all together.[38]

Third, if targets are used to get rid of poor performance, by either sacking those who fail, or – more usual – bringing everyone up to uniform standards, then they signal virtually nothing, because everyone's performance is identical. The government's Research Assessment Exercises (RAEs) are intended to justify university funding by measuring their research. At the last RAE round, every university did very well, having learned to play the system, but the pot of funding for which they were competing did not grow. Hence lots of universities made huge changes, at great cost to themselves, and yet were not rewarded.

The problem is that targets need to be sophisticated, fine-grained and constantly monitored and updated to be effective (and even then they are not guaranteed to be). But to be a cheap method of enforcing discipline on public servants, they need to be relatively simple (so that public servants can understand them and react to the signals they give), coarse-grained (so that there are only a few targets to be reached, not lots of small ones), and kept stable (so that people don't have to keep learning new sets of rules and filling in new lots of forms every year). Unsurprisingly, many have concluded that targets to set outcomes will never be sufficiently flexible or useful to ensure good public services.

The moral is straightforward: planning is, at best, extremely difficult. First, planners are unlikely, given a complex and dynamic society under inevitable conditions of uncertainty, to be able to achieve their goals. Second, even if they do manage to succeed, this is likely to cause unintended side-effects or perverse outcomes. And third, even if planners do achieve their goals without too many bad side-effects, the price of their control may be the erosion of important ethical and professional codes.

Where is the knowledge? Its distribution

Does this mean that there is no knowledge that can be gained from and about an economy? Are we forever doomed to blunder about in the half-light of ignorance?

Not quite. As individual economic agents, we have some knowledge about our own circumstances, which enables us to make our own small plans. We can plan for certain outcomes, we can substitute one set of exchanges for another. If I have £5 in my pocket, and I see that I can buy four cans of my favourite beer for £5 from the off-licence, or a copy of Rosebery's biography of Pitt from the bookshop next door for the same price, I can decide which of those two treats – or neither – I should buy. I do that on the basis of some self-knowledge. Someone who knows me well could also make the same choice, and indeed someone who knows me better than I know myself might be able to spend £5 on something I would never have thought of, but which I will enjoy very much. Of course, the knowledge to which I refer is rapidly changing, and not fully certain in application. It may well be that I bought the wrong thing. But I had enough knowledge about my finances and my preferences – at that particular point in time – to make a reasonable plan.

The knowledge that is essential for economic decisions is often of this sort, as argued by one of the leading economists of the Austrian tradition, Friedrich von Hayek (1899–1992). Even when we move out of the sphere of the individual decision, it is easy to see that the knowledge required to make good economic plans is of relevance only in highly circumscribed contexts. The context of operation is central to the usefulness of knowledge.

> We need to remember only how much we have to learn in any occupation after we have completed our theoretical training, how big a part of our working life we spend learning particular jobs, and how valuable an asset in all walks of life is knowledge of people, of local conditions, and of special circumstances.

To know of and put to use a machine not fully employed, or somebody's skill which could be better utilized, or to be aware of a surplus stock which can be drawn upon during an interruption of supplies, is socially quite as useful as the knowledge of better alternative techniques. The shipper who earns his living from using otherwise empty or half-filled journeys of tramp-steamers, or the estate agent whose whole knowledge is almost exclusively one of temporary opportunities, or the arbitrageur who gains from local differences of commodity prices – are all performing eminently useful functions based on special knowledge of circumstances of the fleeting moment not known to others.[39]

And because the relevant economic knowledge depends on 'the circumstances of the fleeting moment', it is virtually impossible to pass that sort of knowledge up the political hierarchy, to the 'men from the ministry', in a timely or cost-effective way. Indeed, bureaucrats explicitly try *not* to deal with particulars. They abstract away from the detail, often using statistical techniques, to produce a much more stable body of knowledge. But experts cannot be relied upon to develop effective models for the economy, or indeed wider society; economic modelling is much more an art than a science.[40] Expert prediction, particularly of the effects of change, is not particularly good; the aggregated opinions of groups of experts tend to be more accurate than those of individual experts, and – perhaps more surprisingly, when opinions of laypeople or non-experts are added to the mix, the resulting aggregate is even more accurate. The bringing together of diverse opinions – especially including the opinions of those who know little about a topic – results in much better performance than consulting the opinions of the relatively homogeneous band of experts.[41]

Modelling is a perfectly legitimate way of understanding the environment, and a government or big company that did not do this would be negligent. But this does not mean that the economic detail goes away.

Even the large and highly mechanized plant keeps going largely because of an environment upon which it can draw for all sorts of unexpected needs: tiles for its roof, stationery for its forms, and all the thousand and one kinds of equipment in which it cannot be self-contained and which the plans for the operation of the plant require to be readily available in the market.[42]

This level of detail cannot be communicated to the large-scale economic planner, and we might therefore assume that economic decisions at that level of detail are beyond the planner's purview.

In other words, the knowledge about the economy that a planner would ideally get hold of is actually distributed around the economy, held by millions of individuals, often tacitly and unconsciously. The knowledge is about conditions that affect the transactions of now; it is more often than not out of date before it is articulated.

On Hayek's view, there is one heuristic abstraction (i.e. a distillation of the relevant information that is more likely than not to be helpful) of the sum of all the individual economic contexts affecting the demand for and supply of a particular good, and that is the *price* of that good as determined in a competitive bidding market. This theory, of course, is the basis of the neo-liberal philosophy of free market economics, which is beyond the scope of this chapter. But it is an important topic in the understanding of the meaning (if any) of conservatism in the 21st century, and we will return to Hayek and the price function in Chapter Six below.

Knowledge, wisdom, institutions, tradition

This distribution of knowledge around the economy need not always be fleetingly or otherwise contained in anyone's head. It may be that important knowledge about how to achieve social goals or realise corporate aims gets ossified in procedures within institutions and organisations. In other words, when an organisation (whether formal or informal) is used to perform some task, perhaps on a regular basis, then, even though at the outset it is people doing the work, over time the organisation will take over and actually perform the task itself.[43]

How so? One example of the sort of way this happens is when a task is relatively routine. Suppose the task can be set out as a checklist of mundane subtasks, for instance a service for a car, with the mechanic going through a checklist of tests on a form, ticking the boxes as he goes. The form might initially be intended to serve as an *aide memoire* for the service mechanic, who knows all about the cars in question. But when the firm expands, the form might be copied and distributed to apprentice workers, who can perform the tasks as structured (check tyre pressure, test windscreen wipers ...), even though they lack the overall knowledge to understand the car as a unity.

The firm may expand further, and begin to employ people in specialist roles; for example, there might be a person with responsibility for exhaust systems, another for ignition, and so on. Then when a car is serviced, the manager of the service process will go down the checklist, sending the car to the specialist units as appropriate. Under this system, none of the specialists need know anything about the car as a whole, only about the subsystems for which they are responsible; the checklist has become a management strategy. The person managing the servicing process need only understand the routine of going down the form, and which unit is responsible for which checkbox.

Finally, suppose the original expert mechanic now retires. In that case, the new expanded firm might actually employ nobody who possesses all the knowledge about the car as a single object. The knowledge is distributed around the firm in the specialist units. But note also that some key knowledge, the knowledge of how to perform a service, and how to coordinate the servicing resources most efficiently while ensuring that every part of the car is tested, is possessed by no one at all, not even by a computer. The important knowledge is contained in the servicing form, together with the instruction to the manager to go down the form, doling out the tests in order. Some of the knowledge is no longer stored in a human mind.[44]

In the wider social context, there is much knowledge – to do with how to perform social tasks, how to manage limited resources, for example – that is spread around a wider society, between people and artefacts, in this way. Many formal processes or institutions are dramatically simplified by being grafted onto existing social practices; those practices may be as important to the outcome as the formal processes themselves. For instance, free markets are artificial, rule-based creations that sit on top of various important social structures, such as the rule of law (particularly contract law), non-arbitrary government, well-respected property rights and the Protestant work ethic.[45] When these structures are not in place, the imposition of market economics can be quite disruptive.

We have seen how planning outcomes can often distort existing practices or cause unfortunate side effects. Unplanned development of practices can, as it were, encode wisdom in tradition. If a society has 'always done it that way', there will be a reason. If the traditional practice was harmful to that society, then either the practice or the society, or both, would not tend to survive. Hence there is at least a presumption that a long-standing tradition serves some sort of useful purpose, encodes some 'folk wisdom', and stamping it out will mean that that purpose will no longer be served. Note that this presumption is related to the need for a public reason defence of conservatism; the assumption is that irrationality serves some function, and we do not merely enjoy irrationality for the sake of it.[46]

The presumption is not that the traditional practice is the best system possible, only that it is likely to encode knowledge about how a purpose can be achieved by that social group. Even outmoded or otherwise inefficient traditions can do this. For example, the open field system of agriculture was no doubt inefficient in various ways, but it achieved a number of useful purposes. It ensured a relatively even distribution of the good and the bad tillage; it helped the farmers of the village interact, and therefore spread good ideas among themselves; it helped equalise the resources that each villager had access to. The ending of that system produced efficiency, at the cost of losing the benefits of the system. The system itself encoded traditional wisdom about how members of a society should get along together. Its relative inefficiency as a system of agriculture, which resulted in its falling into disrepute, has to be balanced against the social solidarity it supported, at least in assessing the part it played in medieval society.

There are many examples of traditions and practices that encode important knowledge about a community. The identity of a community through time (over generations) is often sustained by obscure (to the participants) rituals that implicitly exclude others, or practices of allowing only people with certain genealogy access to group-owned resources.[47] Religions are particularly potent identity-conferring traditions. Each new generation may alter the tradition, reinterpret it, but all they are doing is adjusting the pre-existing social practices that are embedded in social order. Such flexible, organically growing traditions both help unify a society, and perform certain social tasks in such a way as not to disturb what may be a delicate social order.[48]

The British system of Common Law is perhaps the classic example of a system of transmission of wisdom via tradition through generations. Under a system of common law, people are allowed to get on with their own lives until a dispute develops. The dispute is then taken to an agreed arbitration system, which will provide a principled resolution of the dispute. In future disputes, that judgement can be reused; the parties to the future dispute have the task of showing whether their dispute resembles earlier ones, and if so, in what respects. The 'rules' are not laid down by any individual; rather they develop over time, via a series of judgements about problematic cases. With such an underlying system, when more formal rules are required they can be overlaid onto the existing system, as has happened in Britain.[49] Much of law is made by judges' decisions, not by the Houses of Parliament; at the very least, judges play a giant role in interpreting the legislation laid down by Parliament. In this way, the abstract, dry, context-free meaning of a law receives its life from the attempt by the judiciary to place the law in the context of current behaviour and past judgements.[50]

The claim, then, is that traditional practices and systems that have developed organically, planned not by a remote central authority, but rather over a period of trial and error by the community itself, often encode useful knowledge learned by the community over the trial period (but which might not be known consciously by any individual member of that community), in the same way as the form encodes the knowledge of how to service a car. Particular solutions to internal tensions and external pressures will have been crafted, often in an *ad hoc* manner, and the practices and institutions that embody these solutions preserve the balance between those tensions and forces in the long term, well beyond anyone's capacity to remember the reason for them.[51] The traditions act as the *communal memory*. Because the knowledge is not necessarily known consciously by anyone, it may well be that no one is alert to the potential disruption to the community that would be caused by rationalising or dismantling the system.

The second tenet of conservatism: the knowledge principle

To summarise the epistemological arguments of the last three sections, the knowledge that is required to coordinate and direct a complex, dynamic society is almost certainly beyond the ken of an individual person, or even a hierarchical bureaucratic machine. So interconnected is a modern society that an attempt to plan its future development is likely to result in many side effects that cannot be anticipated. The knowledge that is relevant to the planning of a society or an economy will be distributed across that society, and furthermore at least some of it will be encoded in practices, texts or rituals so that no individual can be said to possess that knowledge him- or herself. This makes up the second tenet of conservatism, which we shall call the **knowledge principle**. We have seen the knowledge principle foreshadowed through the Pyrrhonism of Sextus Empiricus, Montaigne, Browne, Hume and Balfour.

The knowledge principle links with the change principle to create an elegant but powerful conservative philosophy. If we accept the change principle, we accept that the concrete benefits of an existing society are given greater weight over the potential benefits of an abstract theory. The knowledge principle, when added to that, suggests that an abstract theory about something as complex and dynamic as a society, even a relatively rigidly structured one, will almost certainly be inadequate, that there will be unintended side effects of major changes that will threaten those concrete benefits. Worse, the knowledge principle enjoins us to be highly sceptical that the advertised potential will ever appear. As philosopher Hannah Arendt put it, action has infinitely many consequences, and can't be undone.

> Since we always act into a web of relationships, the consequences of each deed are boundless, every action touches off not only a reaction but a chain reaction, every process is the cause of unpredictable new processes. This boundlessness is inescapable; it could not be cured by restricting one's acting to a limited graspable framework or circumstances or by feeding all pertinent material into giant computers. ...
>
> Action processes are not only unpredictable, they are also irreversible; there is no author or maker who can undo, destroy, what he has done if he does not like it or when the consequences prove to be disastrous.[52]

Arendt, who wrote extensively about the Holocaust and the prosecution of the Second World War, resolved this problem by invoking the redemptive power of forgiveness, as a direct recognition of human frailty and uncertainty. One need not contradict this humanitarian view by pointing out that judicious restriction of one's horizons of action will also reduce the damage one does, and the need for one to seek forgiveness.

This result backs up the instinct articulated by Oakeshott that innovation always carries a risk. The conservative will turn away from innovation as much as he possibly can – and continue to bear in mind that innovation *includes* the dubious practice of trying to turn the clock back to restore some golden past.

Compare the effect of substituting Freeden's 'extra-human' idea for the knowledge principle. We have already aired several arguments that knowledge and certainty are hard to obtain, arrogant to assume. But a thinker who is positive about the extra-human origins of the social order will *be* certain; his handicap *is* arrogance. The assumption, for example, that the world is God's creation brings with it the disastrous certitude that holy writ should steer political action. Small 'c' conservatism is premised on the avoidance, not the fostering, of fundamentalism, on the humble assumption of ignorance, not arrogant certainty.

The sceptical conservative philosophy does not contradict the idea that some complex organisations, for example very large firms, require innovation. The knowledge principle still operates in such environments, for sure. But there are important dis-analogies between a society and a large organisation, however complex (and there are corporations that are larger and more complex than many societies). The organisation, unlike a society, has *goals*, and the imperative to reach those goals will on many occasions rule out adherence to the change principle. If an organisation is not on course to reach its goals, then it has to change, even though – in the commercial world, *because* – it involves risk.

Neither does conservatism deny that sometimes we learn things that tell us we need to innovate. Serious damage to societies often happens via extraneous circumstances outside the control of the inhabitants, but sometimes not. Sometimes people create harm by acting perversely, in full awareness of the likely consequences, often through conflicts of interests that mean some members of a group take actions that harm the group as a whole (environmental calamities can be of this type, such as deforestation, overfishing or bad water management).[53] In such cases, as we have argued, the change principle allows us to adjust. But equally, we should note that spotting such circumstances is very hard within a functioning society, and always controversial, as vested interests are involved. It is infinitely easier to spot problems in retrospect, as the ruins of the dead societies are there for us to inspect. The fact that societies can drive themselves to destruction on occasion does not mean that we should lower the burden of proof on the innovator.

Does the conservative philosophy, endorsing the sum of the change principle and the knowledge principle, mean stasis, a boring, unadventurous society? No, unless that society is boring by inclination. If a society is dynamic and changes under its own steam, then it is certainly not the business of the conservative to impede that. As long as the changes are the results of people in their own spheres of influence, exploiting the small amount of economic knowledge that they possess about their own circumstances, being prepared to take risks upon themselves, then there is no problem.

Does the conservative philosophy mean inactive government that stands by to allow injustice and economic failure? This is not at all implied by either the change principle or the knowledge principle. In the first place, the change principle depends on the concrete benefits of an existing society being tangible. In a dysfunctional society, the change principle becomes less applicable as the society provides fewer benefits for its members. Whether change is actively sought will depend on how bad the society is, what abstract benefits are in the offing from possible innovations, and the plausibility of those innovations. It is, of course, a political question, to be answered at the time, as to when potential benefits become worth exploring.

Some, like Bruce Pilbeam, have argued that this is problematic.

> It is flawed because it leaves too vague the circumstances requiring conservatives' defensive efforts: for example, how long must an institution have been in existence before it is considered established? Equally, in that few conservatives have ever opposed all change, without further principled appeal the line between unacceptable 'radical' and acceptable gradual change is similarly unclear.[54]

However, the conservative ideology of course reflexively applies to itself. No conservative ideologue would wish to lay down in advance the circumstances in which innovation is allowable. The decision is a political one, and therefore to be taken in accordance with the democratic political decision-making processes operative in the society at the time. A conservative government in the early 21st century in Britain could well move in a number of policy directions; my aim in Part Two of this book is to focus on policy arguments in the context of David Cameron's leadership.

If a conservative government did move in the direction of change, then the knowledge principle also provides some guidance. The knowledge principle says that the government will of necessity be unaware of the effects of its innovations. That suggests that managed change should be incremental, rather than thorough-going, and, where possible, reversible. Incrementally changing policy or institutions should mean that the effects of changes can be measured, and unfortunate side effects detected early. In practice, the difference between a conservative government and those of other ideologies is that the conservatives will be in favour only of incremental changes; their ambition will be smaller, their scepticism higher.

Does this all mean that conservatism is empty? That we should avoid change, except when it can't be avoided? The appearance of vacuity here is appearance only. No ideology can *dictate* political action in a concrete circumstance – how could it, any more than a speed limit can dictate slower driving? Liberalism says that freedom is important; a liberal government ensures freedom, except where people's freedom needs to be curbed. Socialism recommends equality; a socialist government ensures equality, except where things have to be unequal. Free market governments still collect taxes, green governments still allow industry. An ideology is but one pressure on a government. Ironically, most ideologies, being absolutist in tone, will find that difficult to explain, whereas conservatism explicitly accepts that the political context will play a massive role in determining what can and can't, what must and mustn't, be done. Like all ideologies, conservatism is a guide to action, a rallying cry for the party, a political and moral compass. These are all important functions, but a government in a complex democracy responds to much more than that.

A conservative government will be sceptical of its power to solve problems (even sceptical of its power to *diagnose* problems). It will be conscious that institutions, practices and processes, unguided by interfering hand, are likely to be better regulators of a society, because rooted in that society, because going with the grain of that society, than clever theories imposed from outside. This is what marks out conservative governments from those of other types.

One final wrinkle about conservatism is that, historically, it can be highly inconsistent. There are certainly conservatives who resisted change way beyond what was wise – the Duke of Wellington springs to mind. But on the other hand many conservatives have adopted really quite progressive measures. Disraeli and even Salisbury were known to enact Liberal policies in a weakened form, as we noted in Chapter Three. The effect of such reforms is to inoculate the body politic against the wider and deeper reform efforts of their opponents. How is it possible that conservative reformers exist? In the same way that doctors, who intend to make us well, inject us with doses of pathogens in order to boost our immune system, conservatives often use a similar trick, a trick we can call the *vaccination strategy*.

The idea is that the conservative, who is not, of course, worried about change while he is in power, may well worry in the longer term about what the opposition might do. In a democracy, his fear, both for the country and more prosaically, for his own political career, will be that the radical opposition will win elections. Hence the vaccination strategy: the conservative takes over the process of change, providing enough of the radicals' programme to satisfy some of its voters, thereby inoculating the future against radicalism by a small injection of the virus now. To be sure, the conservative will not do this with any great enthusiasm, but he will hope to preserve social unity, and to ensure that as many people as possible retain their loyalty to the state as it is. Examples of the vaccination strategy in Britain include Peel's repeal of the Corn Laws, Disraeli's, and to a lesser extent Salisbury's, social reforms, and the development of the Butskellite policy to manage the post-war settlement in the long period of Conservative government from 1951 to 1964.

The conservative recognises that it is vital not to allow a large constituency for change to develop. Hence it is important not to demonise the radical opposition, but rather it is sensible to make a limited number of concessions – often in the teeth of the most reactionary of conservative allies – in order to ensure that the radical element is kept small. But the result can certainly be internal strife *between* conservatives, because when to operate the vaccination strategy is a fine judgement. There was a falling-out of this very kind between Disraeli and Salisbury over the Second Reform Act in 1867; Disraeli wanted to extend the voting franchise to poorer voters using precisely the vaccination strategy, whereas Salisbury thought the result would be permanent Liberal Party government and strongly opposed him in Cabinet. In the end, Disraeli won the day and Salisbury resigned;[55] Disraeli was proved right in the end. Salisbury as Prime Minister found himself adopting the vaccination strategy in social policy.

So the conservative can manage change after all, and can support progressive developments while ensuring the basic attitudes and institutions for social harmony are kept in place; in this way, progressive policies don't end up throwing out the baby with the bathwater. But what happens when change is all around and endemic, and society seems to be fragmenting, when it's all bathwater and no baby? How can conservatism survive then? Investigation of that issue is our task for the next chapter.

CHAPTER FIVE

IS CONSERVATISM DEAD?

Mad world

The world is changing all the time, more quickly than many of us can keep up with. New technologies are proliferating: information and communication technology, biotechnology, nanotechnology all have revolutionary potential. Just when we thought that the future was online, with the development of the World Wide Web and mobile telephony revolutionising our personal lives, and with exciting (and possibly dangerous) innovations such as the Semantic Web and ubiquitous computing just around the corner, the focus shifts. The science for the 21st century seems to be biology, where our mastery of genetic engineering increases with new discoveries almost every day, and all sorts of incredible advances against disease or hunger are promised.

But this fantastic scientific world has its own dangers, of course. How will routine genetic manipulation affect our view of ourselves as humans? The facilitation of communications between people is surely a good thing, but it will certainly promote globalisation, which has many detractors. It may also create strange intellectual ghettos, where extremists talk to extremists and are increasingly able to filter out moderating voices. And while many of the arguments against genetic engineering, genetic modification of crops and nanotechnology are no more than Luddite throwbacks, the deployment of new technologies certainly creates risks that are very hard to quantify.

The advances of science, our ability to harvest more data, and our phenomenal information processing capabilities also mean that we are able to understand our environment a little more. We can discover the weak signals in the noisy input from a complex world. And what we hear is, by and large, not good. Much environmentalism overstates its case, relying on multiple worst case hypotheses and ignoring the ability of humans to innovate out of crises. But equally there is absolutely no doubt that environmental degradation is not being halted despite our greater awareness. And the evidence for climate change grows daily, with tangible negative effects, while the best computer climate models we have (which are admittedly primitive) are starting to show horrendous feedback loops that will, if anything, accelerate change. So little is known about the way that climate works that we are simply unaware of how this will affect particular parts of the world. The UK, for instance, might become much hotter as less of the sun's energy is reflected away from the Earth. Or it might become much colder, as the cycle that feeds the Gulf Stream peters out.

Politically, things look even worse, if that were possible. From 1945 to 1989, international politics were characterised by a tense but stable stand off between two superpowers. There were plenty of lower-level conflicts, notably in the Middle East, sub-Saharan Africa and South-East Asia, but these were orchestrated by the USA, the USSR and their proxies and were unlikely – in retrospect, though it did not seem like this at the time – to escalate to the extent of engulfing both big players. This was an unsatisfactory system to say the least, but it had the merit of everyone knowing where they stood.

In 1989, America and Ronald Reagan won the Cold War, and the Soviet Union collapsed. For a decade things looked rosy. The USA was the world's sole superpower, and being the good guy it was hoped that international relations might become a little more ethical and a little less realist. The appalling treatment, in Rwanda, the former Yugoslavia, Kosovo, Sierra Leone and Somalia among other places, of citizens by their own governments, would-be governments or proxies for them, prompted a move for more activist governments in the West, grouped around the USA, the United Nations and NATO. The model was the Gulf War, where Iraq's invasion of Kuwait was reversed without the catastrophes predicted by the faint of heart. It was recognised that a set of principles needed to be developed to justify such intervention, and many proposed interventions went very badly. America was scared out of Somalia by losses in Mogadishu. Genocide in Rwanda was allowed to take place almost unhindered. European diplomacy was powerless in Yugoslavia, until backed up by American muscle. But there still seemed to be the germ of a system coming into being.

Two problems were emerging, though. The first, in a system that relied so much on American wisdom, force, know-how and willingness, was that so much depended on the person of the President. George Bush Sr was a limited, unimaginative man, but serious and careful. His years as Vice-President to Ronald Reagan had shown him the value of ideals ('the vision thing', as he had been known to say). He was a good man for this new world, as was Bill Clinton, devious but intelligent and capable of taking a nuanced view of the world. Each made mistakes, but they were at least capable of understanding the importance of America's role. In contrast, George W. Bush was a disastrous choice as head of the sole superpower. Enough has been written about President Bush; I need not add to it here. But the 'new world order' which George Bush Sr proclaimed in 1991 could not survive the crass simplifications, unilateral nationalism and disregard of alternative voices that are the trademarks of his son and the inadequate cronies surrounding him.

The second problem was that, with advances in weaponry, the sheer incompetence of many totalitarian governments worldwide and the fragmentation of ideology that followed the discrediting of Marxism and socialist planning, states were not the only significant actors. Many non-state organisations arose, and they have proved to be stronger and harder to address (where they are malignant) than states, which after all have territory, armies and personnel with which one can engage. Some were political actors, such as the Palestine Liberation Organisation, the Muslim Brotherhood and Hamas, Hizbollah, the Tamil Tigers, FARC, the Shining Path and so on, while others were purely and simply organised criminals taking advantage of the possibilities of globalisation for communications, transfer of people and goods, and money laundering. At the same time, states themselves have proved weaker at holding their nations together, with a number of them, most notably in Somalia and Afghanistan, falling apart entirely. The result was lawlessness and poverty – grim for the victims, but at least not our problem.

Such was the position twelve years after the end of the Cold War – a more complex world, potentially harsher for many, but not looking too bad. At least nuclear annihilation was no longer on the cards. Then came that unforgettable day of 11 September 2001, when the evil, barbarous destruction of the World Trade Center in New York and related terrorist attacks sponsored by al-Qaeda captivated the world's media audiences. The world, in truth, did not change, but Western perceptions of it did. And so was launched the war on terror, which at the time of writing looks like being as successful as the war on drugs, but which all decent-minded people must hope will ultimately be successful. Regime change in Afghanistan followed immediately, and few regretted the passing of the Taliban. But then followed Iraq, Guantánamo and the whole sorry mess. We will discuss Iraq a little later, but it's a story we are all aware of – and surely no one now will assume without question that America, now that even its commitment to human rights and the due process of law is in doubt, can once again straightforwardly play the role of the world's policeman.

Meanwhile, slowly shaking themselves free from the shackles of socialist ideology, China and India are putting on the economic weight that is giving them political oomph. A staunchly nationalist Russia is being more assertive too. Ideologically if not militarily or economically, France is trying to set itself up as a counterweight to American hegemony, though the efforts of Jacques Chirac, whose incompetence rivals that of Mr Bush, have been predictably lame. But it is certain that the period of American domination of the international scene is coming to a close. We are back to a *de facto* multipolar world, with new alliances to be made, new histories to live down, new uncertainties to face.

Politically, on the British domestic front, things are none too cool either. The euphoria that greeted Mr Blair's victory in 1997 has long since melted away, but the residue seems to be a collapse of trust in all politicians (prompted at least in part by his own relentless attacks on Tory sleaze), and a catastrophic decline of interest in the political parties. Many voters see things through the distorting lens of single-issue politics. Many commentators worry that, despite freedom and prosperity, people are not happy. Extremism makes its mark, with animal rights protesters second only to Islamic neo-fundamentalists in their disregard for the niceties of democratic debate. The tone of much political debate is set, for the worse, by the tabloid newspapers and hectoring TV and radio interviewers, who either do not know or do not care that the hurried legislation that follows their campaigns always has the most malign effects. Thoughtful debate is somewhat hard to find (a number of MPs, of all parties, have said to me at one time or another that such-and-such an approach to a problem is politically impossible because it can't be explained to John Humphrys in a ten second soundbite), and its traditional institutional vehicles – the political parties – are moribund, unloved and starved of funds.

In such a world, there are good reasons for thinking that conservatism is dead, that no reasonable constituency of people would wish to develop the philosophy of scepticism outlined in Chapter Four and to focus on preservation and conservation. Surely every politician, every voter in his or her right mind, will want to tear up society by the roots? Surely it is time for a bonfire of the vanities?

As we saw in Chapter Four, the change principle does not rule out the possibility that society should be changed, even radically; it only insists that the burden of proof falls upon the innovator. Many thinkers, even conservative ones, have understood that conservatism might be undermined simply by the perceived unpleasantness of the world as it stands; Michael Oakeshott points out the importance of there being something worth preserving.

> If the present is arid, offering little or nothing to be used or enjoyed, then [the conservative] inclination will be weak or absent; if the present is remarkably unsettled, it will display itself in a search for a firmer foothold and consequently in a recourse to and an exploration of the past; but it asserts itself characteristically when there is much to be enjoyed, and it will be strongest when this is combined with evident risk of loss. In short, it is a disposition appropriate to a man who is acutely aware of having something to lose which he has learned to care for; a man in some degree rich in opportunities for enjoyment, but not so rich that he can afford to be indifferent to loss. It will appear more naturally in the old man than in the young, not because the old are more sensitive to loss but because they are apt to be more fully aware of the resources of their world and therefore less likely to find them inadequate. In some people this disposition is weak merely because they are ignorant of what their world has to offer them: the present appears to them only as a residue of inopportunities.[1]

Can conservatism flourish in our mad world?

The hollowing out of Tory Britain

A number of commentators have argued that not only can conservatism *not* flourish, but the fact that it cannot is largely, even entirely, the fault of the Conservative Party. This was argued most forcibly and cogently by John Gray, towards the end of the period of Conservative dominance of British politics.

[T]he conditions under which conservatism as a coherent form of political thought and practice are possible exist no longer; ... conservatism has for us a Cheshire Cat quality, in that what it proposes to conserve is a spectral thing, voided of substance, partly by the policies of recent conservative governments, and partly by aspects of modern societies which such policies have reinforced; and that conservative parties and movements have in all Western countries been captured by neo-liberal ideas, more properly thought of as those of fundamentalist or classical liberalism, that in their utopian projects of world-improvement and their expectation of convergence on a universal civilization are alien to the forms of thought and practice most characteristic of a conservative outlook as that used to be understood. ... In short, the subversive effects of unhampered market institutions on traditional forms of life makes free-market conservatism an inherently unstable and, over time, a self-undermining political project. For these reasons, I conclude that a genuinely conservative form of political thought and practice, the lineaments of which we can discern as at least one element in our cultural history, is no longer a real possibility for us.[2]

The charge falls, in effect, into two halves. The first is that the Conservative Party (I focus, of course, on the British context) has been hijacked by neo-liberals – the Thatcherites. I will not spend any time disputing this; it is certainly my view (see Chapter Three) that the Conservative Party was the ground for an ideological battle between liberals and conservatives for almost a century, though 'hijacked' is a strong term and for the most part the two ideological groups were fighting side by side in the trenches against collectivism and socialism. The neo-liberal heritage of the Conservative Party, Gray seems to say, will make its return to conservatism difficult.

So we will focus on the second half; which is that the Thatcherite neo-liberals in effect removed the institutional core of British public and political life that provided continuity with the past and was a useful source of knowledge about British social relations.

> A fundamental objection to the paleo-liberal regime of incessant economic change under unfettered market institutions, then, is that in devaluing traditional knowledge it renders social and economic life ever less understandable to its human participants. In so doing, unfettered market institutions tend to deplete the cultural identities of their practitioners – upon which these institutions themselves depend. Market institutions will enhance human wellbeing, and will be stably renewed across the generations, when they do not go against the grain of the particular cultures that harbour them, but on the contrary assist those cultures to reproduce themselves. By imposing on people a regime of incessant change and permanent revolution, unencumbered market institutions deplete the stock of historical memory on which cultural identity depends. The common cliché that globalized markets tend to yield cultural uniformity is therefore not without an element of truth. What such cultural homogenization signifies is perhaps less obvious: a breach in historical memory which disrupts, or empties of significance, the narratives in terms of which people make sense of their lives. If, as any conservative who is also a sceptic is bound to think, the meaning of life for all of us is a local matter, this junking of local knowledge by unencumbered market processes is no small matter.[3]

Roger Scruton makes a similar point in *England: An Elegy*. After developing the interplay between England's institutions, culture and politics, and insisting that these very institutions are required to underpin the good things in English life, he bemoans their loss, and, like Gray, blames the Conservative Party at least in part. He also accepts that there is no way back, and the England that Scruton celebrates is now, like Ancient Rome, part of history.[4] Geoffrey

Wheatcroft, focusing partly on tactics, as well as the collapse in patrician ideals within the Tory Party, is careful not to close the door on the Tories, but wants much greater humility, and willingness to learn from non-conservative political thinkers (George Orwell most prominently).[5]

Gray agrees that, as dislocation has been made more rapid by the economic and social changes ushered in by the liberalism of the last quarter of the 20th century, it is impossible for conservatism to keep pace.

The Old Right project of cultural fundamentalism is best understood as an ill-thought-out response to the modern dissolution of old forms of moral life that contemporary conservative policy has itself promoted or accelerated. This is not to say that all such older forms of community and moral life lacked value. On the contrary, the reactionary perception of cultural loss as a real historical phenomenon is sometimes well founded ...; but that does not mean that the old forms of life can, or even should, be reconstituted. Not only is the current conservative clamour about family breakdown dishonest in repressing the role that market-driven economic changes – sometimes occurring over several generations, but greatly accelerated since the mid 1970s, as with female participation in the workforce – have played in transforming family life, but also it is self-deceiving in imagining that older forms of family life can conceivably be revived in which modern Western demands for choice and self-fulfilment – which are in other areas elevated by conservatives to the status of fetishes – are denied. The current neo-fundamentalist clamour for a return to the traditional family is, in other words, misconceived and frivolous in the highest degree. It expresses no serious concern for the needs of people in families, nor any understanding of the diverse forms in which the institution of the family is now to be found. Such vulgar clamour is symptomatic of contemporary conservative thought in the unreality of its perception of real people and their needs.[6]

So local knowledge has been devalued and extinguished, and older forms of social interaction have been rendered irrelevant or irrecoverable by changes partly, maybe largely, brought in under the freedom facilitated by market liberalism. We cannot go back to a world in which that knowledge and those social norms obtain; it is also hard to see how a conservative could deal with a world that is inherently unstable, without continuity with past forms of life, and with a dramatically decreasing local element as globalisation continues to promote cultural homogeneity.

Conservatism as realistic social criticism

This is a tough argument; certainly the world is very different from the world in 1974 when conservatives were prominent in the Conservative Party and as commentators in the right-wing press. Indeed, it is probably fair to say that a conservatism that deliberately centres on the continuity of English, or British, institutions, or of particular elements in English, or British, society, in order to emphasise the need to preserve continuity – in the way that, say, Stanley Baldwin used to do very successfully in the 1930s – really is in the sort of trouble that John Gray describes. The sort of conservatism espoused by Enoch Powell, which made great play of the almost unique 1,000-year history of English institutions,[7] or the sort described by Quintin Hogg, which made the Christian, specifically Anglican, religion central,[8] are surely doomed.

On the other hand, it is an intriguing thought that the market that arguably brought about most change was the market in *labour* – a market weighed down by many controls, indeed that is barely free at all, but which at various times has resulted in the influx into Britain of large numbers of immigrants. This change in the character of Britain, in terms of religion and of whatever cultural unity existed previously, certainly makes the traditional form of conservatism harder, which was the burden of Powell's anti-immigration case in his more thoughtful, less controversialist, moments.[9] But it is hard to argue that, as swingeing immigration quotas still hold sway, and as newspapers spread scares about the hordes of Eastern Europeans about to flood into the United Kingdom from the new members of the European Union, these changes are the result of a *free* market, or indeed of the British people's ignorance of the so-called 'dangers'.

Another key social development, highlighted by Gray, for which we can thank the labour market, is the increase in the number of women in work, and the consequent changes to the structure of 'typical' family life. Once more the influence of the free market is perhaps smaller than might be assumed. Powell, among many others, always maintained that markets were gender-blind, and that the panoply of equal opportunities bodies was therefore out of place, but as all the evidence is still of women being underpaid compared with men, one can hardly argue that women are being seriously induced into the labour market.

It also has to be said that 'Britishness' never ran particularly deep, and that the British national identity, such as it is, was always deeply contested. Some, such as Linda Colley, have argued that Britishness was relatively artificial and oppositional (i.e. we're not the French).[10] To the extent that the British are driven less by ideas and principles – which certainly contrasts with the French, and Americans for that matter – and more by the business-oriented pragmatism that followed from our development as an island nation that lived on trade, that may well be true (another topic upon which Powell had much to say[11]). A recent survey pugnaciously reported that many of the distinctive symbols of Britishness are related to our not-so-good cuisine; fish and chips, and roast beef and Yorkshire pudding were voted equal first in a 'league table' of national symbols, to the mild amusement of foreigners.[12]

Though Gray's criticisms may well discomfit those whose conservatism, like Scruton's, Powell's or Hogg's, rests on a particular vision of society, they have rather less purchase on the conservatism defined in Chapter Four, a sceptical conservatism that has taken a Rawlsian turn. In other words, the conservatism I have been describing is not anchored to a particular way of life, a particular view of the good, or a particular culture or society. It is an epistemological argument that, in so far as it is persuasive at all, is persuasive for intellectual reasons and not sentimental ones.

Neither the change principle nor the knowledge principle demands particular views of society. If British society, no matter how fast-moving or multicultural it has become, is more or less satisfactory to enough people, then governmental interference with it should surely be limited to the incremental adjustment of regulation in order not to disturb what may be very delicate social balances. Indeed, if British society has become more fast-moving, then it is likely that society is more delicately balanced than ever before, and therefore the risk aversion of those who would mould society should be even greater.

Gray is understandably perturbed by the loss of institutional knowledge. But free markets also rely on the deployment of local knowledge, tacit and often untranslatable into new contexts. And the influx of new people into a society will anyway require the evolution of new institutions and ways of, for instance, managing social services. The compromises of political and bureaucratic processes are of great importance here. There is no doubt a great problem of principle about, for example, how to disburse funds intended for women or girls to a community that may well have a strong cultural bias towards keeping women subservient to men. The problem of principle may be insoluble, but the *ad hoc* methods that a local council will have to develop on the fly, offensive to somebody's principles though they will inevitably be, may be of great practical use, and will encode a great deal of social learning about the interaction between the indigenous and the immigrant culture. On the other hand, principled approaches, like the French government's ban on Muslim headscarves in schools, are rather less responsive to the changes within the indigenous culture, though undoubtedly more in line with a conservative tradition of an authoritarian kidney.

The conservatism I describe should be applicable in any society, and at any time. The 'better' the society is – and that, of course, will be very much in the eye of the beholder – the more likely conservatism is to gain support. We expect this from the change principle. The loss of important cultural knowledge, via what Gray has called the 'hollowing out' of British institutions, is no doubt to be regretted. But that does not tell against the change principle, which says that one should recognise the great risks involved in trying to engineer a society, nor against the knowledge principle, which says that societies are too complex and dynamic to be fully understood from the centre. That an important source of knowledge has been lost (viz., the institutions Gray mourns) cannot mean that sceptical conservatism is made harder, as its whole premise is the difficulty of establishing knowledge about society.

A distinctive conservative identity

So there is a role for conservatism, but that may not be enough to save it. The negative, critical role is important but cannot be constitutive of a political programme. We still require some positive sense of what conservatism can deliver in policy terms. This will be the task of Part Two of this book, where we will examine where conservatism sits in the context of David Cameron's thought. Chapter Six will look at a major fault line in right-wing thought (and increasingly in left-wing thought too), that of the role of free markets in determining the allocation of resources. Chapter Seven will get back to the Conservative Party's greatest embarrassment, its seemingly irrevocable association with Mrs Thatcher's widely quoted remark that there is no such thing as society. Chapter Eight looks at how conservatism might be a response to one of the biggest perceived crises in British political life, the decline of trust.

Part Two

Conservatism and the Modern Conservative Party

But the human character, however it may be exalted or depressed by a temporary enthusiasm, will return by degrees to its proper and natural level, and will resume those passions that seem the most adapted to its present condition.

Edward Gibbon, *Decline and Fall of the Roman Empire*

It's like the fashions. A hat may be as new-fashioned as you like, but it must stick on a woman's head.

Joyce Cary, *Herself Surprised*

CHAPTER SIX

CONSERVATISM AND MARKETS

The allocation of resources and the knowledge principle

We have argued at some length that conservatism and the free market liberalism that has become important, even fashionable on occasion, in the last couple of decades are two separate ideologies. That does not mean that a conservative has to be opposed to free markets; conservatism is all about preserving one's culture, and if the culture to be preserved values free markets, then the conservative will try to support them.

The liberal underpinning of American political society means that, in that country, conservatives sound like free market liberals. Britain has a long tradition of free trade and free markets. Indeed, Britain has always been a major trading nation. In France, on the other hand, top civil servants and politicians share a common political culture of planning and centralised control and often training from the elite École Nationale d'Administration. There are clear differences between these three countries, and the conservative should respect them.

British conservatism has a distinctive position with respect to free markets, not wedded to them but neither deeply opposed. The charge against markets, made for example by John Gray, is that they are too disruptive to society to be compatible with conservatism. On the other hand, the free market has played a key part in British economic history, and in the person of Adam Smith it was Britain which supplied their greatest theorist. The questions for this chapter are how the conservative, in the British context, should balance claims for and against markets, and how that discussion maps onto the positions being sketched out by David Cameron. The Labour Party under Mr Blair, and probably under Mr Brown as well, seems to have been persuaded of the merits of markets in at least some circumstances, although whether the rank and file agree is perhaps moot. So Mr Cameron's job is not only to develop a line on free markets, but also to distance himself from the government he opposes.

An extra dimension is that voters are, generally speaking, less enamoured of free markets than the politicians they elect. Many of these anti-market feelings are based on rather unrealistic views of what is possible and on unduly negative views of the effects of free markets. David Willetts, for example, has vented his frustration at four particular commonly held fallacies: free markets mean every man for himself and the devil take the hindmost; if you are rich, then others must be poor; there is no real competition in big business; and markets are immoral because everything has a price.[1] Adam Smith certainly strongly opposed the first of these. But even after correction for these fallacies, there is little public appetite for the extension of economic liberalism.

Conservatism is the conjunction of the change principle and the knowledge principle. Hence if free market ideology is to be consistent with conservatism, then it should not contravene either of those principles. The knowledge principle appears to be unproblematic – the failure of various planning regimes, not least in the former Soviet Union, but also, on a much smaller scale, in the corporatist Britain of 1945–79, shows that allowing markets to allocate resources at least produces comparatively good results. Free market liberals, of course, are at one with conservatives about this, and distrust any attempt to try to engineer particular outcomes, as stated for example by F.A. Hayek.

> Strictly speaking … there are two reasons why all controls of prices and quantities are incompatible with a free system: one

is that all such controls must be arbitrary, and the other is that it is impossible to exercise them in such a manner as to allow the market to function adequately. A free system can adapt itself to almost any set of data, almost any general prohibition or regulation, so long as the adjusting mechanism itself is kept functioning. And it is mainly changes in prices that bring about the necessary adjustments.[2]

For Hayek, there is literally no sensible decision to be taken about price and production except relative to what people want, and what they want to exchange for what they want. These are the only parameters that matter, and nothing will tell you about them except the state of a free market. The more that a government interferes with the freedoms of a market, the less useful that market's signalling will be. Moreover, the beauty of the price system is that the knowledge that a consumer requires is actually tiny: all he or she needs to know is what he or she wants, and what he or she is prepared to pay for it.

The Hayekian neo-liberal generally goes further than the conservative on this point by arguing that government interference in resource allocation and price control is actually the first step to totalitarianism,[3] which the conservative need not go along with (in fact, European experience with welfare states shows it to be false). It may be that government needs to allocate resources or fix prices for some reason other than economic efficiency, in which case it would have to attempt to 'buck the market'; the conservative, who should not wish to rule out anything in advance, must accept that as a possibility at least. Although the conservative would also accept that such interference is likely to have unpredictable consequences, and in the long run may well be positively harmful, he or she shouldn't think that it is necessarily sinister.

However, when it comes to the change principle, conservatives and neo-liberals part company. Let us illustrate this idea by contrasting Hayek with the ideas of a self-proclaimed conservative, Enoch Powell.

Markets and the change principle

Powell was very pro-markets. For Powell, markets were a conservative mechanism – it was central planning, equated by Powell with socialism, that caused change to go too quickly and too far. Markets are important mechanisms for telling us about the consequences of our desires and financial decisions, better than journalists, better than politicians, better than academics, better than clergymen. They do not flatter.

> I hear people complaining about the high prices of building land for houses. But prices are only telling us the truth about the consequences of our own actions. The price an article will fetch in a given set of circumstances is its value in those circumstances. To rail at prices and threaten to control them is to behave like a petulant child who smashes the clock because he wishes it were a different time of day.[4]

Rigging markets will skew the natural 'flow' of development in society, no matter how well-meant the attempt. Powell takes the view that the 'impulses to growth and change' should not be hampered, because then the change will be unnatural and costly. Furthermore, in many if not all areas of society, a free market is the only mechanism that will allow this 'organic' change to happen at society's preferred pace. Anything else either holds society back, or pushes it forward in directions that it does not necessarily wish to go. Hence one function of a free market, according to Powell, is to ensure adherence to the change principle.

Ironically, Hayek agreed with pretty well everything that Powell says here. Hayek, like Powell, is very much in favour of free markets. The difference between them is that Powell (believes he) is a conservative, while Hayek (believes he) is not. Hayek would also accept much of the stringent critique of conservatism put forward by John Gray, whom we met in Chapter Five. The idea that markets can cause rapid change, possibly even going so far as to produce what we might call 'creative destruction', was part of what attracted him. An Austrian who had witnessed the rise of fascism, Hayek saw in markets the potential for people to be the masters of their own fate. When individual economic decisions were given their proper weight, dictatorship became next to impossible. If the cost of liberty was a certain chaos in public affairs, Hayek didn't mind; indeed, he wasn't even sure it was a cost as opposed to a benefit, at least for those nimble enough to take advantage of opportunities as they fleetingly became available.

> As has often been acknowledged by conservative writers, one of the fundamental traits of the conservative attitude is a fear of change, a timid distrust of the new as such, while the liberal position is based on courage and confidence, on a preparedness to let change run its course even if we cannot predict where it will lead. There would not be much to object to if the conservatives merely disliked too rapid change in institutions and public policy; here the case for caution and slow progress is indeed strong. But the conservatives are inclined to use the powers of government to prevent change or to limit its rate to whatever appeals to the more timid mind. In looking forward, they lack the faith in the spontaneous forces of adjustment which makes the liberal accept changes without apprehension, even though he does not know how the necessary adaptations will be brought about.[5]

Aside from a contrast in loaded vocabulary – 'fear', 'timid', 'courage', 'confidence' – Hayek welcomes markets as potential agents for great change, and agrees with Powell that they liberate the consumer. But Powell also values the continuity that conservatism hopes to protect; he sees government as the threat to it, not markets.

> All government rests ... upon habit, upon being exercised in the same way or a similar way to that in which the governed

remember or believe that it was exercised before. Brute force can break with habit; but as soon as brute force begins to turn into government, it does so by starting to observe habitual modes of behaviour. Habitual forms or institutions for counsel and consent are thus of the essence of government.

These institutions and forms persist while all other realities are changing around them.[6]

The problem for conservatives, as Gray and Hayek point out, is that free markets themselves are highly disruptive of settled forms of social interaction. They even, as they evolve, demand new forms of government (Bill Clinton's advisor James Carville once said that if there was reincarnation he would like to come back as the bond market: 'You can intimidate everybody'). It is unrealistic to suggest that far-reaching social and economic changes will not affect the continuity of government that Powell values so highly. The alteration of a law to admit more market exchanges will always produce unintended and unpredictable alterations in social arrangements. This is not to say that these unintended alterations will always be bad – far from it. It is only to state the corollary of the change principle that, if society is in a happy state prior to the change (even if obviously not optimal), then the risk of change needs to be taken very seriously.

Let's take an example that is very close to home. Britain has always been a nation of relatively uncouth beer drinkers (I am one myself, so I am not being snooty here). Mr Blair's New Labour government, in its early days of 'rebranding Britain' as 'cool Britannia', wished to change the ingrained habit of pub drinking, with its predominantly male ethos, uncool beery denizens, lack of atmosphere and lousy food, and licensing laws that inconveniently deposited thousands of drunken young men together on the streets at closing time.

The preferred model was the continental bar, the café culture of Europe. The Labour government wished to develop Euro-style licences, to encourage Euro-style drinking. In fact, Britons do not drink a particularly large amount compared with their European cousins, but they tend to cram it all into short periods. By 2000, the government was seriously worried by the problem of bingeing, but wasn't about to change tack. Though Alcohol Concern reckoned that in any particular year the cost to the nation of boozing was £3.3 billion, and 33,000 deaths,[7] liberating the licensing laws remained a priority.

But the café culture never arrived.

Advocates of 24-hour cities argue that they have improved the quality of life in Romford. That may be true of the daytime. But it is at dusk that the problems start.

For by night, South Street turns into a very different place. The street becomes a mass of 18–26-year-olds, drinking as much as they can. For anyone else, the place becomes almost a no-go area. Gillian Balfe, the council's town-centre manager and a strong supporter of the 'leisuring' of South Street, concedes that the crowds become uncontrollable, and the atmosphere quickly turns 'hostile and threatening'. Buses are now barred from going down South Street after 9.30pm: there are too many drunken people milling about.

In a survey for the local council done last year, 49% of the residents of the surrounding borough of Havering confessed that they did not want to come to the city centre any more for fear of crime. The local police concede that they are virtually overwhelmed. Violence is commonplace. There has only been one consequent fatality in the area in the past couple of years, but the police say that this is mainly thanks to the merciful proximity of the local hospital.[8]

The end result? By 2004, the Prime Minister's Strategy Unit acknowledged Britain's drinking problem cost the country £20 billion per year.[9] If Mr Blair ever thought that his strategy of rebranding Britain as a 24/7 happening place would lead to our youngsters donning berets and discussing the relative merits of

Sartre and Camus over a calvados at a pavement café as the sun set over South Street, Romford, he has presumably long since been disabused of that notion. The market reforms, the liberalising of the licensing laws, brought with them dramatic changes in society, in the use and function of our city centres, in our health and in our institutions, such as the police. None of these changes was foreseen; all were produced by people voluntarily doing what they were legally entitled to do. Hayek's 'spontaneous forces of adjustment' do not necessarily produce results that all would welcome.

The price signal and the knowledge principle

What should the conservative say about markets and knowledge? Hayek argued that conservatives 'lack the faith in the spontaneous forces of adjustment which makes the liberal accept changes without apprehension, even though he does not know how the necessary adaptations will be brought about'.[10] This is undeniable. In general, conservatives should lack faith; faith is a bad predictor of events. It is true that, under certain assumptions, markets distribute resources in the most efficient way. But this is, as economist and Nobel laureate Kenneth Arrow has pointed out, more of a theorem than a fact.[11] It may well be true by definition that markets will reach a balance inevitably; there is still surely a question about the desirability of the balance reached. A balance was achieved in Romford between the drunken revellers and the people of Havering by in effect terrifying the latter from entering the town centre.

So the liberal adherence to free markets appears to respect the knowledge principle while covertly contravening it. The liberal assumption that the most efficient allocation of resources is equivalent to the best outcome is exactly the type of theoretical fiat that is *ruled out* by the knowledge principle. The world is a complex place, says the knowledge principle, and knowledge of its operations is almost certainly impossible to get (or impossible to recognise when, by chance, it is achieved). To assume that the price system will automatically produce the best outcome is to place too much faith in the theory of free markets – the faith that the conservative refuses to have. There is more to social life – more even to economic life – than this. The price system tells us more than other systems, sure, but that does not mean that it tells us everything we want to know; nor does it mean that, *pace* Hayek, we should be meekly accepting of whatever outcomes free markets produce. Attempts to reconcile Hayek with the knowledge principle ultimately require altering something fundamental in his philosophy, to square the circle.[12]

Markets have their limitations like any system, and the conservative will have to agree with Hayek, *contra* Powell, that if they operate unchecked there is little control over outcomes. To assume that outcomes can be left to look after themselves is to assume that markets will always work – a faith in theory that the knowledge principle simply will not allow. As Oakeshott is said to have said about Hayek's philosophy, 'I suppose a plan not to have a plan is better than most plans.' Salisbury, for example, was a keen promoter of free market policies, and in fact for pretty much the same reasons as Powell, but when he detected unfortunate outcomes he was prepared to turn to, in Andrew Roberts' phrase, 'enlightened quasi-public bodies' subsidised by government to reverse them.[13] There is a big difference between being a free market liberal, and being in favour of free markets except when they do not work; a conservative can clearly be the latter.

Important though this result is, it is *not* to say that conservatives are always, or even often, opposed to the free operation of markets. Much will depend on the market orientation of the traditions of the society in which the conservative lives. And much will depend on the outcomes of the markets themselves; in many markets, a number of factors go to determine price, including social constraints, and economists have time and again discovered a lack of connection between levels of demand and levels of price.[14] In Britain, we have a highly developed market tradition, and a British conservative will take notice of that, but support for markets *cannot* be uncritical, or based solely on ideology.

So how will this difference in emphasis pan out in practice? That will be the subject of the investigations of the rest of this chapter.

Autonomy, markets and well-being

One particular aspect of neo-liberal free market philosophy that should draw the attention of the conservative is that of the autonomy of the individual. This means, in effect, that society should not interfere with the legitimate decisions made by an individual, at least as long as that individual does not propose to interfere with anyone else. A man with a £5 note should be able to buy an improving book, make a charitable donation, get a packet of cigarettes, invest it in a building society account or place it on a horse as he sees fit; he no doubt has preferences as to which of these and other options are superior, as far as he is concerned and at this particular moment, and those preferences should be sovereign. It may be that others have opinions about what this gentleman's interests are (and therefore what his preferences should ideally be). It may be that such persons would wish to try to persuade, cajole or even force him to pursue his 'correct' interests, as opposed to the interests he believes he has. But if the observer is committed to regarding the consumer as autonomous, then he must eschew any temptation to interfere with the consumer's choice.

The conservative has a somewhat different view. He wonders precisely what the *conditions* of autonomy are for the consumer, who is after all not an abstract entity; any individual, any consumer is a *person* existing in some social milieu. Our identities are functions of many influences; we are immersed in societies that have incalculable effects on us. To focus only on autonomy is to risk an unhealthy preoccupation with our narcissistic sides. Pressure is placed on people to be the creators of their own identities, to be the authors of their own values, and the effect is to disconnect them from the values of their own societies and cultures. Cultural conformity appears to be a failure of individuality. The result, in Britain at least, is a peculiar obsession with celebrity, exhibitionism and hedonism; everyone wants to be 'doing it' on the telly.

But the bizarre twist is that, with less support from the rich nexus of cultural and social values that help determine identity and preference, autonomy is arguably being *undermined*. Young men have always found beer and sex deeply enjoyable no doubt, but we live in an age where, for some reason, they *all* seem to prefer Jordan to anyone else. Young women, given much greater freedoms than almost all of their sisters at almost any other time in human history, appear not to have chosen very many different ways of exploring that freedom – to the extent, it seems, that every girl between the ages of fifteen and thirty has an identical tattoo on the small of her back. That we have turned out a generation of FCUKwits is probably not so terrible. But we should not confuse growth in respect for individual autonomy with growth in autonomy itself.[15]

A particular problem with markets is that they send quite specific signals and focus effort on a relatively circumscribed set of rewards. It has been observed, often by extremely wealthy people, that the best things in life are free. 'Imagine no possessions', sang John Lennon so beautifully on his white grand piano before setting off in his white Rolls-Royce, but *pace* Mr Lennon, it *is* quite hard to do. When one has worked one's socks off for a day or a week or a year or a lifetime, it does seem to make more sense to exploit the extra earning power one has thereby accrued. We get locked into a work–spend–work–spend cycle.

So, as David Willetts has argued, there is a sense that in promoting markets during the 1980s, the Tories came to be seen as the economics party, the party who never thought beyond the bottom line; they became committed to the narrow focus of markets. This may or may not have been a fair characterisation, but it is certainly a handicap now. Mr Cameron's strategy to deal with this has been to cast doubt on the very notion of markets as methods for identifying and satisfying wants. He has spent much time discussing well-being, which he now, in a slightly sinister if not Orwellian manner, has capitalised as General Well-Being (or even, sometimes, GWB).

> Well-Being can't be measured by money or traded in markets. It's about the beauty of our surroundings, the quality of our culture, and above all the strength of our relationships. Improving our society's sense of well-being is, I believe, the central political challenge of our times. The idea that there's more to life than money is hardly new. We have always known that money can't buy happiness. But politics in Britain has too often sounded as though it was just about economic growth. Of course economic growth is vital. Capitalism is the engine of progress, and it has brought us unprecedented prosperity and opportunity. There is, however, a yearning for more – for capitalism with commitment, for work that has meaning and for relationships that are about more than just money and markets. A yearning for social growth and green growth as well as economic growth. Politics needs to respond to that yearning. It needs to recognise the value of relationships with family, friends and the world around us. It needs to find the words to articulate, and the means to fulfil, the nation's longing for a General Well-Being that goes beyond economic prosperity.[16]

This is all to the good, and chimes in with a recent trend in social policy research, which has focused on the apparent decline in happiness that has accompanied the 'unprecedented prosperity and opportunity' that Mr Cameron describes. For instance, Richard Layard, an economist, has tried to shift the aim of governmental social policy from creating wealth to fostering happiness.[17] But surely the conservative attitude of scepticism is needed here more than anywhere. How on earth can a government make people happy?

Lord Layard believes that there are more or less objective measures of happiness – indeed, he thinks that there are key neuropsychological indicators of happiness, although it will surely be many years before such indicators, which rely on the detection and accurate reporting of brain processing, will be usable for policy purposes. Even if we did develop a portable MRI scanner that could decide on the spot whether or not people were happy, it would still not tell us how to aggregate those measures (is it better to have five moderately happy people, or three very happy and two unhappy?). Furthermore, he also believes that happiness is unidimensional – that is, that there is only one way of being happy, which makes comparison of disparate states and feelings possible.[18] Ultimately, Lord Layard advocates a return to the utilitarian principle of engineering society to produce the greatest happiness of the greatest number.[19]

But it is hard to see how governments can make these things happen, even if they were as theoretically feasible as Lord Layard claims, and hard to see how markets could be arranged to make them more likely. For instance, a major theme of Mr Cameron's time as leader has been the importance of family life, and quite right too. He is very keen on progressive, family-friendly policies at work.

Flexible working and an understanding of the need for trusting relationships is good for business and good for individual employees. Companies are competing more and more to be good employers, to attract and retain the best talent. It saves money and it increases productivity. At BT, flexible working policies reduced absenteeism to 3.1%, compared to a national average of 8.5%. Their home working policies have resulted in a 31% increase in productivity, with savings of £69 million each year from reduced accommodation and overhead costs. And 99% of women return after maternity leave, compared to a national average of 47%. ...

For other companies ... technology – particularly

broadband internet connections – is now a huge driver of homeworking. And even in some parts of our public sector, employers are creating opportunities for parents to have term-time jobs so they can be with their children in the school holidays. These and other employers are showing how it's possible to combine organisational success with a culture that values human relationships and contributes to individual well-being.[20]

But it is noticeable that, in the many cases he cites, there is a business case for family-friendly policies – BT *et al.* are convinced they get a competitive advantage. So the market does help after all? It is unclear, a mixed message. If the labour market is not producing the right effects, then action needs to be taken to amend or ameliorate the action of the markets, but actually Mr Cameron is saying that markets should result in precisely the family-friendly policies he advocates.

Mr Cameron is right to insist that markets will not provide happiness, nor even necessarily create the conditions for happiness to occur.

I think there are a number of forces driving a desire for dramatic change. The first is the growing tension between two very different sources of human satisfaction. On the one hand we want to be heroic individuals, making our own way in the world and shaping our own fate. One of the ways we express ourselves is when we exercise our sovereign power of choice. These aspirations are expressed by politicians – especially Conservative ones – in the language of opportunity, mobility and freedom. This belief in freedom and mobility generates the pace and the excitement of much of modern working life. And when we Conservatives reformed Britain's economy in the 1980s it was this kind of picture of a modern society that we appealed to. But there is a second very different aspiration too. We know there is a deep satisfaction which comes from belonging to someone and to some place. There comes a point when you can't keep on choosing, you have to commit. If so much of our modern globalised consumer culture ultimately seems unsatisfying then it is because it fails to satisfy this deep human need.[21]

Of course there are better things to do than make money, and it will do the Tories no harm for Mr Cameron to point this out. But the problem is not as simple as removing the pressure of markets from people's lives. It just happens to be an inconvenient fact that if people can make their own choices, they make some choices that seem, to an outsider, to be against their own interests. This, after all, has been a key tenet of socialism for years – false consciousness results in people thinking it is in their interests to consume the products of capitalism, whereas actually their interests lie in class solidarity.

When someone is doing a job of work, she may well be required to work for long, inflexible and inconvenient hours. This will diminish her ability to enjoy her family growing up, and to engage in her parental duties. It may be that this does not matter to her – she may feel that the extra money is needed to provide material comfort and that is enough to fulfil her duties to her children and partner. But if it does matter to her, and if the employer demands that she work those hours to earn her money, then there is certainly an argument for saying that she is in the wrong job.

This is not to say that people are never pressured into poor working conditions, or feel powerless to resist their bosses; they often are, and we rightly deplore such cases. But equally when people are given the choice between working for the two sources of human satisfaction that Mr Cameron discusses, very often they focus on the first. So the question is what Mr Cameron can do about that. Can he *make* people focus on the second aspiration, for belonging? He can certainly raise the issue, as he has done, and no bad thing. He can exhort companies to be more understanding and people to be less focused on making money. All to the good.

But it is not clear that, ultimately, there is much he can do beyond that. The reason that markets, and associated phenomena such as globalisation, can be so destructive of communities is that left to their own devices people make choices as if they are Mr Cameron's 'heroic individuals'. The question the conservative must raise is whether it is the politician's job to prevent them from doing that.

Public services

Markets, by allowing people their own choices, reduce the space for experts, and those in authority to direct their lives. Small 'c' conservatives, from Lord Salisbury downwards, have always had something of a problem with experts, but in a complex society it seems sensible to outsource some decision-making to people with special training or experience (doctors, mechanics, scientists, etc.). Sadly, they are sometimes wrong, and it is hard to hold them to account when they are. Furthermore, their message is often complex and nuanced, and can be drowned out by simpler, more populist messages. This can mean experts feel they have to respond with equally simplistic messages, which can in turn result in them making claims that are too strong, promises that can't be kept.

The relation between ourselves and our experts is complex. For example, one could follow government guidelines on obesity, say, but equally, as one has freedom to spend one's pound where one wishes, then there is nothing to prevent one from buying burger and chips as opposed to one or two of the five helpings of fruit and vegetables that practically no one in the country eats because they are boring. We all accept that exercise is good for us, but as it is so mind-bogglingly tedious it is noticeable that only quite dull people spend any time doing it. The general consensus is that this combination of our stuffing our faces and not otherwise moving is a medical timebomb. The problem is that it is much more agreeable to give in to temptation than resist it, unless one is a sad puritan whose vices of choice are nut cutlets and several hours in the gym.

So when, as has happened in the UK, obesity gets out of control,[22] the temptation of many commentators is to blame the government. There is a problem, it has been foreseen, nothing seems to have been done – it is the government's fault. But this is not something a conservative should say. Conservatives are sceptical of the government's ability to solve any problem with a widespread set of social causes, and after all, health care professionals tend to see the world through their own microscopes, and understand human behaviour less. So it is a hard call for a conservative when the government fails to do very much to prevent obesity happening; perhaps the best route is to attack the government for pretending that there is very much it can do.

When Mr Cameron called for the education system to turn out fully 'rounded people',[23] he was not condoning the Labour government's failure to reduce obesity. Instead, the Conservative Party's response in 2006 was to attack the government for failing to tackle the problem. Shadow Health Secretary Andrew Lansley was certainly correct to worry about Labour gimmickry, especially in the face of a critical government report on obesity, but by demanding 'effective ... initiatives involving communities and individuals',[24] he did rather beg the question of what he would do in the face of people who do not take advice, particularly where weakness of the will, rather than ignorance, seems to be at the root of the problem. Mr Cameron himself argued not long before Mr Lansley's speech that 'well-being can't simply be required by law or delivered by government'.[25] Consequently, when he went on to discuss obesity, and related questions such as smoking and sexual health, he argued that the solutions here couldn't lie with the NHS. Rather, he advocated a shared responsibility, but was perforce not terribly specific about what that would actually mean. Beyond an advertising campaign about the dangers of junk food, what is any government going to do to stop me wolfing down a Big Mac if that is actually what I desire?

For ourselves, individualism rules, and the markets – much despised as they are – reflect that. We have a range of choices, some sober but boring, some harmful but enjoyable, and, by and large, we make the harmful choices often enough to cause harm. I am not talking merely of chavvish types who are incapable of making salads or cooking vegetables, and subsist on burgers and takeouts. Being unable to drive, I travel everywhere by bus, and I can certainly testify that the middle-class types who worry about there being too many cars on the road don't seem to have flooded onto public transport, at least in my home town. One will often discover that one's greenest friends have just jetted back from a holiday somewhere exotic, where (a) their presence, and their spending dollar, will be transforming society (for the worst, if one extrapolates from their opinions on others' holidays), and (b) their flight will have deposited a fair wodge of CO_2 and nitrogen oxides directly into the ozone layer. Some airlines allow one to pay a premium to cover the environmental costs of travelling, but not many people have salved their consciences in this way.[26] Our ids, it seems, are triumphing over our superegos, and free markets make it harder for our egos to hold the ring.

It is probably fruitless to argue about what is cause and what effect. The decline of deference may have helped free markets take off as the chief mechanism for presenting choices to us, or alternatively it may be that the creeping progress of free markets has chipped away at deference. Maybe the two are both symptoms of wider changes in society. No doubt social historians will get to grips with these issues. But whatever the facts of the matter, it is undeniable that we do live in a less deferential society, and removing market-driven methods of making choices will involve a level of interference by governments, experts, politicians and social theorists that many will in practice find hard to stomach, however tempting social engineering seems when one is reading about the collapse in society in one's *Grauniad*, *Torygraph* or *Mail*. However the issue of causation is finally resolved, if at all, there remains a real dilemma as to how to engineer the provision of essential services, the distribution of important advice and the preservation of what seem like vital social structures.

In a fascinating study, economist and social scientist Julian Le Grand has traced the history of governments' understanding of public service during the half century of the welfare state.[27] In particular he looks at the different views of providers' motivations and recipients' capabilities. He argues that, roughly speaking, the view of the entire structure of the welfare state has gone from a social democratic view at its beginning, to a neo-liberal view now.[28]

What has this meant in practice? First, with respect to service providers, the civil servants, doctors and other professionals, the view has changed, in Le Grand's terminology, from seeing them as 'knights' to seeing them as 'knaves'. In other words, the social democratic view of the founders of the welfare state that public service providers were focused on the interests of their clients, has morphed into the modern, neo-liberal view that they are self-interested, requiring incentives to work in others' interests. Second, the understanding of the recipients of welfare has changed. The social democratic founders of the welfare state looked upon them as 'pawns', as passive receivers of help in standardised form. Today's neo-liberals see them as 'queens', actively seeking the best services tailored for their own purposes.

The problem with this from the conservative point of view is that it is patently obvious that service providers actually have many knightly characteristics, and that they are not always self-interested knaves.[29] Indeed, their view of their job differs dramatically from that of comparable people in the private sector. Professionalism has always carried a large quantity of weight in the system, but the professional ethos is in distinct danger of being undermined by market structures that reward self-interest and penalise altruism. It is certainly a good sign that Mr Cameron wishes to 'liberate the enterprise of public sector professionals, freeing them from the constraints of centralised targets and bureaucracy'.[30] But the use of that word 'enterprise' jars. The Tories in general seem to be swinging in the right direction, with a report by their public service improvement policy group admitting that previous Tory governments have exaggerated what public servants have to learn from the private sector, and correspondingly underestimated the contribution that their expertise in service provision makes.[31]

On the other hand, it is no trivial matter simply to switch from neo-liberal marketisation back to social democratic trust. Even if it were known for a fact (which it is not) that all welfare service providers are knights, it is very clear that many recipients have indeed made the move from being pawns to queens. Trust of the expert, and deference to his or her expertise, has diminished dramatically.[32] The idea that patients might sit in militaristic wards snatching sleep where possible and eating horrible food to a timetable set largely for the benefit of the ward's ancillary staff seems quaintly old-fashioned now. I may err in thinking that all significant social developments from the mid-50s to the mid-70s are chronicled by the *Carry On* films, but nevertheless if one compares *Carry On Nurse*, made in late 1958, where the patients are kept regimented in Colditz-style accommodation, *Carry On Doctor* from 1967, where the patients revolt and attack surgeon Kenneth Williams to get him to change the regime, and *Carry On Again, Doctor* from 1969, where the patients (fat ladies) are demanding particular treatments and willing to pay good money for them, one cannot help but detect a pattern. This decline in trust makes it unlikely that the social democratic system could satisfy the new more active clientele (I hesitate to use Le Grand's terminology of 'active queens' here to avoid a *Carry On-*style *double entendre*). The change principle prevents us from trying to recreate the past, as well as from engineering an ideal future.

The third sector

There seems to be something of a problem, felt by the higher echelons of both major political parties in Britain today. The rank and file Tories may retain their faith in the free market, while

Labour's grass roots would agree with the Liberal Democrats that government can and should deliver much more. But those who have wrestled with the real problems of steering the ship of state can testify that neither system works terribly well in these interstitial areas that require us to behave as we do not wish to.

Is there another option? In the 1990s, Tony Blair invented the Third Way, of service delivery that did not rely on government direction or free markets. Unfortunately, the Third Way was a placeholder for a gap, an empty space; it was a hope, rather than an assumption, that such a space existed and could be populated by an efficient and accountable delivery method.

Now the leaders of the two major parties are beginning to reach a consensus. The Third Way has quietly been dropped, but we are now to admire the third sector, which is not capitalised. The third sector is the area of society that is not driven by profit or controlled by the government; rather it is run by volunteers. Mr Blair (and, it appears, Mr Brown) sees the third sector as a means for delivering public service without costing taxpayers a fortune, or requiring the poor to pay above their means. Mr Cameron sees it as a method for keeping inefficient government out of service provision, and taxes correspondingly low, without making false promises about the abilities of markets to deliver, and lending some substance to his desire to distance the Tories from Thatcherism.

> We need a government that is prepared to trust the third sector more. Sometimes that will mean letting go, taking risks, saying sometimes, we're doing a lousy job rehabilitating drug users or helping excluded kids back into school – you have a go. And it will always mean – before taking any decision, before setting up any new bureaucracy – asking the question: what is the third sector, charities, voluntary bodies and social enterprises already doing and what more can they do? And I also want to see greater levels of community engagement by the people who have done really well in the world. We already have great philanthropists like Sir Peter Lampl – I want to see

more, our own home-grown Bill Gateses and Warren Buffetts.[33]

The idea of involving the voluntary sector in service provision is certainly not a bad idea, and Mr Cameron would be silly not to pursue it, especially as Mr Blair, and his fellow enthusiasts in government such as Work and Pensions Secretary John Hutton, will take the first tricky steps, and may, by the time the next Tory Prime Minister comes on the scene, have moulded Whitehall to a greater acceptance of the idea. However, it is one thing to pursue the idea, quite another to rely on it.

Any conservative worth his salt will be pleased to involve Burke's 'little platoons'. A voluntary organisation developed from the bottom up, to solve some particular problem, with no thought of engineering society in some particular direction, would seem to promise just the sort of understanding of users and dedication to the job that is needed. But there is much more to service provision than that.

Mr Cameron has made no secret that he wants the third sector to play a much larger role in service provision.

> The fact is that the system is institutionally hostile to voluntary bodies and community groups. All in all, guess what proportion of government spending goes on voluntary organisations? Less than half a per cent. And guess what the government's target was to raise this by last year? Five per cent. So they planned to raise spending on the voluntary sector from 0.5 per cent to 0.525 per cent. That's not exactly ambitious. Worst of all, the Government doesn't even know where this money goes – though they do confess that the poorest communities benefit least.[34]

As noted, there is nothing wrong with this, but it is not enough for a conservative simply to insist that local groups are competent to deal with problems. It is one part of the story that the state's increasing power since the Second World War has tended to push non-state actors out of civil life, but another part of the story is that there was, in truth, something of a vacuum for the state to fill. Unlike the United States, the British tradition of volunteerism has not been sufficient to perform all those difficult distributional things that markets don't do. As we noted in Chapter One, we don't have as many religious people or philanthropists as the Americans, which is why American solutions won't necessarily work in the UK. The immediate ancestor of Mr Blair's and Mr Cameron's thinking on the third sector is George Bush's compassionate conservatism, which we have already argued is not by itself a way forward, however attractive it may seem at first blush.

Not only are there not enough volunteers to do as much work as Mr Cameron wants, it is not clear that the retirees and well-meaning people who man tea urns, make sandwiches and rattle collecting tins in front of us of a Saturday have the level of professionalism that is required. No doubt many organisations could be and are being trained up, but it would have to be done extremely quickly if the voluntary sector is to increase its proportion of government spending beyond the level upon which Mr Cameron has already poured his scorn.

To take one obvious example of the requirements of professionalism, Mr Cameron laughs at the government not knowing where its 5 per cent of spending on volunteers goes. He is, of course, correct – it is mad for the government to spend any money on any sector without knowing what happens to it. So the logic of his position, then, is that the government should trace the usage of these monies. And that means tedious forms for the little platoons to fill in. All those volunteers, many of whose motivation stems at least partly from freedom from the boring constraints of the nine-to-fiver, will find themselves with forms in triplicate, or some complex online system that they have to master every time they steer a homeless person towards a bed, or a former prisoner towards a job.

We must always remember Montaigne's lesson – it doesn't matter what our own vision is, we must go with society's grain. Many services have been delivered by the state for decades, and people are more or less happy with that. It will not be possible, with the best will in the world, to change that in any short period of time. To state the obvious, volunteers volunteer. They cannot be conjured up out of thin air (because then they would not be volunteers, they would be conscripts or employees), and it is risky to change their conditions of operation radically (because they may well find their operating conditions are not those they would want, voluntarily, to work in). Mocking Mr Blair for the glacial increase in the third sector's growth is storing up trouble for when Mr Cameron himself occupies 10 Downing Street and faces the same inevitable problems – problems that are predicted by the conservative philosophy.

Alternative sources of value?

The third sector focuses on particular outcomes for society – fewer homeless people, fewer drug addicts, or what have you. The particular reason that such a goal-driven approach goes against market philosophy is that it doesn't make allowances for comparison of values. Price, which is a heuristic parameter on a numerical scale, can be fixed as a value to anything, and so allows comparison. The advantage of this is that different goals can be ordered – so, for example, a safety system for the railways can be rated according not just to the number of lives saved, but the amount of money spent to save each life. For some, this is sensible prioritisation; for others, outrageous callousness. One philosopher recently wrote, in a piece of ludicrous hyperbole, that economists who theorise about the monetary value that can be placed on life, or on deeply important relationships such as friendship or marriage, 'have abdicated the right to be considered human'.[35] Presumably he has no insurance.

The third sector ignores questions of priority by focusing on particular problems, no matter what the cost. They never have enough money to do all they can do, so they concentrate on raising the profile of the problem, and fostering a marketplace of giving – they try to attract money from the general public, and government, to solve whatever social problem they specialise in. This is a somewhat dangerous line to go down, in that it in effect pits third sector marketing departments against each other in the goal of extracting loot from you and I and hapless government departments which have found themselves incapable of doing what they are supposed to do.

This kind of goal-driven approach, characteristic of the third sector, is not properly described as stemming from alternative sources of value. A third sector organisation has goals which it can only shed at the cost of its own identity. It considers the goal to be of paramount importance. The Royal Society for the Protection of Birds corporately considers birds to be the end of all its actions. It may say that it is 'working to secure a healthy environment for birds and wildlife, helping to create a better world for us all'.[36] It may pretend that what is good for birds is good for all wildlife, and indeed part and parcel of the better world for us all. But fundamentally, deep down, it must believe, as an organisation, that birds trump anything. If it gets money it must spend it on birds. If it received $1m to address the problem of HIV/AIDS in sub-Saharan Africa, it couldn't do it. Birds, for the RSPB, are non-negotiable, more important, by definition, than sick or orphaned Africans.

That does not mean that the RSPB, or bird-lovers generally, have alternative values from the rest of us. I am extremely fond of birds myself. It's just that I have *competing* values. My love of birds goes as far as three bird-feeders in my postage-stamp-sized back garden, which I maintain at a relatively small cost. I have other values – books, music, food, clothes, travel, warmth, security and so on – and limited funds. Birds get some of my funds, other charities get some, the bulk is spent on me and my own comfort. After all, no one else will do the last of those. The RSPB, in contrast, has no competing alternatives, which means it can sound inordinately and superhumanly generous on topics avian, if not on any other. I, in contrast, sound stingy because I put strict limits on what birds get out of my wallet.

One finds oneself out in the glorious British countryside, looking at one of the splendid vistas unique to our island, and someone will say 'Look at that. How can you put a monetary value on that?' The implication being, of course, that anyone who does is obviously a baboon with no soul. This cuts both ways, though: our nature-lover refuses to put a value on it at all. Which means that he or she actually contributes nothing to its upkeep, except to complain whenever someone decides to drive a motorway through it or make a nice golf course. Which is the same as valuing it at zero. This, incidentally, is why we have so many vile motorways and boring golf courses over our green and pleasant land – because no one will contribute anything other than hot air to its preservation, whereas the developers are at least prepared to put their money where their mouths are. Unprincipled baboons they may be, but they get their own way, thanks to inaction justified by sanctimony.

Vote blue, go green?

All too often, politicians exploit this sanctimony, by demanding something be done about some problem or other without explaining where the resources will come from. If a particular goal matters to a politician, then he or she should explain why, and explain how much of our taxes should be diverted from roads, prisons, schools, foreign aid, paying off the national debt, defence and so forth, to meet the problem, or, alternatively, to suggest how much *more* tax we should pay.

To his great credit, David Cameron and his Tory team have done precisely that with respect to the environment. There are good reasons to protect the environment, and perhaps the most pressing is the evidence, absolutely convincing to my mind, of climate change.[37] Some economists and thinkers have tried to quantify the cost of addressing global warming – some, including Bjørn Lomborg's Copenhagen Consensus initiative, have argued that the costs of addressing the challenges of climate change are so large that more bang can be got for the charitable buck elsewhere (for instance, minor improvements to basic health care or water sanitation worldwide would save many more lives for much less money).[38]

As noted above, this sort of investigation is not at all illegitimate – the economists in question can still, as far as I am concerned, be admitted into the human race. But equally, they are operating, as they themselves admit, under conditions of enormous uncertainty. A conservative is entitled to be very sceptical about their claims (and indeed sceptical about climate change as well). No one knows very much in this area at all. The evidence for climate change has piled up and is very hard to gainsay, but that does not mean that predictions of the effects and costs of that change are much more than guesswork. Will Britain's climate get hotter (because of global warming), or cooler (because of the failure of the Gulf Stream)? Will malaria or frostbite be endemic in Hampshire in 2050? We simply do not know. But the conservative's suspicion of change entitles him or her to try to ameliorate the risks. We have already seen the early effects of climate change in Britain, and the result has been a diminution of the unique qualities of the British environment – summer is less temperate, autumn a dim memory of mists and mellow fruitfulness and snow non-existent. These are relatively minor irritations, of course, but important if for no other reason than that they put extra distance between ourselves and the glorious nature poets and Romantics of the British tradition. The world of Gawain and the Green Knight, or Keats, or John Clare is already remote – do we wish to make it more so?

The lazy assumption that the Conservative Party is the party of business, and the even lazier conflation of conservatism and the Conservative Party, mean that many people simply assume that Tories are opposed to greenery and natural beauty. Actually, there are interesting parallels between conservatism and environmentalism; indeed Bruce Pilbeam, no friend of conservatism, lists no fewer than ten.[39] The common etymology of the words 'conservative' and 'conservation' is, of course, no coincidence. By rejecting accounts of instrumental reason, the conservative is open to the idea of value as something beyond mere exchange value, although, unlike many nature-lovers, a properly conservative government has to be prepared to shell out to preserve that worth preserving (and Shadow Chancellor George Osborne has already talked of 'painful' rises in green taxes[40]). Many a conservative includes the landscape, and architectural beauty, as among the important aspects of a society that should be preserved. The conservative, also like the green, is suspicious of the idea of individual autonomy; an individual's actions affect everyone, and politics is not simply a matter of ensuring, as neo-liberals might think, that individuals' preferences can be met by an economy. David Cameron has become the first Conservative Party leader for some time to exploit the congruence between the two ideologies of conservatism and environmentalism.

A particularly interesting convergence is their joint concern with intergenerational justice and equity. Each ideology concerns itself with people who are not currently alive. Edmund Burke, mocking the idea that one might have a superficial contractual relationship with the society into which one was born, put this clearly in a famous passage.

Society is indeed a contract. ... It is a partnership in all science; a partnership in all art; a partnership in every virtue, and in all perfection. As the ends of such a partnership cannot be obtained in many generations, it becomes a partnership not only between those who are living, but between those who are living, those who are dead, and those who are to be born. Each contract of each particular state is but a clause in the great primaeval contract of eternal society, linking the lower with the higher natures, connecting the visible and the invisible world, according to a fixed compact sanctioned by the inviolable oath which holds all physical and all moral natures, each in their appointed place.[41]

There is much in there that the green would endorse. The main difference between the two is that the environmentalist is concerned almost exclusively with future generations, whereas the conservative looks both forward and backward; indeed, many conservatives are much more concerned with the dead than the yet-to-be-born. There are also important differences in the way they conceptualise our relationship with the environment. Its value, says the conservative, stems from its contribution to society as a whole, for example by providing it with important symbols of continuity, by supporting particular ways of life that cement the link between a community and its locality, by emphasising the distinction between a community and others, and by providing a historically interpretable landscape. For the green, of course, the natural environment has a value in itself, and on its own terms.

Conservatives (small 'c') certainly diverge from radical environmentalists who wish to change society in order to preserve the environment. At best, such people will be seen as bossy bobble-hatted fanatics wanting to impose their own highly controversial interpretation of the good life upon everybody, and whose attempts at policing will include intolerable levels of intrusion. At worst, as with professional weirdos like John Aspinall or James Goldsmith, the prescriptions go beyond socialistic communism and start to resemble the theories of Pol Pot. For instance, Aspinall's musing that the ideal human population of the world is 200,000,000[42] makes one wonder not only how he arrives at that figure, not only what definition of 'ideal' he is working with, but also how the 5,800,000,000 of us that should 'ideally' make way should react. It is almost as scary when they are taken seriously by thinkers such as John Gray.[43]

The big test of the Tories' green credentials is how far they are prepared to override the interests of those in the present, whose material interests involve exploiting the resources now available, and assuming that increased growth will pay for a clean-up of pollution by future generations, just as we have been able to clean up after the Industrial Revolution with the huge windfall income that industrial growth since the 19th century has provided. As noted, George Osborne has mused about greener taxes – under Mr Blair, the proportion of tax raised from green levies has fallen from 7.7 per cent to 6.2 per cent during his period of office – but this is the least that the Tories could do following their sustained effort to promote their green credentials.

Steve Norris, who leads the Tories' policy task force on transport, did claim that a reversion to the fuel duty escalator (a measure to increase fuel duties annually by more than inflation) was inevitable. This would be an interesting move: there is a false belief that Labour's instincts are greener than the Tories'. But Mr Norris is merely setting the story straight; after all, the escalator was a Tory measure introduced by Norman Lamont in 1993, and accelerated by Kenneth Clarke. It was dropped by Gordon Brown, a cowardly tactical retreat in the face of fuel protests in 2000, shortly after the Labour government insisted the escalator was not negotiable. And, as Mr Norris argued, increasing green taxes could easily be offset with decreasing non-green taxes (his favourite was the council tax).[44]

But Mr Norris, as leader of a task force, has deniability – senior Tories have generally welcomed his original thinking-out-of-the-box, but have hardly fallen over themselves to endorse his position – and the same will be true, in spades, for whatever Zac Goldsmith suggests as part of the Quality of Life review, however hopeful Mr Goldsmith is about the reception he is getting.[45] The Tories' interim energy review, under Alan Duncan, varies between the relatively bold (some intelligent and thoughtful musings about a 'cap and trade' regime for carbon emissions that promises to be a fairly firm long-term framework), and the bland (a 'level playing field' to give green energy a chance – since much of the energy argument revolves around how tilted the playing field is, between long and short term, low emission and high emission, diverse and narrow supplies, price and security, wanting a level playing field is tantamount to saying they will make a decision when the time comes, i.e. saying nothing).[46] And anyway, it also has that blessed deniability – in fact, these reports and suggestions have not one but two opportunities to be ignored, since they feed into the Quality of Life review, which then feeds into the policy review process under Oliver Letwin prior to drafting the manifesto.

The Tories have pushed greenery further up the political agenda than it has been since the heights of the 1989 European Election when the Green Party, manifestly inadequate for office as it was, took 15 per cent of the vote. But, Mr Osborne's speech aside, there has been relatively little discussion of the potential for pain. The Tories' campaign for the local elections in 2006 urged voters to vote blue, and thereby go green (prompting the invention of lovable Dave the Chameleon), but Mr Cameron's speech on the topic actually stressed the importance of local measures, and the successes of various Tory councils in picking up litter or running school buses.

> So where people have voted blue, their councils have gone green. If Conservatives are successful on [election day] May the 4th they'll help to make a change with tough targets and real action:
> - In Barnet, a Conservative council will set a new target for waste recycling – up from 32 per cent today to 40 per cent by 2011.
> - In Camden, Conservatives have promised to give incentives to residents who swap their petrol-driven car for an electric one.
> - And if they win in Lambeth, a Conservative council will plant more than 1,000 new trees.[47]

These initiatives may well be welcome, but they are hardly tough. Barnet's recycling will only have increased by a quarter in the next five years, while Camden's incentives could be large or very very small. And even if the Tories didn't win in Lambeth, there would be very little stopping them planting trees anyway. Have they no gardens? Localism is, in general, a very good thing, but as is well-known in environmental politics where global action is required, it can produce free riding and the not-in-my-back-yard attitude.

We are seeing the Tories develop a green, conservation-minded outlook which is very welcome after the neo-liberalism of the Thatcher era and the historically- and aesthetically-blind Blair years. But it should not be confused with greenery *per se*. Mr Cameron has quite rightly emphasised the Tories' greater propensity for valuing a pleasant environment, which has tended to contrast with the Labour Party's comparative indifference – until recently, Labour was the party of the big industrial heartlands, not the middle-class outfit it is morphing into. The local measures that Mr Cameron celebrated in his April speech will not have any noticeable effect on the variables underlying climate change; that is not a reason not to do them, of course, nor a reason not to trumpet them, but he should beware of overclaiming. His much-photographed bicycling to work did him some good (he made a good joke about this, at the expense of the BBC, in his first speech as Tory leader[48]), until it was discovered that he still used an official car to ferry his papers and clothes around;[49] he should not let this disappointment act as a metaphor for Tory green policies.

Sceptical of liberal economists' sanguine acceptance of the power of economic growth to repair our damaged environment, sceptical of easy assumptions that dramatic lifestyle changes can be made in a very short space of time, scathing about greens' desire to restrict prosperity and growth in the developing world, and mindful of the uncertainties in the science: in many ways, Mr Cameron's policies are admirably conservative. Our environment is a wonderful thing, and a major component of our British identity. It deserves a very high value indeed (not *no* value – a high value). Messrs Cameron, Osborne, Norris and others clearly place such a value on it, and this is a genuinely conservative position. It is greener than any position that Messrs Blair and Brown have adopted, but it is not thereby green. Mr Cameron's position, in an age of environmental concern and awareness among the very voters he is pursuing, is a good one to have; he needs to ensure that it is not swept away in a backlash against what has been called his 'green spin'.

Markets and communities

We have talked so far about getting a distinctive conservative position on free markets in terms of increasing the distance from neo-liberalism's uncritical Hayekian support for markets. We have quite properly drawn attention to the damage that the assumption of and respect for individual autonomy can do to communities, and to authority, and to the provision and delivery of public services. But on the other hand free markets do sit rather well in British society with its traditionally 'hands off' approach to its citizens, its relative lack of social solidarity and its trading outlook, as argued by David Willetts.

> So it is not the case that Britain had the Industrial Revolution and then became a market society. It is the other way round – it is because we were a market society that we were the place where the Industrial Revolution started. *Britain has always been far more of a market economy than the Continent.* So when we talk of the cash economy, the rise of the market or individualism, we are not speaking of some extraordinary alien import from America that arrived in 1963. We are talking about a fundamental feature of English society. ... Again, can you imagine a Labour MP, even Tony Blair, speaking in praise of Britain as the world's first market economy and praising the fact that we historically have been a far more individualistic culture than the continent? They still cannot do it and yet it is true.[50]

Market economics sits on top of a particular world view, which is prevalent in British society: the emphasis on hard work, and on the rewards of that work going to the worker; the uncomplicated view of social mobility and the acceptance of self-made men in the higher echelons of society; the robust individualism. This world view, at least since Weber's analysis of it,[51] has been associated with the puritan spirit whose rise coincided with the rise of capitalism and the explosion of personal wealth in the Western world. That puritan spirit has certainly been a theme in British history, though it has always met resistance, and was much more likely, at least until the leadership of Mrs Thatcher, to be represented in the roundheaded Labour Party than the cavalier Tories. Mr Cameron has explicitly moved back in the traditional Tory direction by distancing himself from talk of the work ethic.

> We have to care about working life, and we have to show that politics can make a positive difference. My aim is to show how Conservative instincts and Conservative values provide the right solutions. Our goal is clear: to move beyond a belief in the Protestant work ethic alone to a modern vision of ethical work.[52]

'Ethical work' is perhaps an odd phrase, but Mr Cameron recognises that the long hours that people have been working, as a direct result of the Tory reforms of the 1980s, have been undermining family life, and therefore, indirectly, communities. He believes the pursuit of wealth is not enough, and supports a vision of people being able to specify their own hours of work, work from home, enjoy extended sabbaticals and take time off to help bring up children, or even grandchildren. We have already discussed the question of whether Mr Cameron will be able to square the circle of trying to bring in such policies in business without legislation or regulation; the issue is whether such ideas will help communities to thrive.

Markets do sit very successfully on top of British society. But the problem for most commentators, especially John Gray and Roger Scruton,[53] is not that people cannot spend as much time with their offspring (or down the pub) as they would otherwise like, but rather that the bracing economic flux welcomed by Hayek is in fact terrifying for people. Competition should not appear too threatening, and the creative destruction that is its forte should not be overdone. If people's jobs are perceived as being perpetually under threat, then that will obviate the security that people need.

If someone believed that his or her job was completely safe under any circumstances, then his or her planning for the future would be seriously distorted under the moral hazard that 'someone else will provide'. But equally, conservatism values stable conditions. The idea of *closure*, the idea that one can stop striving and settle down to live the same way for a period of years, is very important. Many people, though certainly not all, are temperamentally opposed to the continuous climbing of the greasy pole; they aim to achieve a particular standard of living or social status, and then they wish to enjoy that as a reward. Indeed, since it is everyone's striving for themselves and their families that drives the economy, and since many people wish to enter the rat race only if there is a decent prospect of winning it, even moderate market liberals should think in terms of platforms and safety nets. Markets provide massive disincentives to the idea of closure, and a conservative should be wary of this.

Mr Cameron hasn't focused quite so much on this destructive aspect of markets; instead his recipe for boosting community involves removing restrictions from the third sector and increasing local democracy.[54] We can take the latter with a pinch of salt – the last leader of the opposition to go into an election proposing to centralise power rather than devolve it to local communities was Mrs Thatcher in 1979, and as we know no British Prime Minister, given the choice, gives power away when push comes to shove.

Surely a sign of a functioning local community is that people, when they go about their daily business and doing their own thing, get their supplies, victuals, entertainment and pleasures from that community. They eschew the convenience of big supermarkets with big car parks and instead buy their goods from local shops. They look for jobs within easy reach of their homes. They do not have to drive miles to see their friends, who live nearby within walking distance, or within walking distance of a convenient and friendly café, bistro or pub.

Such is the ideal. The problem, to reiterate, is that given any kind of a choice, people tend to desert their local haunts, and would rather drive miles to a Tesco or Wal-Mart. They do not enjoy local pubs, and if they do they don't talk to the people in them; friendships do not tend to develop from leisure time activities any more. They look for jobs in the national newspapers or online, not in the local paper or labour exchange, and are prepared to move to get work. The problem with rescuing communities is to put a halt to that sort of outwardly directed behaviour, and the issue is how this can be done without being overly prescriptive. Once free markets arrived and made it easier for these conditions to obtain, it automatically became much more difficult to get back to a more locally based existence.

The problem is not so much with the fifteen or twenty million Britons who do volunteer work,[55] as with the rest of us. The 'community', however we define that, has little to do with volunteer *workers*, and more to do with people consuming and living there voluntarily. The presence of the state in a community need not be inimical to it – for instance, with oft-repeated calls for more 'bobbies on the beat'. The presence of volunteer community officers in bright orange jackets meets Mr Cameron's criteria, but hasn't as yet diminished the fear of crime that has undermined communities so much.

Restricting market freedoms is, to an extent, possible, even for the party of Margaret Thatcher. Planning permission for out of town shopping malls is being given less frequently. Brave councils may try to restrict the use of cars, with pedestrianisation schemes, congestion charges, reduced numbers of parking spaces, and so on. There is a distinct trend for new housing schemes to be composed of traditionally designed houses in close proximity, in geometric arrangements rather than the rambling, relatively spacious estates of two-storey houses customary in previous decades.[56] Some even ban external taps, to discourage watering the garden. But it is not at all clear that such measures can do more than just tinker round the edges. New housing schemes, for instance, are often intended to discourage car use, but have not succeeded in doing so.

On the other hand, the mood music is important. Small 'c' conservatism is based around a preference for the actual over the abstract, the concrete over the potential.[57] Any conservative message should therefore stress the actual advantages of stable and contented communities over and above the abstract advantages of dynamic market-based economies. Even Margaret Thatcher and Enoch Powell were known to make that case in their milder moments.[58] So Mr Cameron is right to pursue the issue.

How does that chime with the tendency to assume that enterprise and entrepreneurialism are the keys to improving communities? The Tories' statement of their aims and values, *Built to Last*, advocates

> Harnessing the entrepreneurial spirit in our communities to tackle poverty and deprivation by removing the barriers that hold back the expansion of the social enterprise sector, community organisations, voluntary bodies and charities.[59]

This is a way of seeing the world that the Conservative Party has imported from America,[60] and is not necessarily accurate as a way of diagnosing the malaise. The fact is that transport, money, communications technologies and the lack of regulation allow us to ignore (relatively speaking) our neighbours, and given that opportunity, most of us do.

There is a converse way of looking at things, though, which is that the success of markets depends on there being strong communities, in particular the rule of law and respect for property and fair play, underlying them. They may not be the sorts of communities that were common 50 years ago – and there are grounds for thinking that the communities that are now idolised were rare, generally rural, and, at the time, unpopular.* But the fact that rich and full lives can be lived easily and without hindrance in many areas should not be gainsaid. It is one of those existing positive states that we tend not to value very highly when we look at politics. The very fact that free markets work as well as they do entails that they remain integrated effectively with a strong underlying community that may be wider than the imagined communities of planners and nostalgists, but is functional. People show very little inclination to go back to the narrower communities of earlier days, but that does not mean that markets are dismantling communities. They are enabling communities to evolve alongside the technological marvels that have stretched our horizons in the last century, and though there have been plenty of difficulties and troubles (as there have always been in any human society since Cain and Abel), there seems to be little reason as yet for nervousness about the future.

The conservative has to believe that, even if only *in extremis*, communities trump markets. But it is equally hard to imagine a conservative going very far in impeding the operation of markets in order to save a notion of 'community' when the people living in those communities take little action, given the choice, of saving them themselves.

---

* See, for example, the fascinating essays of the founding editor of *The Countryman*, Robertson Scott, showing his (low) opinion of rural England in the 1920s and 1940s: J.W. Robertson Scott, *England's Green and Pleasant Land* (Revised and extended edition, Penguin, Harmondsworth, 1947). In one essay, Scott even gives the label 'liberal conservative' to perhaps the first of the breed, 80 years before David Cameron claimed it (pp. 129–35). Scott's simple definition of this particular liberal conservative's beliefs expresses the spirit of genuine conservatism in admirably concise terms. 'There are other things an Englishman … considers before history and logic. There is old custom, there are relationships, convenience, neighbourliness, civility, peace' (p. 131). Hear hear.

CHAPTER SEVEN

CONSERVATISM AND SOCIETIES

'There is no such thing as society'

The magazine *Woman's Own* has rarely been the centre of major political controversy in its 70-odd years of existence. But in 1987, an interview with Mrs Thatcher included a passage that has caused immense embarrassment to the Tories ever since. The key section is very well known and oft-quoted. It goes as follows:

> We've been through a period where too many people have been given to understand that if they have a problem, it's the government's job to cope with it. 'I have a problem, I'll get a grant.' 'I'm homeless, the government must house me.' They're casting their problems on society. And you know, there's no such thing as society. There are individual men and women, there are families. And no government can do anything except through people, and people must look after themselves first. It's our duty to look after ourselves and then, also, to look after our neighbours.[1]

Doubtless the hoo-hah came as some surprise to Mrs Thatcher's team. The so-called dependency trap enmeshes people who do not think it worth their while to work, to plan their own lives or to try to be independent. Though the state offers a very low standard of living as its safety net, nevertheless many people, sometimes on

211

the basis of calculation, sometimes merely because they lack the skills to forge their own independent existence, prefer to stay in the net rather than striking out on their own. This moral hazard is worrying for conservatives, and the *Woman's Own* interview is unobjectionable from that point of view.

Nevertheless, carefully crafted or not, one sentence has become immortal – 'there's no such thing as society'. That single clause seems to encapsulate the 'I'm all right Jack' individualism of the 1980s that so many voters found, and still find, so distasteful. Taken thus, Mrs Thatcher seems to be saying that people can divest themselves of their moral responsibility for their fellows, and legitimately pursue their own interests instead, although she certainly denied this interpretation hotly.

> My meaning, clear at the time but subsequently distorted beyond recognition, was that society was not an abstraction, separate from the men and women who composed it, but a living structure of individuals, families, neighbours and voluntary associations. I expected great things from society in this sense because I believed that as economic wealth grew, individuals and voluntary groups should assume more responsibility for their neighbours' misfortunes. The error to which I was objecting was the confusion of society with the state as the helper of first resort. Whenever I heard people complain that 'society' should not permit some particular misfortune, I would retort, 'And what are you doing about it, then?' Society for me was not an excuse, it was a source of obligation.[2]

However that may be, the quote was disastrous for the image of the Tories, and they have been living it down ever since. Mr Major was clearly a Tory of a different kidney from Mrs Thatcher, but early on in his period of office, the 'no such thing' argument received rather more scholarly flesh than *Woman's Own* might have been able to support. David Willetts:

Reading the full text of the 1987 interview, it is clear that all she meant was that we could not evade personal responsibility for our actions by saying everything we did wrong was really society's fault. And if we want 'government' or 'society' to do something, that means putting a duty on other people and collecting taxes from them. But Mrs Thatcher did not mean that we had no responsibilities to others, or could lead any meaningful existence outside society. Indeed, one of her preoccupations was with reconciling the world of economic calculation with our moral obligations to our fellow-citizens. For her that reconciliation was achieved through her strong sense of religious obligation.[3]

By 1997, disabusing the British people of the idea that Tories believed that there was no such thing as society was becoming imperative. In a book brought out for the general election of that year, David Willetts called one chapter 'Is there such a thing as society?' and answered his own question with a paragraph consisting of a single word: 'Yes.'[4] In 2002, Iain Duncan Smith, expressing his personal credo, dispensed with Willetts' interrogative, and merely asserted that there *was* such a thing as society.[5] Incredibly, fifteen years after the original unfortunate remark, intellectual heavy hitters – this time Oliver Letwin[6] – were still being brought in to try to explain the misunderstanding, and the protesting continued during Michael Howard's leadership, led by Damien Green.[7] So when David Cameron, upon election to the leadership of the Conservative Party in December 2005 said, in his acceptance speech, 'There is such a thing as society, it's just not the same thing as the state',[8] the BBC's headline that 'Cameron offers something new'[9] was not strictly accurate.

It is extraordinary that one backfiring remark in a popular ladies' magazine could still dog the Tories today, but it does. Partly this may be because the quote has now been rather over-interpreted, with the various glosses on it being none too consistent with each other. But more importantly, there is a sense that Mrs

Thatcher made a sort of Freudian slip, that the 'no such thing' slogan, though it is not what she meant to say, does rather sum up the vision of society as being made up of nothing above and beyond the individualistic interests of its members. Society is not, therefore, something that you can destroy, break down or otherwise harm. Perhaps more to the point, on Mrs Thatcher's implicit view, a society is not something, unlike an individual, that can have causal powers. If someone does something, they are entirely responsible for it.

The struggle for Tories such as Willetts and Letwin, who are after all trying to reconcile two different ideological traditions, is that the British conservative simply does not believe this to be true, though the neo-liberal might. The question that we must address in this chapter is whether David Cameron has the ability or inclination to reconcile the two traditions. The Tories are less trusted than the Labour Party to deal with social problems, although people are generally speaking not terribly happy with Mr Blair's record here.[10] But there is an opportunity for Mr Cameron, and he has begun to take it. If it is accepted that there is such a thing as society, then society needs to be understood as something with causal powers that can affect the behaviour of individuals. In his famous (or infamous) 'hug a hoodie' speech, Mr Cameron came closer than any senior Tory has for years in accepting that implication.

> Crime, drugs, underage sex – this behaviour is wrong, but simply blaming the kids who get involved in it doesn't really get us much further. It is what the culture around them encourages. Imagine a housing estate with a little park next to it. The estate has 'no ballgames' and 'no skateboarding' notices all over it. The park is just an empty space. And then imagine you are 14 years old, and you live in a flat four storeys up. It's the summer holidays and you don't have any pocket money. That's your life. What will you get up to today? Take in a concert, perhaps? Go to a football game? Go to the seaside?

No – you're talking £30 or £50 to do any of that. You can't kick a ball around on your own doorstep. So what do you do? You hang around in the streets, and you are bored, bored, bored. And you look around you. Who isn't bored? Who isn't hanging around because they don't have any money? Who has the cars, the clothes, the power? … Even if you're not interested in crime, it's difficult to avoid the culture. Of course, not everyone who grows up in a deprived neighbourhood turns to crime – just as not everyone who grows up in a rich neighbourhood stays on the straight and narrow. Individuals are responsible for their actions – and every individual has the choice between doing right and doing wrong. But there are connections between circumstances and behaviour.[11]

There is an opportunity here, but much hard work still needs to be done to live down the Tories' bad rep.

Personal morality

One issue that has dogged the Conservative Party for a number of years is that of personal morality: when should we respect, and when should we not respect, the personal autonomy of individuals in areas of behaviour that affect no one else? Much personal behaviour, of course, offends those with strong moral tastes. Furthermore, the broadly liberal direction in which society is moving means that those of a conservative disposition will be ranged against increasing *freedom*.

The dangers for the Conservative Party when it takes a reactionary stand against changes in personal morality are threefold. The first is that, because by definition the actions being criticised by Tories affect no one other than the individual involved (and other consenting adults), nothing tangible is gained by any prohibition, and much is lost, including personal liberty and the resources of policing authorities who have to track down unfairly criminalised people. The second is that, by making something against the law, the wherewithal for an illegal supply industry, attracting juicy price premiums, will have been created. And third, moral rectitude can attract charges of hypocrisy if members of one's own party are caught out indulging.

Many Tories have been arguing for the need to 'move with the times', perhaps most notably Alan Duncan, at the time of writing Shadow Secretary of State for Trade, Industry and Energy.[12] Pollster Andrew Cooper warns about the dangers of reactionary 'grumpy old man' thinking into which the Tories often threaten to lapse, and which pervades their image even today.

> When Tories get together and talk about Britain, what often unfolds is one vast harrumph about what Britain has become. Rather than reach out to a mass market, the Conservative Party has seemed content to become the campaigning arm of the Daily Mail, fanzine of 1950s Britain and, it must be remembered, an institution that, unlike the Conservative Party, can go on forever while appealing only to a hard core of a few million nostalgics.
>
> It has often been remarked that the Tory Party needs to look more like Britain but it has remained overwhelmingly a white party of grumpy old people which, at best, patronises women, gays and ethnic minorities. With no vision for a better future, the Conservative Party has come to represent little more than the last stand of yesterday over tomorrow.[13]

It is indeed the press that seems to oppress the Tories most, and to prevent them from, in Alan Duncan's words, 'getting real'. The *Daily Mail* is certainly a cheerleader here, as is the *Daily Telegraph* (one commentator generally sympathetic to the Tories blames the *Torygraph* for most of the Tories' problems post-1990[14]), where the real Tory opposition to Mr Cameron, led by Simon Heffer, is based. And it is the area of personal morality that really gets people going and sets Tory upon Tory.

In this context, we'll look briefly at a couple of difficult areas of personal choice where attitudes are changing and yet problems still remain. We'll look initially at the issue of homosexuality, and then move on to the more complex case of drug abuse.

Homosexuality is condemned by the Bible quite explicitly. If you take your Bible without layers of interpretation, you should be against it. This is the basis for the traditional conservative rejection of homosexuality, which meant that the activity was criminalised for a long period in Britain, being legalised only in the 1960s. All well and good. This is not a sufficient rationale, however. In the first place, many perfectly innocuous activities are explicitly condemned by the Bible, and few if any people argue that they all should be criminalised (adultery, for example). And second, we have recommended that conservatism should take a Rawlsian turn: that is, it should not rest its arguments on disputed views of society, or particular moral or cultural perspectives that may not be shared. That homosexuality is condemned in the Bible is of course sufficient for some – by no means all – Christians, but the rest of us who are not Christian are unlikely to be swayed if the argument does not go beyond that into a more public realm of reason (which it doesn't).

The taboo surrounding homosexuality is disappearing from British society. Gay couples live together quite openly without condemnation. Even if one were not a liberal, and refused to agree that in the personal sphere the individual should be sovereign, one might still accept homosexuality because it is so obviously harmless to its practitioners, and to everyone else. The major problems with gay behaviour stem from the social stigma attached, which could be and is being dispelled to some extent by the equalisation of treatment by the authorities (and anyway is hardly gay people's *fault*), and, in the British context, the greater risk compared with heterosexual couples of contracting AIDS, which is a function of promiscuity rather than homosexuality *per se*. In short, discrimination against gay people is unjust, pure and simple.

Let us make a further point here. Conservatives (small 'c') need to deal with society as it is, whether or not they are happy with it.

Even if conservatives are opposed to homosexual behaviour, this is not sufficient reason to try to prevent it. Gay relationships are clearly common in society, are frowned upon by few, do no one any serious harm and make a lot of people very happy. Surely the change principle must weigh against trying to engineer society to discourage the practice.

Mr Cameron dipped a tentative toe in these waters at the 2006 party conference, putting in a plug for civil partnerships, even though he managed to avoid using the word 'gay'.

> When you stand up there, in front of your friends and your family, in front of the world, whether it's in a church or anywhere else, what you're doing really means something. ... And by the way, it means something whether you're a man and a woman, a woman and a woman or a man and another man. That's why we were right to support civil partnerships, and I'm proud of that.[15]

This is an important step for Mr Cameron. Commentators have focused on his change agenda since he became leader, but we should not lose sight of his 'Dave the Chameleon' side. Before he hit the limelight, Mr Cameron made a bit of a point of fitting in with his surroundings, even when those surroundings were the illiberal Tories of old. Most notably he was the author of the 2005 manifesto, but he also voted for a continuation of the notorious section 28 legislation, that banned public bodies from promoting homosexuality (whatever that means), in 2003. Before that he had spoken against repeal of section 28 in 2000, and in favour in 2002.[16]

On the other hand, now that he is leader, he does speak for gay rights, and has tried to ensure that gay politicians are not given a hard time by his party. Affairs, both heterosexual and homosexual, by front benchers have not been punished under the Cameron regime, which is all to the good (despite vain attempts by the *Daily Telegraph* and *Daily Mail* to create some outrage[17]). The gay pressure group Stonewall points out that Mr Cameron's rhetoric goes further than that of the Labour Party. Of course it is easy to sound liberal in opposition, perhaps harder when in government. Mr Cameron has never really addressed his voting record on this issue, although a spokesman argued that he voted with the Tories' manifesto commitment in 2001.[18] But the mood music will help revive the Tory vote, and perhaps will help move the Tory Party in the right direction.

The recreational use of drugs is a much more complex case for the conservative (as for any politician of any ideology). The issue has caused a great deal of difficulty for the Tories in their years of opposition, most notably at the party conference of 2000, when Shadow Home Secretary Ann Widdecombe outlined a zero tolerance strategy, only to be sandbagged as seven of her Shadow Cabinet colleagues admitted to taking recreational drugs in the past and the Police Federation condemned the policy as unworkable.[19] In 2005 Mr Cameron himself came under very uncomfortable pressure to reveal whether or not he had taken drugs at university.[20] 'I led a normal university life', said he, in response to a question about drug-taking, and he seemed happy to go along with the innuendo that that implied, that the real answer to the question was 'yes'. He came out of it pretty well, seeming like a modern leader, not hide-bound in the attitudes of the past. On the other hand, maybe the cherubic Mr Cameron had led a boringly blameless student career, and his refusal to answer the question made people think he was hipper than he actually was. We shall probably never know.

Few ideologies are so specific that they determine a right and a wrong drug policy (except for libertarianism, which recommends legalisation of course). Conservatives (small 'c') are not naturally drawn to the liberating properties of drugs, nor to the artificial and chaotic lifestyle of the user. Why should a conservative wish to cleanse the doors of perception? But on the other hand, the conservative has always prided him- or herself on being able to look at the facts with an unsentimental eye. What sort of arguments should he or she take seriously?

Some arguments are irrelevant. First of all, the personal liberty argument, that recreational drug users are being prevented from pursuing their own idea of the good life, is not, in itself, interesting to the conservative. Assuming drug users do no harm, the conservative's instinct should be to respect personal liberty. But whether drug users do harm is precisely the issue; they can be responsible for crime, and they also require a criminal infrastructure to supply the needs of their habit. So until that issue is resolved favourably, the infringement of liberty argument does not feature on the conservative's radar.

Second, there is an argument that some drugs, such as cannabis or ecstasy, are notably less harmful to society and their users than other drugs that are legal, most obviously tobacco and alcohol. All that is true, but the conservative is unimpressed. Admittedly, to make drug laws consistent with alcohol and tobacco laws it is necessary to either legalise soft drugs or make alcohol and tobacco illegal. But who said that laws need to be consistent as long as they are clear? Granted that, all things being equal, it is good for laws to be consistent, it does not follow that where laws are adequate yet inconsistent they should be altered to make them consistent. For that may stop them being adequate.

There are plenty of arguments for keeping drug laws as they stand. One would invoke the change principle on the need to avoid change. A second, related argument goes beyond the law and looks at how the law interacts with society; laws do not exist in the abstract, and one cannot gauge the effect of a law merely by analysing its content. The combined effect of the law being as it is, policing policy being as it is (i.e. cracking down much harder on hard drugs such as heroin), and social mores being as they are, is that the recreational use of cannabis and ecstasy is relatively less risky for users. Indeed, anyone worried about illegality can fairly easily make their way to places, such as Amsterdam, where the practice is tolerated. As a matter of fact, goes this second argument, cannabis or ecstasy users are barely impinged on, while heroin and cocaine users are given a much harder time, which is more or less commensurate with the effects of the drugs. Hence, as *the system as a whole* is much more punitive towards hard drugs, there is no need to change things round. Any liberalisation, on the other hand, would send quite the wrong signals.

A third argument is that drugs undermine human dignity, and erode community relationships; such an argument clearly resonates with conservatives.[21] Heroin is severely addictive and leads users very easily into crime; crack cocaine can turn abusers into one-man crime waves. Crime patterns vary with patterns of drug abuse.[22] And the attraction of any kind of tolerant zone for criminal activity means that criminality will tend to spread anyway to other members of the community beyond the drug-using element. It is essential to prevent drugs getting a hold of society, and similarly essential for governments to give out strong anti-drugs messages.

The arguments for decriminalisation fall into two types. The first type recognises that drug use is widespread and tolerated by many people; as with the arguments about homosexuality, this view says that conservatives need to recognise that society is tolerant, and that the change principle entails that that tolerance should be respected. The second accepts the challenge of the change principle by insisting that the current situation is completely unsatisfactory, and that therefore change, if only incremental change, is legitimate in this case; any harm done is likely to be less harmful than the law as it stands. For example, the so-called war on drugs has done little other than create astonishingly lucrative networks of organised crime, notably in South America (based on the cocaine trade) and the Middle East (opium). These networks are prepared to undertake the small risks of supply to meet the giant demand for drugs in the rich world, creating the conditions for the generation of astonishing quantities of money. Much of the opium money goes to fund Al-Qaeda, and so the war on drugs undermines the war on terror. Furthermore, current drugs policies are not keeping vulnerable people from drugs at all; a medically based strategy of intervention, rehabilitation and support might be a better policy (and indeed Tory Shadow Home Affairs minister Edward Garnier has indicated tentative support for applications of that approach, including setting up injection centres for drug addicts[23]). And, given the large number of young people who take ecstasy of a Friday night while clubbing, a conservative might reasonably worry about the effects on millions of youngsters' respect for the rule of law of their making criminals of themselves with impunity on a weekly basis.

None of these arguments, either for or against the current system, is decisive. But we can at least see how the conservative will expect to argue and be argued against. Arguments addressing the health of the community should be regarded as over and above arguments about personal liberty. Arguments should take the facts as they stand, public attitudes as they are, over and above any preferences about how society should be run. Justice should count for more than making laws consistent or 'modern'.

Education

Education is a social issue that, like personal morality, divides groups; indeed, so complex an issue is it that it is hard to frame obviously fair and sensible policies. There will always be awkward cases that threaten to fall between various stools; sweeping statements or wide-ranging laws will always be embarrassed eventually.

In this section I want to adumbrate four lines of thought along conservative principles to show what a conservative critique of the current system would look like. I do not suggest that these four criticisms are the only ones that a conservative would want to make, nor that only conservatives would make them. These criticisms provide a means for judging the import of current Tory thinking.

The first criticism is perhaps the most obvious: there is no need for a comprehensive system or a national curriculum. Education officials cannot know, even in broad outline, what type of education is better for everyone. Children have wildly varying needs. Neighbourhoods have important requirements too: a leafy suburb might well want schools that prepare its offspring for university, while an inner city estate would actually benefit from prioritising good behaviour and social awareness, and an area with a large proportion of recent immigrants might focus on language (if it is then argued that the suburban children are thereby getting an unfairly better start in life, the rejoinder has to be that the education they receive is a symptom of that, not its cause). Hence a conservative will work towards a system with as fine a grain as is feasible. As much control as possible should be devolved to as local a level as possible.

A second criticism goes to the heart of what education is. The problem is this: there is actually remarkably little agreement about the purpose of education. Is it supposed to impart the values and heritage of a particular culture? To create the citizens of the future? To equip youngsters for the future? To make youngsters independent and able to pursue their own ideas of the good life? To make youngsters willing and able to contribute to the community? To impart currently understood knowledge across a range of subjects? To give youngsters the skills they need to be economically successful? To produce an educated, knowledge-rich workforce to increase the future wealth of the nation? To instil discipline? Should children be seen and not heard? Or should we encourage them to explore their own values, make their own decisions and have confidence in their own independently reached ideas?

Given the lack of consensus, and corresponding lack of direction from central government, it is hardly surprising that comprehensive education has flaws, or that the national curriculum is overloaded and complex. Education is not something that you plonk down on top of a society; education remakes society in various ways that are hard to measure, hard to spot and next to impossible to reverse.

A third conservative criticism of the education system as it stands is that standards are being neglected. Much of this goes back to the incentives to meet performance targets, but there is also an unfortunate move to make education more 'relevant' to today's young people. Given that educational achievement is a major predictor of wealth, health and social status, how relevant do you want it to be?

Moves to tailor standards to the desires, rather than the needs, of children actually hurt the children of the poorer and less educated classes more. In such systems no one gets taught the skills that seem too hard or too boring. In which case, preference in later life goes to those who imbibed them at their parents' knees. Faced with a large number of graduates, employers are actually finding that those old stand-bys 'literacy, numeracy and the right attitude' are more useful predictors of who will be a good employee.[24]

The fourth conservative criticism is of the helter-skelter expansion of universities during the Blair years. There has been a dramatic increase in the percentage of school leavers going to what is now termed 'uni', despite the fact that universities themselves have not been properly funded to cope with the influx of students. Residential capacity has not grown, and many areas of university towns and cities have been effectively taken over by student flats, while teaching standards have plummeted as relatively few resources have followed the influx of students. Universities are given incentives to take on more students, but the incentives for individual lecturers still focus on their performance of research rather than teaching. No doubt it is a good thing to receive a higher education. But, as the conservative would remind the government, the unintended consequences of this dramatic expansion will soon outweigh the intended ones (if the latter ever happen at all).

The upshot of these criticisms, taken as a whole, is that education ought to be a rich experience, whose goals are far more nebulous and ambitious than the target-driven educational culture that has been the result of Mr Blair's focus on 'education, education, education'. We have seen that the large-scale goals of education are highly contested. But the small-scale aim, the day-to-day aim, seems paradoxically simple: receiving an education in a subject involves achieving mastery of that subject, which mastery may be used to enhance one's earning capacity or merely to make one a better person. Conservatives (small 'c') should never be afraid of speaking the language of improvement, even while they remain convinced that humans are not perfectible. As we noted in the previous chapter, the target-setting culture misses some of the most important qualities of an interaction, and this is certainly true in education. Shadow Education Secretary David Willetts makes the case.

> When we have talked about education exclusively in terms of league tables and targets, we have separated ourselves from parents and teachers who feel that there is something missing. Much of what is valuable in education cannot be measured in tests and league tables, just as the value of life is not only about prices and markets. It doesn't mean education should decline into 'edutainment' interspersed by tests. Education must be a route to deeper happiness – the real fulfilment that comes from mastering an idea, mastering a skill, mastering a subject. There is the fulfilment that comes from rising to a challenge, doing something difficult, pushing yourself harder.[25]

There isn't a great deal that can be gleaned from Mr Cameron's utterances on education, either as leader[26] or in his brief incarnation as Mr Willetts' predecessor as Shadow Education Secretary,[27] a post that we understand he expressly asked then-leader Michael Howard for. The Tory statement of principles *Built to Last* is somewhat more encouraging, promising the promotion of streaming of children, greater rigour in exams, and allowing schools and universities more independence.[28] Increasing diversity and standards simultaneously is exactly what a conservative should be aiming for, and the best way to do that is to relax controls and make it possible to close failing schools and other educational institutions. It is important that this does not lead to further disadvantages for poor students, and so the devil is in the detail of any proposal.

But as we noted above, there is no reason why all children ought to be taught the same things. There is no consensus on what the wider goals of education are, and no reason to impose any on society. Standards are more important than targets, bearing in mind that one way of meeting targets is to lower standards. And there is no reason to cram everyone through university. In this context, so far Mr Cameron's team deserve a tick, and if, in government, they have the confidence to decentralise education policy and to make room for the deeper experiences that Mr Willetts talked about, then they should get a gold star.

The public services revisited

Education is something of a special case, on the assumption (not usually examined deeply) that it is responsible for transmitting cultural values across generations. Space precludes us from examining every public service in equivalent detail, but we can make a few notes on what a conservative policy on public services would look like.

The public services remain popular, on the twin grounds that people like to know that there is a recognised supplier not after commercial advantage, and they like to think that the poor will not be disadvantaged by being unable to meet the costs. People seem prepared to be tolerant of a less than efficient service. And they tell pollsters that they are prepared to pay more tax to receive one (though they may be lying when they say that). So Tory calls for reform of public services do not necessarily meet with universal joy, even with regular, and frustrated, users. The Tories have been severely handicapped over the last two or three decades by the fissure that has opened up between them and public servants and service users. They have shown little nose for opinion in the public sector (on either side of the counter), and have relied on often savage and ambitious reports from various free market think tanks, which have the reduction of the public sector as part of their mission statements after all. Most of the Tories' conversations have been with people who think the unthinkable, and they have rather lost touch with those who think the thinkable.

Even now, a disputed interview with Oliver Letwin, in which he claimed that there were 'no limits' about which NHS functions could be contracted out to the private sector, caused a huge amount of trouble at the outset of the 2006 Party Conference.[29] Their reputation goes before them. Mr Letwin's point was that if there was a part of the NHS that could be improved by private provision, then that could and should be investigated. But language is everything. The inference his form of words allows ill-wishers to draw is that he would contemplate privatising the whole lot. This is not what he said, certainly not what he meant. But more care is needed.

There are three major problems with the Tories' desire to reform public services, understandable though this desire is. First, the balance between public and private provision is less a matter of quantity than of distribution; the type of services people expect from a government depends on the piecemeal way that public service provision has developed over the decades. Such untidy provision reflects what people of that country are prepared to pay, what they are prepared to pay for, and what has not been provided traditionally in an affordable and reliable form by charities or the private sector. This will vary from country to country, and so practice from other nations will be hard to import.[30] No doubt reforms are always desirable to some extent, and no doubt the British like nothing more than a good grumble about their public services, but the central importance of those services to people's expectations of society entails, on the change principle, that reform should be patient, quiet and incremental.

Second, the Labour government from 1997 has indulged in quite a quantity of reform itself, under self-consciously prudent Chancellor Gordon Brown. No doubt much of that reform has had the unfortunate side-effects that the change principle and the knowledge principle would predict, but equally statistics are trickling out to show that Labour's reforms have been successful in many areas. The conservative principles, though of course allowing organic and incremental change, also imply that, once reform is carried out, it should be given time to work. This means that (a) it is possible to check that changes are really a result of the reforms, rather than some other temporary or otherwise unpredicted cause, and (b) a little more knowledge can be gained about the system by seeing what the effects of particular reforms are.

Third, public servants are under a great deal of pressure. Placing performance targets on the public services often warps their work patterns, gives them perverse incentives, and deters many of their most altruistic instincts. We must also not forget the vast quantity of change – usually entailing dramatic increases in paperwork – that public servants have had to endure since 1979. One's work is an important part of one's identity, and when it ceases to be a vocation, and becomes an endless round of form-filling, that is very undermining of morale.

Different services will require different levels of change, reform and attention; it is hard to generalise across defence, policing, health, energy, transport and so on. But the above reflections suggest a potential line of conservative policy. Labour has carried out many reforms. It has, indeed, often responded, when reforms don't seem to have worked immediately, with further rounds of reforms. Reforms built on reforms, a hyperactive government; the public sector is in flux.

It follows that a conservative response to issues in the public sector is a careful review of reforms, and of their effects. It should not be assumed that a behemoth like the National Health Service, the world's third largest employer after the Chinese Red Army and the Indian Railways, will suddenly show vast improvements after a few months. Reform has to be given time to bed down, and to pile reforms on more reforms, when the effects of the first reforms remain unknown, contravenes both the change principle and the knowledge principle. The Tories can't criticise Labour for being hyperactive and simultaneously boast about the radical reforms they will bring in.

And any further change will result in possibly large transaction costs, and won't necessarily save much money. For instance, if the public is to choose its hospitals, then there has to be greater capacity to make the choice meaningful, while the localism that is likely to govern Tory attempts at reform (see Chapter Nine for more on this), by devolving more decisions down to the level of individual users of the system and local administrators, will add further uncertainty. We are currently extremely unaware whether users will be able to take such decisions (about which school, hospital or route for a new road is best) with any competence or confidence without first gaining a good deal of experience.

Furthermore, as noted public servants have been under incredible pressure, morale is low and the desire for some stability high. It therefore follows, pragmatically, that a cautious conservative approach as outlined may well translate into a number of Tory votes from public servants. This is deeply significant, because the public services have been a Tory-free zone since May 1979. Furthermore, Wales, Scotland and the North of England have economies where the public sector is much larger than in the South of England, and the Tories' perceived attitude to public services is hindering their ability to win parliamentary and council seats in these regions; hence a more conservative attitude to the public sector might also help the Tories escape from their South-East bunker. Quantitative work done by political scientist David Sanders tends to show the same thing: the Tories moving to the centre will alone add something like 5 percentage points to their share of the vote in 2009–10, but more is needed, and targeting the votes of disgruntled public servants alienated by micro-management could well supply the numbers of votes needed.[31]

None of this, it should be added, would connote opposition to private sector provision of services, or indeed less of a commitment to reform. It would simply show that the Tories, for good conservative reasons, understood the complex dynamics and

229

epistemology of reform, and appreciated that it does not work overnight, or produce simple, easy-to-evaluate effects.

Despite the obvious advantages to the Tories, Mr Cameron was initially opposed to such a line. As he argued in his review of the first edition of this book:

> However, his [i.e. my, Kieron O'Hara's] proposal that we should freeze the process of reform in the public sector is way off the mark. The reason Labour's reforms have not worked is because they do not accord with Conservative principles – they have been top-down, centralising, and have assumed that bureaucrats setting targets and measuring performance have perfect knowledge.[32]

Mr Cameron's diagnosis of the problems with Labour's reforms is spot on. But that does not mean that those reforms won't have good effects – they might, though we can doubt it. And it does not mean that a new Tory government achieving office in 2009 will have much of a clue as to what the effects of several years of Labour reforms (and spending increases) will be having – it won't have the foggiest. So suggestions in 2007 as to what a government will do in 2009 in response to reforms, some of which will not yet have been enacted, and all of whose medium term effects will be unknown, are no less misguided than shots in the dark.

As we saw in Chapter Six, Mr Cameron's initial instinct has been to promote the third sector to take up at least some of the slack, but we won't repeat our scepticism about the possibilities of that well-intentioned part of the economy being ready to take on a big burden anytime soon. So until recently, it looked bad for public service workers.

But the Public Services Improvement Policy Group rides to the rescue! In their interim report, the co-chairs signalled a timely and rational retreat from the entrenched position the Tories have found themselves in.

At a time when the commercial world has understood the power of aspiration, politicians have seemed content to be regarded as destructive and negative. In doing so, they have demeaned the political process, and lost countless opportunities to articulate any sense of national shared vision or common purpose. Equally, there has been a vastly overstated focus on what the public sector can learn from the private sector. This seems to have occurred without any consideration that the end experience of the user is driven by the professional delivering the service, regardless of public or private sector.

In no field of policy is this need for a change of approach more obvious than in discussion of the public services. The political culture has often required the Conservatives to belittle the efforts of people whose objectives we share, and to defend indefensible consequences of policies for which the previous Conservative Government was responsible.

Despite these exaggerated rhetorical differences, the reality is that there is in truth a broad consensus within the electorate about the values which they believe should shape the public services, and this consensus is widely shared among politicians of all parties. It is one of the more puzzling aspects of modern politics that the politicians have appeared to be content that this fact should remain a state secret.

That is not to say that there are no areas of disagreement, still less that there are no areas where policy development does not hold out the prospect of service improvement. Quite the contrary.

The problem has been a disconnect between the political debate in which politicians have sought to paint their opponents into ever more implausible ideological corners, and the experience of the users of public services who have seen an ever-widening gap between aspiration and reality.[33]

This is a welcome switch to a more consensual approach to the public services. It is, at present, somewhat ambiguous as to whether the consensus is to be engineered between the Tories and the Labour government (bad idea), or the Tories and the 'knights' of the public service professions (good idea). And an interim report from a policy group (that deniability again) need not necessarily leave any traces in the manifesto. Nevertheless, the Tories' policy chief Oliver Letwin welcomed the report as a decisive turning point.[34] If so, it would be the first time for many years that a conservative policy on public services had broken through the ideological stalemate in this area.

Tax

This takes us to the sensitive area of tax. Since Mrs Thatcher demonstrated the reluctance of the British to pay tax (shown perhaps most graphically after her departure when Chris Patten's 'double whammy' campaign was so successful against Shadow Chancellor John Smith's shadow budget of 1992), the political parties in Britain have vied with each other to be tax cutters. This has generally meant, of course, being sneakier tax *raisers* who would never on any pretext raise income tax, one of the fairest methods of taxing, because it is that that features in the news headlines.

The government, in effect, has three sources of money: taxation, borrowing it or printing it. Any government will try to seek the sensible balance between the three. Borrowing pushes up interest rates and depresses the economy; printing money is inflationary. Hence it is inevitable that if public spending has to rise for any unforeseen reason – say, for instance, a giant war and reconstruction effort in a large country thousands of miles away – there will be some pressure on taxes to rise.

A conservative approach to taxes should never preclude tax rises, because sometimes tax rises are needed, and better than borrowing or printing more money. Income tax and straightforward consumption taxes between them are fairer than any alternatives, because they will be so much less distorting of the economy. That is not to say that conservatives *want* to raise taxes; far from it. As we have seen, conservatives are not very confident that government activity will be fruitful, and all things being equal a conservative government would be much less active than a socialist one, say, or the Gladstonian one that we have now. Nevertheless, the conservative, unlike the neo-liberal, is quite happy for the government to do some things, particularly things which it always has done, or which its voters wish it to do, and doing things costs money, and money has to be raised somehow.

This has to act in the Tories' interests. The Tories have a well-established brand as enemies of tax, which they should exploit. Even if the Tories put taxes up for whatever reason, very few people actually think that taxes will be lower under Labour. There is, to reiterate, nothing wrong with reducing public spending. But equally there is no 'correct' level of public spending – society, and *a fortiori* the economy, does not have a 'best' form, to which it should be moulded if it does not conform.

However, the Tory urge to cut taxes will be a serious source of pressure for Mr Cameron. His economic competitive policy group, run by John Redwood, has already produced its interim report, which hints at an eventual recommendation of tax cuts.[35] Mr Redwood wrote an introduction to a pamphlet to coincide with the Tory conference in October 2006 urging Mr Cameron to make the moral case for tax cuts.[36] There have been many instances, in the run up to the 2006 conference season, of right-wingers demanding tax cuts.[37]

And one of the biggest tactical errors of the Cameron period was the setting up of a tax reform commission under the chairmanship of Thatcherite ultra Michael Forsyth, which duly reported in October 2006 demanding £21 billion of tax cuts.[38] Not only that, but the cuts suggested benefited the rich much more than the poor – not helpful when the Tories are trying to live down their image of being the party of the rich. This is the problem with the independent commissions that the Tories have used in policymaking – they have deniability, but only up to a point. They are associated with the Tories, and can be presented as the secret Tory agenda. It is great to be able to welcome the report of the Public Services Improvement Policy Group, but then you have to live down the Tax Reform Commission.

To promise tax cuts, in advance of knowing what circumstances the decision will have to be made in, is an obvious and elementary error, although the problem is to some extent presentational. One point made by tax cutters, though more often than not privately, is that the tax-cutting message is simple. It can be a simple soundbite, easy to defend against the Humphrys and Paxmans of this world, as opposed to the line above that taxes should be as low as possible, and cut as and when the unknown circumstances of 2009 onwards allow. This is true; the tax-cutting line is straightforward. Unfortunately, it won't get past the Paxmen because it suggests another simple, straightforward question: if you cut taxes, what services will you cut? That, of course, is hard to answer.

Tax cutters such as Mr Redwood make the perfectly correct point in response that lower taxes often generate more money, so the apparent requirement to cut services doesn't follow. But that is no longer a simple soundbite for the *Today* programme. So the simplicity argument doesn't hold. It may be simpler to get over your tax policy, but it makes it correspondingly harder to get over your spending policy, unless you want to come clean about cutting spending.

And of course it should, but doesn't, go without saying that not promising to cut taxes is not the same as promising not to cut taxes. The Tory policy ought to be the fairly simple one of taxes being as low as is necessary. The state might well be shrunk, but it is plainly unconservative to shrink it at any kind of pace. The reduction of support for various people (whether or not they are undeserving), and the shift in expenditure in the economy from public to private sector would be a massive shock, and should not be undertaken lightly. When Mrs Thatcher undertook shock therapy in the 80s, the British economy was a basket case, and the risks were on balance worth it. But it was an awfully painful process, involving riots, strikes and crushing unemployment. That unemployment may have been transitory, but the human cost, and that on some communities, was large. In 2006, in contrast, as the economy trundles along quite happily, with blips here and booms there, any risk-taking clearly contravenes the change principle.

None of that means that careful adjustment of spending priorities wouldn't result in lower taxes. It just means eschewing rash promises. In 1988, George Bush Sr, in accepting the Presidential nomination of the Republican Party at the New Orleans convention, said, famously: 'Read my lips: no new taxes'. But he found himself as a President with a Democratic majority in both the Senate and the House of Representatives, and in order to get anything done, compromise was the order of the day. Compromise is no bad thing – that is one of the deeper messages of this book. To get the 1990 budget agreement through, in order to cut the massive budget deficit which Ronald Reagan had built up and which was being exacerbated by a recession, spending was cut but taxes also rose.

This was entirely sensible of Mr Bush, it must be said. The deficit needed to be tackled, and the Gulf War was just around the corner (not a cheap excursion, though substantially cheaper than the return match with Saddam). Consensus across the political spectrum was the only way to do it, and the 1990 deal laid the foundations for tackling the budget deficit. By the time Bill Clinton left office, it was no longer a problem. Mr Bush had made his own contribution in a statesmanlike way.

If only he hadn't made that damned promise. The pressure on Mr Bush came not from his nominal opponents in the Democratic Party, who of course supported the tax rises. They came from his nominal colleagues on the right. Pat Buchanan stood against Mr Bush in the 1992 primaries, and the unwise promise was the stick with which Mr Buchanan armed himself. Mr Bush eventually saw off the challenge, and duly received the Republican nomination for a second time. But he was severely wounded, and made things worse by apologising: 'I did it, and I regret it.' The damage was not to perceptions of Mr Bush's economic competence, but rather to his credibility. His promise in 1992 not to raise taxes again was, of course, not taken terribly seriously. Much worse, his opponent Mr Clinton had trust problems of his own in spades (even before Monica Lewinsky), which Mr Bush was unable to exploit because of his *volte face*. In raising taxes, Mr Bush had taken a step that was no doubt unpalatable to him, but which was felt necessary by most commentators at the time. Having raised them, it was his own right wing which crucified him for it. But for the promise made in New Orleans in 1988, Mr Buchanan would have had very little to attack with.

Mr Cameron and his Shadow Chancellor George Osborne seem to have learned the lesson. The *Built to Last* policy document is unambiguous about the deleterious effect of high taxes,[39] but it equally makes very clear that taxes are not going to be cut come what may. Instead, the document advocates 'creating stable foundations for enterprise and economic growth by strengthening the independence of the Bank of England and putting economic stability and fiscal responsibility ahead of promises to cut taxes', and 'sharing the proceeds of growth between investment in public services and tax reduction'.[40] They also seem more set on simplifying taxes, which have grown noticeably more complex during Gordon Brown's period of office, as the tax system has been used to try to achieve various social ends (Mr Osborne even floated the idea of a flat tax at one stage[41]).

So far, so sensible, and the political debate is switching anyway from the correct level of tax to the best methods for taxing (New Labour man Stephen Byers has, for instance, suggested scrapping inheritance taxes). Mr Osborne, somewhat cheekily as befits someone barely out of short trousers, has taken to pointing out that even Mrs Thatcher didn't promise to cut taxes: in 1979 she said she would reform the system and cut some taxes, but not to reduce the overall tax burden.[42] And because she made no rash promises, she was insulated from criticism when her Chancellor

Sir Geoffrey Howe, whose brief was to cut inflation, was forced to raise taxes in the first couple of years of her period of office.

The dangers of making promises that one cannot know whether one can keep are obvious. And there is an interesting circularity here, in that those urging promises of tax cuts are precisely the people who will attack if those promises have to be broken. Nothing Messrs Cameron and Osborne have said implies that they wish to raise taxes. This is all well and good. They need, and should, say no more.

The constitution

If we move from the sphere of concern of the private individual to the construction of an arena for public life, we are drawn inexorably to the constitution, where Mr Blair has been very active in his period of office. It is, after all, a cheap way of being radical. As well as introducing a Freedom of Information Act, and bringing the European Convention on Human Rights into British law for the first time, he devolved power to Scotland, Wales, London and Northern Ireland. Unfortunately, these made his life trickier than he anticipated. Playing with the constitution, he should have realised, is not a simple matter – as our constitution is so intertwined, having grown organically over centuries in response to vastly different circumstances, it is in a very delicate balance. My own study of a particular constitutional novelty, the European referendum of 1975 (still the only national referendum that has taken place in the United Kingdom) shows how its unintended consequences spread far and wide, and indeed how hardly any of the intended consequences happened at all.[43]

In Scotland, where devolution was generally if not universally welcomed, the new Parliament managed to get itself embroiled in an unseemly argument, not about politics, but the building in which it is housed. Initial estimates of a cost of £40 million were impressively incorrect; the final cost of the Parliament building in Holyrood, when it opened three years late, was £431 million (and even then the debating chamber had to be evacuated in 2006 when a beam collapsed during a debate). Personally, I have no problem with these costs. Indeed, a conservative, sensitive as ever to the importance of symbolism and myth, should support the use of imposing and grand buildings for government – and they do not come cheap. Equally, the conservative, in the tradition of Lord Salisbury, wouldn't have believed the estimate in the first place.

Wales and London provided different problems for Mr Blair. An inveterate centraliser, he was loath to devolve power unless he knew how it was going to be used (which isn't devolving power at all). In the end he had to eat humble pie, and accept Rhodri Morgan and Ken Livingstone against his chosen placemen.

The worst area of Blairite indecision, of radicalism combined with a fatal lack of bravado, is of course in the reform of the House of Lords. Many a conservative voice, Enoch Powell's perhaps the loudest, has counselled against reform over the years. The executive, the Commons, the judiciary, the Lords, all these have various powers and a certain amount of legitimacy, and though no one would set up a system like this, the British system has grown so that those without the legitimacy of a democratic mandate have limited powers to restrict those who have. The balance is crucial, and the system worked reasonably well (compared, say, with the impeccably democratic American system which often silts up with bi-partisan brinkmanship and tit-for-tat vetoes). When Labour was elected in 1997, its radical rhetoric led most people to assume that there would be a wholly elected chamber. But Mr Blair does not now wish this to happen – an elected chamber, he believes, would challenge the primacy of the Commons.

Well, no doubt it would. That's what happens if you hope to set up a chamber to monitor and act as a check on the Commons and give it sufficient power so to do. The trick is to produce a system where the monitors have just enough power to restrain the Commons, yet not enough to usurp its functions. The slow evolution of the British system over time achieved that. A completely new system designed from scratch is a much harder proposition.

The conservative will, of course, smile smugly at the confusion, with an 'I told you so' expression on his or her face. The constitution is always in a state of delicate balance. All politicians and officials work to try to increase their responsibility, and their budgets; they oppose each other in subtle ways that have usually grown out of long experience. The baroque structure that is the constitution therefore encodes a huge amount of practical wisdom from centuries of lawmaking, legislating and protecting the rights of the citizen. Hence mucking about with it will cause problems. If you devolve power, for example, you don't have it any more. Goes without saying.

But it is here that Mr Cameron made one of his biggest mistakes as leader, in an ill-advised attempt to challenge the Human Rights Act.[44] The HRA was drafted into British law by the Labour government to regularise an anomaly in the law, whereby as signatories to the European Convention on Human Rights the government had to respect those rights. However, the rights themselves were not part of British law. So anyone who felt their human rights had been breached had to exhaust the appeals process within British law (which was not able to make the required judgement) before taking a further appeal to the European Court. By incorporating the Convention into British law as the Human Rights Act, many if not all rights-based questions could be sorted out more easily and quickly.

Many have been dissatisfied with this state of affairs, largely because of the odd occasions where malefactors or evil-doers, or just unpopular people, had successfully sued because of a breach of their human rights. Mr Cameron, in a speech to the Centre for Policy Studies, offered to repeal the HRA, and replace it with a Bill of Rights. But he didn't offer to leave the European Convention, which is fortunate since that would be a very serious constitutional matter indeed – it would involve, for instance, leaving the European Union. So the rights in question would still be held by malefactors and evil-doers, but the situation would be complicated still further by the Bill of Rights.

Add to this the fact that the European Convention was largely drafted by British lawyers to preserve the British Common Law experience, which has generally been humane and successful in preventing tyranny and protecting the weak, and that therefore little in the Convention is alien to British law as it stood before the HRA, and Mr Cameron's suggestion seems remarkably odd and ill-judged. The constitution is a delicate thing. Mr Blair has done it no good whatsoever, and Mr Cameron needs to show much more care than he has so far.

Race, multiculturalism and immigration

The politics of race are fraught for conservatives. The reason is obvious. New entrants to a country, from markedly different cultures, will threaten to alter the indigenous culture. The change principle looks as if it will be violated. The problem with this is that the negative position will skirt very close to racism. And even if it were possible to mark out a distinctively conservative position that was just, respected human rights and could be shown to be non-racist, in our multicultural country it could still be electorally disastrous.

Conservatives (small 'c') must accept that Britain undoubtedly *is* a multicultural country. Some cities have very large populations from the ethnic minorities, and as a whole 4.5 million people obviously make a giant contribution to British culture. It is the job of the conservative to meet society as it is, not as he or she would wish it to be; indeed, unlike other ideologues, the *whole point* of the conservative's philosophy is that his or her wishes about how society be governed and constituted are explicitly understood to be irrelevant. The conservative imposes as little as possible on his or her fellow citizens.

The irony is that immigrant communities in the United Kingdom contain many whose instincts chime in fairly naturally with a number of aspects of conservative philosophy. There are some close parallels between conservative thinking and religiously based ideologies, which deserve some exploration. Religion is the foundation of many societies, and contains, in a suite of rituals and moral precepts, much of a society's inherited wisdom, and many important aspects of a culture's identity. So conservatives can join with, say, Islamists[45] or Christian fundamentalists[46] to oppose progressive attempts to impose an instrumental reason (that is, reason directed towards the attainment of a particular ideological or material end) over and above the practical reason expressed in the institutions and practices of those religions. Tory leaders have not been backward at this tactic for a while, and Mr Cameron is as willing as anyone to try a bit of the old flannel to religious and community leaders from ethnic minorities.[47]

That there is more than a touch of self-interest in Mr Cameron's speeches here, and for that matter those of Messrs Hague, Duncan Smith and Howard before him, should not obscure the fact that the sort of practical reason embedded in community institutions is of deep importance to many conservatives.[48] For example, Quintin Hogg wrote in 1947 that:

> For myself I say quite plainly that I can see no hope for secular society unless it be based on a fundamental recognition of the spiritual nature of man and the providence of God, and in return I believe that religion owes to secular society the debt of recognizing that without the stability of the social order a full religious life becomes impossible except in the hermit's cell or in the monastery.[49]

A cleavage appears between the religious ideologies and conservatism, though, in two ways. First of all, much depends on the society. A religious society, as for example America or many of the conservative Muslim states of the Middle East, with a high level of belief and observance, might well require religious precepts to be enacted at a political level in order to respect the change principle. In that case, conservatives would at a minimum not wish to impose anti-religious policies on such a society. On the other hand, in a secular society, the imposition of religiously inspired law from a position of political authority would clearly violate the change principle, even if the perception was of a society that was formerly devout but now not. In a secular society, the conservative has no business imposing religion.

And second, there is a question of what religion brings to our understanding of the world. If the religion brings certainty about the constitution of the world, moral precepts and the social order, then it is hard to see how it can be reconciled with either the change principle or the knowledge principle. It goes without saying that the knowledge principle shows that we can never achieve such certainty about society. And anyway, religiously guided politicians will find themselves either preserving a godly society and *preventing* its organic change and development, or actively *engineering* a godless society in a particular direction; in either case violating the change principle.

Religion and conservatism sit together most happily when the religious aspect brings a deep sense of spiritual mystery, a sense that, though there is an order to things underpinned by God, that order is forever and tragically beyond our grasp. Lord Salisbury, perhaps the most religious of our conservative thinkers, was driven precisely by this sense of devout mystery, which fitted into his pessimistic conservatism from an early age. But the ideology that follows is remote from the writings of the Christian right, or the Islamist.

'The light is too dazzling for our weakened eyes,' [Salisbury] wrote to his sister Blanche from Cape Town about the doctrines of Original Sin and the Fall of Man; 'we must turn from it, lest it blind us. At the proper time we may logically test these doctrines, and if true accept them. But as a habit we must not think of them.' Yet for [Salisbury] there never was a proper time. He preferred to take the view that the ways of God were too unfathomable to be explicable to man, that no human experience could possibly come close enough to His to make any attempt to employ reason or logic worth while.

'God is all-powerful, and God is all-loving, and the world is what it is!' he would say to his children when they attempted to apply logic to their faith: 'How are you going to explain *that*?'[50]

Britain is, as I have said, a multicultural place. No getting around that, and silly to try. But a real debate, in the context of the alienation that has led to racial unrest in some cities, and in extreme cases terrorism, about governmental and social attitudes towards multicultural*ism* has begun. Basically, the problem is whether those whose identities are at least partly created in the context of non-indigenous cultures are under any obligation to sublimate those aspects of their identities and instead meet various cultural demands determined by the host nation. In many countries – the United States and France come to mind – the national identity is fairly well-understood in terms of a set of principles that you ultimately have to go along with as an immigrant. The United Kingdom, however, as a trading nation, has always prided itself as being a hands-off sort of place; institutions such as the Académie Française strike us as bossy, while American-style flag-worship makes our toes curl. The British version of multiculturalism has generally tended to allow people to do their own thing, to follow their own creeds and observe their religions in their own way.

Small 'c' conservatism about multiculturalism can, in fact, go either way. The conservative is worried about change, and so the influx of obviously foreign people can be seen as threatening. Furthermore, in the most extreme versions of multiculturalism, the role of the state gets adapted to meet the needs or preferences of all communities; the state is there not only to protect the cultural specificities of immigrant communities, but also to foster and encourage them. In its worst form, the idea seems to be that all cultures are equal, except that of the English, which is inferior to everyone else's. It is in schools where the arguments here are most heated, when Christmas is not celebrated, or British history is represented as a litany of imperialist outrages, or Shakespeare, Donne, Swift, Dickens and Hardy dismissed as so many dead white males (Jane Austen and George Eliot become honorary males for these purposes), and therefore *irrelevant* – the worst insult that can be thought of. This kind of psychopathic political correctness is easy to disparage, but very tenacious, and certainly a legitimate target for conservative attack. But it is important to realise that, though extreme multiculturalism takes this form, there are many more moderate voices who see within cultures much of value, and who are uncomfortable forcing anyone to adopt a particular way of life.

On the other hand, British culture and political institutions have always eschewed a canonical way of life, and if there is any particular theme that runs through British history it is that of toleration and the protection of those who wish to be unusual. Of course, there have always been periods of intolerant persecution, but these have been relatively minimal compared to any other country, relatively short-lived, and always overcome in the long run. Hence it was that, famously, Karl Marx wrote his greatest works in Britain where he was safe from persecution, and nowadays hundreds of politics lecturers can devote their time to bad-mouthing the British government, while not only being perfectly safe from its retaliation but also on its payroll. The idea of citizenship tests, language tests and all the flag-saluting panoply seems somewhat unBritish.

So a conservative line on multiculturalism has to pick its way carefully through a minefield, avoiding the twin dangers of a *Guardian* or *Daily Mail* mentality. The corresponding risk is of being devoid of content. Mr Cameron has form here.

> And I want to say something this morning about integration – about how we build stronger, more cohesive communities. It is a vital task. British Hindus are truly British, but have achieved this without giving up their religious and cultural traditions. And if you prefer to be referred to as British Hindus

or British Indians rather than as simply Asians, we should welcome that as a positive thing. Out of a misplaced sense of politeness, politicians have too often spoken of ethnic and religious minorities as though they are independent blocs who share nothing with the so-called 'host' nation, other than the same set of borders. Politicians may have adopted such a tone to avoid offending anybody, but the effect was that many minorities who were keen to integrate got the impression that they could never truly be British. That is wrong. It is time for a different approach – one that talks about the country we are building together. In fact, few nations are more suited to making a multi-ethnic society work than Britain. After all, Britishness evolved, in part, as a way of uniting the ethnically different nations of these Isles under a common civic identity. It's time for that idea to be renewed. Britain should not just be, in the words of the professor Lord Bhiku Parekh, a community of communities. There should be over-arching values which unite every individual and give meaning to our citizenship. These values need to be reinforced through institutions and shared culture and experiences. Those values – of hard work, tolerance and family – are ones you and I share. They are transmitted from parents to children and within communities. This happens spontaneously through human interaction and, of course, government cannot, by itself, impose values on people. Nevertheless, at a time of rapid change we all have a shared responsibility to consider what needs to be done to bind the nation together.[51]

This is certainly striking the right sort of note – no sign here of anything like Lord Tebbit's notorious 'cricket test', which poisoned relations between immigrant communities and the host for some years. And certainly no sign of the intolerance of the 2005 election manifesto, which Mr Cameron was instrumental in creating. But the 'values' that Mr Cameron ultimately gets around to mentioning are somewhat underwhelming.

In the first place, they are, as he says, values shared by many communities; maybe all communities understand the importance of families and hard work. If all communities share the values of hard work, tolerance and family, then they will have had these values in their own home nations, and brought them to Britain. In fact, hard work, tolerance and family are more likely to be rejected by the host population than most immigrants. If everyone agrees, then where's the problem? What sources of tension can there be? Why do those in the ethnic minorities feel it is difficult to feel British if that is all that is involved? Mr Cameron, in this speech, often sounds as if he is talking to the dissolute ethnic majority, not minorities.

No, if you are going to back away from multiculturalism to the extent of looking for values that are to do the job of uniting us, then there is no way round some painful decisions. To the extent that multiculturalism is seen to have failed, there must be values that have to be instilled into immigrant communities, values that will help promote unity in the nation at large, and which are either rejected by or irrelevant to minority groups. Furthermore, there must also be sticks as well as carrots; there must be some method of encouraging recalcitrant groups to play along. That, of course, is much harder – particularly for a British conservative who is fundamentally tolerant.

Tolerance is a value that is not shared by all. The Conservative Party has been a home for intolerant people for some years, which is one reason why its recovery has been so tricky, and why Mr Cameron has to make careful speeches like the one quoted above. But many immigrant communities have been less than liberal over the years. The furores surrounding the publication of Salman Rushdie's *The Satanic Verses* and a series of cartoons depicting Mohammed in a Danish journal show that toleration is sometimes a hard choice for a deeply religious community. Equally, the response of British authorities was hardly robust either. Inflammatory threats against Mr Rushdie were not pursued by Mrs Thatcher's government, although he was put under government protection, and diplomatic relations with Iran were severed (and not reinstated until Iran had softened its position). But not much was done to address the affronted Muslim spokesmen in Britain itself.

It is not clear that things have got any better. Because former Foreign Secretary Jack Straw's constituency has a sizeable Muslim population, and because he will forever be associated with the disastrous invasion of Iraq (see below), he was not in a good position to protest when demonstrators against the Danish cartoons in 2006 carried placards such as 'Slay those who insult Islam'. In fact his ire was reserved for those who published the cartoons. Meanwhile, as a resurgent Iran reiterated the *fatwa* against Mr Rushdie in 2005 and again in 2006, and offered a reward of $2.8m for his life, very little was, or could be, done.

It is easy to poke holes in multiculturalism. But backing away from multiculturalism is harder than its opponents make it seem. It will of necessity involve a rather unBritish intolerance of intolerant people, and will also require a more aggressive attitude to be taken towards people who are already alienated. The risk, as is obvious, is that their alienation is increased, and that therefore the risk of terrorism and social unrest increases with it. There is nothing wrong with Mr Cameron, and other British politicians, addressing audiences of Hindus, Muslims or whoever, and dishing out a bit of flattery about the fine qualities immigrants bring to Britain. That is all to the good, and true as well. But requiring us to unite about a set of values will also involve lecturing and hectoring, if it is to be meaningful. If we all agree about those values, then we are already united around them; if we are not united, then we do not agree, and a firm debate has to be started. And such a debate might well exacerbate the very alienation it is supposed to prevent.

This is the sort of job that David Davis feels comfortable with.[52] Nevertheless, Mr Cameron has on occasion sounded a little more aggressive.

On community cohesion, we need firm leadership from moderate Muslim opinion, and leadership from the Government. In particular, we need follow-through when the headlines have moved on. A year ago, we were promised tough and concerted action to deal with the community crisis in our midst. But precious little has actually been done. While I certainly do not agree with all sixty-four recommendations of the Preventing Extremism Together Working Group, the Government should explain why it has acted on so few of them. And why is the Government still funding conferences addressed by Yusuf Qaradawi, the preacher who said, 'We must plant the love of death in the Islamic nation'? Why has so little been done to minimise the impact of imams who come to Britain and preach, often with little knowledge or appreciation of British values? Again, we have made constructive suggestions to strengthen the fabric of our society, including proposals for school exchanges and a national school leaver programme, teaching English to new arrivals, and proper teaching of history to all our children. A year ago I supported the proposal by Dr Siddiqui, Leader of the Muslim Parliament, for the establishment of a Mosques Commission to provide proper regulatory oversight of mosques, and ensure the involvement of young people in their management committees.[53]

This is a stronger speech, but the aggression is much more firmly towards the government, rather than the moderate Muslim leadership, which is criticised implicitly but not explicitly. And again, it is somewhat harsh on the imams who have little knowledge or appreciation of British values, when so few British politicians have much of an idea of what those values are either.

The problem is that the arguments about multiculturalism and alienation tend to assume that people are malleable, and that they are easily moveable. Neither of those is true. Setting out a group of values that can unite us as British people is no bad thing. But it will not be possible simply to throw anyone out of the country who does not subscribe to them. Multiculturalism has not succeeded in creating the harmonious nation that we would all like to see, but there are no simple and painless alternatives. It may well be that intra-British exchange programmes, and a scheme for school leavers to do public service, may go some way to causing people of different ethnic backgrounds to mix, as Mr Cameron has suggested,[54] but can we really believe that such experiences as these, lasting a few hours a week for a limited period, can create the sort of bonding and camaraderie that the total immersion in national service for two years produced, whose effects he hopes to replicate?

It should also be said that a reversion to the outright hostility towards immigrants that has surfaced off and on in the Tory Party, most notably in the politics of Enoch Powell, is not an option either. A change in the constitution of the population has occurred, and it is the conservative's business to *manage* that change, not to prevent it, nor to reverse it. We are currently living through a period of giant migrations, which our immigration laws are designed to prevent (or, rather, to deflect elsewhere). As Lord Salisbury would no doubt have reminded us, this is irresistibly reminiscent of King Cnut trying to hold back the tide, especially at a time when short-term labour shortages and the long-term aging of the population mean an *increase* in demand for immigrant labour, both short-term and long-term. It is futile to stand in the way of great social changes.

The result of our being silly Cnuts has been obvious. Some of those who wish to emigrate legally to the United Kingdom have been put off, and continue to live less productive lives in less productive parts of the world (rather than being able to send remittances back to their country of origin – and remittances from émigrés, at $100 *billion* annually on official figures alone, dwarf development aid[55]).

But many pay large sums of money to illegal people smugglers, and incidentally put their lives at risk, as several tragic incidents have recently demonstrated. It is not at all clear why people prepared to pay large sums of money to come to the United Kingdom, and prepared to work very hard, are not simply allowed to do so in somewhat greater numbers. Indeed, given that illegal people smugglers can charge large fees, why can't the authorities undercut the gangs' source of profits by charging a somewhat lower, but still substantial, fee for immigration? And if immigration and working in Britain was made easier, then immigrants would feel less obliged to stay for long periods if they felt that they could come and go somewhat more freely, thereby reducing pressures on population and culture. The attempt to restrict immigration, as with drugs, has created all sorts of criminal opportunities. That is not to say that the existence of criminality should lead automatically to deregulation; far from it. But when considering the situation from the point of view of the change principle and the knowledge principle, it is still an important datum. It is at least in Mr Cameron's favour that arguments about immigration and asylum, which seemed very pressing when the first edition of this work was published in early 2005, are now much more amenable to rational discussion.

Europe

Having looked all too briefly at the personal and the formal aspects of British society, we should look at the relationship between British society and others. To begin with, we should grasp what has been a stinging nettle indeed for the Tories: Europe.

We needn't spend a great deal of time over a conservative attitude to the big European questions. Britain has been in the EU for some 30 years now; it affects our financial governance, our political governance, our diplomacy, our employment patterns and our law. The effects have been enormous. Withdrawal from the EU altogether is not a conservative option (even if it were feasible). But while we should remain within the EU, quite obviously a conservative in Britain at this time should be Euro-sceptic.

It is hard to imagine a less conservative course of action than, for example, changing the currency and putting its control in the hands of bankers over whom one has no control at all, or rewriting the constitution. Even where less overarching policies come from Brussels, it is clear that Eurocrats have little democratic mandate and relatively little knowledge of British society and politics. In general, it is not their job to ensure that policies fit into the warp and weft of life in Britain (or any other country, for that matter), and there is no reason to think, *ab initio*, that European-inspired legislation will not have serious unintended consequences for British society.

David Cameron clearly subscribes more or less to this conservative vision of the relationship between Britain and Europe, and was of course stung by his involvement in Black Wednesday as one of Norman Lamont's advisors. This has produced a Euroscepticism in him, which is perfectly reasonable in itself, except he has unfortunately upset the carefully balanced settlement brought in by William Hague, as a result of a rash promise made during the darkest days of his campaign for the leadership of the party. At a time when no one was taking a great deal of notice of him, he promised to pull Britain out of the centre right grouping in the European Parliament, the European People's Parties, on the ground that parties in the EPP – most of the mainstream right, including Angela Merkel's Christian Democrats in Germany, Jacques Chirac's UMP, Jose-Luis Aznar's Partido Popular and Silvio Berlusconi's Forza Italia – generally espoused a federalist vision of deepening European Union.

Such a vision is of course anathema to conservatives, to Tories and in general to most sides of British politics. However, it is not obvious that leaving the EPP was a wise move, since on continental Europe, right-wingers who are opposed to the deepening of intra-EU relations are a loony lot on the whole, and many enjoyed the spectacle of the über-fragrant Mr Cameron rubbing metaphorical shoulders with the ghastly Jean-Marie le Pen, the weird and not-so-wonderful Kaczyński twins and a certain Robert Kilroy-Silk.

According to reports, Mr Cameron had not consulted widely about the plan, and had relied on the advice of one MEP and *Telegraph* leader-writer who rather misled him about the political situation in the European Parliament.[56] Actually, there was a lot of support within the Tory MEPs for remaining in the EPP, and good strategic reasons for so doing.[57] Certainly he could hardly have expected his Shadow Foreign Secretary, Mr Hague, to put everything into forming a new group, as it was the same Mr Hague who had created the post-1997 European settlement in the Tory Party in the first place. In the end, Mr Cameron had to climb down; the new grouping was put back to 2009, though he still remained bullish about its prospects and critical of the EPP when announcing this climb-down.[58] No party, certainly not the Tories, functions well when it is out on a political limb. Mr Cameron has kicked this issue into the long grass, and anyone who wishes the Tories well must hope that is where it stays.

Iraq and neoconservatism

On the international scene, one cannot really avoid brief mention of the crisis in Iraq. Britain has remained a close ally of the USA throughout the whole *imbroglio*, which at least demonstrated a very conservative understanding of the nature of political power and its relation to the ability to apply force. Compare the British stance with that of France, which almost seemed determined to provoke the Americans into an illegal invasion (had President Chirac wanted that result, it is not clear what, in the run up to the invasion, he would have done differently).

The Americans themselves were principally driven, in the aftermath of the attack of 11 September 2001, by the neoconservative analysis of people such as Paul Wolfowitz, Richard Perle and William Kristol. These commentators and politicians had a particular view of the Middle East, and argued for a reversal of traditional US policy in the region of garnering support by making friendly gestures towards Arab regimes, most notably Saudi Arabia – key to American energy requirements – and Egypt, the latter in return for its more compliant stance towards Israel. The neocons (as they have become known) argued that, given that all Arab regimes are undemocratic, and most of them corrupt, this policy, while it may have short-term benefits, is disastrous long-term, because ultimately most Arabs see their own governments, rightly, as major obstacles to their freedom and prosperity. Hence cutting deals with unsavoury Arab regimes merely fuels future anti-American terrorism. On the neocon analysis, then, the smart thing to do would be to remodel the Arab world in democratic fashion.

But who are the neocons? Is the remodelling of the Arab world to be done for reasons of principle (a somewhat arrogant viewpoint), or for the long-term security of America (an even more arrogant viewpoint)? One thing is sure – the neocons aren't conservatives proper, because conservatives are wary of remodelling anything. The neocons have a fairly chequered history, with many inconsistencies between their major thinkers (as with any other ideological position – this is not a criticism), but one can discern a number of themes in their thought. Their chief formative experiences were opposition to Stalinism after the Second World War, and to the leftist counterculture from the 1960s onwards, including the 'culture wars' in the 1990s and onwards. Hence they have cleaved to a conservative-sounding position against social engineering, and have opposed the changes that the broad left has tried to impose on American society, such as a revision of gender roles, toleration of alternative sexual lifestyles including sexual promiscuity, toleration of and even proselytising about drugs, and a willingness to consider alternative family forms, including same-sex couples and communal living.[59]

On the other hand, neoconservatives are unlike authentic conservatives in three important ways. In the first place, they fight, and are fighting, tooth and nail to preserve the various institutions they feel important, such as the family. Now, there is no doubt that the family is a vital institution, and nothing whatsoever wrong with intervening to make living together easier, especially for couples with children. No conservative would ever gainsay the importance of the family. But equally, the assumption that there is a knowable ideal familial form is deeply unconservative because it transgresses the knowledge principle; society is way too complex to make such judgements straightforwardly. And the further assumption that, despite decades-long social movements, it is the politician's job to hold back the tide (even if that were possible) contravenes the change principle – as we have often had cause to say, holding back undesirable social development is as much social engineering as is trying to make desirable social development happen.

In the second place, the neoconservatives hold a (possibly sanitised) view of mid-century America as in some sense their ideal. There is nothing wrong with this either – after all, it was a nice place – but conservatism proper has to be imbued with a sense of place. A conservative from one place preserves things from that place; he does not export them to other places, because that, once more, is social engineering, not conservatism. So neoconservatism, with its respect for the American constitution, democracy, freedom, economy and family structures, may – just about – be regarded as conservative in the American context, but is actually very radical in other contexts, such as the United Kingdom. This is why the various attempts by Tory opposition leaders to emulate George Bush's compassionate conservatism have run into quicksand.

The third problem stems from the neocons' strong foreign policy dimension. They contend that in dealings between states, the internal character of the states with which one deals also matters. Propping up horrible dictators is un-American, and foreign policy must reflect the deeper values of liberal democracies. Neocon foreign policy analysts point to many occasions, from the two world wars to the Balkans, when America has used her massive firepower to moral effect.

Furthermore, the neocons are sceptical of the legitimacy and effectiveness of international institutions. This in itself is somewhat unconservative, because the legitimacy of institutions depends to a large extent on their effective dealing with crises, and their responses (rarely laid down in advance) to situations where their competencies are stretched (just as with legal institutions in domestic polities). Effectiveness, of course, can be measured, but without American support few international institutions could really cope anyway. It is certainly true that the Geneva Conventions do not cope very well with the concept of a global *jihad*, as opposed to conventional warfare. But that is no reason to scrap Geneva and behave as if all rules or constraints have gone.

These thoughts about the international world led the neocons close to George Bush to push for regime change in Afghanistan and Iraq. Afghanistan was one thing, a dreadful place that was certainly dysfunctional enough to justify overriding the change principle. But having got rid of the Taliban, the coalition forces then characteristically neglected the recovery, allowed the Taliban to regain a foothold in the South on the border with Pakistan, underfunded the relief effort and undermanned the security services. Afghanistan is now back supplying the world with all sorts of nasties again, and the judgement that it is a better place than it was in 2001 is now harder to make with confidence.

Iraq is a different kettle of fish. The most stunning fact about the whole debacle is that the Americans seem to have gone into Iraq after months (if Washington insiders are to be believed, years) of military and diplomatic preparation, without a single clear idea of what they would do when they won the war (and, extrapolating counterfactually, presumably what they would do if they lost). It seems that barely a single one of the famously superintelligent Republican wonks in the Washington Beltway gave any thought to reconstructing a complex society of 25 million people, or even anticipated much difficulty. Even given the natural (though in the event false) assumption that American liberators would be welcomed with open arms, putting together a democracy in a country known for authoritarian misrule was unlikely ever to be straightforward.

No conservative of the sceptical tradition would have made this elementary mistake. No sceptical conservative would have missed the potential for a power vacuum developing upon Saddam Hussein's removal; *all* attempts to reconfigure power structures leave vacuums. That Iraq is a complex place, with millions of people, including three different antagonistic ethnic/religious groups, and a set of traditions distinctly uncongenial to democracy and market systems of exchange, makes the problem even harder.

It beggars belief – particularly after the difficult, though not uniformly unsuccessful experience of transforming the economics of the former Soviet Union in Eastern Europe from socialist to capitalist – that the Americans thought that Iraq would be a breeze. Societies are not prone, like the lion from whose paw Androcles removed the thorn, to gratitude, to a long-term view of their own best interests, to having their problems sorted for them by professionalised outsiders. As the conservative argues so forcefully, societies bite back.

Which is why the international institutions' legitimacy outstrips neocons' estimates of it. A world order based on American hegemony will not work, because that type of order requires too much of the 'world's policeman'. As Francis Fukuyama noted wryly, 'the hegemon has to be not just well-intentioned but also prudent and smart in its exercise of power'.[60] Prudent indeed, because when ambitious neocon rhetoric is put into action, the unintended consequences are vast, with global scope. Changing regimes are about as geopolitically wild as it gets. To take the most obvious unintended consequence of recent American action in the Middle East, the revolutionary Shia government in Iran has been strengthened enormously by the removal of its two big regional Sunni threats, the Taliban and the Ba'ath regime of Saddam Hussein. The world is only just beginning to grapple with the malign consequences of that.

Mr Cameron is not a foreign policy buff, but chose the fifth anniversary of the destruction of the World Trade Center to deliver his first keynote, which shows at least a sense of symbolism.[61]

The trick for Mr Cameron is to deliver the right sort of message, a disavowal of the neoconservative assumptions that Mr Blair has had to swallow, more or less willingly, in the five years since the attack, without resorting to anti-Americanism or, more stupidly, the desire to pull forces out precipitately (it does not follow that, just because one thinks it was silly to send in troops in the first place, one can pull them out willy-nilly – sometimes one has to help clear up one's own mess). Mr Blair's consistent support of George Bush, and the *contretemps* between Mr Cameron's predecessor Michael Howard and George Bush's spin doctor Karl Rove, makes it a little more palatable for the leader of a traditionally Atlanticist party to point out the error of the neocons' ways.

> Britain does not need to establish her identity by recklessly poking the United States in the eye, as some like to do. But we will serve neither our own, nor America's, nor the world's interests if we are seen as America's unconditional associate in every endeavour. Our duty is to our own citizens, and to our own conception of what is right for the world. We should be solid but not slavish in our friendship with America.[62]

So, given that Mr Cameron is not anti-American, but a robust and honestly critical friend, what is the substance of his foreign policy position?

> But I believe that in the last five years we have suffered from the absence of two crucial qualities which should always condition foreign policy-making. Humility, and patience. These are not warlike words. They are not so glamorous and exciting as the easy sound-bites we have grown used to in recent years. But these sound-bites had the failing of all foreign policy designed to fit into a headline. They were unrealistic and simplistic. They represented a view which sees only light and darkness in the world – and which believes that one can be turned to the other as quickly as flicking a switch. I do not see

things that way. I am a liberal conservative, rather than a neo-conservative. Liberal – because I support the aim of spreading freedom and democracy, and support humanitarian intervention. Conservative – because I recognise the complexities of human nature, and am sceptical of grand schemes to remake the world.[63]

That is, in truth, a not-terribly-deeply coded attack on the neocon view of the world, and none the worse for that. Conservatism (small 'c') *is* about humility and patience, about understanding that one has no monopoly of wisdom.

But what does liberal conservatism entail in this context?

A liberal conservative approach to foreign policy today is based on five propositions. First, that we should understand fully the threat we face. Second, that democracy cannot quickly be imposed from outside. Third, that our strategy needs to go far beyond military action. Fourth, that we need a new multilateralism to tackle the new global challenges we face. And fifth, that we must strive to act with moral authority.[64]

Well, maybe that is a large enough dose of motherhood and apple pie for anyone to swallow. But Mr Cameron's conservative instincts here are very sound indeed. The lacuna in his speech is the extremely difficult part about what interventions in the Middle East, now, would meet the demands of these propositions. No one really knows that – it is a conservative assumption that destruction is infinitely easier than construction, and no conservative should be surprised that it is the wholly destructive insurgents who are the only force with any idea of what to do in Iraq.

Nevertheless, Mr Cameron's analysis of the problem, its causes and the respective failings of Messrs Bush, Rumsfeld and Blair, are absolutely convincing, and his 11 September speech may well go down as one of his most effective. Britain, as I have argued, is an increasingly liberal place, for good or ill, and a genuinely liberal conservatism would be an important tool for the Conservative Party. Like neoconservatism, Mr Cameron's liberal conservatism has only really looked three-dimensional in the foreign policy arena, and more flesh needs to be put on the bones. But no one can doubt that he has learned the important lessons of the Iraqi failure.

Terrorism and security

The mistakes of Iraq, of course, bring us back to the United Kingdom. There are many causes of Islamic terrorism, and Iraq is only one of them – serious attacks on Western targets long pre-date the 2003 invasion. However that may be, there is no doubt that Western societies, Britain especially, are under the threat of unprecedentedly bloody terror. The IRA conducted operations for decades, but they had, ultimately, a political aim; there is, of course, an argument about whether bombing one's way to the negotiating table is acceptable in a democracy, but at least in the IRA's demands there was always the germ of a political solution, even if that solution was impractical. But al-Qaeda is a different kettle of fish. It has no reasonable or sensible aims; it is as outraged and exercised by the expulsion of the Moors from Spain in 1492 as it is about American troops on Saudi soil – and says much more about both of these subjects than it does about more obvious problems such as the Israeli/Palestinian conflict. Its aim is to produce a global ummah by bombing the world back to the Middle Ages. Negotiation is not even an option.

The problem for the Western democracies, of course, is how to balance the demands of an open society against its security. Using obvious racial or religious markers to underpin security policy (not letting Muslims travel on aeroplanes, for instance) is a nonstarter. The threat level of terror will remain high for years, and so security will of necessity have to remain tighter than we have been historically used to.

We are unlikely to get the balance right – no conservative would believe such a utopian result possible. The question for policy-makers is whether to err on the side of liberty or caution. Do we protect our liberties or our society? There are obviously clear arguments for keeping those ancient liberties – not particularly because they are liberties, but because they are ancient. They are part of our society, and have evolved (they were never designed) to keep government from stifling social life while ensuring safety as far as possible. Innovations such as identity cards, or revocations of liberties such as the reduction of access to trial by jury, should clearly be worrying for conservatives.

It also goes without saying that there is a prominent authoritarian faction in the Tory Party that has often, if not always, carried the day against Tory libertarians. Such a debate, between liberty and security, is going on under Mr Cameron at the moment,[65] much less publicly than the debate over tax cuts, but it is a much deeper argument and a fundamental one, with profound consequences for all of us. Outside the party, in the grey 'deniability' zone, former chairman of the Joint Intelligence Committee Dame Pauline Neville-Jones, whose hawkish views include support for ID cards, is leading the National and International Security Policy Group, and will almost certainly weigh in with a plea to tighten up security against terrorism when that particular policy group reports. There are reportedly a number of heavyweights in the Shadow Cabinet who will support that line. Ranged against them are those with a stronger commitment to civil liberties. This debate has been conducted in relative silence, although a *Telegraph* report suggests that David Davis and Oliver Letwin are lined up with the doves, and David Willetts and George Osborne with the hawks.[66] That's a pretty equal fight. Given Mr Cameron's hoodie-hugging credentials, it may well be that his instincts veer towards liberty, and he will naturally award himself the casting vote.

There is a related, but separate question of tactics here. Labour, at the time of writing, is acting tough on security, and John Reid is the latest of a fairly long line of illiberal Home Secretaries. Under

Mr Blair Labour has assiduously ensured that it cannot be accused of being soft on crime and security – a constant charge during the 1980s – and the Tories are in danger of being outflanked on the right. The tactical question is whether there are more libertarian votes to the left of Labour, or whether the Tories will lose a number of core voters by deserting their traditional authoritarian territory. That's a tricky judgement, and not one that I would want to judge without a large amount of empirical evidence.

The ideological question is amenable to philosophical discussion, however. Britain's liberties are important, and should be preserved. But the fabric of society is also central; our freedoms have to be exercised in a secure framework, because otherwise fear makes us unfree. Protecting liberty from those bent on destroying it is as important as protecting it from encroaching governments. At different times, the balance between the two will alter; there seems to be little doubt that security has to be a priority for a conservative at an historical moment when there are people who wish to engineer change through the ruthless use of violent means. It is a deep shame that that is so, and it will always be important to nurture the love of civil liberties within the Conservative Party. There are few more important debates in society at the moment, and it is quite right that the Conservatives are having it. It may be here that the background of Mr Cameron counts against him: Old Etonians are impeccable at seeing the point of view of the badly off, rather less good at taking into account the concerns of the nervous middle classes.

Political science vs political engineering

As an image for the difference between conservatism and its ideological rivals, consider the distinction between science and engineering. Science is glamorous, it is the creation of knowledge, the discovery of the eternal truths about mankind's environment, about the universe, about the Earth, about all living things. Engineering is rather a second-class thing to want to do. The engineer doesn't worry about great truths, he or she worries about getting a thing to work. Design matters to the engineer. Things aren't abstract, or isolated, or theoretical: they are typically part of some wider system with which they have to interact, and the engineer's job is to worry not about the eternal, but about the immediate and contingent trade-offs. If I make this aero engine more powerful, that will make it heavier, which will reduce passenger capacity. If I design this lift to carry twelve people, then we will need to widen the counterweight shaft at the rear. Engineering's truths are not eternal. The systems engineers design are as robust as possible, and they have to be monitored constantly to ensure that they remain robust as the context changes.

Most ideologies try to produce some version of what we might call a political science. Conservatism (small 'c'), on the other hand, is political *engineering*. There may be ideals about how people should relate to each other, but those ideals bear a very tenuous relation to real life. Real societies have to work. They have to be pleasant environments for their populations; they have to interact reasonably well with other societies. All this takes place in a world constantly changing, where the context can never be taken for granted.*

The political scientist *par excellence* was Gladstone, whose idealistic pursuit of the greater good of mankind drove both Disraeli and Salisbury towards their often cynical positions, and Mr Blair certainly has tried to cast himself in the Gladstonian mould. When he is convinced of the moral rectitude of what he is doing – and I do not for an instant want to suggest that Mr Blair is

---

* In passing, another way of looking at this is to extend Hannah Arendt's idea (in a different context) that politics is a performative art. Liberalism and socialism, and indeed most non-conservative progressive ideologies, are after a product, a particular outcome. Conservatism (small 'c'), in contrast, focuses on the *process*, the *performance*. As Arendt puts it, political institutions 'depend for continued existence upon acting men'; they are embedded, and it is the acting that counts, not the Platonic ideal of the play. Cf. Hannah Arendt, 'What Is Freedom?' in Peter Baehr (ed.), *The Portable Hannah Arendt* (Penguin, New York, 2000), pp. 438–61, at p. 446.

not a man of great moral seriousness and sophistication – he is tireless and virtually unstoppable. I say 'virtually unstoppable' because reality often intervenes.

It is not credible that Mr Blair's vision of regime change in Iraq was as naïve as that of the neocons surrounding Mr Bush, but nevertheless the period following the successful toppling of Saddam has been difficult for Mr Blair in a way that he could never have expected. And back in Blighty, the attempt to create 'Cool Britannia' has not worked, as our public services remain poor, our transport systems threadbare, our population under-educated and unproductive. The impression is sometimes left (particularly when one has encountered a large group of Brits abroad) of Mr Blair as a denim-shirted Prospero governing a crumbling island of Calibans.

Where Mr Blair has succeeded – and the problem for the Tories is that his record is comparatively good for a British Prime Minister – is in the areas where his ministers have rolled up their sleeves and done the serious, painstaking, unglamorous work of examining services, testing and evaluating improvements objectively, finding the money, and – not least – not burdening the system with Prime Ministerial expectations. This is all political engineering in the conservative tradition.

The Conservative Party's secret weapon may be that this is not what Mr Blair wants to be remembered for.

CHAPTER EIGHT

CONSERVATISM AND TRUST

The crisis of trust: the official story

In the new politics of the 21st century, 'trust' is the watchword. Like 'inflation' and 'unemployment' in the 20th, the 'T' word is the key to understanding a remarkable proportion of the things that politicians in the mature democracies do. The official story is that politicians have overused their authority and power, and that there is a huge disconnection between them and the voters; the latter are confused and bored by the new politics. Politicians seem strangely powerless to do anything about the great globalising forces that batter the country and the economy. Bizarre regulations are passed down from unaccountable officials in Brussels independently of our wishes. The concerns of the public are ignored by politicians, who focus instead on the needs of business. British interests are all too often trumped by American interests. The Iraq war, hugely unpopular with voters, was nevertheless unstoppable. A sense of *ennui* has settled over the democratic process. No wonder that voters are disengaged.

This is reflected ideologically. The 60s, 70s and to an extent the 80s were characterised by ideologies emphasising various types of social *solidarity*. Not only conservatism on the right, but also socialism on the left and paternal liberalism in the centre were premised on the pooling of one's interests with others. The argument for politicians of the post-war period was how far one should sublimate one's own preferences for the greater good, and

265

which social groups one should see one's own wider interests resting with.

Nowadays the ideological universe is completely different. On the right, neo-liberalism rules. The radical left takes a postmodernist line (in the early days it was often argued that postmodernism was inherently conservative,[1] but it doesn't take much study of the scene nowadays to realise that, despite superficial similarities to conservatism, the anti-authoritarian power of postmodernist creativity is being exploited by the oppositional left). In the centre, egalitarian liberalism still holds sway, but in the adaptation developed by John Rawls,[2] which lays stress on the liberal's attempt to ensure that people are as free as possible to pursue their own individual idea of the good. The difference is that today's ideologies place a great deal of importance on people's individuality and autonomy.

The modern scene is almost unique in the widespread rejection of social hierarchies. Many commentators have detected a decline of trust well beyond the world of politics. We no longer trust scientists' claims about, for example, vaccines or GM foods in the wake of the BSE crisis. We do not trust businesspeople after Enron and Parmalat. According to many surveys, we do not even trust our fellow human beings very much at all; one widely quoted work worries aloud about our decreasing tendency to form social groups.[3]

So the crisis of trust has the potential to be something of a disaster. It threatens to undermine Western society exactly at the point at which some perceive it as being under threat from more vigorous traditions. Is there a role for conservatism here? Is it possible that conservatism has anything interesting to say that the new individualistic ideologies cannot?

Crisis?

The official version of the crisis of trust actually can be made to pack quite an anti-authoritarian message. At its most pungent, it says, in a nutshell, that the powers that be have been inadequate for various reasons (sometimes incompetence, sometimes venality), and that, as people have valued their individuality and autonomy more, they have ceased to be the supine citizens they were in the 1950s, say, and now are complaining and questioning more. We probably should be somewhat suspicious of such a glib reading of events. As philosopher Onora O'Neill puts it:

> Growing mistrust would be a reasonable response to growing untrustworthiness; but the evidence that people or institutions are less trustworthy is elusive. In fact I think there isn't even very good evidence that we trust less. There *is* good evidence that we *say* we trust less: we tell the pollsters, they tell the media, and the news that we say we do not trust is then put into circulation. But saying repeatedly that we don't trust no more shows that we trust less, than an echo shows the truth of the echoed words; still less does it show that others are less trustworthy.
>
> Could our actions provide better evidence than our words and show that we do indeed trust less than we used to? Curiously I think that our action often provides evidence that we still trust. We may *say* we don't trust hospital consultants, and yet apparently we want operations – and we are pretty cross if they get delayed. We may *say* that we don't trust the police, but then we call them when trouble threatens. We may *say* that we don't trust scientists and engineers, but then we rely on hi-tech clinical tests and medical devices. The supposed 'crisis of trust' may be more a matter of what we tell inquisitive pollsters than of any active refusal of trust, let alone of conclusive evidence of reduced trustworthiness. The supposed 'crisis of trust' is, I think, first and foremost a culture of suspicion.[4]

This is not to say that there is not a crisis, only that the nature of the crisis is that people are needlessly critical of professionals, public servants and others. Granted, many politicians actively inflate expectations for electoral purposes. Higher public spending without raising taxes, sir? Certainly. We'll just cut red tape and eliminate bureaucratic waste. Such politicians should not be surprised when they are rejected when shown to be hypocrites, too cowardly to tell the electorate the truth. But cowards make bullies, and the danger is that public expectations about what is possible become completely disconnected from the real world. It may be that the problems are with voters, not politicians.

And note that trust actually affects voting patterns surprisingly little; we do not often prefer the politicians we trust. Polls abounded saying how little trusted, in the wake of the Iraq war, Mr Blair was in the run-up to the 2005 general election; trust was going to be the big issue, where he was vulnerable. Yet even with this handicap, Mr Blair won comfortably, albeit with a reduced majority. But if trust ratings in opinion polls were informative, he would have had virtually no chance of winning. In one telling poll, voters were asked which politician, of a choice of four, they trusted: they trusted Gordon Brown the most, then Michael Howard, then Charles Kennedy, and last of all Tony Blair. Asked in the next question which politician, from the same choice, they would rather share a long train journey with, they preferred Mr Blair, then Mr Kennedy, then Mr Howard, and then Mr Brown.

In fact, Mr Blair, master of spin, has *never* been trusted by voters, and his three spectacular electoral successes measure up nicely to the records of other distrusted Prime Ministers, such as Harold Wilson (four general election victories out of five) and Margaret Thatcher (three out of three). On the other hand, more trusted leaders have failed dismally: Michael Foot, John Major, Edward Heath. This is a pattern repeated across the mature democracies; we do not seem to value a leader's trustworthiness particularly highly, certainly not compared with his or her effectiveness and ability to embody the *Zeitgeist*.[5]

Turnout and disengagement

But is this too sanguine a view? In March 2006, the POWER Commission published its report into the lack of public confidence in and engagement with politics, and it said almost exactly the opposite.[6] It worried about lowered turnouts, the estrangement of whole sections of the community from politics, the weakening of effective dialogue between governed and governors, the lack of recruitment into politics, the rise of undemocratic forces in society, and of authoritarianism in government.

POWER's research showed that apathy was not the problem; interest in political issues is high, and there is increasing participation in 'pressure politics' (e.g. consumer boycotts, signing petitions), and what is often called single-issue politics (focusing on one policy rather than an ideologically-driven range of policies).[7] It isn't obvious to me that that is a good thing.

The commission seemed to believe that the shift in voters' interests from party politics towards a more narrowly conceived idea of engagement showed that their political instincts had remained constant, but that they had been deserted by professional politicians. Nothing could be further from the truth.

One can support or oppose a political platform, but a platform has the advantage of involving a necessary balance of activities across the important fields of government. A government has finite resources, and it must make hard decisions about how much to devote to defence, education, health care, transport, trade, sport, women's rights and so on, and how much effort to spend on legislation and how much on administration. These are trade-offs. On the other hand, a single-issue party or group, as we have already had cause to note, focuses on its mission and nothing else. One can never satisfy a single-issue organisation, because it will always feel it has lost out in the inevitable scramble for resources.

Furthermore, because single-issue organisations do not seek to put forward a balanced political programme, they do not seek election into government (or very rarely – the UK Independence

Party is one exception, but not a happy example). This means that they never take any kind of responsibility for failure to achieve their aims. A famine in Africa will bring Bono and Bob Geldof to our screens, but it would not occur to them that the famine shows that their tactics for averting starvation are inadequate, and that they therefore should resign from public life, even though that is a plausible interpretation of the facts.

A programme developed by a political party involves the painstaking assembly of a series of promises that is intended to be coherent and affordable, at the end point of a process of negotiation and compromise. Such a programme is an institutional expression that a series of interests are willing to work together for a common goal, and are willing to sacrifice many of their demands in the face either of opposition to them, or of a lack of time or money to implement them. And such compromises, given the finite resources of government, are the only alternative to government by coercion.[8] Political opposition has to include within it the commitment to keep the political system going, even while trying to thwart the schemes of the government of the day.[9]

Being a democrat involves accepting democratic outcomes, which may mean the defeat of some proposal about which one might feel very strongly. But a single-issue group sees its purpose as being the opposite: it needs to keep up the assault even if its aims are defeated or demonstrably lacking in support. In the most extreme example of this kind in domestic politics, some animal rights protesters, in the face of widespread public indifference and opposition to their aims, have launched increasingly violent and unsavoury campaigns against those who are going about their lawful business. The commission may well be correct to say that voters do not have a 'weak sense of civic duty',[10] but if more people are refusing to accept the inevitable compromises of democratic politics and instead concentrating their energies on individual issues, we surely have to say that such voters' senses of civic duty are strong, but deeply mistaken and misguided.

The commission divines six reasons why voters are turned off by mainstream politics.[11] It is certainly regrettable that these six perceptions of politics have led to a dramatic reduction of public interest in mainstream politics, and it is reasonable to want to do something about it. But is it not worth pointing out that none of them is actually a *good* reason to avoid politics? Let's look at them, one by one.

1. Citizens do not feel that the processes of formal democracy offer them enough influence over political decisions – this includes party members who feel they have no say in policy making and are increasingly disaffected.

But citizens have more say over policy than virtually ever before, in any society, anywhere; Mr Blair was criticised for years for his reliance on focus groups, and was often told that he must show leadership. When he did show leadership, by supporting the invasion of Iraq, he was accused of a 'quiet authoritarianism'.[12] Which may well be another way of telling him to consult more focus groups.

Members of the three major parties have, it is true, been sidelined from the policy development process somewhat over the last few years, but only because they tended to come up with cretinous policies that prevented their leaders from attaining office. And ultimately, the desire to ditch party politics because one cannot get one's own way is an example of exactly the same pathology that drives single-issue politics, the inability to compromise.

2. The main political parties are widely perceived to be too similar and lacking in principle.

Too similar, eh? Unlike, say, the 1960s and 1970s, when red-blooded ideologues like Tony Benn and Enoch Powell, Margaret Thatcher and Barbara Castle bawled at each other like mastodons

271

bellowing across the primeval swamp (to misquote P.G. Wodehouse). I have tried to present a sketch of this extraordinary period elsewhere.[13] One certainly reads of worries about the

> tendency to abandon ideological commitment, sometimes of old date, in favour of short-term, pragmatic policies. ... Can the giving up of ideological positions lead to a loss of esteem with the public? ... The traditional antagonisms of class allegiance and doctrinal pledges have been toned down to contrasting views of the application of public policies, broadly agreed upon by both the electoral channel and the party leadership. The central sectors of both parties, relatively large in comparison with their outer fringes, show an obvious tendency to come together, submerging other longstanding divisions. ... To some extent this accounts for the general feeling that party programmes are interchangeable, that there is 'no alternative' ... and that politics have become very dull. It also leads many to feel a certain impatience with the very idea of party politics, now that there is no really substantial difference between the parties.[14]

This is exactly the feeling that the POWER Commission has detected. Except that those words were written in 1968, while the left of the Labour Party was hoping to end capitalism and right-wing Tories wanted to throw all the blacks out. This feeling that the parties are too similar is perennial; it is usually a symptom of a lack of understanding of the nature of politics, and a failure to engage with political history. And is it really better to be in a world of extremes? American politics has become much more polarised in recent years since the culture wars flared up, and is a worse-governed place as a direct result.

3. The electoral system is widely perceived as leading to unequal and wasted votes.

This one beggars belief, in one sense. The general perception that one's vote is wasted is, of course, true. All votes are wasted. In my home constituency, the sitting Labour MP won with a majority of 6,939. I did vote, as it happened, and it is clear that my vote made absolutely no difference to the result (except it affected the majority by one). So by that criterion, my vote was wasted. Indeed, in any constituency where the majority is two or more, each vote is wasted. No single vote will ever make a difference in any system designed to choose a few hundred representatives for tens of millions of people.

4. Political parties and elections require citizens to commit to too broad a range of policies.

It is perfectly reasonable that voters should dissent from some of the policies each party puts forward. One is faced with a number of policy slates, all of which will contain (a) policies one agrees with, (b) policies one disagrees with and (c) policies about which one could not give two hoots one way or the other. When one votes, one is not 'committed' to any of these policies. I might vote Labour because I think they will be more egalitarian than the Tories, though I disapprove of their Iraq policy. I might vote Tory because I think the state sector is too large, though I disagree with their line on immigration. It might be that no party has a slate of policies which enthuses me, or it might be that the only party that has what I consider decent policies has no chance of winning. Many people even vote for a party they do not support in order to prevent another party coming to power (tactical voting). It is unclear how such people are committed to anything that they have voted for.

And if anything, the parties are promoting fewer and fewer policies. Mr Blair asked, in 1997, to be judged on a political programme written on a credit card (one up, I suppose, on a fag packet). Michael Howard got his 2005 campaign down to ten words. Who is this too broad for?

273

5. Many people feel they lack information or knowledge about formal politics.

This is perhaps the most bizarre of the lot. Why do such voters not find out what they want to know? It's not hard.

6. Voting procedures are regarded by some as inconvenient and unattractive.

One wants to say: 'tough'. If someone can't summon up enough gumption to walk to the local church hall or scout hut to put a cross on a piece of paper, or to register for a postal vote, then I think I'm allowed to be sceptical of their 'sense of civic duty'.

The commission worries that political parties are after victory in general elections, rather than any wider goal. This is a perfectly fair comment: as psephology improves, political parties are competing for ever-smaller numbers of swing voters ('Basildon Man', 'Worcester Woman' and various other suburban homunculi). So parties' messages are targeted at ever-smaller numbers of key voters, ignoring the rest of us; no wonder we lose interest. This is not to say that the parties are coming together, only that they have a much stronger sense of who will definitely vote for them (and can therefore be ignored), and who needs to be wooed. Then factor in woeful ignorance and wilful cynicism on the part of many of us, to give us the net result of pipsqueak turnouts and the occasional brief flourish of silly populist parties such as the UK Independence Party.

The commission instead wants us to engage more democratically. Well, yes, all well and good. Let's have proper debates about things. But how is that to be managed? Here is one (genuine) and suitably ludicrous vision of a democratic future.

It feels very different to be a citizen in this new political system. ...

The start of the [election] campaign is marked by all

political parties emphasising the breadth of their manifesto policies rather than emphasising just five key pledges. Costed manifestos (and a merciless Audit Commission) have radically changed the style of campaigning from a negative attack on the other parties' spending plans to a positive promotion of their own policies. Gone too is the 'beauty contest' between individual party leaders as parties stress instead the broad range of their candidates, especially their women and ethnic minorities candidates. ...

The Alternative AV+ system empowers voters to choose their policy priorities in the sure knowledge that these choices will be reflected in the new parliament. Voters therefore do not mind spending up to fifteen minutes in the voting booth numbering their preferences from the three page ballot paper. Turnout reaches 90% as polling is spread across the Spring Bank Holiday every four years. Increasingly, voters use ICT facilities to examine the manifestos and research the options available before voting electronically during the three day election. ...

The local government elections produce mandates across the country for local hypothecated schemes covering everything from more drop-in centres for the homeless to more pre-school places. Electoral turnouts increase, doubling in local elections, as voters take control of the future of their public services through the proportional voting system.[15]

Sounds as ghastly as it is unlikely. Are 90 per cent of us really such nerds that we would forsake our precious holiday to stand in a booth for fifteen minutes reading three pages of guff? Oh, the queues that would engender! The shouts of 'GET ON WITH IT' one would have to endure! You don't have to think very much about the detail of democratic engagement to see the point of a system that delegates political work to specialists.

Add to all this the facts that those countries which do indulge regularly in very heavy doses of direct democracy (the United

States and Switzerland, most obviously) labour under pipsqueak turnouts; that the six explanations for what the POWER Commission persists in calling 'the disconnect' have all been true for decades; and that the phenomena causing such hand-wringing in the UK are common to many countries across Europe, and are noticeably worse in some places, such as France and Italy. The result is that, although the falling turnout is a bad thing, and although it would be nice to have lots of voters like they did in the more deferential 50s, it's not clear that we need to change the British constitution to the extent of the 30 recommendations of the commission.

A conservative attitude to the crisis of trust

The crisis in trust, then, is of somewhat debatable significance. Given that, there are three obvious questions the conservative needs to ask. First, as trust has a fairly tenuous connection with voting behaviour, should the conservative bother with the problem at all? Second, if the answer to the first question is 'yes', then what policies should he or she endorse to arrest the decline? Third, is it possible that the revival of conservatism as a realistic ideology in the 21st century would itself help address the problem of trust? We will answer the first two questions in this section, while the remainder of the chapter will be given over to answering the third.

The answer to the first question is pretty straightforward: yes, the conservative should wish to bolster trust in politicians and the political process. Grant that the public is not very trusting of politicians. An optimistic explanation of that is that they are properly understanding of the need for dissembling, even outright mendacity, in order to get things done in a complex world of constantly changing interests. A pessimistic one is that they are needlessly cynical. But either way, the conservative should be interested in fostering trust.

It is an axiom of conservative politics that a functioning society is inherently valuable. Society, at least sometimes and for at least some purposes, should come before the preferences of individuals. But trust is exceedingly important for that conception. After all, if citizens are going to (be asked to) defer or even eschew certain anticipated gratifications for a common good, then those making sacrifices must be confident that others will play their part as well. In particular, those in positions of power must be perceived to have clean hands, for it is they who formulate the choices that people must make, and who, in effect, suggest the sacrifices that must be made.

Hence trust throughout society, and trust in the political class in particular, is essential if people are going to be prepared, generally, to put the interests of society before their own. Note that this is to a surprisingly large extent an issue of *perception*: what is important is not so much that politicians are *trustworthy* (most of them are, pretty well), but that voters and citizens *think* they are – and as of September 2006 only 29 per cent of voters thought MPs trustworthy, while ministers scored a mere 23 per cent[16]). The task of any politician who wishes the interests of society to be felt to be more important than the interests of the individual is to foster the networks of trust that allow individuals to feel confident enough to put their interests to one side. Mr Cameron has a sensible line on this, advocating independent commissions to determine MPs' salaries and investigate breaches of the ministers' code, and cementing the independence of the civil service[17] (though whether this will prevent the squeals whenever MPs get a pay rise is perhaps another matter).

So moving to our second question: how should a conservative go about arresting the decline in trust? Politicians, perhaps more than most people, want to be loved, and if they think they are not, they are likely to act. Politicians worry about low turnouts and poor opinion poll ratings, however temporary these may be (or alternatively, however consistent with other social phenomena of disengagement they may be), and are often tempted to tinker with voting methods, or representational forms, in order to boost popularity. These changes, small as they usually are, can have far-reaching effects on the constitution. For instance, recent attempts in Britain to provide different methods of voting alongside the traditional polling booth – or indeed as replacements for the polling booth – will inevitably alter the profile of the constituency. Votes by post or mobile phone will be cast at varying times during the course of an election campaign, rather than, as now, at the climax of it. These changes may have negligible effect, or positive effect, or negative effect – there is no way of telling. The early indications are that they have led to a massive increase in electoral fraud.[18] They will tend to accentuate the divorce between people and their locality, merely by removing the requirement to stroll to the church or the town hall or whatever every so often. Combined with other electoral developments, like the introduction of the faceless proportional party list system in some elections, the result is to reward disengagement in politics. Is that a good thing or a bad thing? It is hard to tell, but the knowledge principle says that the constitutional meddlers do not know, and the change principle says that the risks are too great to endure.

Trust is extremely hard to drive; it cannot be created to order.[19] So it is not surprising that the knowledge principle tells us that we can never know if our trust-building measures will work, or indeed what unintended consequences they will have. The change principle tells us that radically reforming our political system in the hopes that trust will be achieved is very risky, and should only be done if the system is already shot to pieces.

Conservatives (small 'c') should therefore resist constitutional change, particularly on the scale envisaged by the POWER Commission. But changes in political *behaviour* are a different matter. They should trust their opponents to be trying to do their best for society, even if they don't think that the policies being suggested actually will help. They should trust voters. And they should not be afraid to give credit where it is due to ideological opponents; as we have had cause to note before, conservatives should be prepared to make U-turns when risky policies they have opposed turn out to have good effects. Conservatism is a humble ideology; not only does it not claim to have all the answers, it specifically claims that it does not. Others may have some answers, and if they have a mandate to experiment in some directions, the conservative, though he or she may warn of potential consequences, should not try to stand in the way.

Signalling trustworthiness

The issues discussed so far in this chapter have much to do with the daily rough and tumble of British politics, and with the media flurry around trust that has dominated political discourse for the last few years. But there is more here: it is my contention that conservatism has a stronger message with respect to trust than other ideologies, because of its strong connection with social continuity and epistemological scepticism. In the rest of this chapter, I want to explore some themes relevant to the sociology of trust, and to show how those themes resonate very strongly with the conservative.

To begin with, let us consider the distinction between *trust* and *trustworthiness*.[20] Trustworthiness is a property of a person (or institution, or system, or anything else that makes claims about performance – for the rest of this section I will limit my discussion to the case of individuals), which is that that person will typically do what she claims she will. If she is making a claim about her identity, then that claim will be true. If she claims to be acting in another's interests, then she will be so acting.

Trust, on the other hand, is an action of an observer; the observer *imputes* trustworthiness to an actor. If I trust you, then I have *come to believe* that you are trustworthy. If you claim to act in my interests, and if I trust you, then I may leave you to defend my interests, and take no action myself. If you claim to be about to perform some action, and I trust you, then I may make my future plans on the assumption that that action will be performed.

When I trust you, I make a judgement on the basis of what I can see. I cannot, of course, trust you to mend my car after seeing you mending my car, because my trust must come *in advance* of your action. So I look for by-products of trustworthiness, things that trustworthy people tend to do, or to say, and that untrustworthy people don't. If you do or say those things, then that is a decent reason to trust you. Appearing trustworthy is an art in itself; I should smile a lot, wear a suit, look concerned at others' troubles, and so on. I should display my certificates from professional bodies. Experiments have even shown that we are more likely to trust people who have symmetric faces.

It should go without saying that the best way to foster trust is to be trustworthy. But the connection is not solid: I may trust you without your being trustworthy; you may be trustworthy without being trusted. One might be trustworthy, at some cost to oneself, without being trusted.

Question: is it better to be trusted or trustworthy?

In a highly interactive world, being trusted is essential. Which means I had better *appear* to be trustworthy. But that doesn't actually *mean* that I am trustworthy. Just because I wear a suit that does not mean that I will not sell you a dud car, or run off with the church funds. We associate the outer forms that trustworthy people adopt with trustworthiness. Such forms – suits, smiles, certificates – then become *signals* of trustworthiness. I can signal my trustworthiness by wearing a suit and smiling. But then, once the signalling system is widely adopted, others who are not trustworthy can follow my example; untrustworthy people can wear suits and smile, and then they might be trusted too. The signals can be faked. Instead of being produced accidentally by trustworthy behaviour, they are produced on purpose, to create a deliberate impression.

This is the heart of the New Labour approach. Old Labour was not trusted, and the imperative was to regain trust. So New Labour focused on sending out those signals of trustworthiness. Out went the beards. Out went the jeans and pullovers. New Labourites wore suits. They were neat. The party colours were toned down from red to pink. A rose was used as the new logo. Certain words were dropped from the lexicon ('socialist' perhaps the most prominent). Clause 4, which committed the party to nationalising British industry, was noisily dumped (though not even Old Labour governments took it very seriously).

This was all a very conscious effort to send out different signals from those of the unpopular rabble that was Labour in the 80s. The rationale was that, to get anything done at a policy level, it was important to be trusted enough as a party to win elections. The Labour Party, by common consent unelectable, said it had changed; that message had to be trusted if it was to get back into power. Independently of whether New Labour was actually trustworthy, it was essential that it sent out enough signals to contradict any claim that underneath it was still the same old party.

Tory campaigns against New Labour at first tried to exploit the gap between the signals and their perception of reality. The famous 'demon eyes' campaign of 1997, showing the still-youthful, fresh-faced Mr Blair with red demonic eyes, supposedly conveyed that, however cosy he looked, he was really a front man for trade unionists, communists, loony lefties and so on (absurd as it now seems). The posters tried to persuade us that the signals Mr Blair was so assiduously sending out concealed his real character.

Of course they failed, and the position is now reversed. It is the Tories that are not trusted, and they are trying to send signals that they have changed, that they don't hate single mothers, or gays, and that they really do think there is such a thing as society. Like Labour, they have taken the simple expedient of changing their logo from the blue torch into a green scribble (at a cost of £40,000 – see Chapter Nine). Mr Cameron has attempted to show how he represents a changed party, following Mr Blair's strategy from the 1990s of borrowing the language of other parties, and demonstrating the same concerns as their supporters. For Liberal Democrat audiences, Mr Cameron is a liberal conservative; for Greens he is green, and so on. This led to his caricaturing by the

Labour Party in the run-up to the 2006 local elections as lovable squamate Dave the Chameleon.

> Dave changes from one colour to another, depending on whatever he thinks his audience wants to hear. To supporters of the blue party, he changes deepest blue and tells them he is 'Conservative to the core'. To supporters of the red party he changes into finest red, and tells them he is the 'heir to Blair'. And to supporters of the yellow party, he changes into brightest yellow and says he is a 'liberal Conservative'. He flip-flops from one position to another, depending on whatever he thinks you want to hear. But underneath it all David Cameron will always remain true blue through and through. 'I am Conservative to the core of my being, as those who know me best will testify'.[21]

This is the wrong argument. The signals Mr Cameron sends, and the signals Mr Blair is sending us too for that matter, are *all* bogus. They are literally irrelevant to the question of the trustworthiness of the two principals, because they are consciously sent in *order* to convince us of trustworthiness. Whether or not Messrs Cameron and Blair are trustworthy has nothing to do with their public faces, which are constructed entirely by professionals to attract our trust. The signals that they send out are not by-products of their trustworthy behaviour, but instead are manufactured to imply trustworthiness. That does not mean that they are not trustworthy, only that the signals are irrelevant to the question. And when signals matter more than their causes, we have a sign of the culture of spin.

This is not intended as a criticism of Messrs Blair and Cameron – if we voters persist in voting according to the headlines rather than the facts, then we cannot blame politicians for trying to change the headlines rather than the facts. If we vote against bald men, or beardies, then everyone will start the day with a combover and a shave. If it is our demand that MPs wear suits, then anyone with a few hundred quid can hurdle that obstacle.

If that is how we vote, that is the behaviour we will engender. It is our own fault if we don't like what we get.

Trustworthiness in politics

Trustworthiness involves much more than sending out comforting signals. In the political context, the concept has much to do with *reliability*, with adherence to *principles*, with pursuing the *common interest*; and with a certain *predictability* based on good faith.

These various attributes of the trustworthy politician can come into quite stark conflict with each other. For instance, consider the pursuit of the common interest. There will always be problems, in a complex society, in defining the common interest, and politicians will often struggle to do it persuasively. Politicians have a great deal of power (given to them in trust), and they may use it in their own interests. The trustworthy politician will, on the other hand, try to calculate the general interest and make decisions accordingly. But if the politician is not trusted, then voters may come to believe that she has not made any genuine attempt to take the interests of others into account. Instead, they may believe that the politician is covertly making decisions in her own interests, be they to make her richer, or more powerful, or to help out her friends.

Quite often, of course, answering the question of whose interests a politician is pursuing is not easy. A working-class politician who promotes the interests of the working class, a businesswoman promoting the interests of the business community, a gay politician promoting the interests of the gay community; each of these is arguably promoting her own interests as well as those of a wider group of people, and disentangling the personal from the public can be little more than a matter of (often ill-informed) opinion in many cases. 'The way of even the most justifiable revolutions is prepared by personal impulses disguised into creeds.'[22] Given the complexity and inequality of most Western societies, there will be several possible interpretations of 'the common interest', so it is not as though we can expect to discover obvious yardsticks for measuring a politician's trust-worthiness.

With Mr Cameron, such problems of interpretation are no less present. For instance, does he rail against the British political culture from self-interest (because he thinks there are votes in doing it), or conviction?

> And we need to change, and we will change, the way we behave. I'm fed up with the Punch and Judy politics of Westminster, the name calling, backbiting, point scoring, finger pointing. I want and I will lead a Conservative Party that when the Government does the right thing, we will work with them, and when they do the wrong thing we will call them to account and criticise them. We won't play politics with the long term future of this country, we will work to get it right.[23]

For example, right at the beginning of Mr Cameron's leadership, he was able to take advantage of an intra-Labour Party spat about an Education White Paper, setting out the government's vision of 'independent state schools' and promoting choice for parents and pupils, which would allow some schools to manage their own budgets and admissions, and to compete for parents. Mention of the 'c' word spooked Labour backbenchers, who were worried that if schools could decide who they taught, this would lead to a selective system. No bad thing for the conservative, of course. Mr Cameron's response was cunning: he offered his support for the bill, knowing that this would spook the government benches even more.[24] Mr Blair was, in effect, presented with the choice of turning the white paper into a bill, which might well only pass with Tory support, or to dilute the bill and suffer an obvious defeat at the hands of his own people. In ye olden days, the Tories would have opposed the bill, and Mr Blair could use that opposition to coax enough of his backbenchers into loyal, if grudging, support to get the bill through.

But is that a movement away from 'Punch and Judy'? Or is it a clever wheeze to wrong-foot Mr Blair while appearing to be ever-so-supportive? Many commentators went with the latter interpretation. Whether or not it is a correct view of Mr Cameron's motivation, supporting the Education White Paper had the effect of being just another move in the game. The same was felt to be true when Mr Cameron held out an olive branch to the Liberal Democrats[25] (as Mr Blair had done in his opposition years, only to drop them after the 1997 landslide). We should certainly also note that such wheezes are somewhat risky and not always clever. The tactic of claiming that Mr Blair is in his heart of hearts a Tory, and only that nasty centraliser Mr Brown prevents him from being true to his reforming instincts has actually been tried before, by Iain Duncan Smith and his team in 2002.[26] At the risk of stating the obvious, it didn't work then.

A trustworthy politician is supposed to be principled. Fair enough. However, it may be that she feels that actively pursuing her principles may contradict her desire to act in the common interest. For instance, it may be that trying to achieve some outcome that is in the common interest will involve some subterfuge, perhaps some dissembling, perhaps a bit of unsavoury political roughhouse. Such personal dishonesty is not very principled behaviour; however, it might make a politician more effective in the public interest. Salisbury was particularly shameless in lying for the greater good of British interests.

Indeed, it seems virtually impossible to see how a politician could function at all without some element of personal dishonesty. For example, any negotiation she undertakes will of necessity involve the concealment of information. And few politicians can be of much use without being elected, which may well demand carefully crafted representations of their work in different ways for different audiences (i.e. spin). We must beware of holding our politicians up to ridiculous standards of probity that the rest of us could never achieve.

Conservatism, trust and tradition

Hence trustworthiness in politics, at least in the naïve sense outlined above, is trickier to produce than one might think. The question then is how trust in politics can be supported (without being misplaced), and how conservatism in particular could help that process.

If we borrow a framework from sociologist Barbara Misztal,[27] trust is a social phenomenon that performs three major functions. It helps provide social *stability*; that is, it helps people to cope in a world that is uncertain, complex, contingent and arbitrary. Second, it underpins values, faith and friendship as bonds which help society to *cohere*. Third, it enables *cooperation* between otherwise independent agents to take place.

For the conservative, stability is central. Both coherence and cooperation are possible only when people's social roles are predictable, and therefore when one can enter into long-term relationships with them with confidence that their interests aren't going to change in the interim. The aim of the conservative politician, then, is to create and foster social stability, and then to stand aside and let the bonds of coherence form, and allow people to develop forms of cooperative behaviour.

So how does stability come about, and can the conservative make the claim that he or she is better placed to create it? Since anyone can do anything at any time, and all sorts of interactions can take place, it looks like the world ought to be so unpredictable that it will be almost impossible to deal with.[28] However, in societies with a modicum of social order (which happy state does not exist in all societies, of course), the impression we get is of regularity and reliability; people's actions are *legible*. People do more or less what they are expected to do, and the variation from expectations is actually kept within very strict limits. The bank manager may not do exactly what we expect; for example, he may refuse my reasonable request for a loan. But he is very unlikely to deviate from what we might consider bankmanagerly behaviour;

he is unlikely, for example, to spit at me, proposition me sexually, burn a £50 note under my nose or push an ice cream cone into my face.

> Hence, trust plays the role of a protective mechanism, which prevents chaos and disorder by helping us to cope with the volume and complexity of information. It reduces the anxiety caused by ambiguity and the uncertainty of many social situations. It also tends to endow social order with meaning and neutralizes its arbitrariness.[29]

How is this stability produced? By a number of mechanisms, some embedded in individual behaviour, some in social constraints and norms. For example, there is the idea of *habit*, of responding to a present situation more or less as one has responded in the past. Behaviour is routine, assumptions and rituals constant. Artists, teenagers and rebels of all stripes have complained about habit since time immemorial, but it provides an underlying substratum of stability which enables life to be comprehensible (and, among other things, gives rebels something against which to rebel).

Collective memory is another mechanism for producing stability. Various public objects, including texts such as histories and narratives, artworks such as statuary, traditions such as rituals, (interpretations of) phenomena such as landscape, together provide a background against which the past of a community can be made sense of, and in terms of which the present and future can be planned and understood. The identity of a community can be transmitted via such collective memories.[30] This is not to say that collective memory always provides unambiguous and consistent accounts, nor that it is never degenerate or manipulated (as, for example, in the former Yugoslavia); only that it helps provide continuity of experience.

Finally, there is an important role for *authority*. The conservative, perhaps more than all other democratic political thinkers, is a respecter of authority and a promoter of obedience to it where it is legitimate. Indeed, the conservative, with a mixture of realism, *Realpolitik* and a love of order, even takes illegitimate authority seriously; he or she is mindful of the suffering caused by conflict, and will not treat the illegality of a seizure of power as necessarily entailing intervention. Authority can help promote trust by providing sanction and constraint for the untrustworthy. Such authority must be applied justly, of course; arbitrary authority is deeply undermining of trust. It is in his support for the authority of Parliament against the executive where Mr Cameron's impact should be highest. Mr Cameron has spoken of the importance of holding the government to account, of strengthening the powers of MPs and select committees.[31] Given the low standard of legislation that has resulted from the greater centralisation of power over the last few years (under both Tory and Labour governments), this is a reasonable innovation, bolstering a weakened institution that is central to our political life and national expression of values.

So a conservative attitude can help supply stability. The second function of trust, coherence or bonding, depends on common values and beliefs, and once more conservatism is an aid here, particularly in supporting collective memories and ideas, and a common view. Small 'c' conservatism does not see individualism and the rights-based culture as an unqualified good; it also contains the imperative to sustain the common good, and understands rights to determine responsibilities as well. Small 'c' conservatives understand that there are many links underpinning relationships between people beyond self-interest.

The third function, that of cooperation, finds conservative support from the desire not to interfere, not to impose plans or rules from the top down. In fact, cooperation and coherence are simultaneously supported by support for localism and context-based solutions to problems, derived, where possible, by the very people affected by those problems. The conservative celebrates local communities developing local, possibly idiosyncratic, institutions and policies; the lack of top-down direction promotes cooperation, and the process of development helps foster coherence. It is all to the good that terms like 'localism' are often heard on Mr Cameron's lips. One serious problem, in conservative eyes, with Mrs Thatcher's premiership was that though she talked of setting the people free, she never really trusted local communities to do the right thing, so she actually centralised power. Certain favoured local authorities, who voluntarily followed Thatcherite policies, were subsidised massively from central government; those that wanted to go their own way were not. The result was to subdue local communities, not to empower them. Mrs Thatcher, like Mr Blair, never really trusted the British people.

All these mechanisms for providing trust make sense of the present in terms of the past. Social stability is rooted in a continuity that makes few cognitive demands on an individual. It goes without saying that conservatism, being the ideology specifically designed to maximise that continuity, fits well into the provision of social stability through trust. The conservative, who values that stability, happens also to value many of the mechanisms that can bring it about, such as tradition, habit and the repression of innovation.

Conservatism, then, can make an important contribution to the restoration of trust in public life, not necessarily because conservative politicians are more trustworthy than their green, socialist, liberal, feminist or social democratic opponents, but rather because unlike those other ideologies, conservatism is compatible with many of the mechanisms within society that are known to preserve and foster trust. It is on the *content* of conservatism, not the *character* of conservatives, that the argument rests.

Conservatism and the Conservatives

Part One of this book described the development of a type of conservatism based on Pyrrhonism, or scepticism, and tried to show how such a model of conservatism could thrive even in the 21st century. Part Two has now fleshed out the theoretical details in the practical context of the direction taken by David Cameron's Conservative Party, looking at three of the major dilemmas of the time: how to deal with free markets and arrange our economic relationships; how to understand society and its relation to the individuals in it; and how to foster social trust. Obviously those three dilemmas are very much connected; just as obviously they hardly cover the whole of political space. Nevertheless, the aim of Part Two was to suggest what a conservative government could achieve in those areas, in such a way as to retain an ideological link to Conservative governments of the past, while simultaneously appealing to the voters who have deserted the Tories in droves to follow Mr Blair, and who might well, in the aftermath of Iraq and others of Labour's difficulties, be beginning to cast about for an alternative.

Since the catastrophic defeat of 1997 the Conservatives have half-acknowledged that the legacy of the government of 1979–97 has not been wholly positive (which does not imply, of course, that Conservatives should *repudiate* the actions of the Thatcher and Major governments; only that they might consider moderating their principles in the future). But it is fair to say that the big issue confronting all Tory leaders since 1997 has been the way to deal with that legacy, and how to appeal to an electorate which turned strongly towards Mr Blair. We will conclude our look at Mr Cameron's Conservative Party in Part Three with an examination of its prospects.

PART THREE

ESCAPE FROM THE WILDERNESS?

Unfortunately, nine-tenths of the time of any political leader must be spent not on defeating his opponents, but on manipulating the stupidities of his own side.

Doris Lessing, *A Proper Marriage*

CHAPTER NINE

CONSERVATIVE MODERNISATION: OXYMORON OR NO-BRAINER?

Learning from Labour

On 10 June 1983, Britain woke up to the fact that it had changed, and radically. The previous day, two ideologies had clashed in a general election. The Conservative Party had finally made a convincing move to the liberal right (after promising to do it for several years). Labour had whizzed off in the opposite direction, chosen a grand old man of the literate left as leader, and produced a bold manifesto. Not only that, the centre ground was now occupied by a credible third party (or parties – an alliance of the Liberals and the breakaway Social Democratic Party). People sensed a shifting of the ground – Roy Jenkins had talked of 'breaking the mould' of British politics. And there had been civil strife, with riots on the streets of many cities, particularly during the fervid summer of 1981.

This election was a test of where the British people stood, and it was a decisive one. The Tories received 13 million votes, Labour 8.5 million and the Alliance 7.9 million. Because of Labour's geographical concentration, they did much better in the election than the Alliance, but still disastrously, with only a little more than half the number of seats that the Tories won. With a mere 209 MPs, Labour appeared to be finished. The popular image of Labour was rooted in three caricatures: the cloth capped trade unionist who went on and on about 'paragraph 4(b) of composite motion 257 amended by the Associated Society of Locomotive Engineers and Firemen'; the spotty firebrand shouting 'Maggie Maggie Maggie, out out out!'; and the pipe-smoking Hampstead resident keen to draw parallels between a British Leyland spot welder sacked for falling asleep on the job and the Tolpuddle Martyrs. It is safe to say that none of these three caricatured figures was palatable to the Great British Public.

Labour was old-fashioned and tedious. It had been this way for some time. In the 1950s, senior Labour politicians would complain about American films ('We want bacon, not Bogart, from the Americans', said Hugh Dalton) or the growth of consumerism (for some reason, many Labour politicians were particularly opposed to the washing machine, completely uninterested as they were in liberating workers' wives from monotonous and onerous housework) or mass tourism. But at a time when many people were still mired in poverty, and workers needed protection, Labour was tolerated, and people appreciated having more secure jobs and a National Health Service. Still, as Labour and Tory governments alike succeeded in pulling more people out of poverty, the joys of Puritanism seemed rather less compelling to the newly affluent than the evils of consumerism. Labour had not moved with the times, and had become increasingly unpopular among a population which it had taken for granted and ceased to resemble. Neil Kinnock, John Smith and Tony Blair, in their very different ways, dragged the party back to normality.

So fast forward from 1983 to 2005 and we see the same thing, except that the Tories have even fewer MPs than Michael Foot's Labour Party (and even that is by some measure the highest number they have gained in an election since 1992). The world has moved on, and left the Tories behind. And they know it.

We have a fading brand driven by people who represent a diminishing minority of the general public some of whom radiate values which are not shared by much of contemporary Britain. The problem is fundamental and the problem is us.[1]

The message ... is that the Conservative Party is not seen to represent the interests of all society. When we asked what put people off a political party, the Conservative Party led on five of the worst eight attributes. Although Labour was seen as being untruthful and being all spin, the Conservative Party was seen as overwhelmingly standing for business and the rich, being old-fashioned, extreme, not representing 'people like me' and having no new ideas.[2]

The most widely chosen phrase to describe how the Conservatives had come across during the campaign was 'old fashioned'. More than six times as many people selected this description (43%) as chose 'modern' (7%). Only 14% had seen the party as 'trustworthy', compared to more than a quarter (26%) who thought it had come across as 'dishonest'. Nearly a fifth of voters (18%) thought the Conservatives seemed 'normal', but more than one in ten (11%) regarded them as 'weird'. Only half as many voters thought the party appeared 'concerned about people like me' (17%) as thought it was 'not concerned about people like me', and while a fifth believed the Conservatives were 'in it for what they believe is best for the country', more than a third (36%) thought they were 'in it only for themselves'.[3]

Two great demonstrations were held in London to protest against the hunting Bill, in March 2000 and September 2002, far more people than had ever ridden to hounds marching in the largest such rallies the capital had ever seen, apart from the equally unsuccessful demonstration against the Iraq war. And yet it was audibly a last hurrah. To watch that parade of the rural classes and what was left of the landed gentry was like peering at something from a nature reserve. As Ian

Kilbannock might have said, 'Delightful fellows, but the Wrong Period. Hopelessly upper class. "The Fine Flower of the Nation". And it *won't do*.'[4]

There are worries about the Conservative brand.[5] Theresa May famously called her own party the 'nasty party'. Jo-Anne Nadler, a self-proclaimed 'Tory rock chick', entitled her memoir *Too Nice to be a Tory*.[6] The message has got through.

But …

There are two 'buts'. One is the sense of *déjà vu*.

Even after two crushing defeats, and flatlining at the polls at about 30 per cent for most of the last eight years, the Conservative Party still contains a remarkably large number of people who can't, or won't, accept the truth of how we are seen by others, or the reality that this means the party must change fundamentally or die.[7]

We are like a major brand which has lost the confidence of its customers. Without stretching the analogy too far, perhaps we are like Marks and Spencer before its recent recovery: a declining number of loyal customers, some products seen as worth buying, but overall perceived as out of date, out of touch, and with products which just won't sell. Like Marks and Spencer, we have to win customers back through a new image and improved products. As yet, however, the act of buying into our brand is not seen as a positive, forward-looking, exciting statement of who you are.[8]

Perhaps best not to stretch the analogy, given that the most popular M&S products are pants. Anyhow, these articles, and many like them, were written in the aftermath of the 2001 electoral defeat, even heavier than that of 2005. Yet nothing obvious was done in the interim: the Tories, as we have seen, went into the 2005 general election with a negative manifesto that enthused nobody. It is quite possible to be aware of a difficulty without doing anything sensible about it.

The Tories' small recovery in 2005 – a gain of 32 seats – was certainly not evidence that they had begun to act on these warnings; their percentage of the vote rose very slightly but not significantly, and their gains were generally due to third-placed Liberal Democrats picking up enough disgruntled Labour voters to drop some sitting Labour MPs into second place.[9]

During 1997–2001, there was an excuse for ignoring the outside world and looking inward – the party had got completely out of hand, and it was part of William Hague's brief to create a settlement between the various factions to allow it to function. He had a reasonable go at this, although the Cabinet itself became notorious for backbiting and plotting.[10] After the second massive thrashing in 2001, there was no excuse at all – yet neither Iain Duncan Smith nor Michael Howard made adequate attempts to shift the party.

David Cameron has clearly been much more ambitious, for example with his greenery, so we shouldn't worry that nothing is being done. Changes such as this, experience shows, have to be driven down into a party from the top. We must remember Labour's problems; the top end of that party is made up of committed modernisers who tried all sorts of tactics, some fair, some foul, to keep control of as many levers of party power as they could. But the urge to modernise does not run deep, and there is still a decently sized constituency in the Labour Party and its supporters who are nostalgic for the 'suicide note' of 1983. Such people were quiescent as long as Mr Blair delivered landslides, and didn't offend their principles too much. But over ten years or so their stoicism has been sorely tested, not least over the Iraq war, and the lid may well be about to blow off. Mr Cameron has to worry about taking his party with him as he goes. This will be a long process. I argued in the first edition of *After Blair* that any Tory leader needs to be in it for the long haul, but it is not clear that either the higher echelons of the party or the grass roots understand how difficult it is to show patience.

The leadership contest

There is a second 'but'. The defeat in 2005 led to a general consensus that the Tories must modernise or die. In the words of former treasurer Michael Ashcroft, most Tory workers woke up and smelt the coffee. Michael Howard announced his intention to resign as leader in the wake of the defeat, and the leadership election was expected to settle the modernisation question once and for all. Candidates moved into position.

Liam Fox addressed the Centre for Policy Studies, a centre-left think tank, in September with a paper called *Modern Conservatism*.[11] David Davis had actually addressed the same organisation in July, with a paper called, er, *Modern Conservatism*.[12] David Cameron, with his modernising reputation, had been able to disguise his talk of modernisation (in any case prior to the 2005 defeat) in his Sir Keith Joseph lecture, by calling it *Practical Conservatism*,[13] but by November he felt he had to go back to the CPS with a piece billed as *Modern Compassionate Conservatism*.[14] Only the old jazz-loving, cigar-smoking recidivist Kenneth Clarke felt able to ignore the modernisation trend. He came last.

Modernisation certainly was a consensus position after the 2005 defeat. In the first vote of MPs in the leadership contest, 160 of the 198 Tories voted for a modernising candidate. Personalities seem to have played a part too. Mr Cameron was perceived as a nice young bloke with a refreshingly direct manner, and all were impressed with his speech at the party conference in October; this got him a number of supporters who perhaps aren't natural Cameronians, such as one right-wing MP who noted that 'we are looking for someone to get us back into government, and Cameron ticks all the boxes'.[15] There was also a bit of needle against Mr Davis, who was a somewhat divisive character perceived as something of a plotter – although he had been the first to lay claim to the 'modernising candidate' label, during his candidacy in 2001 when beaten into fourth place. But of course leadership voting can't be based entirely on personalities. Ideology must come into it somewhere.

As indeed it did. Upon inspection, 'modernisation' meant very different things to the modernising candidates. Dr Fox had a very clear set of goals: a social policy to be promoted by supporting the family; a prosperity agenda driven by reducing taxes; and a global agenda consisting of pushing the EU into halting the progress towards 'ever closer union', adopting a free trade position, and staying in Iraq. Mr Davis preferred localism and low taxes. Mr Cameron argued that the Tories had revelled in the triumphs of the Thatcher years, and had failed to move on to consider the challenges of the future: insecurity in the face of globalisation, degradation of the environment, and rising expectations of public services. He also threw in a bit of localism and a *soupçon* of Euro-scepticism for good measure, while in November, closing in relentlessly on his eventual victory over Mr Davis, he warned us against high taxes, hostility to capitalism, the regulatory culture of Europe again, inadequate public infrastructure and Britain's deplorable lack of human capital in terms of the skills of the population. The most eye-catching part of the speech was his ruling out markets as a *complete* solution to these problems; markets were necessary but not sufficient.

So some differences and some similarities remained. All three candidates were worried about high taxes. Messrs Fox and Cameron discussed international affairs, although they took different lines; Dr Fox wanted to sort out the Middle East and project British power, while Mr Cameron preferred to eliminate world poverty. Neither was terribly keen on the EU. Mr Davis was a limited government sort of chap, Dr Fox almost Reaganite, Mr Cameron, though non-committal on the topic, seemed to envisage more intervention than the other two, given the larger number of problems he wanted to get sorted.

The leadership contest also contained a key modernisation moment, a moment where nothing happened – the dog that did not bark in the night. Mr Cameron, asked by Andrew Rawnsley at the Tory conference about whether his university years had been as strait-laced as one might expect from an Old Etonian would-be

Tory leader, gave an evasive answer, and implied strongly that he had had the odd puff, or possibly even done the odd line, while beavering away in the dreaming spires. As we noted in Chapter Seven, we do not have to believe the implication, but at least it was a bit classier than Mr Hague's possibly fictional fourteen pints of beer.

There was a collective deep breath from all concerned with the contest. Many commentators worried that this would be the defining issue of the campaign;[16] some of the tears shed were of the crocodile variety, others more genuine. These hints of drug-taking had the potential to play an analogous part in 2005 to the revelations of Michael Portillo's gay past in the 2001 contest, which seriously derailed his campaign. Timing was important. The sequence of events was that David Davis gave his conference speech, and then Mr Cameron his interview. So at the time of the interview, Mr Cameron was not the front-runner. It was the poor press that Mr Davis received the next morning that catapulted Mr Cameron into the limelight, and raised the profile of the interview. Maybe had he been the favourite already he might not have allowed us to draw the strongest implications.

Mr Davis, a man whose instincts are stern, and who at the time was Shadow Home Secretary, might well have banged the law and order gong. He chose not to. The *Telegraph* was supportive, and kept relatively quiet.[17] The *Mail* and the *Standard* huffed and puffed, but blew nothing down. The *News of the World* tried its best to nail Mr Cameron, but the best it could do was a front page lead consisting of a twelve-year-old photograph of Mr Cameron's campaign manager with a friend's girlfriend (now known as 'Mistress Pain'), under the headline 'Top Tory, Coke and the Hooker', a pathetic attempt which the top Tory in question was able to laugh off.[18] The minor candidates, Kenneth Clarke, Liam Fox and even the normally level-headed Sir Malcolm Rifkind, at the time still in the race, made coded and snide attacks which gained them little headway.

It was Mr Davis who made the correct decision beyond a shadow of a doubt, though it may have removed his last chance of winning. But winning a negative contest would not have left Mr Davis in charge of a party at ease with itself. And the Tories' commitment to tracking change in Britain would have been seriously compromised. Too many people have experimented with drugs for any mainstream party to try to kick them out of public life, as William Hague pointed out. That is not to say – again, see Chapter Seven – that the Tories need condone drug-taking, or support legalisation, or cease to consider the very real public health dangers that the drug scene creates. But society is more tolerant of drug use, and no conservative government could ever try to create an organic framework of law and health care on the basis of demonising a large minority of the country.

The revelations had little effect on Mr Cameron's poll ratings, seemed to spark relatively little outrage in the country at large and obviously did not shift the final result much. A severe row about the contents of Mr Cameron's nostrils would have set the Tories' recovery back a little bit further; the mature way that the party dealt with the allegations may not have created any positive momentum, but at least did no harm.

The rumours also pointed up the differences in outlook between the modernising candidates. Broadly, Mr Cameron was supposed to be left wing and liberal, Messrs Davis and Fox right wing and authoritarian, although all three candidates preferred not to talk in such terms – and we can judge for ourselves how accurate or useful these labels were by looking at their speeches. The total number of votes going to the two right-wing modernisers in the two ballots of MPs was pretty constant, 104 in the first and 108 in the second. Mr Cameron received 56 votes in the first ballot, and 90 in the second. After the MPs' ballots were over, it was Mr Cameron who received more pledges of votes (we must be cautious about these, as a pledge to support is not a real vote, but there is no doubt that MPs generally saw Mr Cameron as the likely winner). In the showdown ballot of all the party members, Mr Cameron prevailed by better than two to one.

So everybody agreed that modernisation was the thing. Mr

Cameron triumphed in the end, but equally it's not clear that a consensus was reached on what 'modernisation' actually meant. On the day the result was announced, a YouGov poll showed that 45 per cent of party members wanted to move towards the centre, while 48 per cent preferred a more aggressive right-wing agenda.[19] But that is not how they actually voted, unless they chose to decode the campaign remarks of Mr Cameron and Mr Davis somewhat differently to the commentariat.

The modernisation debate

The Centre for Policy Studies has been following, and to some extent orchestrating, the modernisation debate, and during the leadership election campaign backed a series of meetings to find a common frame of reference between modernisers and traditionalists. *Rapporteuse* Janet Daley was pleased, in September as the leadership contest was well under way (i.e. before the fateful party conference, and before the first ballot of MPs), to note the commonalities between the contenders.

> There now appears to be at least a weak consensus on what must be the central themes of a Conservative revival: the political and economic cost of high taxation; the importance of the role of community in society; developing a distinctly Tory account of what constitutes social justice; and a programme for the reform of the public services.[20]

This statement is actually weaker than it seems. Not only was the consensus weak, but it was only on themes, rather than solutions. There was a fair bit of distance over questions such as tax cuts, or how far to go in supporting the family. But this was a fair summary of a fairly happy position. The issues that were divisive between Tories were not particularly corrosive: how far to take the poor out of the tax system, and whether public sector reform would lead to costs savings immediately or only in the medium term. Meanwhile, the constant talk of localism subtended a clear set of public service reforms, and the focus on the Tory redefinition of social justice gave some useful continuity to recent history (former leader Iain Duncan Smith had set up a Centre for Social Justice to continue his concern for the relief of poverty).

Outside the leadership candidates themselves, there was general agreement across the party that the tax cuts that Michael Howard had offered in the run-up to 2005 were too weedy to be of much interest.[21] They were not large enough to catch the eye, or even to distinguish the party from Labour. Furthermore, by costing tax cuts with correspondingly detailed accounts of spending cuts, credence is given to the link between the two, whereas most Tories generally believe that lowering taxes can lead to greater tax revenues, and therefore (if required) higher spending.

But how to react to the failure of the Howard tax cuts. More and bigger tax cuts? Or not to offer any at all? During the leadership campaign (which, in contrast to those of 1995, 1997 and 2001, was sweetness and light) this seemed like a tactical issue. Tax cuts, ultimately, would be on the table, and no one was going to go to the wall one way or the other, as Ms Daley pointed out.

A practical objection to early promises of lower tax is made by those who believe that the first priority for any incoming Conservative Government will be to reform the public services – the failings of which are thought to be the most important form of public dissatisfaction with Labour.

The reforms which most progressive Conservatives favour, involving more consumer choice and the general empowerment of the public who use the services, will require quite heavy 'transition costs'. For example, if genuine parental choice in state schools is to become a reality, then there needs to be more slack in the system: popular schools will have to be allowed much more flexibility to expand and seed money will have to be made available for new schools to be created to meet parental demand. This will create at least a short-term demand for extra funding until the system is established. So, it is argued, immediate tax cuts would not be consistent with the extra expense of such reforms.

The proponents of early tax cuts counter that reformed public services will inevitably be more cost effective, and thus not be an additional burden on revenue. This is clearly a continuing debate; but it is one about timing. It is not an ideological schism.[22]

This was perhaps a somewhat rose-tinted view in retrospect.

The other point where violent agreement had broken out during the leadership contest was the importance of community, a solid conservative theme. All three self-proclaimed modernisers were interested in this topic. Mr Davis's upbringing, with a single parent and emphatically not via the public school and Oxbridge route, gave him a personal perspective that was respected. Dr Fox's view of the family as the most important support mechanism for the community appealed to traditionalists, while Mr Cameron, an unashamed toff, preferred to worry about those that society had left behind in a *noblesse oblige* sort of way. All agreed there was too much individualism, and that the connections between people had been neglected. There was hope that the third sector might be better equipped to reconnect people than the state. This view of the importance of community, as opposed to the severe self-help messages common in America and in the rhetoric of the Thatcher years, was seen as not only morally but also pragmatically helpful, in that it would help voters understand that the party had broadened its view.

Attacks on the 'dependency culture' are thought to have unpleasant undertones of blaming the deprived for their own condition. Transforming what was once seen as smug censoriousness about welfare dependence into a positive endorsement of voluntary activism is now widely agreed to be an essential element in constructing a new face for the Party.

For Conservatives, the message must be, not that it is somehow shameful to need help and support, but that people should help each other and be supported in constructing their own community welfare projects.[23]

The early stage of the CPS investigation was obviously conducted in good spirit, like the leadership contest itself. But fault lines were still detectable. Having glossed over the disagreement about taxes as a 'disagreement about timing', Ms Daley then constructed a supposedly consensual position built around the area of disagreement.

Developing what is fashionably called a 'narrative' for the Party on the issue of social justice could plausibly be linked to the commitment to lowering tax, offering greater choice for everyone (not just the rich) in public services, and reviving the social role of the community. The Party has often given the impression over the past decade of having definitively lost the high ground over the language of 'social fairness'. But New Labour's monopoly on this vocabulary can be challenged. Many voters do not regard the outcomes of Labour policy – in education, healthcare, and levels of prosperity – as being fair. There is now a much more confident sense within the Tory Party, especially among the younger generation of MPs, that words like 'opportunity', 'aspiration' and 'fairness' can be reclaimed, provided that the Party has a convincing alternative approach: that is, one that does not see government as the only source of virtue.[24]

There is obviously much to this analysis. But it is contentious in two ways. First of all the keystone of the whole idea is the lowering of tax rates. The problem with that has already been explored in Chapter Seven, but if there is a disagreement about timing then any policy based around tax cuts looks very dodgy. How can there be a disagreement about the timing of the central part of the whole Tory narrative? In practice, of course, the narrative is framed in this way precisely to bounce a putative Tory government into promising early tax cuts, which is, as we have argued, unconservative and politically unwise (just ask George Bush Sr).

Second, this narrative aims at reclaiming traditional Labour vocabulary. But even if voters do not regard the outcomes of Labour policy as fair, that does not mean that their assumptions about fairness have changed. They may well be holding Labour to account over their stewardship of the public services, and baulking at a perceived mismatch between rhetoric and reality. Mr Blair, as we have argued throughout this book, has shifted public opinion over such matters somewhat to the left, and it is unclear whether Ms Daley's proposed narrative accepts this. In particular, the government may not be the only source of virtue, but many voters see it as at least a fair dealer, if not an efficient one, and talk of tax cuts in this context may be unhelpful.

Be that as it may, the sensible, moderate debate over modernisation was fine as long as everyone's options were left open. But the leadership contest had to result in a decision, and it was Mr Cameron, for good or ill, who triumphed. At this point, many of the more right-wing and traditionalist routes were closed off; Mr Cameron certainly supported some traditional Tory positions (a strong Euro-scepticism and support for hunting, for instance), but he looked and sounded so much more like Sir Ian Gilmour than Norman Tebbit.

And looks matter. It was Mr Cameron's aim to change not only the minds of the Tories, but their physical appearance. So before we look at the ideological debate that followed the contest, let's see how well he has done on the personnel front.

Changing the face of the Tories

There was a general feeling that the Tories were basically a group of none-too-appealing middle-aged white men, many of whom had hairy ears. Nine out of ten members of the Tory parliamentary party laboured under this handicap (maybe not the ears).

It is a proper issue as to how worried a conservative should be about this. There is a dogma that the demographic profile of our representatives should collectively reflect that of the represented population as a whole, but like most dogmas there is no reason to subscribe to it in the abstract.

In the real world, though, there are reasons to worry. Many of the Tories' problems stem from their apparent inability to understand how British society has evolved in the last two or three decades (evolved as a direct result of Mrs Thatcher's market-based reforms, ironically), which is bad news from a conservative point of view. The conservative rests his or her philosophy on the functioning institutions and structures in a society, and if he or she is ignorant of these, or has an outdated view of them, then we have an obvious and immediate problem.

The fact is that the experiences of members of ethnic minorities, or women in the workplace, or single parents, or the poor, were barely represented or discussed within the higher echelons of the Tory Party at all. That is a lot of people to neglect. On the Tory benches the ethnic minorities are represented by one black MP and one Asian MP. Nearly 8 per cent of the population is from a non-white background, while the 1 per cent of Tory MPs of a similar background is a historical high. There are seventeen women on the Tory benches, out of 198 – not that many more than they had in 1932. Progress has not been made. At least the Tories can take comfort from the fact that women have overtaken Davids – now a mere sixteen Tory MPs are called David. And, of course, Tory MPs are disproportionately likely to have gone to a public school and/or Oxbridge.[25]

To reiterate, this is not necessarily a problem. Davids are as good as anyone, and should not be ashamed of being called 'David'. More to the point, Oxbridge and public-school-educated men are perfectly capable of governing a country, or at least as capable as those of the under-represented groups. But they are bound to see the world through similar eyes; if there are particular problems or perceptions that affect particular communities, it is not obvious that the Tory Party, currently constituted, will be able to detect and address them. The diversity of a set of thinkers is important for helping those thinkers avoid groupthink and achieve policies that are robust and effective in all circumstances:[26] the lack of diversity of the current Conservative Party is a severe handicap in the particular context of 21st-century Britain.

Having said that, the Tory Party has always had a substantial feminine element. It relies on large numbers of ladies to run its operations behind the scenes. Its views of the family and of the community tend to be structured around an important role for women as mothers and carers. And famously it had Britain's first, and so far only, woman party leader and Prime Minister. The other supposedly more progressive parties have failed dismally to produce a female politician of the same calibre. And anyone who still thinks that sexism is the preserve of the right wing needs to look at the laddish culture of the advisors surrounding New Labour's leaders, or, a little further afield, the incredible abuse heaped upon Ségolène Royal, who will be the socialist Presidential candidate in France in 2007, by her own party.

But despite this strong sense of the role of women in the Tory Party and in society, women tend not to be prominent in the party itself. The female influence would be 'behind the scenes'. It has traditionally been an advantage for a Tory candidate to be married, and so any (male) Tory MP will have one source of feminine influence in his home, and in his constituency office the cohort of lady volunteers will provide another. And, between 1975 and 1990, another major one as his boss. But in a society that is much more concerned with women as individuals, rather than as supports for more publicly active men (the politics of this division date back to Aristotle), this is not good enough. Many women, particularly younger ones, do not see their roles as wives, girlfriends and mothers (and general makers of tea) as being sufficient, and they aren't overly impressed by authoritative middle-aged men.[27] They tend to focus less on their authority and more on their hairy ears.

In other words, the Tories have expertise, but not sufficient knowledge or experience at the top to detect, diagnose and solve problems that exist, or are perceived, by all the people they represent. Tory attitudes to women were adequate until fairly recently, and the women within the party, assertive yet retiring, helped keep the party attuned to the priorities of women voters; ironically, the Tories' advantage with women voters evaporated after Mrs Thatcher became leader. Things have now changed, and the increasing prominence of women in the workplace has been of course one of the major developments of the modern age. Understanding a society is key to conservatism, which is a principled reason to worry about the Tories' lack of representativeness. And if voters think that their problems cannot be understood by an overwhelmingly white, male party, they will tend not to vote for it, which is a pragmatic reason to worry.

The Labour Party has been relatively prescriptive about ensuring it is representative, perhaps most obviously with all-women shortlists. The Tories have generally tried to avoid such centralisation, but Mr Cameron's idea has been to develop an 'A-list' of (initially) a hundred or so favoured candidates. The conservative roots of the Conservative Party, with its decentralised control structures, have dictated that the A-list is a somewhat weak tool, but even so it has proved too strong for some.

In the past, to be an approved Tory candidate, there was a complex process to be negotiated. One applied to the central party HQ, which would then, if one was accepted, invite one to apply for constituency vacancies as they occurred. Each constituency would then go through its own interview process. Up to twenty candidates would be selected on the basis of an application form to make a short speech and answer a series of questions from an interview panel; this would result in a shortlist. Those who got so far, usually two or three, would then make a case before a full meeting of the constituency party.

This of course is a perfectly fair way of doing things. But one obvious problem is that Tory constituency activists are not representative of the public as a whole (being older, maler and very much more right wing). Anecdotally, the process of being interviewed by a gaggle of such people has been found quite scary by a number of women; the thought terrifies me, I have to say. More to the point, although such gatherings are capable of finding high quality candidates, they tend to favour very similar types of people. Women do not get through the process easily. This may be because the system leans toward the sorts of skills that men tend to have, or because sexism rears its ugly head; maybe a combination of the two.

And it is particularly difficult for the Tories to adjust this system, because in general they are stronger on the idea of merit than other major parties. On most Tory views of life (including the conservative view), it is unfair that someone of greater merit should receive fewer or lesser opportunities than others. So any attempt to skew the results of Tory candidate selection – for example, by forcing all-women shortlists on some constituencies – looks like undermining the principle of merit.

So the net result is that Tory candidates look pretty much the same, which is always bad for group decision-making, and means that the party has difficulty communicating with young women in particular. A very similar story can be told about candidates from the ethnic minorities, except that the sensitivities are much stronger here. The Tories' historical record on racism, immigration policy and support for colonialism does not stand them in good stead in 21st-century Britain.

The decentralisation of the selection process means that all that the party can do is to invite candidates to apply, and give some gentle pressure that may or may not be heeded, to local parties. But it is hard to drive a meeting of a few hundred often rather cussed individuals who may be, in the abstract, keen to have more Tory women candidates, but who feel that *here* and *now*, *this* particular male candidate performed better on the day.

So, in short, the modernisers' desire to produce a set of Tory candidates that they hope is more representative of the population is problematic because it undermines two important Tory, and particularly conservative, principles: merit and localism.

The A-list concept was more of an attempt to increase equality rhetoric. A series of impressive candidates was drawn up, designed to be substantially more representative, including women and members of the ethnic minorities in much greater numbers than one would expect in a list of Tories. These candidates received some training, and oodles of praise from Mr Cameron and his modernising chairman Francis Maude. But ultimately, if local party autonomy was to be preserved, there would be nothing that the central party could do to get A-listers into safe seats. Many were wary from the start: Ann Widdecombe, who uses religious imagery more carefully than most, called the idea 'diabolical'.[28] Right-winger John Hayes memorably opined that 'the idea that we can parachute insubstantial and untested candidates with little knowledge of the local scene into key seats is the bizarre theory of people who spend too much time with the pseuds and posers of London's chichi set and not enough time in normal Britain'.[29] There was a strong suspicion that the list contained good-looking lightweights; certainly the inclusion of a former soap opera star was a serious mistake.

The A-list could only improve percentages, so in theory a selection in an individual constituency shouldn't be significant, but unfortunately its first outing was in the Bromley and Chislehurst seat, left vacant by the death of a very right-wing MP who opposed the whole modernisation process. Local party leaders were worried that an A-lister would be imposed on them – one was quoted as saying that there would be a real problem if a gay person took over the mantle of Eric Forth. Mr Cameron was forced to reassure them that the A-list wasn't compulsory.[30] This must have been very frustrating, as Mr Forth's majority of around 13,000 meant that the candidate would become the MP almost automatically. The mood within the local party in practice doomed all A-listers; a local middle-aged man (emphatically not on the A-list, though he also turned out on closer examination not to be a local either) was selected, surprise surprise, and limped home with a majority of 633. Two A-listers were rejected.

By August, the A-list was revamped. Of the twenty or so constituencies which had selected candidates, only a little more than half had chosen A-listers (far fewer than intended), while a third had chosen women, including three in winnable seats. Two had chosen candidates from the ethnic minorities. Neither of these fractions was significantly higher than before. The system was falling between two stools, not approaching the expectations raised by Mr Cameron, while still remaining an object of suspicion for the traditionalists. The list was padded out with more candidates, doubling its size, but this led to accusations that the system had failed.[31]

In the end, Mr Cameron was forced to introduce an element of compulsion. Final shortlists would have to include women, and the final choice of candidate would be carried out by a smaller executive committee from the constituency, which it was hoped would be more malleable than a mass meeting of the membership.[32] The issue has not been fully resolved: such a system is bound to produce more women candidates, but may well be attended by a constant stream of bad publicity about rebellions which could undermine the purpose of the exercise by underlining the very maleness Mr Cameron seeks to reduce.

There were other attempts to give the party a lick of paint. The 2006 Tory Conference was kicked off with the launch of Webcameron,[33] a video blogging and podcasting site for Mr Cameron and others modelled on MySpace. It is not clear whether such a site is intended to appeal to those who have no idea what blogging or podcasting are, or those who do, or indeed whether it is simply intended to give Mr Cameron a bit of fun. The interactive blog space was at least somewhat less moderated and more pithy than Tony Blair's tedious 'big conversation' of two or three years earlier.[34] One contributor, resplendent in the name davethechameleoncom (according to his profile, a 51-year-old enthusiast for truthful politics from Reykjavik), summed things up as well as anyone.

WebCameron: professional political silliness?

David Cameron is to be applauded for seeking to connect with younger voters. But is webcameron the way to go about it?

Trying to connect with his younger prospective voters by offering up a video web-blog is very modern for sure. But standing in the kitchen washing up he seems to be trying to appeal to women and youngsters all in one go. And it hasn't occurred to him that video production has just a bit more to it, than pointing a camera: his own energetic 'young'un' gets almost as much of her message across, as Dave himself does.

Dear David – with all best wishes, you have a centuries-old political party in urgent need of management and redevelopment. Spending your time on this sort of thing could seem like 'froth' to the voters and add nothing to your credibility.

Repairing and refurbishing the creaking but grand old building which is the Conservative Party is where your skills are needed – challenge enough for the hardest working of men. Good luck.[35]

More symbolically, Mr Cameron made moves to change the Tory logo, from a rather stark image of a hand holding a torch, blue on white (with a curious bit of red), to an oak tree with a green scribbly canopy and blue bole and shadow. The website got a softer look too, and a new slogan appeared in advance of the 2006 conference, saying *A New Direction*, with a picture of a cloudless blue sky photographed through the green leaves of a tree.

This created the explosion of hot air that any change of any logo anywhere causes. Some people were for, more against. Bernard Ingham, Mrs Thatcher's former press secretary, thought his party had gone 'completely mad'.[36] The opposition had a good laugh at its expense (leader of the Liberal Democrats Menzies Campbell pointed out that an oak tree takes 50 years to produce any fruit). The world of logos and mission statements is opaque to most of us, so we probably should not spend too much time decoding it. But in general the associations seem quite conservative to me.

After all, a torch is a light to guide people by, a way of illuminating them on the difficult road, to prevent them taking the wrong turning. It is all of a piece with the Thatcherite vision of the Tory Party, as the keeper of the flame, the owners of the secret knowledge of how a society should be run. It is a reminder that neo-liberal principles are not shared by all, and that the Tories have a duty to show benighted people the way. It is, broadly, a statement that the Tories have it right, and everyone else has it wrong. That is not the sort of confidence that one would expect in a genuinely sceptical conservative, not the sense of humility and respect for others' opinions about which Oliver Letwin has written at some length, for example.[37]

Whereas an oak tree is a chaotic pattern of organic growth, leading to strength and beauty. It lasts a long time, it is a resource, it is a shelter. It is archetypically British. It was from its trunk (admittedly not usually blue) that the longbows which defeated the French at Agincourt were hewn. And, hey, it is better than carbon-neutral.

Well, of course this is all guff. Longbows were made from imported yew, for a start, but the logo looks nice and green, and infinitely less arrogant than the torch (as many commentators pointed out, a child of three could have drawn the oak). How many votes is it likely to sway one way or the other? My guess would be nil. But it is a tiny victory for the forces of modernisation, if not equivalent to Tony Blair's rewriting of Clause Four.

The view from the right

The modernisation process, whether understood ideologically, in terms of personnel, or symbolically, came to be associated with the Tory left's attempts to drag the party towards the political centre. Had Mr Cameron lost the leadership contest, it is an interesting question as to whether the new right-wing leader (presumably either Mr Davis or Dr Fox) could have sustained a genuinely modernising effort while keeping clear blue water between Labour and the Tories. Certainly, despite the efforts of Mr Davis, modernisation does seem to be best understood as a leftward move to the post-Blair centre where most urban voters now are. That is how Mr Cameron saw it, and began to shift his party. The voters liked it, but many Tories on the right most emphatically did not. On past experience, this is where the greatest threat to Mr Cameron lies.

The Tory right falls broadly into two overlapping groupings, traditionalists and neo-liberals. The traditionalists are perhaps most strongly represented by the Cornerstone Group, which is roughly clustered around veteran right-winger Edward Leigh. Mr Leigh has form; he was sacked by John Major for his opposition to the Maastricht Treaty, but has in recent times gained credibility for his chairmanship of the Public Accounts Committee. The targets of Cornerstone are fairly predictable: the family is under threat, immigration is uncontrolled, the EU is a danger to the British way of life, political correctness has gone mad. And in particular, the Cornerstone Group believes that the Tories are losing votes because they are not sufficiently Tory; they have compromised too much with the modern world, and as a result have sacrificed support.[38]

Much of Cornerstone's impetus comes from the strong religious feeling of Mr Leigh and many of his supporters. The group is certainly aware of the decline of religion during the 20th century, and of the arguments, some of which I have put forward in this book, against founding political ideologies on religious bases.

> Over the last half century we have moved from a position where there was a broad assumption of Christian values in public life, through the view that a Christian worldview is a valid standpoint to argue in public discourse, but not a universally accepted one, to the position today where there is pressure for faith, especially Christianity, to be relegated entirely to a private matter with no application to public policy at all.[39]

The points that are made from within the Cornerstone Group show both advantages and disadvantages of the mixture of faith and politics. On the one hand, religion, like class solidarity, provides a language to describe and prescribe the sort of decent, socially aware behaviour that any civilised person would wish to promote.

> Perhaps one of the greatest gifts of our Christian heritage has been the transmission of the social virtues of politeness, considerateness and thoughtfulness across society and through the generations. ...
>
> It is the growing erosion of these social virtues that underpinned the common decencies that society took for granted that is at the root of the explosion in anti-social behaviour that makes so many of our fellow citizens' daily lives a misery. Politeness, considerateness and thoughtfulness are a straightforward extrapolation of the injunction to 'love your neighbour as yourself'. As Christian belief has declined across society, these social virtues are no longer practiced by a growing minority of families, with devastating consequences for those affected.[40]

The danger, though, is that such benign social feeling morphs into the more metaphysically-driven and purely ideological strictures that have made the influence of the American religious right so poisonous.

> Christian perspectives on abortion, bio-ethics or euthanasia are regularly treated with disdain by a growing number of politicians and commentators. It should not be so surprising that Christians, Jews, Muslims and others concerned about keeping alive African children have a similar reverence for the unborn and our frail elderly, here in the West.[41]

Nothing *too* worrying here – this is a very moderate statement. But there is a big difference between the debates on embryo research, abortion and euthanasia, and lumping them together as a 'pro-life' attitude – when in the first two instances it is the conception of 'life' itself that is at issue – does not help. There is an American tinge to this, and as we argued in Chapter One and elsewhere, this is a mistake, Britain not being America. It is reasonable to suggest, as Mr Leigh does, that Christianity is a key part of the fabric of British society,[42] as long as the distinction between British and American Christianity is borne in mind. But not only is Britain changing in its religious views, Christianity in Britain is itself evolving. Urban churches are growing, the sorts of rural churches championed by Mr Leigh are shrinking, and the nuanced and socially sensitive credo of the Anglican Church is being displaced by the certainties and enthusiasms of the Pentecostal churches.[43] For any truly conservative mind, certainty and enthusiasm are, if not the enemy, at least things to be suspicious of.

And as churches change and religious belief evolves, a theologically informed policy-making process becomes more complicated. For instance, in March 2003 Mr Leigh, together with Ann Widdecombe, sponsored an amendment to the Local Government Bill opposing repeal of the notorious Section 28, which forbade local authorities from promoting homosexuality. It was Iain Duncan Smith's support of this amendment that was taken as marking the Tories' decisive, and ultimately disastrous, move back to the right.[44] The amendment, which failed, revealed then-current splits in the Tory attitude to modernisation – 70-odd Tories supported the amendment, including not only Mr Duncan Smith but also Mr Davis and perennial leadership hopeful Michael Ancram, while fewer than 30 voted with the Labour majority to oppose it. For the record, Mr Cameron abstained.

The vote was an important moment for the Tories in the 2001–05 Parliament, and no doubt not taken lightly. What underpins the official rhetorical discouragement of homosexuality (which is basically what Section 28 provided)? Mr Leigh and Miss Widdecombe are both Roman Catholics, so there is a fairly straightforward religious basis for their beliefs. But both are also conservatives, and have written about the importance of religion in British life. The established religion in Britain is Anglicanism, though, which is generally liberal towards homosexuality; surely that argues for a more inclusive and humane view? On the other hand, as we noted, the faction of Christianity that is growing most dramatically in Britain, especially the capital, is Pentecostalism, which is the source of deep opposition to homosexuals (certainly a deeper opposition than Mr Leigh's). Maybe that argues for an exclusive view? Possibly, except that the growth of Pentecostalism is almost entirely driven by large numbers of recent immigrants, numbers of whom Mr Leigh would rather like to curb. Its influence is also very localised indeed. The moral is that basing policy-making on religious conviction, on the ground of the centrality of religious life to community life, is not a simple process, and won't necessarily deliver the socially conservative results that the Cornerstone Group champions.

One would not expect the Cornerstone team to support the modernisation process, or Mr Cameron's modish tree-hugging. Many commentators have seen the Cornerstone Group as a major danger. Cornerstone's first post-election intervention was seen by *The Economist* as a 'nutty new prescription for [Tory] success',[45] while we have already seen Cornerstone's chairman John Hayes' opinion of the A-list. The group is also very opposed to shilly-shallying on taxation, and would like a strong and straightforward anti-tax line in the run-up to the next election, as well as radical reforms to health and education.[46]

It is safe to say that the Cornerstone Group is not wholeheartedly in the Cameron camp. But equally, the danger to Mr Cameron's modernisation process from that direction should not be exaggerated. In the first place, the group's backward-looking stance puts it at odds with most Tories, who generally feel that it is the party that has got it wrong in the post-Thatcher period, and that some movement with the times is inevitable (even if the direction of that movement is still the cause of debate). This has meant a certain impotence for the Cornerstones, and in the war of influence they have had to move further towards Mr Cameron than he towards them.

They had ideas to put up a candidate in the leadership contest, but didn't really get their act together (they seem not to have expected Michael Howard's rapid resignation in May 2005). Mr Leigh was still apparently musing about a leadership bid in September 2005, which was taken seriously enough at least by Liam Fox, who moved to the right on abortion in response.[47] But any serious bid would have required six months' more preparation, and the whole thing fizzled out. The net result of this is that Cornerstone wasn't really able to present itself as a united faction, able to apply pressure to the leading candidates, and in the end some Cornerstone MPs announced their support for Mr Cameron – not the more right-wing Mr Davis – after their favourite Mr Fox was eliminated on 20 October.[48] Mr Cameron gratefully accepted their support, but there is little evidence that he moved far to accommodate them.

But second, Cornerstone's brand of conservatism can actually be a support for at least some of Mr Cameron's positions. Mr Leigh's Anglo-Catholicism, on the wrong side of history as far as religious attendance is concerned,[49] at least provides a basis for resisting the advance of liberalism. Mr Cameron has many liberal moments, and indeed Britain is becoming a very liberal place, so some measure of liberalism is required by any genuinely conservative ideology at this particular point in history. Resisting the tectonic shifts of society is always a mistake. But Mr Leigh is aware of the gap between the neo-liberalism and libertarianism of some of the wilder-eyed Tories, and the needs of British society.

> Allowing libertarian thought to gain a foothold in the Party would be a betrayal of foundational conservative values. As Lord Griffiths of Fforestfach has said, 'Conservatism has always stood against libertarianism, as the negation of every-thing it stands for'. Adopting libertarian thought into the

Party would also be foolish; it suffers from huge problems in its theoretical coherence. Finally, it would be disastrous. The pursuit of a libertarian agenda would cause widespread breakdown in society, potentially precipitating authoritarian policies by the state. There would then, quite literally, be 'no such thing as society'.[50]

The Cornerstone MPs detect in Mr Cameron a high Tory, not a Blairite sham. There are a number of points of contact between Cornerstone and Mr Cameron, perhaps most notably on green issues and corporate social responsibility. Cornerstone's mission is to work for a 'Conservatism that contrasts the quality of life with soulless utility and community with selfish individualism'.[51] That is not a million miles away from much of the substance of Mr Cameron's ideas.

The same uneasy truce could not be detected between the sterner, market-oriented type of Tory, however. For example, during the leadership contest, the debates about modernisation run by the Centre for Policy Studies, mentioned above, were well-mannered and consensus-oriented. Afterwards, while it would not be quite true to say that all hell broke loose, the unity that had been detected began to dissipate. As the supposedly neutral *rapporteuse* Janet Daley put it.

> The critical question was: could there be a common language acceptable to traditionalists and modernisers, in which future party philosophy and principle could be discussed? It soon became apparent during the later discussions that there was still no clear agreement on whether the modernising agenda was about the language (or presentation) of Conservative politics; or about re-assessing its most basic principles.[52]

This actually is a hard question, thanks to the indeterminacy between whether the principles being re-assessed are conservative with a small or a large 'c' (which, given the context of Ms Daley's brief, is not at all her fault). Adopting conservative views, at the expense of neo-liberal ones, will shift the Tories to the centre, but will also involve an adjustment of what the Tory Party stands for. But that is not a re-assessment of its most basic principles; if anything it is a rebalancing of the party's stance from liberalism to conservatism.

Nevertheless, having to face this issue is causing a clear rift. Ms Daley, dropping almost all pretence of neutrality, spits out her description of the debate through clenched teeth. She makes it very clear whom she believes the villains are. They are those elected by the British people, not those without responsibilities to anyone; they are those whose job it is to represent the broad range of opinion in their constituencies, not the ideologues and theorists.

Unsurprisingly, think-tank representatives were generally more radical – but not necessarily more right-wing – in their views than MPs who believed themselves to be constrained by the limits of what was electorally prudent. This political caution, or 'realism', tended to err on the side of retrenchment from what are often seen as traditional Conservative objectives such as reducing the role of the state. There also seemed to be an assumption among the politicians that, particularly with regard to the public services, talk of a smaller state frightened voters who saw it as a code either for cut-backs in provision or for privatisation. There was little appetite for educating public opinion in the realities of, for example, European models of health care provision which were based on mixed funding or government-regulated social insurance.

The conflict between policies which research had shown to be both practicable and advisable, and what MPs believed politically possible, was a recurrent theme. To put it bluntly, a large proportion of the Parliamentary Party seems to have lost its nerve over proposing any reform of public services or the tax and benefit system which threatens to cause public alarm – even when that alarm is based on economic illiteracy or practical ignorance. This could mean that the modernising programme of the new leadership is simply a way of pandering to an almost superstitious level of anxiety on the part of the electorate. If this proves to be true, then the chance will have been lost to offer truly progressive solutions to Britain's systemic problems.[53]

This is an extraordinary passage, borne presumably of the frustration of someone who feels Mr Cameron is missing an opportunity to produce a strongly ideological right-wing agenda (many left-wingers felt the same frustration with Mr Blair after the 1997 landslide). Voters are described using a deeply negative vocabulary – frightened, illiterate, ignorant, superstitious and anxious. MPs' realism is presented in inverted commas. The results of the wonks' research is emphatically not doubted.

What the passage really shows, especially in conjunction with the companion report from September, is that there was and is no consensus within the Tory Party on these fronts, especially tax. When ultras such as Ms Daley or John Redwood advocate cutting taxes, they build a timetable into their claims: they want tax cuts yesterday, or at worst, now. So any dispute over timing is exactly what Ms Daley says it is not: an ideological schism.

And note that the strong policy charge that Ms Daley advocates is definitively unconservative, on three grounds. First, it demands a solid promise to do something (cut taxes) on grounds of ideology and theory (driven by the policy wonks), irrespective of the actual conditions that obtain in 2009 or 2010 when the Tories might conceivably come to power. Second, dissenting voices are stigmatised as those of the illiterate, ignorant or 'frit'. There is not even a nod towards the conservative principle of the dangers of utopian theory and the wisdom of the crowd. Third, as she herself notes, the programme is progressive, and radical.

The attacks from the ultras on the right, neo-liberal economically though often, like Ms Daley, illiberal on social issues, continued throughout 2006. Stuart Wheeler, whose large donations to the

Tory Party have made him someone to listen to, criticised Mr Cameron's education policy and the commitment to addressing climate change; on the other hand, he sounded a generally conciliatory note, and was supportive of Mr Cameron's drive to make the Tories 'likeable'.[54] Lord Kalms, another big donor, was more worried by the lack of evidence of tax cuts, and sounded much less patient.[55] In August it was the turn of Mr Cameron's old mentor, Norman Lamont, who wanted to see more policies being delivered (up to four years before the next general election!), which it is safest to read as an early commitment to tax cuts.[56] The UK Independence Party specifically sought to capitalise on this discontent by announcing tax cuts and a return to grammar schools, in the unlikely event that they would ever have the opportunity to do something about them. 'We're parking our tanks on David Cameron's abandoned lawn', one of their MEPs explained, obliquely.[57] Mr Cameron responded by calling UKIP 'fruitcakes', 'loonies' and 'closet racists'.[58]

But it was not only single issues that worried the headbanging right. There was a general sense, possibly shared, if mildly, by the Cornerstone people, that the Tories who brought Mrs Thatcher to victory were being deserted by Mr Cameron. There were arguments against this. Ideologically, John Gray had already argued at length that these aspirational people were betrayed by the system itself; the neo-liberal Toryism that had allowed them to reach the top of the greasy pole by the same token kept the pole greasy so they were just as liable to slide back down again.[59] Pragmatically, the evidence of recent history was that the Tory core vote was unable to deliver victory on its own, and so far removed from other British voters that no compromise position was available. These arguments carried little weight with the Tory core itself, of course.

Norman Tebbit, whose instincts as to the direction in which Mr Cameron was determined to go were sound, weighed in as early as January, less than two months after Mr Cameron's victory, with a diatribe about the abandonment of the true believers. Mr Cameron's attempt to 'purge the memory of Thatcherism', said

Lord Tebbit, was an action worthy of Pol Pot.[60] This extraordinary piece of hyperbole, an exaggeration as ludicrous as it is tasteless, ruffled surprisingly few feathers, but it was a harbinger of things to come. Robin Harris, a former member of Mrs Thatcher's policy unit, said it was a huge risk to think that the core Tory voters would stay put, adding that the think-tankers viewed Mr Cameron and his strategies with 'thinly-disguised contempt'.[61] Lord Lamont too worried that it was dangerous to alienate the core Tory vote.[62] But the main attack from the back benches has come from Derek Conway. Mr Conway is a man to worry about – he played a major part in the toppling of Iain Duncan Smith – but as one of Mr Davis's campaign managers he was too partisan to cause trouble at this early stage.[63] Keeping the parliamentary party onside is one of the most important tasks of a Tory leader,[64] and Janet Daley's criticisms of the MPs on the topic of modernisation show conversely that most of them remain in line.

There has been a great deal of suspicion of the policy groups that Mr Cameron has set up. Janet Daley was keen for the front bench to listen to outsiders, as long as they agreed with her.

> For … research and policy development work to be fruitful, there will have to be a genuine partnership with the leadership: a commitment from the Conservative front bench to be open-minded, seriously engaged with new solutions and prepared to take some political risks. This was presented as the explicit intention in establishing a number of commissions to study and report on policy development. (Unfortunately, in the weeks since these discussions ended, there has been a discouraging tendency for the leadership to announce definitively that some areas of debate and policy direction were being ruled out of consideration, which suggests that the work of these commissions might be pre-empted by short-term political strategy.)[65]

Mr Wheeler was worried by some of the more outlandish elements, particularly the move towards environmental awareness and addressing climate change.[66] Oliver Letwin, in charge of the policy review, tried to dampen anxieties by stressing the coherence of the policy documents that must emerge from the review process, and that not every suggestion will be taken on board.[67] That may be taken as good news or bad. The policy review process may well include relatively wild anti-globalisation, anti-capitalism or green measures prompted by Bob Geldof or Zac Goldsmith, relatively sane ideas about the public services from Stephen Dorrell, or John Redwood's stern tax-cutting suggestions, and someone keen to rule out one lot of schemes might well wish to keep others. Mr Letwin, in effect, kept everybody guessing.

Meanwhile, Mr Cameron has kept swinging. His response to Lord Tebbit was to refuse to be drawn rightwards. Using arguments very like those given in this book, he pointed out the self-defeating nature of a move to the right.

> But the Conservative reaction in the 1990s to the changes Labour made then had serious consequences. As Labour moved towards the centre ground, the Conservative Party moved to the right. Instead of focusing on the areas where we now agreed with Labour on our aims ... highlighting the different prescriptions that arose from our different values and principles ... we ended up focusing on those areas where we didn't agree. Tax cuts. Immigration. Europe. This was despite the best efforts of successive Conservative leaders, all of whom understood the need for change. William Hague spoke in his first party conference speech about the need to make the Party less extreme. Iain Duncan Smith initiated a new emphasis on 'helping the vulnerable', a legacy which we are building on to this day. Michael Howard spoke in his famous remarks at the Saatchi Gallery of the need for the Conservative Party to stand for 'for all Britain and all Britons'. But well-intentioned cheerleaders on the right exerted a powerful gravitational pull. The force of the gravitational pull

was increased by one of the inherent difficulties of opposition: unless you say something strikingly different, no one pays much attention. Embracing a 'new politics' and accepting that in many areas New Labour was closer to the Conservative Party was a difficult thing to do. But nevertheless it was the right thing to do. Not least because it's true. And make no mistake – I will stick to this path. The alternative to fighting for the centre-ground is irrelevance, defeat and failure.[68]

Mr Cameron is clear that he will stick to his guns (if he can). And he hints that much of the time it will be a slog. The danger is not so much that he will be forced rightwards while things are going well; it is that if the Tory recovery stalls, and he finds himself in the same position that Messrs Hague, Duncan Smith and Howard found themselves in, then the short or even medium term gains from a move to the centre might be very intangible indeed.

Mr Cameron's position is like that of a spin bowler in cricket. Much of their function is to slow the scoring rate down when the shine has been rubbed off the ball. If they can find some rough footmarks, then they can get the ball to turn and thereby hope to get wickets. But on occasion, through no real fault of their own, they can be hit for six if the batsman's eye is in. The danger then is that the captain panics and puts the more glamorous and eye-catching fast bowlers on. But on a slow pitch with an old ball they will be certain to concede runs and – crucially – won't take wickets.

The Cameron route

There are various interpretations, as we have seen, of modernisation of the Tory Party. Mr Cameron's strategy has been quite clear, and consists of two strands.

- First, the Tory brand has to be rescued. This is a little bit of an obsession with the inner circle, especially of Mr Cameron's chief advisor Steve Hilton. There is even, apparently, a Delivering the Cameron Brand Working Party.[69] This is very managementspeak and silly at one level, but fundamentally the Tories are not liked or trusted, and Mr Cameron has worked very hard, exploiting his own likeability, to change perceptions.

- Second, perceptions of Tory motives have to change. There is an idea that the Tories are the party of the rich and powerful (where do such rumours spring from?). So Mr Letwin's policy review process is intended to associate the Tories with ideas to solve various problems that are not the prerogative of the better-off – most notably global poverty and climate change.

This strategy has caused ructions, as we have seen. But as I argued in Part Two of this book, Mr Cameron has said relatively little that contradicts a basic, sceptical conservative philosophy. Indeed, as others have pointed out, he hasn't endorsed much that Tory governments between 1979 and 1997 would have ruled out.[70] For example, *pace* Stuart Wheeler, Mrs Thatcher never opened a grammar school as Prime Minister.

It has been argued that growls from the right are a good thing.[71] Certainly there is agreement that howls of pain from Tebbitosaurus, Hefferlump and other Tory dinosaurs will remind voters how far Mr Cameron has pulled the Tories. Even Simon Heffer himself feels that his own negative reaction to a Cameronian speech will be taken as the major piece of evidence that the Tories have changed.

> On Sunday, hours after 'hug a hoodie' headlines had appeared in newspapers, preceding a speech on social problems by the Leader of the Opposition the next day, I found myself chatting with a seasoned observer of the political scene. He argued, and I did not dissent, that there is now no soundbite so ludicrous, or no opinion so bizarre, that David Cameron will not utter it, or have his minions encourage us to think he has uttered or might utter it.

Perhaps there is still a pale beyond which he will not go: we have yet to hear him, for example, arguing for full agrarian Marxism or greater compassion for child molesters. But, certainly, this expression of love for the sort of person many of us only meet when being mugged was true to that prime motivation of Mr Cameron's, which is to challenge our presumptions and enforce that magical and elusive thing known as 'change'.

There is another consistent trait, which I have mentioned before, but which is highly relevant to this episode. It is that Mr Cameron seeks to say things that will have me fulminating, and have my beloved readers writing in to the editor in their legions, for the simple reason that (as he sees it) there is no finer way to prove his party has changed than to have us foaming at the mouth. It is not for me to point out that this is a high-risk option, but I shall anyway.[72]

However, it is not obvious that internal Tory arguments will always work in their favour. Voters want the Tories to modernise in the direction Mr Cameron has set, but too much resistance from the right may cause them to doubt that he will stay the course.[73]

Undoubtedly the main requirement for Mr Cameron is that he continues to deliver poll leads. His agreeable style of leadership supplied a little kick start; the troubles of both the Labour government and the Liberal Democrats helped him – so busy have they been with other things that Mr Cameron didn't come under sustained criticism for several months after becoming leader, and was basically allowed to introduce himself to the voters. When poll gains were stalling in the spring, there were rumours of trouble ahead if the local elections went badly.[74] In the event, they were a qualified success. But Mr Cameron cannot relax. His poll ratings, and demographic position, as we argued in Chapter One, are nowhere near as favourable as those of the Labour Party at a corresponding stage of the 1992–7 Parliament, and so the stock of goodwill on which he can rely is somewhat smaller.

His position is a good one. He is clearly thought more highly of, by his MPs, the party as a whole, journalists and the electorate, than any of the other post-Thatcher blues. He has been admirably explicit about the direction in which he intends to take his party, and secured a hefty victory among party members in the leadership contest. Most MPs ultimately pledged their support in advance, though he failed to win 50 per cent of their votes in an actual contest. Thanks to his conference speech, he was hardly an unknown quantity.

And most importantly, thanks to research conducted by various well-wishers, there is hard polling evidence of what voters think is wrong with the Tories.[75] There is no alternative direction for Mr Cameron to go in. There must be substance, ultimately, behind the rhetoric, but there is no reason to think that that substance will not be forthcoming. Modernisation must mean more than turning down the volume of the screeching.[76]

We have argued that conservatism, properly understood, will fit the bill as a source of substantial philosophy for the modern Conservative Party. Our final task is to look at the balance sheet. How far is Mr Cameron truly conservative, and how far will his conservatism, such as it is, get him?

CHAPTER TEN

THE BALANCE SHEET

A fresh face

By the next election, David Cameron will be the longest-serving of the major party leaders (barring accidents). And yet he will also be the freshest of face. Indeed, he appears to be about twelve years old. Perceptions of personality matter. Gordon Brown is a brooding, somewhat menacing figure, the proud owner of a 'big clunking fist'. One sees him, like John Jarndyce at Bleak House, retiring to the growlery to rail at the world. Other potential Labour successors to Tony Blair (Alan Johnson? John Reid?) are hardly oil paintings either. Meanwhile, on the opposition benches, Sir Menzies Campbell is a comedy figure out of Gilbert and Sullivan, whose early efforts at Prime Minister's Questions were apparently so disastrous because he is used to being heard in reverential silence (which doesn't explain why he once forgot the end of one of his own questions[1]). Rumours that he keeps a Corby trouser press to keep the crease in his pyjamas may be false, but they are consistent with the picture.[2] In a stupendously ridiculous but amusing poll where people were asked 'if X was a car, what car would he be?' Mr Cameron came out very well, as a sports car; battered Mr Blair was a defunct Rover, and Sir Menzies was an old Jag. Worryingly, Mr Brown was a tank.[3]

Well, image isn't all. Mr Brown is very serious, private and formidable, while Sir Menzies' knowledge of foreign affairs is supposedly impressive. On paper Mr Cameron, with a little bit of experience behind the Tory scenes, and seven years as Director of Corporate Affairs (not sure what that is) at Carlton Communications, is a comparative lightweight. Mr Brown in particular, one of Britain's most successful Chancellors, who eats Blairite pretenders for breakfast (mmm, Alan Milburn, yum!) will be a redoubtable opponent.

But Mr Cameron is clearly a nice chap, gets on with people, carries his privileged birth and impressive academic credentials lightly, and looks like the sort of person you would want to have, if not a beer with, at least a G&T. He connects with voters with his enthusiasm. He makes jokes. His wife has a tattoo. He actually sounds less like a Tory than either Mr Brown or Sir Menzies. He bangs on about the environment, and is photographed with glaciers and icebergs worrying about global warming; the environment is usually Lib Dem territory, but Sir Menzies just isn't associated with these issues in the same way. Mr Cameron gets his message across.

It is not necessarily a good thing when leaders are chosen on the basis of their being more likeable than their opponents (cf. George Bush Jr), but that is hardly Mr Cameron's fault. An important effect of his likeableness is that it gives him a great deal of leverage with his party, which is desperately conscious that it is disliked, so it is not irrelevant to more ideological matters as well. But it is a pragmatic thing.

Our investigation is into ideology, so let's conclude with a brief summary of Cameron's words and deeds, not his cherubic features.

Learning lessons?

We have reviewed Mr Cameron's policy pronouncements in Part Two of this book. They obviously vary – anyone in charge of such a broadly-based party (and wishing to broaden the base still further) cannot afford to draw inspiration from a single ideological well. And the quality of the initiatives and statements certainly varies.

There have been two major failures on Mr Cameron's part. His proposal to rewrite the constitution by getting rid of the Human Rights Act was terribly misguided, and his promise made during the leadership contest to leave the European People's Parties in the European Parliament was not thought through. In each case, there are issues about Mr Cameron's judgement – on neither topic is he an expert, and he seems to have listened to too small a clique of advisors. His conservatism is only partially implicated; euro-scepticism is an important part of British conservatism in the 21st century, but dramatic alterations to the constitution are not.

Aside from those problems, Mr Cameron has been generally effective in his first year as leader. But how conservative has he been, and how conservative is he likely to be? In Chapter One, we set out a short framework, of ten lessons for the Tories to learn from the grim post-Thatcher years. How does Mr Cameron's first year measure up? Has he learned those lessons? And can he take the Tories with him? Let's review progress.

1. Tone down individualism.

✔: Good start here. Much of Mr Cameron's rhetoric at least has been to emphasise the social nature of politics, and the way that individual achievements depend on the public background. Many of his speeches have been given to community centres and community groups, and he has attempted to get himself associated with various effective schemes at the local level; in contrast, he is seen much less often being wined and dined in the City. His localism is a very good antidote to individualism; by focusing on the local, he avoids the temptation to counter individualism with central control (a New Labour tendency).

There is a well-known problem with opposing individualism, which is that you often end up promoting the needs of the community above those of the individual. In many ways this is all very well, but the danger is that it leads to strong communi-tarianism, where the individual is subordinate to the community as a whole. Many cultures are quite happy with this – Singapore comes to mind – but going this far would be a mistake in the individualistic West. Not only would communitarianism go somewhat against the grain of much of Western development over the last century or so, but also, in our radically diverse societies, the notion of what 'the community' is can never be clear. It is all very well to talk about the interests of the community against those of the individual – many phenomena, such as crime or graffiti, are clearly against the interests of the community. But getting down to specifics is much more difficult. Is it in the interests of the community to have another pub? A big branch of Tesco? A library? A railway station? A bypass? A traffic calming system? These should not be ideological matters; rather, they are the sorts of disputes that should be thrashed out, in a democracy, with discussion, argument and voting.

The community efforts with which Mr Cameron has generally been involved have been uncontroversial. They tend to be self-help organisations, often with a core membership drawn from an ethnic minority, which are not intended to impose a particular point of view on a community. He manages thereby to emphasise his empathy for communities, particularly but not exclusively urban ones, and by praising rather than advising, he appears sincere about his hands-off localism. In fact, apart from his greenery, localism and support for self-help for small communities may well be the most prominent theme of his leadership in the first year.

But the tick is not without a caveat. In his ill-advised suggestion of repealing the Human Rights Act, Mr Cameron may have felt that he was pulling our legal system back from the rights-based brink, back to a more Common Law vision where responsibilities are also prominent. However that may be, repealing the HRA won't actually change any of the law, as we argued in Chapter Seven. The idea was a poor one; rights do go alongside an individualistic cast of mind, admittedly, but as the human rights in question are relatively consistent with the British Common Law system (indeed, were drafted with the British experience in mind), and as the rights in question have been important in British law independently of Europe for decades if not longer, a more measured response to the Human Rights Act is required (if, indeed, any kind of response is called for at all).

2. Avoid libertarianism.

✔: Well, Mr Cameron has gone along with suggestions that he may have done a few drugs in his university career. But he has been careful not to condone such behaviour in others. The think-tank-style libertarianism that was briefly in vogue in the 1980s never really took off within the Tory Party, which contained too many censorious people, and businessfolk who like the idea of limits to behaviour.

3. Avoid moral prescriptivism.

✔: Mr Cameron isn't a sanctimonious man (at least not since he became leader, though his voting record on gay rights prior to 2005 is not that of an über-liberal). We all err and stray, as he said himself in the aftermath of his own drug controversy. His infamous hug-a-hoodie speech was controversial, but it certainly fell a long way short of the Manichaean good-and-evil framework that often accompanies discussion of our social ills. In that speech he was prepared to accept that it takes great strength of character to overcome a poor upbringing, in some of our urban wastelands. That is not to say that yobbish behaviour or worse can and should be explained away, but at least that there is something others can do to make such behaviour less likely.

4. Need to be careful on Europe.

✗: Oh dear. Not so good. Mr Cameron's Euro-scepticism is a conservative instinct, and he was obviously badly burned in his formative years by Black Wednesday. It wasn't too bright, however, to make promises about Europe during his leadership campaign, at a point in the campaign when he was struggling to get himself noticed. And given that he is not a foreign policy expert by any manner of means, it was very unwise indeed not to consult more widely on whether to leave the European People's Parties group in the European Parliament. Many of the EPP members are conservative parties with which the Tories would hope to have much in common. Jacques Chirac is not a terribly useful man to have on one's visiting list at the moment, but Angela Merkel certainly is, and irritating her was a bad bit of business.

From a conservative perspective, trying to pull out of the EPP and join up with sundry right-wing loonies across Europe is an awful idea. The sort of moderate, principled opposition to the deepening of European ties that British conservatives espouse doesn't really exist to the same extent in Europe, where history has run a very different course. So the Tories are never going to find soulmates on this topic. Only as part of a bloc of moderate right-wing parties can they exert any leverage in Strasbourg. It is a conservative principle that compromise is essential in politics, and there is no reason at all why the Tories cannot remain in the EPP while agreeing to differ – as in fact they did from 1992. The EPP is not perfect for the Tories, but events have shown that there is no better home for them. The politics of making a splash outweighed the politics of getting things done – the worst mistake for a conservative to make.

5. Don't shift too radically from public to private service provision.

✗: This is a tricky one, but so far this is another cross. Mr Cameron has talked a lot about public sector reform and localism, and was the issue over which he disagreed with the first edition of this book. In general this is defensible – the public services do not work terribly well, and local decisions are much more likely to be sensitive to local conditions than centrally-decided targets or whatever.

However, there are four reasons to believe that Mr Cameron's thinking is not conservative enough. First, there is the straight-forward sceptical conservative point that the public services have gone through several bouts of reform, and Mr Blair clearly believes that reformed public services will be the major legacy of his period of office. Very well, so they may be. But we simply do not know how the reforms are turning out, what their unintended conse-quences are and whether more are required. We do not know if harm or good has followed. We need to see the results of reform, and only the urge to appear hyperactive (true of both Tories and Labour) prevents either side from doing a proper evaluation. Every reform means another learning curve for public servants, makes them less efficient and means they are working for another year under conditions of great uncertainty.

Second, Mr Cameron wants to shift power within the public services to local communities and the third sector. Nothing wrong with either of those ambitions, but it is a mistake to try to do this quickly, as neither untrained people (whether users of public services or elected officials) nor volunteers will necessarily be able to make good decisions immediately. There is nothing wrong with moving towards this arrangement, but Mr Cameron's jibes at the snail's pace of Mr Blair's outsourcing of public service functions to the third sector imply that he wants to speed things up, possibly unsustainably.

Third, it is essential, from a conservative point of view, that politicians go with the grain of a society, not against it. And in fact the Tories' views of the public services, like those of the Blairites, are more radical than those of the British people who rather like their public services, and are willing to tolerate a bit of inefficiency for free provision, paid for in taxes, and fairness of distribution. To repeat myself, that does not mean that reform shouldn't happen, only that its pace should be such that voters can feel comfortable with the changes.

Fourth (this is a pragmatic point, though related to the above), there are many public servants who wish merely to follow their vocation to help those in need, who feel undervalued and overwhelmed by the reforms, and the hostile rhetoric from both parties, not to mention relatively low pay. These people have votes. Not only that, they are often concentrated in geographical areas where the Tories need to have seats.

The reason the cross is tentative is that the mood music is beginning to change, thanks to a positive report from a working party, welcomed by senior Tories. It may be that, were they to become the government in 2009 or 2010, they would be much more circumspect than they seem to be committed to now.

6. Avoid promises of tax cuts.

✔: Back to winning ways here. The tax-cutting right will show no mercy, and it will take nerve on Messrs Cameron's and Osborne's part to avoid being bounced into rash promises. The fate of George Bush Sr, hung out to dry for sensibly cutting America's huge budget deficit, may help concentrate minds. And to reiterate, there is nothing wrong with tax cuts – they are, by and large, good for the economy and need not mean a reduction in public spending. But at any particular moment in time, at a particular level of public provision and external threat, tax cuts may not always be wise. No conservative can pretend to know in advance what levels of tax should be levied, and those who would promise to cut taxes are pretending so to know.

7. 'Core vote' strategies are a mistake.

✔: No one can accuse tree-hugging Mr Cameron of chasing the core vote. How Lords Tebbit and Lamont cannot see how disastrous the strategy was for Mr Hague or Mr Howard (and his unlamented dog-whistle politics) beats me. It may be that Mr Cameron appals more robust Tories, and even drives some of them into the arms of UKIP. But majorities in Tory seats are generally large ones, because Tories are geographically concentrated. Mr Cameron can afford to lose some of the core vote, in order to win many more voters outside the Tory heartlands.

8. Realise that Britain is a liberal nation.

✔: This is another tricky one. Mr Cameron scores highly here, even calling himself a liberal conservative. His genuine concern for green issues also helps. Basically, he does not sound like a Tory on those issues of importance for young urban professional types. All to the good, but his wider task is to convince those professionals – who are not fond of the Tories – that he is more representative of the Tory Party than one might believe. And that task was not at all helped by his ill-fated proposals for constitutional reform and scrapping the Human Rights Act. Liberals tend to like human rights.

9. Strategy more than tactics.

✔: So far, so good. But so far Mr Cameron has been electorally successful. Will we see a different Mr Cameron if the polls don't budge? Labour began seriously to reform after Neil Kinnock became leader in 1983, and even then it was a good twelve years or so before the Labour Party was properly house-trained.

10. Britain is not America.

✗: Oops, no. Mr Cameron keeps mentioning, or being around people who mention, compassionate conservatism. This is a terrible mistake. That George Bush Jr won a Presidential election using that slogan doesn't mean that it will be as compelling in Britain. The third sector, which is strong in religious America, is relatively weak in secular Britain. Mr Bush is not popular in the UK, nor terribly well-disposed to the Tories. It may be that some inspiration for Tory policies might come from America, but I somehow doubt it. What is conservative in America will be radical in Britain, because the two countries are very different in many key areas. We are much closer to Europe in attitudes, and even then I don't advocate adopting European ideas. A conservative should realise that a functioning society is *sui generis*, and other solutions for possibly analogous problems in other contexts will not necessarily transplant.

The balance

So, seven out of ten for Mr Cameron. Pretty good – after all, he is under all sorts of pressure, and no party political leader has the agenda all his own way – but there is still room for improvement. His biggest boob, to revisit the settlement on Europe, was almost entirely self-inflicted. He had wanted to boost his standing at a time when he wasn't making much impact in the Tory leadership race, and possibly also attract a few of the right-wing ultras, but actually it seems that his conference speech did most of the work in building up his support, giving him momentum at a crucial time. Let's hope Mr Cameron learned the lesson of not offering things that aren't required.

The ten lessons were drawn on an analysis, from a conservative perspective, of the Tories' electoral position. If we go on to peruse Part Two of this book, where some of Mr Cameron's policies and rhetoric are analysed from the same perspective, we get the same 'could do better' sort of feel.

He has been groping round for a language to discuss markets and financial matters, but it is not clear that he has been totally successful. This is clearly a sensible strategy to adopt, as the Tories are seen as the economics party, the party of the voracious capitalist, the party that wants to sell off the family silver. These perceptions are not particularly fair, and Mr Cameron is right to want to change them. But equally he shouldn't be too apologetic about markets *per se*. There are good moral reasons, as well as economic ones, to foster free markets, and markets sit particularly well on top of British social structures and stability. That does not mean that we should be in thrall to them, only that they are highly compatible with British life. The danger is that the Tories are still seen as the party that wishes to sell off popular public functions to private enterprise. Privatisation has worked on many occasions, especially in the early days when way too much of the economy was in public hands, and the Tories should never try to undermine or downgrade the intellectual legacy of Mrs Thatcher's government on this topic. But bad news travels faster than good, and for many the key privatisation was the disastrous reorganisation of the rail industry. As gas prices rise for geopolitical reasons independent of privatisation, the energy industry will come under increasing scrutiny. So it is essential for the Tories, for good conservative reasons, to distance themselves from the proposition that markets are the best way to allocate resources. For any conservative, such a universally quantified proposition should be ruled out: time and social context also need to be taken into account. David Willetts put it well when he said 'my personal definition of a Conservative is a free marketeer with children'.[4] Markets work, but – this is crucial for a small 'c' conservative – they bring with them all the risks identified by John Gray and others. If you don't mind bringing those risks on yourself, you should still worry about your children.

Mr Cameron appears to share these instincts, and good for him. But the odd-sounding General Well-Being (GWB) to go alongside GDP is horribly gimmicky, and seems to move into utilitarian territory (always dangerous for a conservative) by implying that individual happiness can be measured. As we have seen, there are such arguments in the ether, popularised by Lord Layard. And there is nothing wrong in shifting the focus of policymaking away from producing prosperity to other measures. As Oliver Letwin points out, a government could also try to foster virtue, or beauty, or truth, or justice.[5] But these are diverse and opposing aims, and Mr Letwin, in his more theoretical moments, would resist strongly their being yoked together into a single parameter such as GWB. Lord Layard insists that this is possible, but a good dose of conservative scepticism is required.

On the other hand, Mr Cameron's championing of corporate social responsibility and flexible, family-friendly working practices is wise and to be welcomed. This actually gives him a link to the Cornerstone Group of MPs, and strengthens his credentials as a politician whose main concern is the wider society. There are inconsistencies here and there in his approach, as we noted in Chapter Six, but many of those are part and parcel of the CSR movement. The main point to note is that Adam Smith's concept of markets included a large chunk of corporate responsibility – the slash-and-burn capitalism that many discerned in the 1980s was a long way from Smith's ideas – and Mr Cameron is sensibly allying himself to the founder of market economics.

His support for the third sector is fine in its own way, but it won't square the circle between those who wish the state to shrink under any circumstance, and those conservatives for whom state involvement has to be judged by results in context, not in ideological terms. Greenery is a sensible move on his part, especially combined with a sympathy for market solutions. His focus on communities and the ways they interact with markets is also the right one. It may help finally to lay to rest the bad publicity that the Tories have received over the last twenty years since Mrs Thatcher's statement that there is no such thing as society.

With respect to conservative attitudes towards society, Mr Cameron's touch has been relatively sure, and is suitably non-punitive on matters such as drugs and homosexuality without spilling over into libertarianism. In particular, the numbers of openly gay Tory MPs and activists have been rising slowly, which is no bad thing. On race and immigration he seems to be making progress. Resisting promises of tax cuts, while hoping to cut tax, is clearly the correct line to take, and ultimately will probably prove his hardest test. Modernising the Conservative Party is a harder task than he may have thought, even after his big win in the leadership contest, but he isn't showing any signs of shirking the battle at this stage.

But Mr Cameron's tendency to stumble hasn't totally left him.

His education policy is hot on localism, but, as Stuart Wheeler has pointed out, not yet so hot on standards. Some of his policies betray the South-East bias of Tory political culture – for instance, he needs to be more generous to the public services, and criticising regional development boards may go down very well in Witney, but in the North they are key parts of the economy.

In the world of high politics, we have already pointed out his mistakes on Europe and the constitution, but they are offset by his masterly denunciation of the neocon simplicities underlying the Iraq invasion. The wider quest of increasing trust for politicians has been helped by his personable ways and his rejection of what he calls 'Punch and Judy' politics, although his embarrassing Mr Blair over the Education White Paper might owe more to Mr Punch's influence than he cares to admit.

To summarise, Mr Cameron is developing a line of strategy that is not far from the sceptical conservatism that was recommended in the first edition of this book, and it is gratifying (to me, as well as to him) to see his rewards in the polls. In the centuries-old struggle between political scientists and political engineers, with which we closed Chapter Seven, Mr Cameron is clearly a political engineer, focusing on processes and means, not outcomes and ends.

He seems willing to try to understand the society in which he lives, not to judge it, and ultimately that is the mark of the true conservative. Most of his policies and pronouncements are solidly in the conservative footsteps of Montaigne, Burke and Hume. Let us hope this brings him some comfort when he is accused of diverging from Tory traditions.

The results (so far)

There is a psephological mountain for the Tories to climb, but they have at least made base camp. In a comprehensive analysis of the first few months of Mr Cameron's leadership, Lewis Baston and Simon Henig show that Mr Cameron is reaping some dividends. But while he is eroding Labour's lead, it is still unlikely that he has developed sufficient momentum just yet to move into 10 Downing Street;[6] this agrees with the analysis of David Sanders that Mr Cameron could still do with votes from beyond the political centre.[7] Messrs Baston and Henig do argue that one indirect effect of Mr Cameron's modernisation drive might be to chip away at the ingrained tactical voting by Labour and Liberal Democrat supporters designed to keep the hated Tories out of office.

The Tories are not yet into the territory that successful oppositions need to be in. They have now recorded several poll leads, and clearly that is causing concern within the Labour Party. But since 1950, all opposition parties that have gone on to form the next government have at some point in the previous Parliament enjoyed poll leads of 15 per cent or more over the government, and the Tories have a long way to go to manage that. Voting intention polls after a year of a Parliament are particularly bad predictors of eventual victory. Mr Cameron's own satisfaction ratings are middling.[8] In the first poll after Mr Cameron's first 100 days, Labour had retaken the lead (although they lost it again shortly afterwards).[9]

His first major electoral tests, the local elections in 2006, were a qualified success: not a long way short of a 40 per cent share of the vote, and many gains of councillors and councils, which was a distinct improvement and certainly better than expectations. As the elections, in May 2006, came at a moment when the grumbling about Mr Cameron's leadership was probably at its height,[10] this was very good timing. But the news was not all good. The Tories did well in London, and so for the first time in a long time had a significant urban presence. But they did not make it northward; though they had big increases in their votes in the South, they actually lost votes north of the Humber. This corralling of Tories in the South would be bad enough, but is made worse by the first past the post system, which rewards a wide geographical spread. There is a long way to go before the next election, but Mr Cameron, a bit of a southern softie, needs to get northern votes from somewhere.

If we look at those polls which have measured where new Tories are coming from, we can start to get a feel of which groups Mr Cameron is appealing to. The shift from the general election result is not large, and no group has swung towards (or indeed against) the Tories in unusually large numbers. Equally many men and women have switched to the Tories in the first year after the election, but they tend to be older men and younger women. Mr Cameron's appeal seems to be greatest for the 35–44 age group, and pensioners. Perhaps the most encouraging sign is the relatively large increase of the Tory vote in the AB social group, a traditionally Tory stratum where the Tory lead has declined dramatically during the Blair era.[11]

Mr Cameron's strategy has paid some dividends, but the Tories aren't there yet. The question is where next?

Where now?

There are four views on what has gone wrong with the Tory drive for power. Why are they not fifteen points ahead in the polls, given Labour's problems? One view, held by the Cameronians and others, is that the Tory brand is so damaged that it is not surprising that they have not made greater progress. The amazing thing is that they have got so far, in the face of such public hostility, in increasing their vote, and indeed leading Labour in the polls. To advance still further, further modernisation will be required. Expect more young smiling women, more photo-opportunities on bicycles, and as many references to the Arctic Monkeys as can be crammed into a speech.

The second view is that actually Britain is pretty fed up with Mr Blair and Labour, and wants to throw the scoundrels out. But being all warm and fuzzy, Mr Cameron is failing to articulate that anger, and so isn't picking up all the votes he should.[12]

A third idea is that Mr Cameron just isn't all that good. He says daft things, people think his media coverage risible and he still has his L-plates on.[13] I don't really subscribe to this, although as a relatively inexperienced front-line politician, we must expect Mr Cameron to make mistakes (which he certainly has done – see Chapters Six to Nine inclusive).

I actually subscribe to a fourth view, which is that the Tories cannot seriously expect to be any further ahead at this stage. We all agree that the period 1992 (from Black Wednesday onwards) to 2005 was a waste. No progress was made, except in so far as by 2005 the Tories had stopped being a total rabble. In the 2005 general election campaign Tory infighting was no longer the story. But other than the removal of one negative, no positives appeared.

At the beginning of Chapter Nine I mentioned Labour and 1983. Labour ceased to become electable at some vague point during the 1974–9 government, when giant Labour majorities were regularly overturned in by-elections, and the Winter of Discontent finished Labour off. They were a shambles for some time, but the modernisation process began under Neil Kinnock, shortly after 1983 (the real effort probably kicking off about 1985). It still took nearly a decade for Labour to become electable. Labour's defeat in 1992 was a surprise, but clearly Mr Kinnock was not trusted by the electorate. It still took further gains to turn Labour's catastrophic performance into soaring success: two popular leaders, Tory sleaze, Tory infighting, Black Wednesday.

So to summarise, in the fall and rise of the Labour Party there were three or four years of doomed government, four wasted years after 1979, nine years of groundwork, and then five more years of opposition in which various events happened to catapult Labour to a massive lead. If we compare this history to the Tories, they had five years of doomed government, and then they wasted a grand total of eight years in opposition. Mr Cameron has begun the groundwork. But we are not very far along the timeline.

The next election will be called in 2009, if the new Labour leader is confident of victory, 2010 otherwise. Even on the assumptions that Mr Cameron makes further progress, that tactical voting against the Tories declines, that the Tories preserve their unity particularly in the House of Commons, and the Liberal Democrats falter under Sir Menzies Campbell, it is hard to see Mr Cameron actually winning the election. The Tories might well be the largest party. Or they may be within striking distance of a resurgent Labour.

Results like these would be successes. It is wishful thinking to assume that all our political assumptions and accumulated wisdom will be thrown out overnight. A political change takes a long time. Labour's success did not happen overnight, and wouldn't have happened any quicker had Tony Blair become Labour leader earlier. Similar levels of success for the Tories depend on similar levels of hard work, as well as a future Labour government imploding. If Mr Cameron wins the next election, it will be a triumph. A hung Parliament would be a good result. And a narrow defeat, though disappointing, would not be a disaster. Just cast your mind back to 2003; what would the Tories have given for such a result at that stage?

There are two dangers for Mr Cameron. The first is that moderate success is interpreted as failure. The second is that the modernisation programme he is putting forward is interpreted as his ditching Tory principles. I have argued in this book that much of his programme is perfectly consistent with sceptical conservatism of a kind that has featured very strongly in the history of the Tory Party. Let me put it as emphatically as I can: his modernisation programme is a genuinely Tory measure.

But if these two dangerous opinions take root, then the Tories will be tempted, yet again, to change tack. And all the good work of changing the minds of British voters will be undone yet again, and set back once more. The Tories have, for good or ill, chosen the road they must travel. U-turns are not an option.

To coin a phrase: there is no alternative.

NOTES

Preface

1 Jared Diamond, *Collapse: How Societies Choose to Fail or Survive* (Allen Lane, London, 2005).
2 Paul Seabright, *The Company of Strangers: A Natural History of Economic Life* (Princeton University Press, Princeton, 2004).
3 James Surowiecki, *The Wisdom of Crowds: Why the Many Are Smarter Than the Few* (Little, Brown, London, 2004).
4 William Easterly, *The White Man's Burden: Why the West's Efforts to Aid the Rest Have Done So Much Ill and So Little Good* (Penguin, New York, 2006).
5 Francis Fukuyama, *After the Neocons: America at the Crossroads* (Profile, London, 2006).
6 David Cameron, 'Do the Right Thing', *Guardian*, 22 January 2005.
7 Danny Kruger, 'Pyrrhic Defeat', *New Statesman*, 11 April 2005.
8 Kruger, 'Pyrrhic defeat'.

1   Well, I wouldn't start from here ...

1 John Harris, *So Now Who Do We Vote For?* (Faber and Faber, London, 2005).
2 Cf. 'Not As Nice As They Look', *The Economist*, 28 April 2005.
3 'What the Tories Are For', *The Economist*, 12 May 2005.
4 Including this author. Kieron O'Hara, 'Howard's Panic Sets Party Back', *Yorkshire Post*, 26 January 2005.
5 Cf. Chris Philp (ed.), *Conservative Revival: Blueprint for a Better Britain* (Politico's, London, 2006), pp. 33–61.
6 Michael A. Ashcroft, *Smell the Coffee: A Wake-Up Call for the Conservative Party* (Michael Ashcroft, 2005).

7 See Chapter Three for more on Salisbury and Balfour.

8 Anthony Seldon and Stuart Ball (eds), *Conservative Century: The Conservative Party Since 1900* (Open University Press, London, 1990).

9 Michael Flanders, introductory monologue to *The Gnu Song*, from the 1959 recording of the Flanders and Swann revue *At the Drop of a Hat*.

10 Michael Freeden, *Ideologies and Political Theory: A Conceptual Approach* (Oxford University Press, Oxford, 1996), p. 318.

11 Robert Eccleshall, 'Conservatism', in Robert Eccleshall, Alan Finlayson, Vincent Geoghegan, Michael Kenny, Moya Lloyd, Iain MacKenzie and Rick Wilford (eds), *Political Ideologies: An Introduction* (3rd edn, Routledge, London, 2003), pp. 47–72, at pp. 49–50.

12 The rationale behind some of these affiliations is given at length in Roger Scruton, *The Meaning of Conservatism* (3rd edn, Palgrave, Basingstoke, 2001).

13 John Gray, 'The undoing of conservatism', in *Enlightenment's Wake: Politics and Culture at the Close of the Modern Age* (Routledge, London, 1995), pp. 87–119, at pp. 93–100.

14 Nigel Lawson, *The View From No. 11: Memoirs of a Tory Radical* (Bantam Press, London, 1992), pp. 63–5, 197–240.

15 Enoch Powell even finds himself apologising for Disraeli's government in *Freedom and Reality* (Elliot Right Way Books, Kingswood, Surrey, 1969), pp. 74–5.

16 Margaret Thatcher, *The Downing Street Years 1979–1990* (HarperCollins, London, 1993), pp. 839–40.

17 John Gray, 'The Tory Endgame', in *Endgames: Questions in Late Modern Political Thought* (Polity Press, Cambridge, 1997), pp. 97–155, at pp. 99–101.

18 Simon Walters, *Tory Wars: Conservatives in Crisis* (Politico's, London, 2001).

19 Mark Garnett and Philip Lynch (eds), *The Conservatives in Crisis* (Manchester University Press, Manchester, 2003).

20 Richard Kelly, 'Organisational Reform and the Extra-parliamentary Party', in Garnett and Lynch, *The Conservatives in Crisis*, pp. 82–106.

21 Walters, *Tory Wars*, p. 101.

22 Kelly, 'Organisational Reform and the Extra-parliamentary Party'.

23 Sarah Womack, 'Gay Past Hit Portillo's Leadership Bid, Says Clarke', *Daily Telegraph*, 7 January 2002. A quick note about references to the *Daily Telegraph*. I do my searches for newspaper articles online, so most references to newspapers, periodicals and magazines can be found on the web. However, whereas most websites make clear distinctions between the different journals that are hosted on them (for instance, the *Guardian*

Unlimited website lets you know whether a report found in its archives was originally published in the *Guardian* or the *Observer*), this is not the case with telegraph.co.uk. On that site, you have to go back through the calendar to work out whether something first appeared in the *Daily Telegraph* or the *Sunday Telegraph*. Life is too short for that, and so my references to the *Daily Telegraph* actually cover both journals.

24 Cf. Anthony Seldon and Peter Snowden, 'The Conservative Campaign', *Parliamentary Affairs* vol. 58 (4), pp. 725–42, at pp. 726–8.

25 Auslan Cramb, 'Tories Must Travel a Long, Hard Road', *Daily Telegraph*, 25 March 2002.

26 Gary Streeter (ed.), *There Is Such a Thing as Society: Twelve Principles of Compassionate Conservatism* (Politico's, London, 2002). See, in particular, Iain Duncan Smith's chapter.

27 Iain Duncan Smith, 'The Renewal of Society', in Streeter, *There Is Such a Thing as Society*, pp. 30–37, at p. 35.

28 Oliver Letwin, 'For Labour There Is No Such Thing as Society, Only the State', in Streeter, *There Is Such a Thing as Society*, pp. 38–51, at p. 45.

29 Benedict Brogan, '"Dance of Death" Sees Off Davis the Kingmaker', *Daily Telegraph*, 30 October 2003.

30 'Howard's New Way', *Guardian*, 20 February 2004.

31 George Jones, 'I'll Be Straight With You, Says Howard, We've Got To Earn Trust Through Action', *Daily Telegraph*, 6 October 2004.

32 Michael Howard, 'I Wouldn't Go That Far', *Guardian*, 28 November 2003.

33 Philip Johnston, 'Davis Talks Tough on the Need to Control Migration', *Daily Telegraph*, 7 October 2004.

34 O'Hara, 'Howard's Panic Sets Party Back', Philp, *Conservative Revival*, pp. 9–12.

35 Michael Howard, 'A Government Which is Honest. A Government You Can Trust', speech to the Conservative Party Conference, October 2004, http://www.conservatives.com/tile.do?def=news.story.page&obj_id=116484&speeches=1.

36 Cf. Philp, *Conservative Revival*, pp. 7–8, Seldon and Snowden, 'The Conservative Campaign', pp. 731–2.

37 The ideological commonalities between the British and American right are described, in what I believe is somewhat exaggerated form, in Bruce Pilbeam, *Conservatism in Crisis? Anglo-American Conservative Ideology After the Cold War* (Palgrave Macmillan, Basingstoke, 2003).

38 Margaret Thatcher, *The Downing Street Years 1979–1990* (HarperCollins, London, 1993), pp. 626–7.

39 Edward Ashbee, 'The US Republicans: Lessons for the Conservatives?', in Garnett and Lynch, *The Conservatives in Crisis*, pp. 29–48, at pp. 39–41.

40 Ashbee, 'The US Republicans', pp. 41–2.

41 Robert Putnam, *Bowling Alone* (Simon and Schuster, New York, 2000).

42 Michael Oakeshott, 'The Voice of Poetry in the Conversation of Mankind', in *Rationalism in Politics and Other Essays* (New and expanded edn, Liberty Fund, Indianapolis, 1991), pp. 488–541.

43 'Something for the Kitchen Table', *The Economist*, 29 April 1999.

44 Sandra Barwick, 'Last Supper as Oxo Family Finally Crumbles', *Daily Telegraph*, 31 August 1999.

45 'The China Syndrome', *The Economist*, 23 August 2001.

46 Rachel Sylvester, 'Duncan Smith Tries on the Leopard-print Kitten Heels', *Daily Telegraph*, 12 October 2002; Colin Brown and Francis Elliott, 'The Week the Kitten Heel Trod on the Polecat', *Daily Telegraph*, 13 October 2002; Benedict Brogan, 'Theresa Given Her Own Range of Shoes', *Daily Telegraph*, 22 November 2002.

47 'A Tale of Two Legacies', *The Economist*, 19 December 2002.

48 Michael Howard, 'I Believe', *The Times*, 2 January 2004.

49 Nicholas Watt, 'Tories' New Credo has US Roots', *Guardian*, 3 January 2004.

50 Matthew Bishop, 'Giving Something Back', *The Economist*, 14 June 2001.

51 Taken from 'A Tale of Two Legacies', *The Economist*, 19 December 2002, in the middle of the Duncan Smith era. Sources: Gallup, MORI, Pew Research Centre, Council for Secular Humanism, *Daily Telegraph*, US Census Bureau, UK Office for National Statistics, Merrill Lynch, *British Medical Journal*, DPIC, IISS, OECD.

52 Such constructive imagemaking is discussed in innumerable editorials, op ed pieces and think-tank pamphlets, but in particular see the Bow Group's book Philp (ed.), *Conservative Revival*.

53 Ashcroft, *Smell the Coffee*.

54 I consider the 2005 leadership contest in Andrew Denham and Kieron O'Hara, *Cameron's 'Mandate': Democracy, Legitimacy and Conservative Leadership* (Manchester University Press, Manchester, forthcoming).

55 David Cameron, 'Change to Win', speech to the 2005 Conservative Party Conference, http://www.conservatives.com/tile.do?def=news.story. page&obj_id=125400&speeches=1.

56 Figures taken from MORI polls, based on voting intentions of all adults naming a party, except where actual general election results (in bold) are cited. See http://www.mori.com/polls/trends/voting-all-trends.shtml.

57 Tania Branigan, 'Donations to Tories Hit Nearly £9m in Three Months', *Guardian*, 26 May 2006.

58 Kieron O'Hara, 'Your Bank Manager's Car', *New Statesman*, 18 April 2005, p. 26.

59 Philp, *Conservative Revival*, pp. 62–87.

60 Ned Temko, 'Tories Bypass A-list to Choose Forth Successor', *Observer*, 4 June 2006.

61 Tania Branigan, 'Narrow Margin of Victory in Bromley Deals Blow to Tory Renaissance Hopes', *Guardian*, 1 July 2006.

62 Simon Heffer, 'Tories Draw Wrong Lessons from Bromley', *Daily Telegraph*, 1 July 2006.

63 Andrew Rawnsley, 'Mr Cameron Must Resist the Siren Call of the Reactionaries', *Observer*, 2 July 2006.

64 Jesse Norman and Janan Ganesh, *Compassionate Conservatism: What It Is, Why We Need It* (Policy Exchange, London, 2006).

65 Norman and Ganesh, *Compassionate Conservatism*, p. 3.

66 Francis Fukuyama, *After the Neocons: America at the Crossroads* (Profile, London, 2006).

67 'The Fight Over a Big Idea', *The Economist*, 20 July 2006.

68 Polly Toynbee, 'Compassionate Conservatism Sounds Uncannily Familiar', *Guardian*, 13 June 2006. The online edition of this article also contains a reply from Jesse Norman in the series of comments posted by readers.

69 *Built to Last: The Aims and Values of the Conservative Party*, August 2006, http://www.conservatives.com/pdf/BuiltToLast-AimsandValues.pdf.

70 David Cameron, 'Foreword', in *Built to Last*, pp. 2–3, at p. 3.

71 Mark Garnett, 'A Question of Definition? Ideology and the Conservative Party 1997–2001', in Garnett and Lynch, *The Conservatives in Crisis*, pp. 107–24.

72 David Willetts, *Modern Conservatism* (Penguin, Harmondsworth, 1992), especially pp. 92–108.

73 Freeden, *Ideologies and Political Theory*, pp. 348–93.

74 W.H. Greenleaf, *The British Political Tradition Volume Two: The Ideological Heritage* (Methuen, London, 1983), p. 195.

75 Bruce Pilbeam, *Conservatism in Crisis? Anglo-American Conservative Ideology After the Cold War* (Palgrave Macmillan, Basingstoke, 2003), pp. 8–9.

76 The speech was spoofed in 'Your Guide to the Forces of Conservatism', *Observer*, 3 October 1999. The speech itself is at http://news.bbc.co.uk/1/hi/uk_politics/460009.stm.

2 The idea of human imperfection

1 Andrew Gregory, *Eureka! The Birth of Science* (Icon Books, Cambridge, 2001).

2 Plato, *Complete Works* (John M. Cooper, ed., D.S. Hutchinson, associate ed., Hackett, Indianapolis, 1997).

3 David Sedley, 'The Motivation of Greek Skepticism', in Myles Burnyeat (ed.), *The Skeptical Tradition* (University of California Press, Berkeley, 1983), pp. 9–29.

4 The major source is a brief philosophical biography written centuries later: Diogenes Laertius, *Lives of Eminent Philosophers* (2 vols, revised edn, R.D. Hicks, trans., Loeb Classical Library, Harvard University Press, Cambridge, MA, 1931), Book IX, pp. 61–108.

5 Though it has been convincingly argued that Pyrrhonism actually doesn't have that many resemblances to the philosophy of Pyrrho. See Richard Bett, *Pyrrho, His Antecedents, and His Legacy* (Oxford University Press, Oxford, 2000).

6 Alan Bailey, *Sextus Empiricus and Pyrrhonean Scepticism* (Oxford University Press, Oxford, 2002), pp. 100–101.

7 Various translations of this are available. The major ones are R.G. Bury (trans.), *Outlines of Pyrrhonism* (Loeb Classical Library, Harvard University Press, Cambridge, MA, 1933); Julia Annas and Jonathan Barnes (eds), *Outlines of Scepticism* (Cambridge University Press, Cambridge, 2000); and Benson Mates, *The Skeptic Way: Sextus Empiricus's* Outlines of Pyrrhonism (Oxford University Press, New York, 1996).

8 Myles Burnyeat, 'Can the Sceptic Live His Scepticism?', in Myles Burnyeat and Michael Frede (eds), *The Original Sceptics: A Controversy* (Hackett, Indianapolis, 1997), pp. 25–57.

9 Michael Frede, 'The Sceptic's Beliefs', in Burnyeat and Frede, *The Original Sceptics*, pp. 1–24.

10 Jonathan Barnes, 'The Beliefs of a Pyrrhonist', in Burnyeat and Frede, *The Original Sceptics*, pp. 58–91.

11 Bailey, *Sextus Empiricus*.

12 Cf. Gisela Striker, 'The Ten Tropes of Aenesidemus', in Burnyeat, *The Skeptical Tradition*, pp. 95–115, and Julia Annas and Jonathan Barnes, *The Modes of Scepticism: Ancient Texts and Modern Interpretations* (Cambridge University Press, Cambridge, 1985).

13 Jonathan Barnes, *The Toils of Scepticism* (Cambridge University Press, Cambridge, 1990).

14 Peter D. Boone, *The Impact of Foreign Aid on Savings and Growth*, CEP working paper no. 677 (1994), 'Politics and the Effectiveness of Foreign Aid', *European Economic Review* vol. 40 (1996), pp. 289–329.

15 Craig Burnside and David Dollar, 'Aid, Policies and Growth', *American Economic Review* vol. 90 (2000), pp. 847–68.

16 William Easterly, Ross Levine and David Roodman, 'New Data, New

Doubts: Comment on "Aid, Policies and Growth" (2000) by Burnside and Dollar', *American Economic Review* vol. 94 (2004), pp. 774–80.

17 Michael Clemens, Steven Radelet and Rikhil Bhavnani, *Counting Chickens When They Hatch: The Short-Term Effect of Aid on Growth*, Center for Global Development working paper no. 44 (2004).

18 William Easterly, *The White Man's Burden: Why the West's Efforts to Aid the Rest Have Done So Much Ill and So Little Good* (Penguin, New York, 2006), pp. 44–51.

19 Gregory, *Eureka!* pp. 115–35.

20 For the debate in medicine about theory and practice, see G.E.R. Lloyd, 'The Epistemological Theory and Practice of Soranus's Methodism', in *Science, Folklore and Ideology: Studies in the Life Sciences in Ancient Greece* (Cambridge University Press, Cambridge, 1983), pp. 182–200.

21 He may have been a physician of a similar type known as a methodist, rather than an empiricist, but for our purposes the issue is not crucial. For the record, he criticises empiricism in the *Outlines* I, pp. 236–7; see Bailey, *Sextus Empiricus*, pp. 92–4.

22 Diogenes, *Lives*, IX, pp. 61, 101, 108.

23 Sextus, *Outlines*, I, pp. 23–4 (Bury translation).

24 Herodotus, *The Histories* (Aubrey de Sélincourt and A.R. Burn, trans., Penguin, Harmondsworth, 1972). It may be suggestive that Enoch Powell began his academic career studying Herodotus.

25 Diogenes, *Lives*, IX, p. 95.

26 Sextus Empiricus, *Against the Mathematicians*, IX, p. 49. Books IX and X of *Against the Mathematicians* are translated as R.G. Bury (trans.), *Against the Physicists* in R.G. Bury (ed.), *Works of Sextus Empiricus Volume III* (Loeb Classical Library, Harvard University Press, Cambridge MA, 1936).

27 Luciano Floridi, *Sextus Empiricus: The Transmission and Recovery of Pyrrhonism* (Oxford University Press, New York, 2002), pp. 20–22.

28 I Corinthians 8:1.

29 Floridi, *Sextus Empiricus*, p. 27.

30 C.B. Schmitt, 'The Rediscovery of Ancient Skepticism in Modern Times', in Burnyeat, *The Skeptical Tradition*, pp. 225–51, at p. 236.

31 Montaigne, *The Complete Essays* (M.A. Screech, ed., Penguin, Harmondsworth, 1991).

32 See, for instance, 'On the Cannibals', *Essays*, pp. 228–41, though there are dozens of examples.

33 Montaigne, 'On Presumption', *Essays*, pp. 718–52, at p. 745.

34 Peter Burke, *Montaigne* (Oxford University Press, Oxford, 1981), p. 28.

35 David Lewis Schaefer, *The Political Philosophy of Montaigne* (Cornell University Press, Ithaca, 1990).

36 Schaefer, *The Political Philosophy of Montaigne*, p. 154.

37 Montaigne, 'On Habit: And On Never Easily Changing a Traditional Law', *Essays*, pp. 122–39, at p. 135.

38 Edmund Spenser, *The Faerie Queene*, V.ii.36. I have taken the liberty of modernising the spelling.

39 I have discussed this aspect of Shakespeare's work elsewhere at greater length. See Kieron O'Hara, *Trust: From Socrates to Spin* (Icon Books, Cambridge, 2004), pp. 36–42.

40 Anthony Holden, *William Shakespeare: His Life and Works* (Abacus, London, 1999), pp. 281–3.

41 Richard H. Popkin, *The History of Scepticism From Erasmus to Spinoza* (4th edn, University of California Press, New York, 1979).

42 Sir Thomas Browne, *The Works of Sir Thomas Browne Volume III* (Sir Geoffrey Keynes, ed., London, 1964), p. 290.

43 Sir Thomas Browne, 'Religio Medici' in C.A. Patrides (ed.), *Sir Thomas Browne: The Major Works* (Penguin, Harmondsworth, 1977), pp. 55–161.

44 *Religio Medici*, p. 66.

45 *Religio Medici*, pp. 147–8.

3 The Conservative Party as the custodian of the conservative tradition

1 Karl Mannheim, *Conservatism: A Contribution to the Sociology of Knowledge* (David Kettler, Volker Meja and Nico Stehr, eds, David Kettler and Volker Meja, trans., Routledge and Kegan Paul, London, 1986), p. 128; Samuel P. Huntington, 'Conservatism as an ideology', *American Political Science Review* vol. 51 (1957), pp. 454–73; Michael Freeden, *Ideologies and Political Theory: A Conceptual Approach* (Oxford University Press, Oxford, 1996), pp. 335–8.

2 Cf. Mannheim, *Conservatism*, p. 95, on the two archetypal ways of experiencing things and the world around them.

3 That right-wing comedians are much funnier than left-wing ones is a fact even acknowledged in the *Guardian*; Andrew Anthony, 'Why Does the Devil Have All the Best Gags?' *Guardian*, 15 April 2004.

4 Louis I. Bredvold, *The Intellectual Milieu of John Dryden: Studies in Some Aspects of Seventeenth-Century Thought* (University of Michigan Press, Michigan, 1934).

5 John Dryden, 'The Medall', ll. 247–50.

6 John Dryden, 'Absalom & Achitophel', ll. 795–800.

7 Basil Williams, *The Whig Supremacy 1714–1760* (2nd edn, C.H. Stuart, rev., Oxford University Press, Oxford, 1960).

8 Edmund Burke, *Reflections on the Revolution in France* (Conor Cruise O'Brien, ed., Penguin, Harmondsworth, 1968).

9 Conor Cruise O'Brien, 'Introduction', in Burke, *Reflections*, pp. 9–76, at pp. 34–41.

10 Hannah Arendt, 'What is Authority?', in Peter Baehr (ed.), *The Portable Hannah Arendt* (Penguin, New York, 2000), pp. 462–507, at pp. 501–02.

11 Cf. e.g. Thomas Paine, 'The Rights of Man' Part One, abridged in Michael Foot and Isaac Kramnick (eds), *The Thomas Paine Reader* (Penguin, Harmondsworth, 1987), pp. 201–364, especially pp. 201–62.

12 O'Brien, 'Introduction', pp. 56–62.

13 Burke, *Reflections*, pp. 89–90.

14 From a letter to Lord Charlemont on 9 August 1789, from Thomas W. Copeland (ed.), *The Correspondence of Edmund Burke Volume VI*. According to O'Brien, this is Burke's earliest known comment on the French Revolution.

15 Burke, *Reflections*, p. 207.

16 Burke, *Reflections*, p. 140.

17 René Descartes, 'Meditations on First Philosophy', in John Cottingham, Robert Stoothoff and Dugald Murdoch (eds), *The Philosophical Writings of Descartes Vol. II* (Cambridge University Press, Cambridge, 1984), pp. 1–62, especially pp. 12–23.

18 See in particular *A Treatise of Human Nature, Enquiry Concerning Human Understanding*, and *Dialogues Concerning Natural Religion*.

19 David Hume, *A Treatise of Human Nature* (L.A. Selby-Bigge and P.H. Nidditch, eds, Oxford University Press, Oxford, 1978), I.iv.i, pp. 180–81. This argument is strikingly reminiscent of the modern case made by Imre Lakatos, *Proofs and Refutations: The Logic of Mathematical Discovery* (Cambridge University Press, Cambridge, 1976).

20 Richard H. Popkin, 'David Hume: His Pyrrhonism and his Critique of Pyrrhonism', in Richard H. Popkin, *The High Road to Pyrrhonism* (Richard A. Watson and James E. Force, eds, Hackett, Indianapolis, 1980), pp. 103–32.

21 David Hume, *Dialogues Concerning Natural Religion* (Henry D. Aiken, ed., Hafner, New York, 1948), XII, p. 87.

22 Richard H. Popkin, 'David Hume and the Pyrrhonian Controversy', in *The High Road to Pyrrhonism*, pp. 133–47.

23 Hume, *Treatise*, I.iv.vii, p. 269.

24 Robert Blake, *The Conservative Party From Peel to Thatcher* (Fontana, London, 1985), pp. 1–9.

25 For an innovative and usable online resource covering the age of Peel, see

Marjie Bloy's *Peel Web*: http://www.historyhome.co.uk/peel/peelhome. htm.

26 John Ramsden, *An Appetite for Power: A History of the Conservative Party Since 1830* (HarperCollins, London, 1998), pp. 47–9.

27 Blake, *The Conservative Party*, pp. 19–27.

28 Blake, *The Conservative Party*, pp. 58–9.

29 Blake, *The Conservative Party*, pp. 18–19, 53–4.

30 Cf. David Willetts, 'The Three Rights of Public Services', speech delivered 9 December 2003, at the Viennese Institute of Human Science. Available from http://www.davidwilletts.org or http://www.conservatives.com/.

31 Benjamin Disraeli, *Coningsby* (Sheila M. Smith, ed., Oxford University Press, Oxford, 1982), II.5, p. 87.

32 Benjamin Disraeli, *Sybil* (Thom Braun, ed., Penguin, Harmondsworth, 1980).

33 Maurice Cowling, *1867: Disraeli, Gladstone and Revolution* (Cambridge University Press, Cambridge, 1967).

34 Blake, *The Conservative Party*, pp. 98–103 summarises the controversy.

35 Anthony Trollope, *Phineas Redux* (John C. Whale, ed., Oxford University Press, Oxford, 1983).

36 Sir Robert Ensor, *England 1870–1914* (Oxford University Press, Oxford, 1936), pp. 20–22.

37 Paul Smith, *Disraelian Conservatism and Social Reform* (Routledge, London, 1967).

38 Quoted in Ramsden, *An Appetite for Power*, p. 530.

39 Blake, *The Conservative Party*, pp. 131–2.

40 Salisbury writing in 1872 about the Irish question; he was also to serve as Secretary of State for India under Disraeli. The passage is taken from Lady Gwendolyn Cecil, *The Life of Robert Marquess of Salisbury Vol. II* (Hodder & Stoughton, London, 1921), pp. 38–9, and quoted in Blake, *The Conservative Party*, p. 133.

41 Andrew Roberts, *Salisbury: Victorian Titan* (Weidenfeld & Nicolson, London, 1999), pp. 85–6.

42 Roberts, *Salisbury*, pp. 282–7.

43 Ramsden, *An Appetite for Power*, p. 537.

44 Ramsden, *An Appetite for Power*, p. 180.

45 Arthur James Balfour, *A Defence of Philosophic Doubt: Being an Essay on the Foundations of Belief* (new edn, Hodder and Stoughton, London, 1920), p. viii; Kenneth Young, *Arthur James Balfour: The Happy Life of the Politician, Prime Minister, Statesman and Philosopher 1848–1930* (G. Bell and Sons, London, 1963), p. 48.

46 Balfour, *Defence*, pp. 296–8.

47 Balfour, *Defence*, pp. 322–3. This position is not a million miles away from ideas of the leading 20th-century conservative philosopher Michael Oakeshott, e.g. 'The Voice of Poetry in the Conversation of Mankind' in Michael Oakeshott, *Rationalism in Politics and Other Essays* (new and expanded edn, Timothy Fuller, ed., Liberty Fund, Indianapolis, 1991), pp. 488–541.

48 Rt Hon. Arthur James Balfour, *The Foundations of Belief: Being Notes Introductory to the Study of Theology* (Longmans, Green & Co., London, 1895), p. 230.

49 As discussed by Willetts, 'The Three Rights of Public Services'.

50 Freeden, *Ideologies and Political Theory*, pp. 139–314.

51 Isaiah Berlin, 'Two Concepts of Liberty', in Anthony Quinton (ed.), *Political Philosophy* (Oxford University Press, Oxford, 1967), pp. 141–52.

52 Willetts, 'The Three Rights of Public Services'.

53 W.H. Greenleaf, *The British Political Tradition Volume Two: The Ideological Heritage* (Methuen, London, 1983), pp. 272–3.

54 David Willetts draws attention to the 'fragmentation, rivalry and jealousy' of the period that prompted the setting up of a 'legion of leagues' in David Willetts with Richard Forsdyke, *After the Landslide: Learning the Lessons from 1906 and 1945* (Centre for Policy Studies, London, 1999), pp. 14–15.

55 Roberts, *Salisbury*, p. 283.

56 E.H.H. Green, 'Conservatism, the State, and Civil Society in the Twentieth Century' in E.H.H. Green, *Ideologies of Conservatism* (Oxford University Press, Oxford, 2002), pp. 240–79, at p. 257.

57 See E.H.H. Green, '"No Settled Convictions"? Arthur Balfour, Political Economy, and Tariff Reform: A Reconsideration', in E.H.H. Green, *Ideologies of Conservatism* (Oxford University Press, Oxford, 2002), pp. 18–41.

58 Blake, *The Conservative Party*, pp. 168–9.

59 Quoted in Young, *Balfour*, p. 214.

60 Robert Eccleshall, 'Conservatism', in Robert Eccleshall, Alan Finlayson, Vincent Geoghegan, Michael Kenny, Moya Lloyd, Iain MacKenzie and Rick Wilford (eds), *Political Ideologies: An Introduction* (3rd edn, Routledge, London, 2003), pp. 47–72.

61 W.H. Greenleaf, *The British Political Tradition Volume Two: The Ideological Heritage* (Methuen, London, 1983), p. 195.

62 J. Enoch Powell, speech to the Royal Society of St George, 22 April 1961, in J. Enoch Powell, *Freedom and Reality* (John Wood, ed., Elliot Right Way Books, Kingswood, 1969), pp. 337–41.

63 J. Enoch Powell, 'Theory and Practice', in G.M.K. Hunt (ed.), *Philosophy*

and Politics (Cambridge University Press, Cambridge, 1990), pp. 1–9, at p. 5.

64 Powell, 'Theory and Practice', p. 7.

65 Powell, speech at Birmingham, 20 April 1968, in *Freedom and Reality*, pp. 281–90.

66 Andrew Denham and Mark Garnett, *Keith Joseph* (Acumen, Chesham, 2001), pp. 245–53.

67 Blake, *The Conservative Party*, pp. 339–40.

68 Cf. e.g. Steve Buckler and David P. Dolowitz, 'Theorizing the Third Way: New Labour and Social Justice', *Journal of Political Ideologies* vol. 5 (2000), pp. 301–20.

4 What is conservatism?

1 Cf. Karl Mannheim, *Conservatism: A Contribution to the Sociology of Knowledge* (David Kettler, Volker Meja and Nico Stehr, eds, David Kettler and Volker Meja, trans., Routledge and Kegan Paul, London, 1986), pp. 72–7.

2 John Rawls, *A Theory of Justice* (Oxford University Press, Oxford, 1971), especially pp. 136–42.

3 Stuart Sim, *Fundamentalist World: The New Dark Age of Dogma* (Icon Books, Cambridge, 2004), pp. 102–34.

4 Mannheim, *Conservatism*, pp. 88–9.

5 Argued by Robert Nozick, for example, in *Anarchy, State and Utopia* (Blackwell, Oxford, 1974).

6 E.g. Robert Eccleshall, 'Conservatism', in Robert Eccleshall, Alan Finlayson, Vincent Geoghegan, Michael Kenny, Moya Lloyd, Iain MacKenzie and Rick Wilford (eds), *Political Ideologies: An Introduction* (3rd edn, Routledge, London, 2003), pp. 47–72; Ted Honderich, *Conservatism: Burke, Nozick, Bush, Blair?* (rev. edn, Pluto Press, London, 2005).

7 Greenleaf, *The Ideological Heritage*, p. 195, in a passage already quoted in Chapter One.

8 Harold Macmillan, *At the End of the Day: 1961–1963* (Macmillan, London, 1973), p. 37. The quote is from Macmillan's diary, from 21 September 1961.

9 See Chapter One.

10 Mike Brewer, Alissa Goodman, Michal Myck, Jonathan Shaw and Andrew Shephard, *Poverty and Inequality in Britain: 2004* (Institute for Fiscal Studies, London, 2004).

11 Mannheim, *Conservatism*, p. 76 and n. 46.

12 Tony Burns, 'John Gray and the Death of Conservatism', *Contemporary Politics*, vol. 5 (1999), pp. 7–24.

13 John Gray, 'The Tory Endgame', in *Endgames: Questions in Late Modern Political Thought* (Polity Press, Cambridge, 1997), pp. 97–155, at pp. 114–15.

14 Michael Freeden, *Ideologies and Political Theory: A Conceptual Approach* (Oxford University Press, Oxford, 1996), pp. 47–95.

15 Victoria Horner and Andrew Whiten, 'Causal Knowledge and Imitation/Emulation Switching in Chimpanzees (*Pan troglodytes*) and Children (*Homo sapiens*)', *Animal Cognition* vol. 8 (3), July 2005, pp. 164–81.

16 Mairi Macleod, 'Just Like Your Mother Taught You', *New Scientist*, 1 April 2006.

17 Cf. Mannheim, *Conservatism*, p. 148.

18 Roger Scruton, *The Meaning of Conservatism* (3rd edn, Palgrave, Basingstoke, 2001), pp. 10, 11.

19 Freeden, *Ideologies and Political Theory*, pp. 332–3.

20 Michael Oakeshott, 'On Being Conservative', in *Rationalism in Politics and Other Essays* (new and expanded edn, Liberty Fund, Indianapolis, 1991), pp. 407–37, at pp. 410–11.

21 Jared Diamond, *Collapse: How Societies Choose to Fail or Survive* (Allen Lane, London, 2005).

22 Diamond, *Collapse*, especially pp. 79–276.

23 Diamond, *Collapse*, pp. 202–03.

24 Mannheim, *Conservatism*, pp. 45–6.

25 Freeden, *Ideologies and Political Theory*, p. 334.

26 Freeden, *Ideologies and Political Theory*, pp. 348–83.

27 Scruton, *The Meaning of Conservatism*.

28 Roger Scruton, *England: An Elegy* (Pimlico, London, 2001).

29 Danny Kruger, 'Pyrrhic Defeat', *New Statesman*, 11 April 2005.

30 Cf. e.g. Larry Arnhart, *Darwinian Conservatism* (Imprint Academic, Exeter, 2005), pp. 85–103.

31 Oliver Letwin, *The Purpose of Politics* (Social Market Foundation, London, 1999), pp. 3–31.

32 F.A. Hayek, *The Constitution of Liberty* (Routledge & Kegan Paul, London, 1960), pp. 397–411.

33 Daniel Kahneman, Paul Slovic and Amos Tversky (eds), *Judgement Under Uncertainty: Heuristics and Biases* (Cambridge University Press, Cambridge, 1982).

34 Bureaucracy has been, for many, the key to modernity. The classic account is in the sociological works of Max Weber (1864–1920), such as in Hans H. Gerth and C. Wright Mills (eds), *From Max Weber: Essays in Sociology*

(Oxford University Press, New York, 1948). See also Kieron O'Hara, *Trust: From Socrates to Spin* (Icon Books, Cambridge, 2004), pp. 55–58, 224–31.

35 'The Trouble with Targets', *The Economist*, 26 April 2001.

36 'Targetitis', *The Economist*, 12 December 2002.

37 Marshall Meyer, 'The Performance Paradox', in B.M. Staw and L. Cummings (eds), *Research in Organizational Behavior Vol. 14* (JAI Press, Greenwich CT, 1994), pp. 309–69.

38 'Missing the Point', *The Economist*, 26 April 2001.

39 F.A. Hayek, 'The Use of Knowledge in Society', *American Economic Review* vol. 35 (1945), pp. 519–30.

40 'Big Questions and Big Numbers', *The Economist*, 13 July 2006.

41 James Surowiecki, *The Wisdom of Crowds: Why the Many are Smarter than the Few* (Little, Brown, London, 2004), pp. 23–39.

42 Hayek, 'The Use of Knowledge in Society', p. 523.

43 Mary Douglas, *How Institutions Think* (Routledge & Kegan Paul, London, 1986).

44 Kieron O'Hara, *Plato and the Internet* (Icon Books, Cambridge, 2002), pp. 32–7, 59–60.

45 David Willetts, *Modern Conservatism* (Penguin, Harmondsworth, 1992), pp. 93–108.

46 Mannheim, *Conservatism*, p. 131.

47 R. Eyerman and B. Turner, 'Outline of a Theory of Generations', *European Journal of Social Theory* vol. 1 (1998), pp. 91–106.

48 Barbara A. Misztal, *Theories of Social Remembering* (Open University Press, Maidenhead, 2003), pp. 91–8.

49 John N. Adams and Roger Brownsword, *Understanding Law* (3rd edn, Sweet & Maxwell, London, 2003), pp. 46–53.

50 Adams and Brownsword, *Understanding Law*, pp. 82–145.

51 Letwin, *The Purpose of Politics*, pp. 32–57.

52 Hannah Arendt, 'Labor, Work, Action', in Peter Baehr (ed.), *The Portable Hannah Arendt* (Penguin, New York, 2000), pp. 167–81, at pp. 180–81.

53 Diamond, *Collapse*, especially pp. 419–40.

54 Bruce Pilbeam, *Conservatism in Crisis: Anglo-American Conservative Ideology at the End of the Cold War* (Palgrave Macmillan, Basingstoke, 2003), p. 8.

55 Roberts, *Salisbury*, pp. 86–98.

5   Is conservatism dead?

1 Michael Oakeshott, 'On Being Conservative', in *Rationalism in Politics and Other Essays* (new and expanded edn, Liberty Fund, Indianapolis, 1991), pp. 407–37, at p. 408.

2 John Gray, 'The Undoing of Conservatism', in *Enlightenment's Wake: Politics and Culture at the Close of the Modern Age* (Routledge, London, 1995), pp. 87–119, at p. 93.

3 Gray, 'The Undoing of Conservatism', p. 106.

4 Roger Scruton, *England: An Elegy* (Pimlico, London, 2001).

5 Geoffrey Wheatcroft, *The Strange Death of Tory England* (Allen Lane, London, 2005).

6 Gray, 'The Undoing of Conservatism', pp. 99–100.

7 Enoch Powell, speech to Royal Society of St George, 22 April 1961, in *Freedom and Reality* (John Wood, ed., Batsford, London, 1969), pp. 337–41.

8 Quintin Hogg, *The Case for Conservatism* (Penguin, West Drayton, 1947).

9 See, for instance, *Freedom and Reality*, pp. 281–314, speech at Wolverhampton, 11 June 1970, in John Wood (ed.), *Powell and the 1970 Election* (Elliot Right Way Books, Kingswood, 1970), pp. 97–104; *Still to Decide* (John Wood, ed., Batsford, London, 1972), pp. 189–212; *A Nation or No Nation? Six Years in British Politics* (Richard Ritchie, ed., Batsford, London, 1978), pp. 160–74.

10 Linda Colley, *Britons: Forging the Nation 1707–1837* (Yale University Press, New Haven, 1992), pp. 24–37.

11 Enoch Powell, *The Common Market: Renegotiate or Come Out* (Elliot Right Way Books, Tadworth, 1973), pp. 66–90.

12 Robin Young, 'Best of British Guts a Nation', *Australian*, 29 April 2004.

6   Conservatism and markets

1 David Willetts, *Why Vote Conservative?* (Penguin, Harmondsworth, 1997), pp. 7–9.

2 F.A. Hayek, *The Constitution of Liberty* (Routledge & Kegan Paul, London, 1960), p. 228.

3 F.A. Hayek, *The Road to Serfdom* (Routledge Press, London, 1944).

4 J. Enoch Powell, speech at Wolverhampton, 6 March 1964, reprinted in *Freedom and Reality* (John Wood, ed., Batsford, London, 1969), pp. 92–4, at p. 94.

5 Hayek, *The Constitution of Liberty*, p. 400.

6 J. Enoch Powell and Keith Wallis, *The House of Lords in the Middle Ages* (Weidenfeld & Nicolson, London, 1968), p. xi.

7 *Britain's Ruin* (Alcohol Concern, London, 2000).

8 'Reclaiming the Night', *The Economist*, 10 August 2000.

9 'In a Pickle', *The Economist*, 18 March 2004.

10 Hayek, *The Constitution of Liberty*, p. 400.

11 Kenneth J. Arrow, *The Limits of Organization* (W.W. Norton, New York, 1974), p. 20.

12 For example, Larry Arnhart, *Darwinian Conservatism* (Imprint Academic, Exeter, 2005), p. 23.

13 Andrew Roberts, *Salisbury: Victorian Titan* (Weidenfeld & Nicolson, London, 1999), pp. 279–87.

14 James Surowiecki, *The Wisdom of Crowds: Why the Many Are Smarter Than the Few* (Little, Brown, London, 2004), pp. 97–101.

15 Richard Sennett, *The Corrosion of Character: The Personal Consequences of Work in the New Capitalism* (W.W. Norton, New York, 1998).

16 David Cameron, speech, 20 July 2006, http://www.conservatives.com/ tile.do?def=news.story.page&obj_id=131047&speeches=1.

17 Richard Layard, *Happiness: Lessons From a New Science* (Allen Lane, London, 2005).

18 Layard, *Happiness*, pp. 11–27.

19 Layard, *Happiness*, pp. 111–25.

20 David Cameron, speech to Google *Zeitgeist* Europe 2006, 22 May 2006, http://www.conservatives.com/tile.do?def=news.story.page&obj_ id=129957&speeches=1.

21 Cameron, speech to Google *Zeitgeist* Europe 2006.

22 Foresight, *Trends and Drivers of Obesity: A Literature Review for the Foresight Project on Obesity*, April 2006, http://www.foresight.gov.uk/ Obesity/Reports/Literature_Review/Literature_Review.pdf.

23 Cameron, speech, 20 July 2006.

24 'Labour's Woeful Track Record on Obesity', Conservative Party website, 23 August 2006, http://www.conservatives.com/tile.do?def=news.story. page&obj_id=131649.

25 Cameron, speech, 20 July 2006.

26 'Virtue for Sale', *The Economist*, 27 October 2005.

27 Julian Le Grand, *Motivation, Agency and Public Policy: Of Knights and Knaves, Pawns and Queens* (Oxford University Press, Oxford, 2003).

28 Le Grand, *Motivation, Agency and Public Policy*, pp. 15–17.

29 Le Grand, *Motivation, Agency and Public Policy*, pp. 23–38, which reviews the empirical literature about this.

30 *Built to Last: The Aims and Values of the Conservative Party*, August 2006,

http://www.conservatives.com/pdf/BuiltToLast-AimsandValues.pdf, at p. 4.

31 Baroness Kelly and Stephen Dorrell, *The Wellbeing of the Nation*, interim report of the Public Service Improvement Policy Group, September 2006, http://www.publicserviceschallenge.com/uploads/tx_ev3evnews/ Public_Service_Policy_Group_Interim_Report.pdf; Will Woodward, 'Tories Admit Past Mistakes Over Public Service Workers', *Guardian*, 4 September 2006.

32 Kieron O'Hara, *Trust: From Socrates to Spin* (Icon Books, Cambridge, 2004), pp. 157–205.

33 David Cameron, Chamberlain lecture on communities, 14 July 2006, http://www.conservatives.com/tile.do?def=news.story.page&obj_ id=130942&speeches=1.

34 Cameron, Chamberlain lecture on communities.

35 Andrew Collier, *Marx* (Oneworld, Oxford, 2004), p. 75.

36 http://www.rspb.org.uk/.

37 For a recent comprehensive summary of the evidence, in a journal not known for its tree-hugging tendencies, see Emma Duncan, 'The Heat Is On', *The Economist*, 9 September 2006.

38 See e.g. http://www.copenhagenconsensus.com/Default.aspx?ID=728.

39 Bruce Pilbeam, *Conservatism in Crisis: Anglo-American Conservative Ideology at the End of the Cold War* (Palgrave Macmillan, Basingstoke, 2003), pp. 173–85.

40 Brendan Carlin, 'Tories Plan "Painful Rises" in Car and Air Tax', *Daily Telegraph*, 1 September 2006.

41 Edmund Burke, *Reflections on the Revolution in France* (Conor Cruise O'Brien, ed., Penguin, Harmondsworth, 1968), pp. 194–5.

42 John Aspinall, *The Best of Friends* (Macmillan, London, 1976), p. 139.

43 John Gray, 'Beginnings', in *Endgames: Questions in Late Modern Political Thought* (Polity Press, Cambridge, 1997), pp. 156–86, at pp. 168–70.

44 Carlin, 'Tories Plan "Painful Rises" in Car and Air Tax'.

45 See http://www.qualityoflifechallenge.com/, and also Zac Goldsmith, 'Climate Change Brings Us an Uncomplicated Choice', *Guardian*, 31 August 2006.

46 *Interim Findings of the Conservative Party's Energy Review*, 6 July 2006, http://www.conservatives.com/pdf/energyreview.pdf.

47 David Cameron, 'Vote Blue, Go Green', speech, 18 April 2006, http:// www.conservatives.com/tile.do?def=news.story.page&obj_ id=129236&speeches=1.

48 David Cameron, 'A Voice for Hope, for Optimism and for Change', speech, 6 December 2005, http://www.conservatives.com/tile.do?def=

news.story.page&obj_id=126757&speeches=1. The joke went 'I tried to make a start [on decreasing carbon emissions] this morning by biking to work. That was a carbon neutral journey until the BBC sent a helicopter following me.'

49 Oliver King, 'Cameron Rejects Accusations of Green Spin', *Guardian*, 2 May 2006.

50 David Willetts, *Who Do We Think We Are?* (Centre for Policy Studies, London, 1998), p. 11.

51 Max Weber, *The Protestant Ethic and the Spirit of Capitalism* (Chas. Scribner's Sons, New York, 1958), and R.H. Tawney, *Religion and the Rise of Capitalism* (Harcourt, Brace and Company, Inc., New York, 1926).

52 Cameron, speech to Google *Zeitgeist* Europe 2006.

53 John Gray, 'The Undoing of Conservatism', in *Enlightenment's Wake: Politics and Culture at the Close of the Modern Age* (Routledge, London, 1995), pp. 87–119; Roger Scruton, *England: An Elegy* (Pimlico, London, 2001).

54 David Cameron, Chamberlain lecture.

55 For an assessment of the third sector as a proportion of the UK economy see Jeremy Kendall and Martin Knapp, *The Third Sector and Welfare State Modernisation: Inputs, Activities and Comparative Performance*, Centre for Civil Society Working Paper no. 14, London School of Economics, December 2000, http://www.lse.ac.uk/collections/CCS/pdf/CSWP/CSWP_14.pdf.

56 'Field of Dreams', *The Economist*, 27 July 2006.

57 Karl Mannheim, *Conservatism: A Contribution to the Sociology of Knowledge* (David Kettler, Volker Meja and Nico Stehr, eds, David Kettler and Volker Meja, trans., Routledge and Kegan Paul, London, 1986), p. 88, and n. 70.

58 Willetts, *Modern Conservatism*, pp. 95–6, J. Enoch Powell, speech at Kensington, 30 November 1970, reprinted in *Still to Decide* (John Wood, ed., Batsford, London, 1972), pp. 11–13.

59 *Built to Last*, p. 4.

60 David Bornstein, *How to Change the World: Social Entrepreneurs and the Power of New Ideas* (Oxford University Press, New York, 2003).

7 Conservatism and societies

1 Interview in *Woman's Own*, 31 October 1987.

2 Margaret Thatcher, *The Downing Street Years 1979–1990* (HarperCollins, London, 1993), p. 626.

3 David Willetts, *Modern Conservatism* (Penguin, Harmondsworth, 1992), p. 48.

4 David Willetts, *Why Vote Conservative?* (Penguin, Harmondsworth, 1997), p. 15.

5 Gary Streeter (ed.), *There Is Such a Thing as Society* (Politico's, London, 2002).

6 Oliver Letwin, 'For Labour There Is No Such Thing as Society, Only the State', in Streeter, *There Is Such a Thing as Society*, pp. 38–51.

7 Damien Green, 'There Is Such a Thing as Society', in Sam Gyimah (ed.), *From the Ashes …: The Future of the Conservative Party* (Politico's, London, 2005), pp. 56–60.

8 David Cameron, 'A Voice for Hope, for Optimism and for Change', speech, 6 December 2005, http://www.conservatives.com/tile.do?def= news.story.page&obj_id=126757&speeches=1.

9 Nick Assinder, *Cameron Offers Something New*, BBC News Online, 6 December 2005, http://news.bbc.co.uk/1/hi/uk_politics/4503982.stm.

10 Bobby Duffy and Rea Robey, *A New British Model?* Ipsos MORI, http:// www.mori.com/publications/rd/a-new-british-model.shtml.

11 David Cameron, 'Making Our Country a Safe and Civilised Place for Everyone', speech to the Centre for Social Justice, Central London, 10 July 2006, http://www.conservatives.com/tile.do?def=news.story.page&obj_ id=130823&speeches=1.

12 Alan Duncan, 'Get Real or Die', in Gyimah, *From the Ashes …*, pp. 52–5.

13 Andrew Cooper, 'What Does the Conservative Party Stand For?' in Gyimah, *From the Ashes …*, pp. 34–43, at p. 42.

14 Geoffrey Wheatcroft, *The Strange Death of Tory England* (Allen Lane, London, 2005), pp. 211–30.

15 David Cameron, 'The Best is Yet to Come', speech to the 2006 Conservative Party Conference, Bournemouth, 4 October 2006, http://www. conservatives.com/tile.do?def=news.story.page&obj_ id=132730&speeches=1.

16 Tania Branigan, 'Cameron Attacked Over Gay Rights Record', *Guardian*, 4 October 2006.

17 Brendan Carlin, David Sapsted and Sally Pook, 'MP's gay affair is just one of those things, say fellow Tories', *Daily Telegraph*, 27 October 2006; Belinda Oaten, '"I know the nightmare you're going through" – an open letter from Belinda Oaten to Celeste', *Daily Mail*, 26 October 2006.

18 Branigan, 'Cameron Attacked Over Gay Rights Record'.

19 Simon Walters, *Tory Wars: Conservatives in Crisis* (Politico's, London, 2001), pp. 72–85.

20 Andrew Sparrow, 'How a Question of Drugs Engulfed Cameron and Hijacked Race for Tory Leadership', *Daily Telegraph*, 15 October 2005.

21 Explored at greater length in Iain McGill and Colin Robertson, 'Drugs

Undermine Human Dignity', in Streeter, *There Is Such a Thing as Society*, pp. 84–95.

22 'The Decline of the English Burglary', *The Economist*, 29 May 2004.

23 Sarah Womack, 'Tories Back Injection Centres for Drug Addicts', *Daily Telegraph*, 24 May 2006.

24 'Skills Filled', *The Economist*, 5 February 2004.

25 *Teaching to Educate, not Teaching to Test*, Conservative Party press release, 20 July 2006, http://www.conservatives.com/tile.do?def=news.story.page&obj_id=131040.

26 David Cameron, 'Higher Quality Education for All', speech, Leeds, 4 April 2006.

27 David Cameron, 'Conservatism – Public Service', in Gyimah, *From the Ashes ...*, pp. 18–26.

28 *Built to Last: The Aims and Values of the Conservative Party*, August 2006, http://www.conservatives.com/pdf/BuiltToLast-AimsandValues.pdf, at p. 7.

29 Isabel Oakeshott and David Cracknell, 'Tories Gung-ho on Privatising NHS', *Sunday Times*, 1 October 2006.

30 So exercises such as Sean Williams, *Alternative Prescriptions: A Survey of International Healthcare Systems* (Conservative Policy Unit, London, 2002) are probably wastes of time.

31 David Sanders, 'Reflections on the 2005 General Election: Can the Tories Win Next Time?' *British Politics*, vol. 1 (2006), pp. 170–94.

32 David Cameron, 'Do the Right Thing', *Guardian*, 22 January 2005.

33 Baroness Kelly and Stephen Dorrell, *The Wellbeing of the Nation*, interim report of the Public Service Improvement Policy Group, September 2006, http://www.publicserviceschallenge.com/uploads/tx_ev3evnews/Public_Service_Policy_Group_Interim_Report.pdf, p. 4.

34 Will Woodward, 'Tories Admit Past Mistakes Over Public Service Workers', *Guardian*, 4 September 2006.

35 *The Economic Competitiveness Review*, Competitive Challenge Policy Group, 13 September 2006, http://www.competitivechallenge.com/uploads/tx_ev3evnews/ECPG_Interim_Report_FINAL.doc.

36 Melissa Kite, 'We Must Cut Tax as a Matter of Morality, Senior Tories Insist', *Daily Telegraph*, 3 September 2006.

37 For instance, Neil Tweedie, 'Right-wing Tories Urge Bold Line on Tax Cuts', *Daily Telegraph*, 28 August 2006.

38 Tax Reform Commission, *Tax Matters: Reforming the Tax System* (Tax Reform Commission, 2006), http://www.taxreformcommission.com/downloads/Tax%20Reform%20Commission%20Report.pdf.

39 *Built to Last*, p. 2.

40 *Built to Last*, p. 4.

41 'A Dip in the Middle', *The Economist*, 8 September 2005.

42 Melissa Kite, 'Those Who Say the Tories Are Tax Cutters Should Look at the Early Years of Mrs Thatcher's Reign', *Daily Telegraph*, 27 August 2006.

43 Kieron O'Hara, *The Referendum Roundabout* (Imprint Academic, Exeter, 2006).

44 David Cameron, 'Balancing Freedom and Security: A Modern British Bill of Rights', speech to Centre for Policy Studies, London, 26 June 2006, http://www.conservatives.com/tile.do?def=news.story.page&obj_id=130572&speeches=1.

45 Phil Marfleet, 'Islamist Political Thought', in Adam Lent (ed.), *New Political Thought: An Introduction* (Lawrence & Wishart, London, 1998), pp. 89–111.

46 Martin Durham, 'The Christian Right', in Lent, *New Political Thought*, pp. 72–88.

47 E.g. David Cameron, speech to Soar Valley Community College, 21 July 2006, http://www.conservatives.com/tile.do?def=news.story.page&obj_id=131074&speeches=1.

48 Bruce Pilbeam, *Conservatism in Crisis? Anglo-American Conservative Ideology at the End of the Cold War* (Palgrave Macmillan, Basingstoke, 2003), pp. 97–9.

49 Quintin Hogg, *The Case for Conservatism* (Penguin, West Drayton, 1947), p. 18.

50 Andrew Roberts, *Salisbury: Victorian Titan* (Weidenfeld & Nicolson, London, 1999), p. 23.

51 Cameron, speech to Soar Valley Community College.

52 David Davis, 'Do Muslims Really Want Apartheid Here?' *Daily Telegraph*, 15 October 2006.

53 David Cameron, 'Achieving Lasting Peace and Security, at Home and Abroad', speech at St Stephen's Club, London, 15 August 2006, http://www.conservatives.com/tile.do?def=news.story.page&obj_id=131435&speeches=1. For the 'Preventing Extremism Together' working groups, see *'Preventing Extremism Together' Working Groups August–October 2005*, http://raceandfaith.communities.gov.uk/raceandfaith/reports_pubs/publications/race_faith/PET-working-groups-aug-0ct05?view=Binary.

54 Cameron, speech to Soar Valley Community College.

55 'A World of Exiles', *The Economist*, 2 January 2003.

56 'A Foolish Promise', *The Economist*, 13 July 2006.

57 Tim Bale, 'Between a Soft and Hard Place? The Conservative Party,

Valence Politics and the Need for a New "Eurorealism"', *Parliamentary Affairs* vol. 59 (2006), pp. 385–400.

58 David Cameron, 'We Have a Future to Fight For', statement, 13 July 2006, http://www.conservatives.com/tile.do?def=news.story.page&obj_id=130928&speeches=1.

59 For an interesting discussion of neoconservatism from a former insider, see Francis Fukuyama, *After the Neocons: America at the Crossroads* (Profile Books, London, 2006), pp. 12–65.

60 Fukuyama, *After the Neocons*, p. 193.

61 David Cameron, *A New Approach to Foreign Affairs – Liberal Conservatism*, J.P. Morgan Lecture at the British American Project, 11 September 2006, http://www.conservatives.com/tile.do?def=news.story.page&obj_id=131904.

62 Cameron, *A New Approach to Foreign Affairs*.

63 Cameron, *A New Approach to Foreign Affairs*.

64 Cameron, *A New Approach to Foreign Affairs*.

65 Rachel Sylvester, 'The Tories Need to be Tough on Crime – Tougher than Labour', *Daily Telegraph*, 3 October 2006.

66 Sylvester, 'The Tories Need to be Tough on Crime – Tougher than Labour'.

8 Conservatism and trust

1 Jürgen Habermas, 'Modernity – An Incomplete Project', in Hal Foster (ed.), *Postmodern Culture* (Pluto Press, London, 1985).

2 John Rawls, *A Theory of Justice* (Oxford University Press, Oxford, 1971).

3 Robert Putnam, *Bowling Alone* (Simon and Schuster, New York, 2000).

4 Onora O'Neill, *A Question of Trust: The BBC Reith Lectures 2002* (Cambridge University Press, Cambridge, 2002), pp. 44–5.

5 Kieron O'Hara, *Trust: From Socrates to Spin* (Icon Books, Cambridge, 2004), pp. 271–6.

6 The POWER Commission, *Power to the People: The Report of POWER: An Independent Inquiry into Britain's Democracy*, March 2006, http://www.powerinquiry.org/report/documents/PowertothePeople_002.pdf.

7 *Power to the People*, p. 16.

8 Bernard Crick, *In Defence of Politics* (Weidenfeld & Nicolson, London, 1962).

9 Ghita Ionescu and Isabel de Madariaga, *Opposition* (C.A. Watts, London, 1968).

10 *Power to the People*, p. 17.

11 *Power to the People*, pp. 17–18, my numbering of the explanations.

12 *Power to the People*, p. 15.

13 Kieron O'Hara, *The Referendum Roundabout* (Imprint Academic, Exeter, 2006).

14 Ionescu and de Madariaga, *Opposition*, pp. 83–4.

15 Andrew Tucker, *Why Trust Has No Part in Modern Politics* (Centre for Reform, London, 1999), pp. 50–54.

16 'Public "Has Little Trust in MPs"', http://news.bbc.co.uk/1/hi/uk/5348238.stm.

17 *Society Has Changed – Politicians Must Change Too*, Conservative Party press release, 29 September 2006, http://www.conservatives.com/tile.do?def=news.story.page&obj_id=132422.

18 'Judge Upholds Vote-rigging Claims', http://news.bbc.co.uk/1/hi/england/west_midlands/4406575.stm.

19 Argued at length in O'Hara, *Trust*.

20 O'Hara, *Trust*, p. 283.

21 http://www.davethechameleon.com/dtchome.

22 Joseph Conrad, *The Secret Agent* (Martin Seymour-Smith, ed., Penguin, Harmondsworth, 1984), p. 102.

23 David Cameron, 'A Voice for Hope, for Optimism and for Change', speech, 6 December 2005, http://www.conservatives.com/tile.do?def=news.story.page&obj_id=126757&speeches=1.

24 'Sorting Out Schools', *The Economist*, 14 December 2005.

25 David Cameron, 'I Say to Liberal Democrats Everywhere: Join Me in My Mission', speech in Hereford, 16 December 2005, http://www.conservatives.com/tile.do?def=news.story.page&obj_id=126938&speeches=1.

26 'Tonier Than Thou', *The Economist*, 10 October 2002.

27 Barbara A. Misztal, *Trust in Modern Societies* (Polity Press, Cambridge, 1996), pp. 95–101.

28 Paul Seabright, *The Company of Strangers: A Natural History of Economic Life* (Princeton University Press, Princeton, 2004).

29 Misztal, *Trust in Modern Societies*, p. 97.

30 Barbara A. Misztal, *Theories of Social Remembering* (Open University Press, Maidenhead, 2003).

31 David Cameron, 'Modernisation With a Purpose', speech launching the Democracy Task Force, 6 February 2006, http://www.conservatives.com/tile.do?def=news.story.page&obj_id=127681&speeches=1.

9 Conservative modernisation: oxymoron or no-brainer?

1 Archie Norman, 'The Problem Is Us', in Sam Gyimah (ed.), *From the Ashes ...: The Future of the Conservative Party* (Politico's, London, 2005), pp. 122–9, at p. 124.

2 Chris Philp (ed.), *Conservative Revival: Blueprint for a Better Britain* (Politico's, London, 2006), pp. xiv–xv.

3 Michael A. Ashcroft, *Smell the Coffee: A Wake-Up Call for the Conservative Party* (Michael Ashcroft, 2005), p. 103.

4 Geoffrey Wheatcroft, *The Strange Death of Tory England* (Allen Lane, London, 2005), p. 272. Ian Kilbannock is a character from Evelyn Waugh's *Sword of Honour* trilogy.

5 Philp, *Conservative Revival*, pp. 33–61.

6 Jo-Anne Nadler, *Too Nice to be a Tory: It's My Party and I'll Cry if I Want To* (Simon & Schuster, London, 2004).

7 Andrew Cooper, 'A Party in a Foreign Land: The Tory Failure to Understand How Britain Has Changed', in Edward Vaizey, Nicholas Boles and Michael Gove (eds), *A Blue Tomorrow: New Visions for Modern Conservatives* (Politico's, London, 2001), pp. 9–29, at p. 23.

8 Andrew Lansley, 'From Values to Policy: The Conservative Challenge', in Mark Garnett and Philip Lynch (eds), *The Conservatives in Crisis* (Manchester University Press, Manchester, 2003), pp. 221–8.

9 Philp, *Conservative Revival*, pp. 2–5.

10 Simon Walters, *Tory Wars: Conservatives in Crisis* (Politico's, London, 2001).

11 Liam Fox, *Modern Conservatism*, Centre for Policy Studies, 15 September 2005, http://www.cps.org.uk/cpsfile.asp?id=108.

12 David Davis, *Modern Conservatism*, Centre for Policy Studies, 4 July 2005, http://www.cps.org.uk/cpsfile.asp?id=106.

13 David Cameron, *Practical Conservatism*, Sir Keith Joseph Memorial Lecture, 10 March 2005, http://www.cps.org.uk/cpsfile.asp?id=102.

14 David Cameron, *Modern Compassionate Conservatism*, Centre for Policy Studies, 8 November 2005, http://www.cps.org.uk/cpsfile.asp?id=109.

15 Quoted in Andrew Denham and Peter Dorey, 'A Tale of Two Speeches? The Conservative Leadership Election of 2005', *Political Quarterly* vol. 77 no. 1 (2006), pp. 35–42, at p. 41.

16 Andrew Sparrow, 'How a Question of Drugs Engulfed Cameron and Hijacked Race for Tory Leadership', *Daily Telegraph*, 15 October 2005.

17 Charles Moore, 'If the Tories Have a Drug Problem, it's their Addiction to Past Quarrels', *Daily Telegraph*, 15 October 2005.

18 Rachel Sylvester, 'Tory Right Has Yet Again Resorted to Playing the Man, Not the Ball,' *Daily Telegraph*, 17 October 2005.

19 Denham and Dorey, 'A Tale of Two Speeches?' p. 41.

20 Janet Daley, *Seeking the Common Ground*, Centre for Policy Studies, September 2005, http://www.cps.org.uk/cpsfile.asp?id=33.

21 'Tories Struggle to be Heard', *The Economist*, 20 January 2005.

22 Daley, *Seeking the Common Ground*, pp. 2–3.

23 Daley, *Seeking the Common Ground*, p. 3.

24 Daley, *Seeking the Common Ground*, pp. 3–4.

25 Philp, *Conservative Revival*, pp. 63–5.

26 James Surowiecki, *The Wisdom of Crowds: Why the Many Are Smarter Than the Few* (Little, Brown, London, 2004), pp. 23–65.

27 Rosie Campbell, Sarah Childs and Joni Lovenduski, 'Women's Equality Guarantees and the Conservative Party', *Political Quarterly* vol. 77 no. 1 (2006), pp. 18–27.

28 David Cracknell and Yuba Bessaoud, 'Tories Rebel at Cameron A-list', *Sunday Times*, 29 January 2006.

29 'Pick 'Em Local and Pick 'Em Early (… and Stand Up for Traditional Values)', Cornerstone Press release, 29 May 2006, http://www.cornerstonegroup.org.uk/Pressrelease.htm.

30 Ros Taylor, 'Cameron: I Won't Impose "A-lister" on Bromley', *Guardian*, 2 June 2006.

31 Tania Branigan, 'Cameron Accused of Retreating on Pledge for 50% Women Candidates', *Guardian*, 2 August 2006.

32 Will Woodward, 'Cameron to Party: Choose More Women Candidates', *Guardian*, 22 August 2006.

33 http://www.webcameron.org.uk/.

34 http://www.thebigconversation.org/.

35 davethechameleoncom, post to the public blog on webcameron, 1 October 2006, http://www.webcameron.org.uk/blogs/list.aspx?role=public.

36 Tania Branigan, 'Cameron Brand is Failing to Set the Tory Grassroots on Fire', *Guardian*, 17 September 2006.

37 Oliver Letwin, *The Purpose of Politics* (Social Market Foundation, London, 1999), pp. 92–101.

38 Edward Leigh, *The Strange Desertion of Tory England: The Conservative Alternative to the Liberal Orthodoxy*, Cornerstone Group, July 2005, http://www.cornerstonegroup.org.uk/the_strange_desertio24c5e0.pdf.

39 Andrew Selous, 'Faith and Politics – Do They Mix?' in *Being Conservative: A Cornerstone of Policies to Revive Tory Britain*, Cornerstone Group, September 2005, http://www.cornerstonegroup.org.uk/reviving_tory_britain.pdf, pp. 63–6, at p. 63.

40 Selous, 'Faith and Politics', p. 64.

41 Selous, 'Faith and Politics', pp. 65–6.

42 Leigh, *The Strange Desertion of Tory England*.

43 'A New Jerusalem', *The Economist*, 23 September 2006.

44 Benedict Brogan, 'Softer Stance on Section 28 in Lords', *Daily Telegraph*, 12 March 2003.

45 'Meanwhile, Back in the Shires', *The Economist*, 28 July 2005.

46 Cf. Edward Leigh, *Set the Schools Free – School Choice: A Human Right – Breaking the State Monopoly Over British Schools*, Cornerstone Group, May 2006, http://www.cornerstonegroup.org.uk/Leigh%20education%2 0cleared.pdf, and the articles in *Being Conservative*.

47 Melissa Kite, 'Fox Courts Religious Right with Plea to Limit Abortion to 12 Weeks', *Daily Telegraph*, 18 September 2005.

48 Melissa Kite, 'Right-wingers Back Cameron for Leader', *Daily Telegraph*, 29 October 2005.

49 'A New Jerusalem'.

50 Leigh, *The Strange Desertion of Tory England*, p. 24.

51 http://www.cornerstonegroup.org.uk/.

52 Janet Daley, *What Does Modernisation Mean?* Centre for Policy Studies, February 2006, http://www.cps.org.uk/cpsfile.asp?id=463, p. 1.

53 Daley, *What Does Modernisation Mean?*, pp. 1–2.

54 George Jones, '£5m Donor Accuses Cameron of Education U-turn', *Daily Telegraph*, 22 February 2006.

55 Tania Branigan and Michael White, 'Senior Tories Voice Fears of Shift to Left', *Guardian*, 23 February 2006.

56 Graeme Wilson, 'Lamont Joins Tory Chorus for More Action on Policies', *Daily Telegraph*, 29 August 2006.

57 Branigan and White, 'Senior Tories Voice Fears of Shift to Left'.

58 Ros Taylor, 'Cameron Refuses to Apologise to Ukip', *Guardian*, 4 April 2006.

59 John Gray, 'The Undoing of Conservatism', in *Enlightenment's Wake: Politics and Culture at the Close of the Modern Age* (Routledge, London, 1995), pp. 87–119; 'The Tory Endgame', in *Endgames: Questions in Late Modern Political Thought* (Polity Press, Cambridge, 1997), pp. 97–155.

60 Toby Helm and David Rennie, 'Don't Be Fooled by Cameron, Tebbit to Warn Right', *Daily Telegraph*, 30 January 2006.

61 George Jones and Brendan Carlin, 'Ditching Thatcher's Legacy "Is A Huge Risk"', *Daily Telegraph*, 21 February 2006.

62 Wilson, 'Lamont Joins Tory Chorus for More Action on Policies'.

63 Jones and Carlin, 'Ditching Thatcher's Legacy "Is A Huge Risk"'.

64 Andrew Denham and Kieron O'Hara, *Cameron's 'Mandate': Democracy, Legitimacy and Conservative Leadership* (Manchester University Press, Manchester, in press).

65 Daley, *What Does Modernisation Mean?*, p. 4

66 Jones, '£5m Donor Accuses Cameron of Education U-turn'.

67 Tania Branigan, 'Letwin Sets Limits on Tory Policy Shakeup', *Guardian*, 17 March 2006.

68 David Cameron, 'Modern Conservatism', speech at Demos, 30 January 2006, http://www.conservatives.com/tile.do?def=news.story.page&obj_id=127560&speeches=1. Ellipses in the original text.

69 Gaby Hinsliff, 'Cameron Brand is Failing to Set the Tory Grassroots on Fire', *Observer*, 17 September 2006.

70 'Cameron's Way', *The Economist*, 19 January 2006.

71 Andrew Rawnsley, 'Cameron Must Prove that his Surgery is More than Cosmetic', *Observer*, 9 April 2006.

72 Simon Heffer, 'Something Needs to be Done, But Does Mr Cameron Know What?' *Daily Telegraph*, 12 July 2006.

73 'It's the Party, Stupid', *The Economist*, 27 April 2006.

74 'It's the Party, Stupid'.

75 Ashcroft, *Smell the Coffee*; Philp, *Conservative Revival*.

76 Theresa May, 'Reassembling the Jigsaw', in Gyimah, *From the Ashes*, pp. 102–09.

10 The balance sheet

1 Matthew Tempest, 'Cameron Urges Blair: Go and Go Soon', *Guardian*, 10 May 2006.

2 Simon Hoggart, 'Watery-eyed at Memories of Leafleting in the Rain', *Guardian*, 19 September 2006.

3 Tania Branigan, 'Three Months On, David Cameron's Star Stops Rising', *Guardian*, 15 March 2006.

4 David Willetts, 'A 20/20 Vision for Britain', in Sam Gyimah (ed.), *From the Ashes …: The Future of the Conservative Party* (Politico's, London, 2005), pp. 142–6, at p. 146.

5 Oliver Letwin, *The Purpose of Politics* (Social Market Foundation, London, 1999), esp. pp. 3–57.

6 Lewis Baston and Simon Henig, 'Has Cameron Turned the Tory Tide?' paper presented at the Annual Elections, Public Opinion and Parties Conference, University of Nottingham, September 2006.

7 David Sanders, 'Reflections on the 2005 General Election: Can the Tories Win Next Time?', *British Politics* vol. 1 (2006), pp. 170–94.

8 Baston and Henig, 'Has Cameron Turned the Tory Tide?'

9 Branigan, 'Three Months On'.

10 Isabel Oakeshott, 'Tory Unease at "Fragile" Cameron', *Sunday Times*, 9 April 2006.

11 Baston and Henig, 'Has Cameron Turned the Tory Tide?', citing poll evidence from IPSOS-MORI.

12 Bruce Anderson, 'David Cameron is Doing Well – But Why Not Better?' *Independent*, 7 August 2006.

13 Robert Philpot, 'Why Aren't the Tories Doing Better?' *Guardian*, 9 August 2006.

CREDITS

The author and publisher wish to thank the following for their permission to reprint copyright material:

Robert Eccleshall et al., *Political Ideologies: An Introduction* (3rd edn, Routledge, London, 2003). Reproduced with permission.

Michael Freeden, *Ideologies and Political Theory* (Oxford University Press, Oxford, 1996). Reproduced by permission of Oxford University Press.

John Gray, *Enlightenment's Wake: Politics and Culture at the Close of the Modern Age* (Routledge, London, 1995). Reproduced with permission.

F.A. Hayek, *The Constitution of Liberty* (Routledge and Kegan Paul, London, 1960). Reproduced with permission.

'Reclaiming the Night', *Economist*, 10 August 2000 © The Economist Newspaper Limited, London 2000.

Margaret Thatcher, *The Downing Street Years 1979–1990* (HarperCollins, London, 1993). Reprinted by permission of HarperCollins Publishers Ltd. © Margaret Thatcher 1993.

Although every effort has been made to contact copyright holders, there are instances where we have been unable to do so. If notified, the publisher will be pleased to acknowledge the use of copyright material in future editions.

INDEX